LUCK IS 33 EGGS

LUCK IS 33 EGGS

EGGS

MEMORIES & PHOTOGRAPHS OF AN RCAF NAVIGATOR

Robert J. Middleton

And

Daniel R. Middleton

This book is dedicated to:
The past, present and future men and women
of the RCAF 431 Iroquois Squadron.
"WARRIORS OF THE AIR"

And

The Custodians of our Canadian Aviation History.
The Canadian Warplane Heritage Museum in Hamilton, Ontario.
The Bomber Command Museum in Nanton, Alberta.
The National Air Force Museum in Trenton, Ontario.

And

Julie, Chris, Lisa, Christine, Leigh,
Colin, Kate, Andrew, Joy,
Austin, Ashley, Lilith,
Zara, Aiden,
Poppy and Holly.

"Three thousand miles across a hunted ocean they came, wearing on the shoulder of their tunics the treasured name, 'Canada', telling the world their origin. Young men and women they were, some still in their teens, fashioned by their Maker to love, not kill, but proud and earnest in their mission to stand, and if it had to be, to die for their country and for freedom.

One day when the history of the twentieth century is finally written, it will be recorded that when human society stood at the crossroads and civilization itself was under siege, the Royal Canadian Air Force was there to fill the breach and help give humanity the victory. And those who had a part in it will have left to posterity a legacy of honour, of courage, and of valour that time can never despoil."

Words spoken by Father J. P. Lardie, Chaplin of 419, 428 Squadron at the dedication of the RCAF Memorial at Middleton St. George June 15, 1985. These words are inscribed on the RCAF Memorial at Middleton St. George in Yorkshire, UK and on the RCAF Bomber Command Memorial at the Bomber Command Museum at Nanton, Alberta, Canada.

CONTENTS

Preface

I have been recounting tales about my life experiences for many years. In 1946 after I had been back in Canada for a while, Mr. Bishop, an older friend told me that I should make a diary of my RCAF experiences so that I would not forget them. I did not do that back then. In 2018 my son Dan was speaking with author, Douglas Gagel, who has written a first person biography about his father, Albin Gagel as a soldier in the German Army during WWII. Douglas Gagel and Albin Gagel wrote the biography together but, Douglas had to finish the book alone after his father passed away before the book was finished. This book, *Führer, Folk and Fatherland: A Soldier's Story* and speaking with Douglas Gagel inspired Dan to become the scribe to record the stories that make up the many parts of my life.

I am extremely fortunate that I have an excellent memory of past events that happened so many years ago. Recently author Ted Barris asked me to do a technical proofread of his book *Dam Busters*. In his book Ted gave me credit for having an "encyclopedic memory."

This book has been written as I would have written it 75 years ago with the pride and sentiments of the war years and our achievements in Bomber Command to bring the Nazi regime to its knees.

We all did our duty to the best of our abilities to stop an evil force that was attempting to dominate the world and enslave and destroy large populations of people. In hindsight many armchair quarterbacks sit back and criticize the work of Bomber Command. If you were not there you have no clue about how serious this life and death conflict was. This was a war where the winner would take it all with no award for second place. If the other side had won, there would be a horribly different world today. Slave labor may be legal, and we would have very few of the freedoms we enjoy today. In August of 1944, the Third

Reich had 7.5 million slave laborers working in occupations from agricultural to industrial.

I believe many people fail to realize that after the Dunkirk evacuation, June 5, 1940 there were no Allied soldiers in occupied Europe for four years until after D-Day on June 6, 1944 when the Allies returned to France. The stories in books and the movies of soldiers fighting in Europe only take place during the last 336 days of the war in Europe. The war in Europe since the September 3, 1939 declaration of war by Britain and France to the end was 2,312 days long. Bomber Command fought in the skies for all those 2,312 days. After Dunkirk, the airmen of Bomber Command and later with the USAAF Eighth Air Force were the only soldiers taking the fight back to Germany in the skies. This is considered the longest continuously running battle in history, day, and night for almost 6 years. The years of bombing by Bomber Command and the USAAF eventually wore down and softened up the Nazi war machine so that the Allied armies could successfully get a foothold in France and finish the job on the land. Out of the 125,000 British Commonwealth, Bomber Command volunteers 55,573 never came home. Of the 50,000 Canadians in Bomber Command 10,250 were killed.

Near the end of WWII there was some sentiment that Bomber Command had taken the bombing of German cities and towns too far and was bombing for no good reason except exact revenge for the bombing of Britain. German cities and towns all had small workshops for the building of items used to wage war on the Allied nations. Britain also had the same small workshops spread out across the country in many cities and towns. The people on both sides in the towns and cities were working to support their side of the war. The German civilians that were working in the factories building the weapons of war had faced many difficulties and were not able to work to their full potential after being displaced from their homes by the unrelenting bombing. Tens of thousands of homes had been destroyed across Germany by the end of the war.

The German people had been convinced by their leaders that they had created a United Europe with a common government. Britain and her friends were the Belligerents, and the German people should fight to the bitter end to defeat their enemy.

During the conflict, the British people were also convinced to fight to the bitter end. "we shall fight on the beaches, we shall fight on the landing grounds, we shall fight in the fields and in the streets, we shall fight in the hills; we shall never surrender." Sir Winston Churchill, KBO, June 4, 1940.

There were many German cities bombed that suffered the loss of thousands of lives in one night. In Dresden about 25,000 to 40,000 people perished. In Hamburg about 35,000 people perished. In Pforzheim about 18,000 people perished. The work we did reduced the ability of the German war machine to wage war and without our sustained efforts of bombing the war may have gone on for many more days, months, or years. The sustained efforts of Bomber Command and the USAAF forced the Nazi war machine into an almost totally defensive position defending the Fatherland. The only real offense the Nazi Army and Air Force could mount against Britain by 1944 was by the use of their V-1 and V-2 missiles from summer 1944 to spring 1945.

This was a war of attrition where the Allied bombers over six years wore down the ability of Germany to wage war. In all the cities in Germany there were about 1.1 million soldiers and citizens operating anti-aircraft guns and 1 million soldiers and civilians tied up in other defensive efforts and clearing rubble and debris from the bombed-out towns. These were all soldiers and civilians that could not be used to muster up an offensive threat to the Allies. By 1944 the German defensive effort had switched 78% of aircraft production to fighter aircraft. Very few bombers were being built.

When Dresden was bombed the Nazi propaganda machine sent photographs of dead Dresden citizens and greatly exaggerated totals on the number of dead to the press in America and Britain with the purpose of turning public sentiment against Bomber Command. It worked. German propaganda was making Sir Arthur Harris, the Commanding-in-Chief of Bomber Command and Sir Winston Churchill, Prime Minister of Great Britain to look like war mongers. The Bully that started the entire affair was now being beaten by his victims who became stronger than he was and had learned how to fight back. The Bully did not like being beaten and was complaining that the Allies were not fighting fair. The Nazis never fought fair. Ask the people of Poland about fighting fair after they were bombed without any declaration of war by Germany. People ask me, "Did you bomb women and children?" I tell them, "Yes we did. They started it and we finished it."

This was the same Nazi regime that had systematically eliminated 8,000 to 10,000 people every day in death camps, concentration camps and slave labor camps. That crime was not widely known by most of the world until after the concentration camps and death camps were liberated and the evidence of the Nazi horrors were seen by the world. Some Nazi sympathizers still deny that it ever happened.

If our bombing efforts shortened the war by only 10 days, then some 100,000 innocent people were saved. The deaths of these people happened because they were not born into Adolf Hitler's pure Aryan master race. Included in the people sent away to be eliminated were people who opposed his regime, people of non-white skin, people of Slavic background, Jewish and Gypsies, homosexuals, developmentally challenged people, people with physical or mental disabilities and many other people who were disliked by the Nazi leaders. The list is quite long.

An example of being saved by mere days is of a Czechoslovakian woman, Gita Cartagena, who was a prisoner at Auschwitz concentration camp during 1944 and 1945. She and others had been transferred there from other camps. She learned from other prisoners the terrifying reality that 6 months after a person arrived at Auschwitz, they were sent to the gas chamber for execution. After Gita arrived, she carved a notch in her bed frame for each day she was there. Gita was two days away from 6 months of notches on February 15, 1945 when the Germans sent her along with other prisoners to Hamburg to clean up rubble and debris created by the Allied bombings. Later Gita ended up at the Bergen-Belsen concentration camp and was freed when it was liberated by Canadian and British soldiers on April 15, 1945.

After the war Sir Arthur Harris, the Commanding-in-Chief of Bomber Command, was shuffled off back home to South Africa without being given any proper recognition of the work he had done with Bomber Command to end the conflict as soon as possible.

Shortly after the war ended the British Commonwealth armed services except for Bomber Command all received a recognition medal for their service in WWII. The few members that were left from Bomber Command did not receive any recognition until 68 years later in 2013. I received a small bar at a small ceremony. It did feel great to be recognized after all those years.

Throughout my story there are some points that I do not remember but, these are few and far between.

In this story I have included all of our combat operations. Some operations have more details than others. The information is from my memories, my collection of personal memorabilia, detailed notes in my logbook and the pilot's notes recorded in the squadron logbooks. There is information from other historical books and publications as per details about the targets and the outcomes of the operations.

Let us all hope and pray that enough people remember the lessons from history and a conflict as terrible as the Second World War never visits mankind again. May humankind quickly be victorious over our current common enemy the COVID-19 virus.

Bob Middleton

Acknowledgements

Alan Sonderstrom for assistance locating maps and photographs taken at Croft and for providing the credit information for the photographs.

Alicia Henneberry, Archives Specialist at the National Archives and Records Administration at College Park, MD for the sailing records of my return trip to North America on the USN Mount Vernon.

Andrew Lewis of the Brooklands Museum Weybridge, Surrey, UK for the supply of Wellington bomber photographs.

Andrew Panton at the Lincolnshire Aviation Heritage Centre at East Kirby, Spilsby, UK for the use of the photograph of the Z equipment on the Lancaster Just Jane.

Andrew Webb at the Imperial War Museum, IWM, for help in securing the print rights for IWM photographs.

Barry Middleton for the use of his photographs.

Bomber Command Museum of Canada for the use of photographs and online squadron archives.

Bill Heron for assistance obtaining LAC photographs, plate numbers and photographs by 431 Flight Officer Michael Bachinski.

Canadian Aviation and Space Museum in Ottawa, Ontario for the use of photographs taken at the museum.

Canadian War Museum and Image Reproduction Technician, Shannyn Johnson for the WWII poster images.

Canadian Warplane Heritage Museum and the members for all their help with details and the permission for use of the Museum's photographs.

Daniel Feher at FreeWorldMaps.net for the creation of the map of operational routes over Europe. Thank you for working through the many changes I made for the final map.

Dave Hogarth family, proprietors of The Tarn End House Hotel for the use of the photograph of The Tarn End House Hotel.

David Walker for the generous use of photographs taken at Croft by his grandparents on March 22, 1945.

Donald Kenneth Anderson print of Lancaster KB-811 at Croft, UK.

Don Root for the generous use of the photograph of the explosion of KB-808 SE-Y over Hildesheim on March 22, 1945. Don Root's father Clayton Root the Mid-Upper Gunner was on board.

Douglas Gagel, author of the book *Führer, Folk and Fatherland: A Soldier's Story* the biography of his father Albin Gagel. Douglas and his father's story inspired Dan to write my biography.

Greg Beaumont (EBay seller ID Slake25) for permission to use the photograph of a Longines RAF Navigators watch he has listed on EBay.

John Desramaux of johnboy Productions for the use of his photographs and his assistance in showing me how to access the National Archives, UK RCAF operation records.

John Gillespie Magee Jr. for the quote from the poem High Flight.

John Hipwell of Wolverine Supplies in Virden, Manitoba for the photograph of a Vickers K machine gun.

Karl Kjarsgaard of Halifax 57 Rescue Canada and the Bomber Command Museum of Canada for Lancaster interior photographs and other photographs.

Katie Martinuzzi for formatting the book for printing.

Kevin Windsor of the National Air Force Museum of Canada in Trenton, Ontario. Thank you for the tours through the Halifax NA-337 bomber for myself and my family members.

Laurel Wheeler for photographs and details of Irene and Bill McIntyre.

Leon Evans, Pilot at the Canadian Warplane Heritage Museum for technical details about the Lancaster Mk. X engines.

Library and Archives Canada, LAC, and Reference Technician, Martin Ruddy for the use of photographs of Croft.

Mark Chin of *The Drive* newsletter for the generous use of his photographs from October 2 and October 3, 2019 of the Collings Foundation B-17G.

Mark Donoghue, artist, Hangar 7 Aviation Art, for his generous use of his V-1 painting "Tipping Point" and his help proofreading the V-1 section.

Mark Evans, Midland Recovery Group, UK, for his assistance in locating the source for the Brooklands Museum Wellington bomber pictures and for proofreading the Honeybourne OTU portion of my story.

Mike Steele-Morgan, artist, Art Prints Direct UK, for the generous use of his Lancaster and Halifax Navigator position paintings.

Miriam Mende of the Archive of Stuttgart for information about Stuttgart flak towers.

National Military Museum in Johannesburg, South Africa for use of photographs taken at the museum.

Nick Ager for the photograph of the Croft Memorial.

Ontario Regiment RCAC Museum in Oshawa, Ontario for the use of photographs taken at the museum.

Paul Gribbons for providing the 431 Squadron records in 1993.

Phil Listemann of RAF in Combat for the picture of the Spitfire with the contra rotating propeller.

Rebecca Middleton from Ajax, Ontario. Thank you for all your time, work editing and proofreading until we got it correct. We would have been lost without your research, suggestions and contributions.

Reginald Harrison, 431 Squadron Pilot from Saskatoon, Saskatchewan for his help with technical details of wartime Lancaster Mk. X aircraft.

Richard Koval for the WWII aerial maps of Croft.

Robert McIntyre of Toronto, Ontario. Thank you, Rob, for your work on the routes map for London No. 4 AOS and the routes map for England. Thank you for designing the book cover and all your time spent cleaning up my sketches, photographs, and numerous documents.

Robert Taylor, artist, for the generous use of his "WELLINGTON" painting in the Honeybourne OTU section.

Ron Passmore and the Archives Committee of the Danforth Collegiate and Technical Institute for the school photograph.

Ted Barris for promoting my book and the use of the Honorary Snowbird photo on the last page.

Theo Czerny-Holownia, Marketing and Communications Administrator for the National Air Force Museum of Canada in Trenton, Ontario for photographs taken at the museum of myself and my family.

The Globe and Mail Inc. For the generous use of my April 27, 1945 homecoming photograph.

The Lightbown family for the generous use of the Lightbown crew photograph taken after their return to Croft from their January 7, 1945 trip to Munich.

The Tiger Boys Aeroplane Works and Museum, in Guelph, Ontario for use of the photographs taken at the Aeroplane Works.

The Toronto Star for the use of newspaper photographs.

Tina Travale and Carla Dicesare for the generous use of the November 11, 2015 photograph taken at the Canadian Warplane Heritage Museum and the photograph of Tina and Carla in 1943.

Chapter 1

<u>EARLY LIFE</u>

I was born in Toronto on Sunday, July 15, 1923. I am told it was a stormy day. Many of the good things that have happened in my life have taken place on stormy days. As I am writing this, I have reached my 97th birthday. We lived in a rented house at number 8 Ashbridge Avenue in Toronto with Mom and Dad (Annie and Robert) and my younger brother Bill. The house was south of Gerrard Street and east of Coxwell Avenue. Ashbridge Avenue no longer exists as the road became part of the east end of the Dundas Street expansion project that took place in the 1950s. The location of the house is shown on the map on page 30. The Toronto 55 Division Police Station is built on the property where the house was on the north side of Dundas Street just east of Coxwell Avenue. The road was made of sand, pea gravel and was tarred regularly. If my Mom caught us playing in the tar after the road was freshly coated in the spring, we would catch a great deal of trouble. We were in trouble a few times.

To go to the washroom at night you had to go through the glassed-in kitchen and down the stairs to the cellar. I had to be wary of the imaginary hands that came out of the wall that tried to grab me when I went up the stairs at night. I could go up the stairs three or four steps at a time. You had to be fast so those hands could not grab you.

My first interest in aviation was sparked very early in my life by the solo crossing of the Atlantic Ocean by Charles Lindbergh on May 20, 1927. I was not quite four years old at the time, but I remember the event and wanting to be an aviator like Charles Lindbergh. Flying the Atlantic solo was just as spectacular a feat in 1927 as when men landed on the Moon July 20, 1969. There are some four year olds that remember Neil Armstrong stepping foot on the Moon. They do not remember a lot of details, but they know it happened by the worldwide excitement.

Charles Lindbergh with his *Spirit of St. Louis* before the flight to Paris. Everett Collection Historical / Alamy Stock Photo CWB17G.

On Friday, May 20, 1927 Charles Lindbergh flew solo, non-stop from New York City to Paris, France. It took 33.5 hours flying over the Atlantic Ocean in his aircraft the *Spirit of St. Louis* built by the Ryan Aircraft Company. A few weeks later when Charles Lindbergh returned to the USA, New York City had a huge ticker tape parade for him on June 13, 1927 attended by an estimated four million people. There was tons of confetti and ticker tape showered on Charles Lindbergh during the four day long hero's welcome. Charles Lindbergh a few days earlier was an unknown aviator. Charles Lindbergh had become the most famous person in the entire world, and he was only 25 years old. Overnight Charles Lindberg went from an unknown person to a celebrity with wealth.

A hod carrier with his hod. Photograph taken by Dan Middleton.

My Dad was not always employed so he did whatever work he could find. For quite some time he was employed as a hod carrier. A hod carrier is the fellow that brings the bricks and mortar up to the brick masons in a three-sided V shaped box called a brick hod. Each hod carrier would supply the materials for two brick layers. The hod carrier would carry up to twelve bricks at a time and climb the scaffolds with the hod on his shoulder. The stack of bricks could weigh 100 pounds. The hod carrier also mixed the mortar for the brick layer. A typical brick layer could lay up to one thousand bricks per day which meant each hod carrier had to move two thousand bricks. Hod carrying was a dangerous and a very labor-intensive occupation. Dad would bring home hods to repair.

I remember Dad walking all over Toronto looking for jobs. My brother Bill was born on Friday, May 17, 1929. I remember the blossoms on the pear tree in our backyard being especially beautiful that day. This year, 2020 my brother Bill is 91 years old.

My brother Bill and I at his 90th birthday party in 2019. I am the person in the foreground speaking. COVID-19 prevented us from having a birthday party for Bill in 2020. Photograph was taken by Dan Middleton.

One day in 1928 as I was coming home from school, I saw our old floor model gramophone going past me in the back of a truck. "Hey that is our gramophone!" Oh, how was I going to listen to my favorite records now? When I got home in the front room there was a new

Stewart-Warner floor model radio. It was such a delight having this radio in our house because up until then we had no radio. Bill and I would go to Cousin Harry's house and listen to the simple two tube radio they had there. They would have two headsets plugged into the radio. There was no speaker. A speaker attached to your radio before 1928 was quite a luxury. A horn speaker would cost two or three months' pay. In 1925 two months' pay bought you the simplest two tube radio and then you had to feed it batteries. Those batteries cost about two weeks' pay and the batteries might last thirty hours. My Uncle Ted would separate the earpieces and we would each listen to one earpiece with one ear. So, the new floor model with the giant twelve inch speaker was living the high life.

1925 Radiola two tube radio with headphones, batteries and horn speaker. Photograph from the Dan Middleton Collection.

In 1928 the radio would have cost $150 at least and Dad was making less than $20 a week if he was working. When the radio was out of date ten or fifteen years later and in much need of service, Dad purchased a new radio for less than $150. The old Stewart-Warner radio hung around in the basement for a while. Eventually Dad cut the middle out of the front of it, made a wooden frame for a door and stretched cellophane across the door frame. The frame had hinges on one side and a latch on the other. Mom now had a small china cabinet. When my Mom had passed away, I gave the china cabinet to my son Dan who collects vintage radios. Many years later Dan surprised my brother Bill and I when we saw the radio totally refinished and working. Bill commented right away that it was Mom's radio. Dan did not have a Stewart-Warner chassis, but he had an Atwater Kent model 55 chassis that when finished looked marvelous.

Mom's restored 1928 Stewart-Warner radio. Photograph from the Dan Middleton Collection.

As a kid I went to the Duke of Connaught Public School. The school went from grade 1 to grade 8. The school is still there located at 70 Woodfield Road just north of Queen Street and six blocks west of Coxwell Avenue. The location of the school is shown on the map on page 30. Our house was located at Coxwell Avenue and Dundas Street.

I used to play with a friend named John Swistanski in public school. We would have make believe battles with our wooden swords. He would say, "Up the Knights of Columbus" and I would say, "Up the

Knights of Columbus." I came home one day, and I said to my Dad who was very prominent in the local Orange Lodge, "Up the Knights of Columbus." Well, I was quickly set straight. As it turned out we were very Orange and Protestant, and the Knights of Columbus are very Catholic. Who knew? In the late 1930s this religious difference was serious.

The front of the Duke of Connaught Public School in 2020. The photograph was taken by Barry Middleton.

Well, Dad told me that the next time my friend John and I play with our wooden swords and John says, "Up the Knights of Columbus" I should say "Up King Billy." The next time we played with our swords I said, "Up King Billy!" John stomped away and we never played together again. After he told his dad he was probably told not to play with me again. Years later when they were moving to Montreal his sister came over and asked me if I wanted to say goodbye before he left. We met and said our goodbyes.

Until about 1973 I took my family, every year, to watch my Dad marching in the Orange Day parade. The parade is always the Sunday closest to July 12th. We always sat on the bridge on Dufferin Street over the Gardiner Expressway, which is just north of the Canadian National Exhibition, CNE for short. The location of the CNE is shown on the map on page 30.

My Dad's Royal Black Preceptory sash and Orangeman's regalia displaying the emblems and badges he earned over many years. Photograph is courtesy of Barry Middleton.

The 12th of July is the most important date in the Orange Order calendar. The celebration marks the anniversary of Protestant King William III's (Billy) victory over the Catholic King James II at the Battle of the Boyne in 1690. Only after my Dad passed away, in 1973 did I discover how high ranking, important and deep into the Orange Lodge he really was. Dad had achieved the highest standing in the Orange Lodge and the highest level, 11, in the Royal Black Preceptory. In Toronto in the first half of the twentieth century many deals and relationships were made at the Orange Lodge. The Orange Order was very powerful and reacted strongly wherever the dominance of the British way appeared to be threatened. All the Mayors of Toronto from 1900 to 1954 were members of the Orange Lodge. In 1954 the Jewish Mayor Nathan Phillips won the Mayoral election being the first to break the Orange Lodge Toronto Mayoral dominance in 54 years. Since 1950 the importance of the Orange Lodge has been greatly diminished with very few Orange Lodges left in Canada.

The Great Depression started with the collapse of Wall Street on October 28 and 29, 1929 when the Dow lost 25 percent over two days. By the time the slide bottomed out the Dow had lost 89 percent of the pre-crash value. Times became tougher for everyone for many years.

Monday, August 11, 1930 the huge 720 foot long and 133 foot wide British R100 airship was floating over Toronto for a few hours. The R100 flying one or two thousand feet in the air could be seen from anywhere in Toronto and our house was only five miles away. We watched it while standing in our front yard. Try to imagine something the size of an ocean liner floating in the air just 1,000 feet above your head. It was a magnificent sight, and this further encouraged my love of all things that flew. The R100 had flown 3,300 miles from Cardington, England to Montreal, Canada in only 78 hours with an average speed of 42 miles per hour. The R100 stayed in Montreal for 12 days and during that time 1.2 million people paid a visit while the airship was at its mooring mast at the Saint-Hubert, Quebec airport. At the end of the week the R100 made a 24 hour passenger flight to Ottawa, Toronto and Niagara Falls before the airship returned to Cardington, England. The return flight to England only took 58 hours. This was much faster than taking trains and a ship back to England.

The R100 airship hovering over the Canadian Imperial Bank Tower. City of Toronto Archives, Fonds 16, Series 71, Item 7921.

The R100 was built by Vickers-Armstrongs, designed by the team led by Barnes Wallis a man whose creations I would experience 13 years later. Barnes Wallis had designed the R100 gas cell with a geodesic frame essentially looking like diamonds. Barnes Wallis would use this geodesic construction in his future designs I would experience.

For a 7-year-old kid in 1930 the sight of the R100 was more spectacular than when the Space Shuttle *Enterprise,* sitting on the back of a Boeing 747, flew over Toronto in June 1983. I was watching the flight in 1983 while standing on the roof of the Bell Telephone building at 100 Borough Drive in Scarborough, Ontario. The R100 airship was cutting edge technology in 1930. The larger sister ship the R101 met with disaster in October 1930. After that disaster the R100 and all airships in England were scrapped forever.

The 747 Shuttle Carrier Aircraft and the Space Shuttle Enterprise in flight. DOD Photo / Alamy Stock Photo CWK7GK.

For many years Dad raised rabbits for food. I had my favorite bunny named Brownie. Brownie the bunny grew up to be a huge rabbit. After Brownie died from old age, we buried him in the backyard. Mom and Dad did not cook him for dinner. Dad had a huge black prize rabbit and one night somebody stole that rabbit. Dad chased the bunny thief all the way up to Gerrard Street, but he never caught up with the thief. Times were difficult and a large rabbit would feed a family.

One day in 1933 when I was 10 years old, I came home from school and asked my Mom if we were poor. Mom or Dad had never said we were poor. When my Mom asked why I asked I told her that my schoolteacher had told me that they were poor. Until that schoolteacher had told me that we were poor I did not know it. I never really questioned why I only had secondhand bicycles and I only got to go to

11

the movies 4 or 5 times a year. In reality we were quite poor but my parents had been able to give Bill and I enough that we did not know we were poor.

A photograph of my brother Bill and I with Brownie my favorite rabbit. I loved Brownie. Dad used to raise chickens and then later he raised rabbits. Photograph from the Bob Middleton Collection.

In 1933 millions of folks were in the same boat. My Dad used to walk many miles anywhere in Toronto looking for work. By walking to employment opportunities and back again he saved the 10 cents round trip transit fare to buy food for the family. A loaf of bread was only pennies. Eventually Dad landed a full-time job with the City of Toronto as a maintenance mechanic at the North Toronto Wastewater Treatment Plant in the Don Valley at Millwood Road and the Don Valley Parkway. Dad would ride his bike to work, and he had to take it up and down the 200 steps to get to the plant from the road.

In the summer of 1933 in Toronto there was a great deal of anti-Semitic activity. I was only 10 at the time and did not understand the terrible treatment of the Jewish people. There were Nazi groups inciting riots in the city and doing damage to Jewish owned shops. There was one large six hour long riot at Christie Pits after a baseball game. There was a great deal of racism against the Jewish people that were arriving in Canada escaping from Europe. The Nazis in Canada were spurred on by hatred that was happening in Germany at that time. I was only 10 but I knew this was worse hatred than the differences between the Protestants and the Catholics in Toronto.

On Wednesday, July 15, 1936 I turned 13 years old. For 8 days from July 8 to July 15, 1936 there was a horrible heat wave in Ontario. By July 13, 1936 220 people had died in Toronto. During the month of July about 550 people in Ontario died from the extreme heat. The thermometer on the back of our house showed 104 degrees Fahrenheit (40°C). Because it had been so extremely hot for such a long period of time that summer the humidity was a low 25 percent. The humidex had not been invented yet, but this would have been a humidex of 113 degrees Fahrenheit (45°C). There was nowhere to hide from this heat. Nowhere was there any mechanical air conditioning. There was one movie theatre in Toronto that had cooling in the form of blowing air across blocks of ice and circulating this cooler air through the theatre. We would go down to the Woodbine beaches to cool off in Lake Ontario but by the time we walked the mile to get back home from the lake we were dripping with sweat again. Thousands of people camped out at night down at the waterfront all the way from Kew Beach to Sunnyside Beach to try to stay cool. The crops in Ontario were ruined as crops perished before the 1936 harvest. These were the great dust bowl years of 1935 to 1938 when so much agricultural land perished, and farmers were left homeless in the Canadian Prairies and the American Midwest. These are the years in the American Midwest that George Steinbeck wrote about in his book *The Grapes of Wrath*.

Violin practice. I am on the right. Photograph from the Bob Middleton Collection.

My Mom wanted Bill and I to learn the violin. I had a difficult time for 6 years learning to play as my fingers were too short. Our violin teacher, Dorothy Daniel was a beautiful young lady and a joy to learn from. The $1.00 per lesson that Mom paid back then was a great deal of money.

In the beginning of the summer of 1937 the first major Polio epidemic of the century began to sweep through Canada. The disease always started up in the warmer weather. Polio is extremely contagious, and it enters through the mouth from direct contact with someone with the virus or contaminated food or water. The cases started climbing by the end of June 1937 and by September 1937 it had peaked. Children were not allowed to play together in playgrounds and generally were kept indoors. I was 14 years old by that time and the risk to me was not as extreme, but my brother Bill was only 8 years old. Mom was so worried about Bill catching Polio.

There was no vaccine or cure for Polio in 1937. It would be another 18 years before the Salk Polio vaccine was available. A child became well, became paralyzed in part of their body or the child died. Parents were frantic, scared and felt helpless. Parents begged doctors for some cure or prevention for their children but there was none. There were two medicines that doctors administered that did absolutely nothing but make parents feel something was being done. In Toronto there were 786 cases, mostly children and 40 died from Polio. Toronto was still suffering through the Depression. To make matters worse for kids and parents the pools, parks and libraries were all closed. Parents were told to keep their kids at home and not allow them to play together. The CNE stayed open that summer but the baby contest was cancelled. The 1937 school year did not start until after Thanksgiving when it was felt that the disease was less contagious. The Polio epidemic of 1937 was as horrible and terrifying to parents then as the COVID-19 pandemic is in 2020. COVID-19 is a severe respiratory virus that is transmitted by close contact through shaking hands, touching something with the virus on it or by respiratory droplets from the nose or the mouth by sneezing, coughing or talking. It can be very mild and give people a fever and cough or very severe causing peoples' lungs to shut down causing death. Currently there is no cure or vaccine for COVID-19 just as it was for Polio in 1937.

In the past few years there are parents who refuse to have their children vaccinated against childhood diseases for many invalid reasons. Recently parents seem to feel there is no risk with Polio or other diseases because these are gone. Currently there are very few cases of Polio in Canada. Within the last 30 years, the only cases in Canada were non-vaccinated residents who had contact with polio-infected visitors from another country. If these anti-vaccination parents could only go back to 1937 in a time machine and see the devastation from the lack of a vaccine and immunity would their eyes be opened? Will these eyes be opened now in 2020? There was a lack of iron lungs to help the victims breathe in 1937. Sick Kids hospital built an iron lung made out of wood by carpenters for a 5-year-old boy that was certain to die in a few hours without some kind of iron lung. The hospital went on to build another 27 iron lungs made from metal. Grace Hospital in Toronto was turned into a rehab clinic for the children affected by Polio. Since 1994, Canada has been certified as a "polio free" country because of the use of the polio vaccine.

```
          A DIP INTO THE FUTURE

SHALL WE SEE- Tom McGall as a speed cop?
 -Bob Middleton flying a plane designed by himself
 -Jim Nelson taking Nelson Eddy's place?
 -Jean Caldwell as president of a Home and School
   Association?
 -Gwen Jackson as the first Lady Mayor of Toronto?
 -Joan Wolfenden as a new Hollywood Star?
 -Crawford Beaton as Postmaster General?
 #Jack Perks as a police inspector?
 -Winnie McCahon as Miss Toronto?
 -Ted Bell as a writer of popular Bedtime Stories?
 -Doris Williams as a Kindergarten Directress?
 -Bill Cheeseman as a Television Star? (due,
    no doubt, to his artistic taste in dress)
 -Jack Davies as an unmasked marvel?
 -Gordon Kingsmill a famous portrait painter?
   (encouraged by his early success at C.N.E.)
 -Alan McCracken a Manual Training Instructor?
```

The last page in the Duke of Connaught grade eight graduation program shows that everybody knew that I was crazy about airplanes and I would be involved with them sometime in my life. The picture is from the Bob Middleton Collection.

The cover page of my grade 8 Duke of Connaught graduation banquet program. The banquet was on Wednesday, October 26, 1938. I was finished grade eight in June 1938. In October 1938 I was in my first year at Danforth Technical School. Little did I know when I was 15 years old that 1938 was the last year of peace before the entire world would be thrown into WWII. The photograph is from the Bob Middleton Collection.

Chapter 2

DANFORTH TECHNICAL SCHOOL AND WAR

Photograph of Danforth Technical School taken in the 1930s. Photograph courtesy of Danforth Collegiate and Technical Institute.

After grade 8 I went to Danforth Technical School which is situated at the south-east corner of Greenwood Avenue and Strathmore Boulevard, about two miles from our house. The location of the school is shown on the map on page 30. It was a four mile round trip each day. Greenwood Avenue was uphill for one mile on the way to the school. I had a single speed bicycle. It was a fabulous way to get exercise getting up that hill. The way home was great however as it was downhill all the way. The odd time going home my speed got away from me and I found myself flying in the air over my handlebars and landing on the road.

On the day before Hallowe'en night, Monday, October 30, 1938 my family and I were listening to the *Jack Benny Show* on Buffalo NBC station WEBR at 970 KHz. At my Aunt Lillian's house about two blocks away from my house they were listening to *The Mercury Theatre on the Air* starring Orson Welles on Buffalo CBS station

WBEN at 930 KHz. At our house we did not think much of The *Mercury Theatre on the Air*. About ten minutes into the *Jack Benny* show Cousin Harry showed up to listen to it with us. Harry said that they were listening to some dumb show about meteors crashing to the earth near some place in New Jersey. They kept interrupting the musical show with news reports. And some Canadian scientist was talking about explosions on Mars. A few minutes later Aunt Lillian called up on the phone and was talking crazy to my Mom about invaders from Mars and thousands of people being killed by heat rays in New Jersey and the end of the world was coming. Lillian told Mom to tune to WBEN to hear the news reports about what was happening. Dad changed the station to WBEN, and we listened to the show. It sounded scary but a couple of minutes after we began to listen to *The Mercury Theatre on the Air* Orson Welles announced that the show tonight was just fiction. It was their little Trick or Treat prank on their listeners. The commercial break happened a minute later. We said phooey and Dad changed the station back to WEBR and the *Jack Benny Show*. We called Aunt Lillian to make sure she knew it was just fiction. Aunt Lillian sure felt dumb. As it turned out this was the first ever fake news on radio. After this show there were groups saying that future dramatic radio shows should be censored. The next day the Toronto newspapers were full of stories about folks calling radio stations and newspapers for information as people were scared to death.

I sold papers at the corner of Queen Street and Coxwell Avenue for 2 cents each. I was one of those kids you see in old movies hawking papers saying, "Get your Star, Tely paper here." On Saturday nights my cousin Wilf would join me as there were many more customers out and about. Once I had some money in my pocket, I could see a few more afternoon matinee serials at the movie houses. These ran from 10:00 AM to 4:00 PM on Saturdays and we took our lunch with us. You did not have to buy food at the theatre in those days. There were many theatres to choose from. The Eastwood on Gerrard Street, the Guild on Gerrard Street a short distance west of Greenwood Avenue, the Grand on Coxwell and the flea pit at the Melba on Queen Street. All of these were less than a 30 minute walk from the house. My favorite serials were *Tailspin Tommy* and *BURN-'EM-UP BARNES*. As with all the serials during the last few minutes of the episode the hero would be in some dire predicament that he could not possibly get out of. By the next episode of course the hero had managed to get out of it.

By 1939 in the theatres there would be many newsreels like the British Pathé *PATHÉ NEWS* and by Time *The March of Time*. Those newsreels carried the news about the troubles in Europe after Adolf Hitler and his thugs in Germany had begun to annex European territories in 1938 and 1939. As I watched these newsreels when I was 16 years old I had no thoughts that I would be joining the conflict in a few years as a member of the military.

During 1938 and 1939 Adolf Hitler had been slowly annexing other counties under the premise that he was repatriating German people with Germany. First, Austria was annexed which was peacefully carried out. Those Austrians who did not like it were convinced or disappeared. Next Adolf Hitler took over part of Czechoslovakia to initially repatriate the Sudetenland and ultimately took the rest of Czechoslovakia later because he was powerful, and no one stopped him. Czechoslovakia laid down their arms and allowed Germany to take over to avoid loss of life as the Czechoslovakian army was out classed by the German armed forces.

During 1939 there was a terrible feeling that something awful was about to descend upon the world. To convey the feelings we felt then, I would say that it was similar to the anxious feeling that we are currently living through in 2020. We do not know who will become ill, when the vaccine will arrive, what the outcome will be, and we do not know how long we have to wait to see the end of the COVID-19 pandemic.

On Friday, September 1, 1939 Germany invaded Poland. This German invasion left 66,000 Polish people dead and 133,700 Polish people wounded. Germany had never declared war on Poland. On Sunday, September 3, 1939 France and the United Kingdom declared war on Germany and the Second World War had officially begun. Adolf Hitler always claimed that France and England were the Belligerents and Sir Winston Churchill was a War Monger because the Allies declared war on Germany. Germany never declared war but wanted others to sign worthless peace treaties with Germany that Hitler would not have honored, like the Molotov-Ribbentrop Pact with the

Soviet Union over Poland where he promised non-aggression thereafter.

September 1, 1939, 2 days before the declaration of war marks the first night that the lights went out all across Britain and did not begin to come back on until April 1945. On nights when there was no moonlight the streets at night were treacherous. The streets were as dark as an unlit cave deep in the ground. The thick English pea soup fog made it even harder to see. That same day because of the fear of German bombing raids or invasion the evacuation of 1.5 million women and children from the cities to the country began. Some children were separated from their parents for years in foster homes. Many families and children returned back to the cities by the end of 1939 when an invasion or bombing did not materialize. After the evacuation of Dunkirk, France in June 1940, and the beginning of the Blitz in September 1940 many families and children returned to the country.

On Sunday, September 10, 1939 Canadian Parliament finally decided to declare war on Germany. For a while there was a question about jumping into another European war like Canada did in the First World War. The Canadian declaration of war was announced on Monday, September 11, 1939. I think it is interesting that September 11 is an infamous date in 1939 and 2001. I was 16 years old in my second year at Danforth Tech where I specialized in machine shop. We had just returned from lunch on Monday, September 11, 1939 and were back in the machine shop class when Mr. Bliss, our teacher, informed us that Canada had declared war on Germany. Gosh this is serious; we are really in the war now. What is this going to mean for me in a few years? How long will this new World War last? Would the world still be at war when I turn 19? Was I going to end up as a soldier? Nobody knew.

This was a very terrible time for the Allies from 1939 to the middle of 1942. The news was always terrible and the same story day after day with no ray of hope at the end of the tunnel. The feelings then are the same as in 2020 while the world is in the grip of the COVID-19 pandemic. All we hear, see, and read constantly, every day in the news media is COVID-19. It seemed like the Germans were going to be taking over Great Britain and then the world. The British Commonwealth forces had been driven out of Europe at Dunkirk,

France on June 4, 1940. We were losing battles in North Africa and England was being bombed day and night. For 27 months until December 7, 1941 Britain and her Commonwealth were all alone fending off the Nazi storm. Britain had to receive military equipment from the USA under a lend-lease agreement as the American people and the American President, Franklin D. Roosevelt, FDR, did not support the war in Europe. The American people would not sanction selling arms to the British Commonwealth but, they could lend-lease equipment. The President's polices at this time were swayed by public opinion. The Americans felt that this was another European war they wanted no part of. The American public opinion was that the outcome of the war in Europe could not possibly have any effect on the USA. The USA did not join the Second World War until the Japanese attacked Pearl Harbor, Hawaii on Sunday morning December 7, 1941. The next day, President Roosevelt said it would be, "a date which will live in infamy."

In high school I would play pickup style baseball games with my friend Bill McIntyre. Bill was a few years older than me, and I met him through my cousin Wilf. Bill was really good at baseball and was on a regular team. I was not that good at baseball. I would tend to miss the ball catching and batting, but the other kids let me play anyway. I found out many years later I am five percent cross-eyed which messes up your depth perception. Sometime when I was 18, I asked Bill if he thought his pretty 16 year old younger sister Pat would teach me how to dance. I had seen her and spoke with her a few times. Pat went to Eastern Commerce Collegiate Institute which was a high school. This was the high school for the arts and sciences. The location of the school is shown on the map on page 30. At first, I only saw her when she came out to watch Bill play ball or when I was at Bill's house. I was shy I suppose, and it was a roundabout way of asking Pat about going on a date with me. Bill told me, "Well sure Pat likes you." Pat and I started dating and before long we were going steady together. We would go to the movies and go down to watch the softball games down at The Beach. These games were great and while the games were going on they would pass around a hat to make donations to their baseball league.

Pat and I went with our friends to the CNE at the end of summer 1941. It was so much more fun going without Mom, Dad, Uncles and Aunts. At the time we did not know that it would be the last time the CNE would be open until after WWII was over. The CNE was great back then with so many fantastic deals in the Food Building. Smiles 'N Chuckles were selling five full size chocolate bars with a model airplane made from metal for 15 cents. Vendors were selling cones of French fries for a nickel. In one building there was a complete cigarette manufacturing machine that took the loose tobacco in at one end and packaged cigarettes came out the other end. In another building there was a manufacturing line set up assembling Bren machine guns. The automotive building was packed full of the next year's 1942 automobiles. Most of them were missing the gear shift knobs that were only threaded on. By July 1942, the CNE grounds and buildings that had been closed to the public were now used only for military purposes. The CNE did not reopen to the public until 1947.

Photograph of German U-Boat U-36. From the Dan Middleton Collection.

During 1942 every day we would listen to Lorne Greene on CBC radio. He could be heard reporting on the hundreds of thousands of tons of Allied shipping being sunk every month by German U-boats (submarines) in the Atlantic Ocean. I remember one month when 1.2

million tons of ships were sunk. Lorne Greene was assigned as the principal newsreader for the CBC news. He had a very deep resonant voice that earned him the nickname "The Voice of Doom." Besides reporting on the sad state of the war in Europe at that time Lorne Greene also had the task of reading the horrible list of soldiers killed in action. Lorne Greene later became well known for playing the character Ben Cartwright on the television series *Bonanza* that ran continuously from 1959 to 1973. In 1964 Lorne Greene had a number one hit song called *Ringo*, a spoken word ballad about a western outlaw Johnny Ringo.

My diorama of a town somewhere in Germany, just bombed by a two engine Handley Page Hampden British bomber. Part of the town under the bomber is actually on fire. The railway has also been demolished. The tracks, trains and buildings were from my model railroad. I built this when I was eighteen in 1941 when real stories and pictures of the war in Europe were in the newspapers and magazines. The Hampton bomber was one of my balsa wood carved models. The photograph is from the Bob Middleton Collection.

While at Danforth Technical School I was building many airplane models. Many were rubber band powered balsa flying wood models like this one covered with tissue paper that was then coated with airplane dope. Others were solid balsa wood that I carved from a block of wood. I spent many hours building my airplanes. This is a model of the American built P-40 Tomahawk fighter aircraft. The photograph is from the Bob Middleton Collection.

Model airplane advertisement from my aircraft recognition scrapbook. From the Bob Middleton Collection.

★ ★ ★

An advertisement from my aircraft recognition scrapbook informing kids they can do their part in the war effort by learning to build and fly model aircraft. The picture is from the Bob Middleton Collection.

GRADUATION CLASSES

——Thomas Kirkland, I 4 M—Called "Kirk" by everyone. Easily recognized in machine shop as he always wears a tie. Likes matwork.

Vincent McAuliffe, I 4 M—A quiet lad who doesn't chase after the girls in the usual I 4 M style. Would be tall if he didn't turn up at the toes.

Robert Middleton, I 4 M—Isn't fat; is just well-muscled. Runs the scraper with his bare hands. Hobby is model-making.

——Eric Robertson, I 4 M—Always *tripping* the light fantastic. In maths is renowned for his, "It's a cinch!" Likes sports.

Thomas Robertson, I 4 M—A former harrier, likes basketball, swimming and girls. His picture doesn't do him justice.

Wilson Rumney, I 4 M—The Quiz Kid of the class; usually stands first. Likes arguing with teachers, and playing basketball and rugby.

The graduation photographs of Tommy Robertson and I from the 1942 Danforth Tech year book called *TECH TATLER*. I am top right and Tommy is middle on the bottom. The photograph is from the Bob Middleton Collection.

High school ended early in April 1942 so young women and men could join the Armed Services or work for the war effort. Young people were needed at home in factories to replace men and women who had gone overseas. There were women building bombs in Scarborough. Factories all over Canada were producing the instruments used to wage war against Nazi Germany.

As I was in the machine shop course at Danforth Technical School the shop teacher managed to land myself and my friend Tommy Robertson a job working at the General Electric transformer factory at Davenport Road and Lansdowne Avenue. The location is shown on the map on page 30. The factory built huge transformers weighing up to 20,000 pounds that were used in power plants, factories, and all sorts of ships. While we were working there an H beam weighing at least a thousand pounds slipped from an overhead crane. The beam fell straight down and landed on a steel toe shoe that a worker was wearing. He no longer had any toenails on one foot, but he was fortunate. If he had he been 6 inches closer to the spot where the beam landed he would have been killed. I think this left an impression and gave me a great respect for wearing the proper safety equipment when performing a task. For the longest time I have been a stickler with people working for me and my sons working safely. I always made my sons wear safety glasses while they were cutting the lawn.

I was working in the tool room which was a plum job in the machine shop. I was working for the manager of the machine shop tool room who was a very stiff, proper gentleman whom no one liked and who wore a grey three-piece suit. I really did not like the manager very much either and it was such a long trip to get to the General Electric transformer factory. It felt like it was 5,000 miles away. To get to the factory I had get up at 5 AM and I would not get back home until 6 PM. I would ride my bike to Tommy Robertson's house near Danforth Avenue and Coxwell Avenue. The bike trip up Coxwell Avenue was uphill all the way. The return trip was easy as it was downhill all the way. I would leave my bike at Tommy's house. Tommy worked at the General Electric transformer factory as well. We had been in shop class together. We would go there together by Danforth Avenue and Bloor Street streetcar for about 20 miles to Lansdowne Avenue and we transferred to the Lansdowne streetcar and rode north up to the General Electric factory at Davenport Road.

After a while Tommy quit working at the GE factory but I would still leave my bike at his house and take the streetcar from there. By the beginning of June of 1942, I was completely fed up with the boss, the rotten hours, the long trip to and from work and I really wanted to fly airplanes. I have loved airplanes all my life. I finally quit working at the GE transformer factory after I decided joining the RCAF would be a great way to learn to fly. The glamorous RCAF recruitment posters did not mention that flying over Nazi Occupied Europe was dangerous and could get you killed.

In 2019 the one remaining Lansdowne GE transformer factory building is now condominium lofts. The photograph was taken by Dan Middleton.

Danforth Technical School
ACTIVE SERVICE

Name Middleton, Robert James
(In full, surname first.)

Reg. No. (R-170904)

J- 37180

Rank AC-2 | F/o   Unit   R.C.A.F.

Date of Enlistment June 17, 1941   Attendance at D.T.S. 1938-41
(Years)

Promotions

Transfers

Casualties

Decorations

Date of Discharge

(OVER)

My Danforth Technical School enlistment card. In error the card shows 1941 instead of 1942. Photograph courtesy of Danforth Collegiate and Technical Institute.

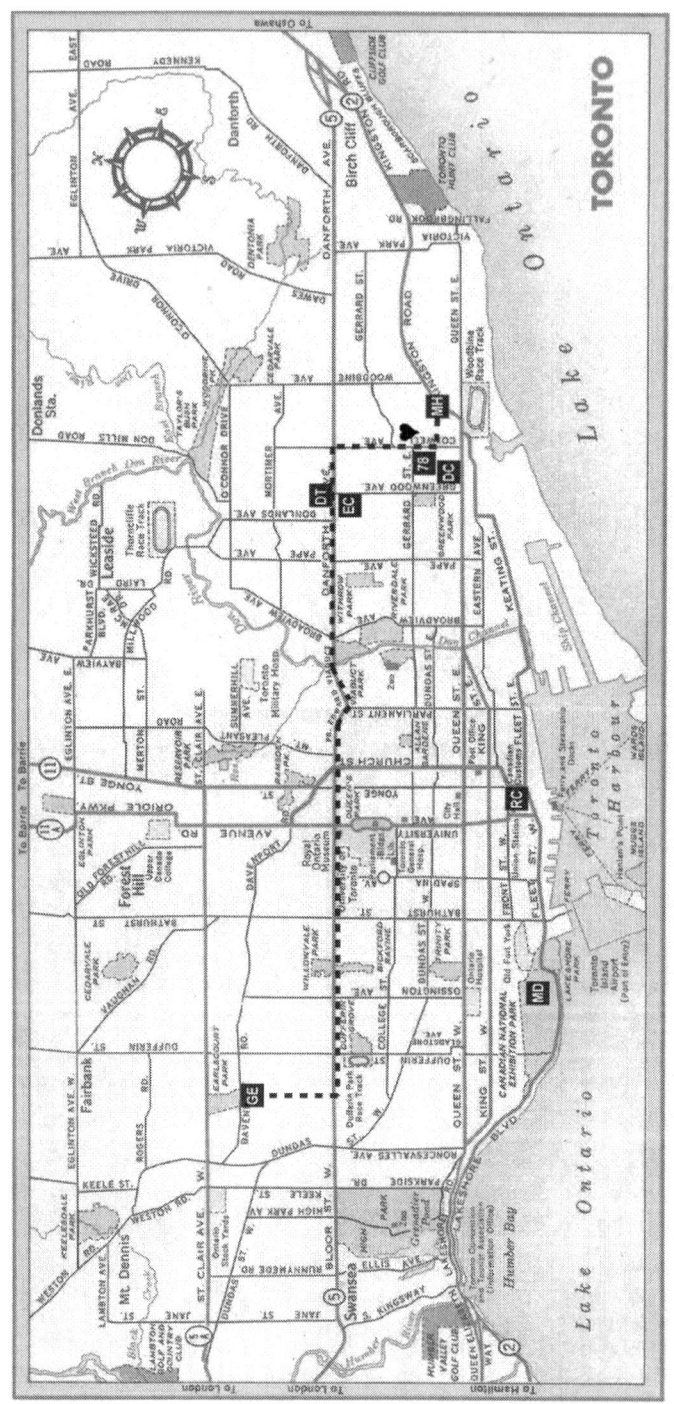

MH Middleton Home 8 Ashbridge Avenue   DT Danforth Technical HS 800 Greenwood Avenue

78 McIntyre Home 78 Ashdale Avenue   GE General Electric Lansdowne Avenue

DC Duke of Connaught PS 70 Woodfield Rd.   RC RCAF Recruitment Centre Bay & Wellington

EC Eastern Commerce HS 16 Phin Avenue   MD #1 Manning Depot Coliseum CNE

Chapter 3

I JOINED THE RCAF

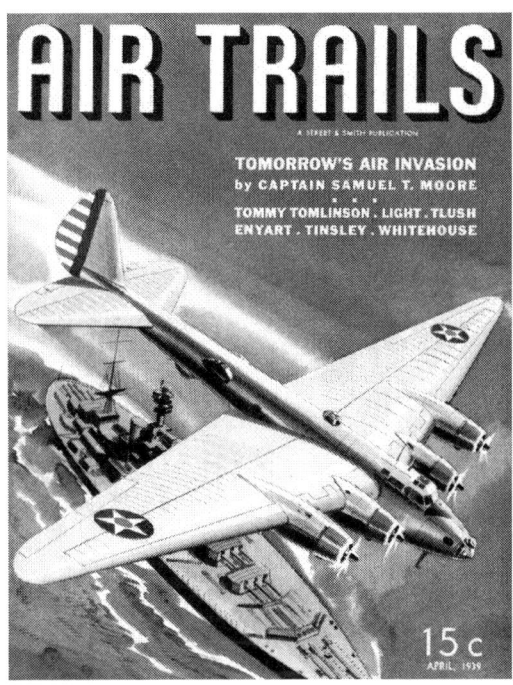

Photograph of an *AIR TRAILS* magazine cover from 1939. The Protected Art Archive / Alamy Stock Photo 2B2DD8T.

I read airplane comics, watched movie serials, and bought *BILL BARNES AIR TRAILS* magazines. These were awfully expensive magazines back then for fifteen cents. I had to sell many two cent newspapers on Dundas Street for the subscription to *BILL BARNES AIR TRAILS*. The stories were great, and, in the stories, Bill Barnes would describe how to use the controls for various aircraft maneuvers. I had been building airplane models for as long as I can remember. There were so many RCAF posters and advertisements posted everywhere showing the glories of airmen in their Spitfires and Hurricane fighter aircraft. I did not want to be in the Army, and I knew that sooner or later there could be a draft and then I would have no choice of which branch of service I would be in. I feared that if I did not volunteer for the RCAF I could eventually be conscripted and end up in a trench or foxhole somewhere in Europe or North Africa with the Infantry of the Canadian Army.

Photograph of an RCAF recruiting poster. Image CWM 19890086-521 coutesy of the Canadian War Museum in Ottawa, Canada.

As it turned out later in the war Prime Minister McKenzie King was terrified of having conscription in Canada as it would not be good for his chances of re-election. Conscription in Canada involved duty with the Home Guard or an essential industry. The people of the province of Quebec, German and Russian immigrants were very much opposed to conscription. It is interesting that Quebec objected to conscription considering that their motherland, France from which their language and culture comes from, had been conquered by the Germans. There were many volunteers from Quebec. Once the Germans attacked Russia the Russian immigrants changed their tune. As a result, no conscripted members of the Armed Forces would go to Europe and see action until after D-Day. The Canadians in the conscripted services received the unenviable nickname "Zombies." By November 1944, the Canadian army was running short of soldiers in Europe after the D-Day invasion of Tuesday, June 6, 1944. MacKenzie King was forced to send 12,000 Zombies to England to fight. By the end of the war on May 8, 1945 only about 2,500 Zombies had actually been involved in any fighting in Europe.

My heroes were all fictional pilots so on Tuesday, June 17, 1942 while I was still only 18 years old, I marched into the RCAF recruiting station on the southwest corner of Bay Street and Wellington Street and I signed my life away to the RCAF for an unknown length of time for an unknown position. I hoped I was on my way to being a fighter pilot. The location is shown on the map on page 30.

When I signed up, I was asked what my religion was. I told the recruiter that we were Protestant. The recruiter asked what type of Protestant? I had to call my Mom at home and ask her. I got off the phone and said, "My Mother says we are Presbyterians." "OK", responded the recruiter and he wrote down Presbyterian. I did not tell my Mom why I was asking. Why couldn't we have a religion I could spell? I would like to say that I joined the RCAF to save the world from an evil tyrant and his thugs, but I was fed up with the job at the General Electric transformer factory and I really wanted to be a RCAF pilot and fly fighter aircraft.

Mom and Dad were not at all happy that night when I told them that I had signed up to serve in the RCAF to go to war. What parent would be happy with their son going off to fight in a war that was not going well? I had June and July to hang around with my girlfriend Pat and all my friends who had not gone off to war yet. On Wednesday, July 15, 1942 it was my birthday, and I was now all of nineteen years old. We went to the Toronto Island a few times, movies, and baseball games. We could not go the CNE that summer as it was turned over to the Government of Canada for military purposes. The Automotive Building became the naval barracks and Royal Canadian Navy recruiting office. The Coliseum became the RCAF No. 1 Manning Depot. The early summer of 1942 was a great time, and I had no idea of what to expect of my future. I was joining a battle that we were not yet winning. I did know that I was going to be flying in airplanes.

Postcard of the CNE Coliseum, No.1 Manning Depot. Postcard is from the Dan Middleton Collection.

On Monday, August 3, 1942 I packed my suitcase and dressed in my best shoes and brand-new suit and went to the No. 1 Manning Depot located in the Toronto CNE Coliseum. The location of the Coliseum is shown on the map on page 30. I was now all of 19 years old and a Leading Aircraftsman, LAC, about as low as you can be in the RCAF. I received a fiber board identity disc, and I was now serial number R170904.

We were all given a new uniform, shoes and a wedge cap so I packed all the new civilian clothes and shoes I had bought back into my suitcase and sent it home. We all had a little propeller on the shoulder of our jackets. There were about 30 of us new recruits in my group. There were thousands of us LACs in the building. We were being paid $1.30 per day which was fantastic. We were all rich beyond our dreams. I had never seen so much money in my life each pay day. The only drawback was that marching all day long in the August heat made a smelly mess of my uniform and it cost me 50 cents to have it cleaned each day. I still had 80 cents per day left. The first two weeks we were indoctrinated in the ways and rules of the RCAF. They would take us out to Centennial Park east of the CNE Princes' Gates and they would march us back and forth in the sun. We learned to stand at attention, stand at ease and we quickly learned that the drill Corporals were God and you did exactly as they commanded.

The identity disc and my serial number that was mine until I graduated from Navigation School at London, Ontario. I was R170904. The word PRES in front of RCAF is short for Presbyterian. The photograph is from the Bob Middleton Collection.

We were lined up for all of our 7 various types of medical shots. They were given in places you did not want them and in places that already were sore from a previous shot including the dreaded TABT shot. This was for typhoid, paratyphoid A and B as well as Tetanus. After all of these shots we were sent out onto the parade grounds in the August heat and humidity to practice parade drill. We had heard that a few of the fellows would faint and the guys on either side of them would have to carry the fellows off of the parade ground to lie down. It was a good way to escape marching drill. There were a few fellows that fainted on the parade ground and we did have to carry them off. That night I was hot, and then I was cold even with my cardigan sweater on in August. Happily, these symptoms only lasted the night. Bunk beds were set up in what had previously been the horse stalls. There were two metal bunk beds per stall with four mattresses. There was still some aroma in the stalls, but I seemed to get used to it. Some fellows with less hardy stomachs had a rougher time.

The first thing I learned as a new recruit was to not volunteer for anything. We were all in the parade groups one day and the Corporal asked who of us could play a piano? That sounded like there could be some interesting musical gig happening. Fifteen fellows stepped forward. The Sargeant told them he needed them to go down to the western gate of the CNE pick up a piano and move it to the Coliseum building for a concert. I am glad I could not play a piano. This was a good lesson in why not to volunteer.

We marched a lot all around the CNE grounds. On Sundays, they marched us to Sunnyside and back again. There was one fellow who no matter how hard he tried could not march in step with the rest of us. I do not know what happened to him as he just disappeared never to be seen again.

There was our manual, the KR Air Book, which had 40 rules that we had to memorize and follow. There was rule number 40 that encompassed anything else that 1 to 39 did not cover. Any violation of these rules would get you 9 days in the jail that was nicknamed The Digger.

Photograph of an Enfield rifle that we practiced with. The photograph was taken by Dan Middleton at the Ontario Regiment RCAC Museum in Oshawa, Ontario.

We had target practice using Enfield rifles with live ammunition. These were 0.303 caliber rifles with a small clip that held five rounds. While at No. 1 Manning Depot we went through many tests for our mental ability. They did psychological testing on us to see what we were made of. We did basic training with lots of physical exercise. At No. 1 Manning Depot they were screening us to determine who should go on as Pilot, Navigator, Wireless Operator, Bomb Aimer or Air Gunner. The recruits with less aptitude would go to Wireless Operator and Air Gunner training. After two weeks of basic training and all the inoculations we were given a mathematics test. My math along with many others was not great and I failed the test. In high school I hated math and I did not have much use for the advanced concepts of grade 12 mathematics and the concepts did not stay with me.

A photograph of Pat and I in her backyard before I went off to Quebec City. I was 19 and Pat was 17. Her Dad loved growing roses. In this picture we just look like kids. This photograph is from the Bob Middleton Collection.

There were a bunch of fellows with less than stellar mathematics abilities that still must have looked like possible Pilot candidates for we were all shipped off for an eight week mathematics course in Quebec City, Quebec. This was so lucky for me. The other fellows with satisfactory math skills that were left behind at Toronto No. 1 Manning Depot did 6 more weeks of parade drill, guard duty and other undesirable menial chores while we were off learning advanced mathematics at a nice school. The school in Quebec City that was being used for the mathematics course was a beautiful old nunnery with great high ceilings and beautiful huge windows. I spent September and

October 1942, at the mathematics course. This was the nicest quarters I ever experienced in all my time with the RCAF. The dormitory where we slept had single beds to sleep in. I did not like the double bunks at other RCAF locations. At the school we learned simultaneous equations, geometry, algebra, and trigonometry. We learned absolutely everything to do with mathematics. We were all given a little red textbook that had everything you ever needed to know about mathematics. While taking this course I found mathematics fun and not hard at all. I thought to myself "What was wrong with you in high school? Why did you hate math so much and did so poorly?" I suppose the reason for my newfound mathematics skill was that if I did well in this RCAF mathematics course I was going to go on to the next step to becoming a Pilot. What a great incentive for a 19-year-old kid who had been dreaming of flying airplanes as long as he could remember. I did fantastic in the Mathematics course and as a reward I was sent to the No. 5 Initial Training School (ITS) in Belleville, Ontario.

The little red math book I was given.
From the Bob Middleton Collection.

Chapter 4

INITIAL TRAINING SCHOOL, BELLEVILLE

No. 5 ITS Belleville on May 17, 2019. The photograph was taken by Dan Middleton.

In November 1942 I was posted to No. 5 Initial Training School (ITS) which in 1942 was just on the outskirts of downtown Belleville, Ontario. This was the ground school operated by the RCAF that opened in 1941 and was located at the former Sir James Whitney School for the Deaf. The school had been requisitioned by the RCAF for the British Commonwealth Air Training Plan, BCATP. The previous students of the school were sent somewhere else. I do not know where. Over the period between 1941 and June 1944 the No. 5 ITS at Belleville trained and graduated 6,664 airmen. Many of these airmen that trained in Belleville ultimately gave their lives.

Posing with my two sons at the No. 5 ITS. The photograph was taken by another visitor.

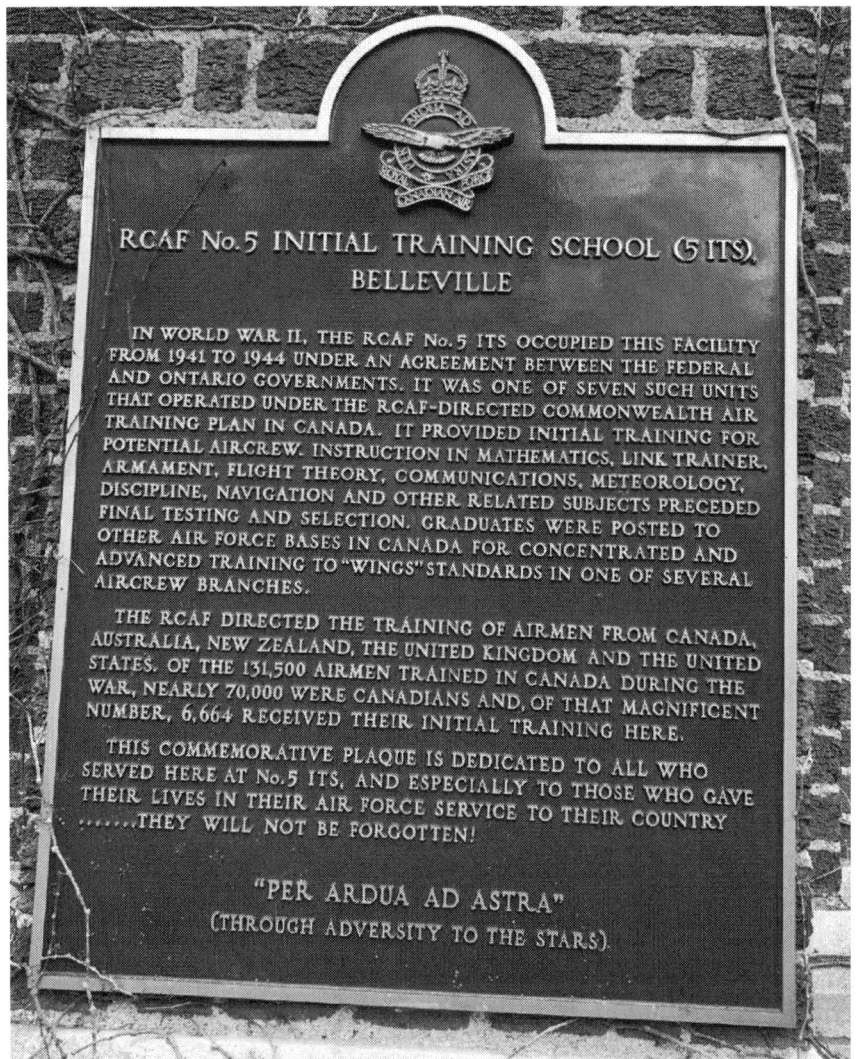

The No. 5 ITS Commemorative Plaque. Photograph taken by Dan Middleton.

A plaque was erected at the site of the school in 1950 to recognize the efforts of No. 5 ITS Belleville and commemorate all those that served in the RCAF and commonwealth countries during the conflict of World War II. The last paragraph on the plaque reads "This commemorative plaque is dedicated to all who served here at No. 5 ITS. And especially to those who gave their lives in their Air Force service to their country. ……..They will not be forgotten!"

The course was 10 weeks long and I learned armaments, theory of flight and navigation. Because I had been sent to the special math course in Quebec City my math was now excellent, and I was placed in the pilot training stream. I received more instructions in advanced math, communications, how to read clouds and meteorology. If your math was not acceptable the stream for you would most likely be Wireless Operator or Air Gunner. Folks with only basic math abilities ended up as Air Gunners.

We learned more of the RCAF dos and don'ts. We would spend an hour every day in the building next door doing physical education. We exercised with 12 pound medicine balls. We stood in two lines across from each other and would throw these back and forth to each other as hard as we could. We were in such good shape after a month of the daily physical education that we would lie on the mats on the floor and another fellow would drop that 12 pound medicine ball on our stomach. We were really tough. We would come back from the gym drenched in sweat and steaming. I remember looking out the second-floor windows at the fellows coming back from the gym and they were surrounded by a great cloud of steam coming out from under their greatcoats.

I went for more medicals. Then we were sent for the hated breath test. To pass the breath test I had to blow into a tube connected to a glass tube filled with mercury. It looked like a barometer tube. I had to blow into that tube and lift that column of mercury until it reached 30 inches high. After the mercury reached the 30 inch mark, I had to hold it there for two minutes. You had to eventually pass this test. For the next two weeks I would practice regularly by inhaling deeply and blowing into my mouth while holding my breath. By the time I tried the official test again I could hold my breath for 3 minutes. I was not sure why we had to do this. It may have been to give us determination or so we could withstand the rigors of flying in unpressurized aircraft at 20,000 feet up in the sky. I never asked.

After I had passed the breath test, I was sent to the decompression chamber where the pressure is reduced to simulate flying at the reduced pressure of high altitudes. This breathing test would acquaint us with high altitude flying using an oxygen mask. In 1942 there were no operational British Commonwealth military aircraft with pressurized cabins.

There were eight of us trainees that would be going up to the equivalent of 24,000 feet in the decompression chamber and we would be wearing oxygen masks. The instructor asked for a volunteer to go up to 24,000 feet without wearing an oxygen mask. The instructor wanted all his students to see and to understand the consequences of not wearing an oxygen mask above 10,000 feet. The oxygen mask was an uncomfortable thing to have to wear for many hours and an airman may be tempted not to wear his mask at all times. Well silly me, I volunteered to be the test victim. I then remembered too late that I should avoid volunteering. But I thought it was scientific and real interesting.

As we reached 12,000 feet the instructor asked me how I felt and I told him I felt fine. I did notice that breathing was a bit difficult but after a while that did not bother me. He then asked me to count backwards from 99 by odd numbers. That sounded easy. So, I started counting, 99, 97, 95, 93, 89, 87, 65, 53 then nothing. All the time while counting it became harder to breathe and I was saying to myself, "It sure is hard to breathe." I was struggling to get a breath before I stopped counting. Eventually I was in the first stage of becoming unconscious from the lack of oxygen. I was not aware of where I was in reality, but I was sure I was doing a great job of counting. The instructor put the oxygen mask back on my face as I was stopping and I thought, "This is great. I can now get along without oxygen." I do not remember him putting the mask on my face. The instructor told me the result of my counting backwards. I did not believe the instructor so I asked if I could try not using the oxygen mask again. The instructor told me, "Absolutely not, nobody does that a second time. We will not be doing that." I persisted so he agreed.

We were already at the 24,000 foot high altitude when I took off my mask this time. The instructor asked me to sign my name as many times as I could. That sounded really easy, and I signed R. J. Middleton once, twice and a third time and then my pencil went off the page and I dropped it on the floor. That was so easy and such a silly test. I felt a bit faint by this point, and it was a hard to breathe but not too bad. It seemed like all of a sudden, I became used to the lack of oxygen and I do not remember a thing after the third signature. While I was signing my name, I thought I was doing a bang up job of it and what was this going to prove? Somehow my breathing became less strained, and I became more aware and somehow found the oxygen mask back on my face. I do not remember the mask being put back on my face.

After my mask was back on I looked at my signatures. The first one was perfect, the second one was somewhat compressed looking, and the third signature was only a scribble of vertical lines and one long line where the pencil went off of the page. While I was sitting there taking in the results of my signatures, I noticed George Lewthwaite who was sitting across from me was holding and looking at a pay book. I told George that his pay book looks just like my pay book. George told me, "It is your pay book." "How did you get my pay book?" "I took it out of your shirt pocket Bob, and you watched me take it. You did not say a word." In the short length of time, it took me to write R. J. Middleton three times I had lost sense of reality while at 24,000 feet without an oxygen mask.

With the reduced oxygen level at 24,000 feet within 60 seconds your mind is not able to function correctly. From this experience I understood what the risk of not using an oxygen mask above 10,000 feet was. You feel that you are functioning simply fine but in reality, it is like being very intoxicated. Little did I know that I would sometime during actual operations experience the lack of oxygen and then have to recover as quickly as I could to preserve all of our lives. If I had not had this experience with lack of oxygen very early on in my training, would I have been panicked and made mistakes and not have made it back home? I appeared to know what to do on that night in the future.

At ITS we had to keep our barracks spotless at all times especially on a Saturday if we expected to go out to the movies. One Saturday found us washing the wooden floors and after that we had to oil the floors. We had our beds made up so nice that a quarter would bounce on the sheets. Perfect. The Duty Officer and his Sargeant came in and looked around. As he was leaving, he ran his fingers across the trim around the top of the door and found some dirt. Saturday night was all over as we now spent another two hours of cleaning, oiling the floors, the doors and the window frames. We did not make it to the movies that night.

The food served at No. 5 ITS was great and we ate like kings. The YMCA provided us with ice cream for our apple pie at dinner.

The YMCA also provided the school with popular music and my favorite tune became *Serenade in Blue*.

My actual Pay Book. The photograph is from the Bob Middleton Collection.

One night after dinner in December 1942 we went into downtown Belleville by bus to watch the new movie *Holiday Inn* with Fred Astaire, Bing Crosby and Virginia Dale. I remember singing *White Christmas* in my head for the longest time. When we got out of the theatre we discovered, to our dismay that the buses were no longer running. It was bitterly cold that night and we had to walk the 2 miles from downtown back to ITS. Even though we discovered that we could unfold our wedge cap down over our ears and button it under our chins every one of us came back with frozen ears that night. The next morning, we all took turns visiting the Medical Officer for our frozen ears. It was about 10 years before I could cover my ears to keep them warm and not have my ears hurt.

After the 10 weeks at No. 5 ITS Belleville was finished, I was selected to continue to Pilot training. I was so excited that I was going to fly Hurricanes or Spitfires one day.

After I graduated from Belleville No. 5 ITS I spent a couple of weeks back home in Toronto. I was so lucky that I could go home for a few days. Some of the other fellows in training had come from other parts of the British Commonwealth and were stuck in Canada until their BCATP training was complete.

While at home I was working on my aircraft recognition scrapbook. I had so many aircraft magazines that I had no shortage of pictures and descriptions. I actually ended up making two scrapbooks as I ran out of pages in the first one. It was a great hobby for an airplane crazy 19-year-old kid. Knowing if an aircraft was Friend or Foe was a matter of life or death.

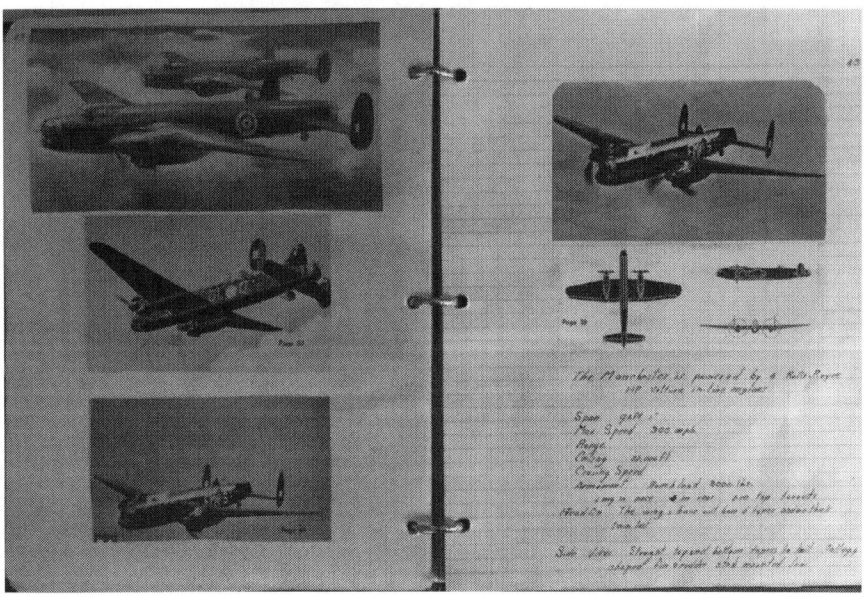

These are two pages from one of my two aircraft recognition scrapbooks. The pages show the Manchester bomber that ultimately became the Lancaster bomber. The photograph is from the Bob Middleton Collection.

Chapter 5

PENDLETON EFTS AND LEARNING TO FLY

In February 1943 I arrived at No. 10 Pendleton Elementary Flying Training School (EFTS) for the eight week course of elementary Pilot training to learn to fly. Pendleton EFTS was initially a private flying club located about 43 miles east of downtown Ottawa, Ontario. It was taken over by the BCATP when No. 10 EFTS, originally located at Mount Hope, Ontario, moved to Pendleton, Ontario. Mount Hope is 8 miles south-west of Hamilton, Ontario. It was a typical EFTS that had the 3 runways each about 2,600 feet long arranged in a triangle with the main runway running east-west.

In 1961 the airfield was purchased by the Gatineau Gliding Club which is a non-profit organization dedicated to promoting unpowered flight.

The BCATP Elementary Flying Schools were using de Havilland Tiger Moth and Fleet Finch biplane trainers. In 1943 the school at Pendleton operated de Havilland Tiger Moth biplane trainers. The Tiger Moths and the Fleet Finch training aircraft were all brightly painted in yellow paint. The bright yellow trainer aircraft were easy to spot in the air to avoid mid-air collisions. The broken Finch or Tiger Moth being searched for from the air could be spotted by the yellow debris lying on the ground or hanging in a tree. I do not know why but Tiger Moths also had the nickname Tiger-Schmidt.

The de Havilland Tiger Moth, DH.82 was designed as a basic trainer biplane by Geoffrey de Havilland in 1930 and 1931.

An aerial view of the buildings in the snow at Pendleton EFTS in February, 1943. Photograph from the Bob Middleton Collection.

A de Havilland Tiger Moth in the Canadian Warplane Heritage Museum collection at Hamilton, Ontario. The photograph is courtesy of the Canadian Warplane Heritage Museum.

The prototype first flew on October 26, 1931. Geoffrey de Havilland was the cousin of actress Dame Olivia de Havilland who appeared in British and American films. She was well known for her portrayals of

Melanie Hamilton Wilkes in the 1939 movie *Gone With the Wind* and as Maid Marion in the 1938 movie *The Adventures of Robin Hood.* Olivia de Havilland turned 104 on July 1, 2020. Sadly, Dame Olivia de Havilland passed away on July 26, 2020.

The Tiger Moth has a wooden frame glued and screwed together with a fabric covering. The Tiger Moth was manufactured from 1931 to 1944 and was used by all the British Commonwealth nations as a basic trainer. The Tiger Moth has an inline, air-cooled, inverted four-cylinder de Havilland 145 horsepower Gipsy Major engine. The Tiger Moth has maximum speed of 107 miles per hour and a cruise speed of 90 miles per hour with a service ceiling of 13,000 feet. The aircraft stalls at about 45 miles per hour and will start to obtain lift and get airborne above 46 miles per hour. An estimated 8,000 Tiger Moths were manufactured with 1,500 being manufactured in Canada at the de Havilland factory where Downsview Park is now located. The Tiger Moth was relatively benign to fly but it did require full time attention to fly it well. A poor pilot would have difficulties that the instructor could easily observe and correct. There are currently about 40 Tiger Moth aircraft in Canada with the majority of these in airworthy condition. There are an estimated 250 Tiger Moth aircraft worldwide that are still airworthy.

A Fleet Finch in the Canadian Warplane Heritage Museum collection at Hamilton, Ontario. The photograph is courtesy of the Canadian Warplane Heritage Museum.

The Fleet Finch was designed as a basic trainer biplane by Fleet Aircraft in Fort Erie, Ontario in 1938 and the prototype first flew in 1939. The Fleet Finch has a welded tubular steel frame with a fabric covering. It was manufactured from 1939 to 1941 and 431 were used by the RCAF in Canada as a basic trainer. The Fleet Finch has a 130 horsepower Kinner five cylinder radial engine. The Fleet Finch has a maximum speed of 104 miles per hour and a cruise speed of 85 miles per hour with a service ceiling of 10,500 feet. The aircraft stalls at about 55 miles per hour and will obtain lift and will get airborne above 56 miles per hour. An estimated 600 Fleet Finch aircraft were built.

Once we were on the base at Pendleton we did not go anywhere for the entire 8 weeks as the deep snow prevented any travel by vehicles with tires. All the supplies were brought into the base by big sleds with skis pulled by a large size D8 Caterpillar bulldozer all the way from the railway station ten miles away. The photograph is from the June 1944 *Pendletonic* magazine.

At this time of the year the entire airfield was covered in 30 to 36 inches of snow so the entire airfield could be used to take off or land on. For the time that the field was snow covered we had skis attached to the aircraft. I really liked having the skis on the Tiger Moth as you could land with a bit of drift if you wanted to. I did not have to worry about keeping the aircraft straight immediately upon touch down.

There were some fellow students at Pendleton who came from Australia and had never seen snow before they arrived in Canada. Well, those chaps had so much snow that they had many opportunities to have snowball fights with teams. A great old time was had by all that participated in the non-sanctioned winter sport. The photograph is from the June 1944 *Pendletonic* magazine.

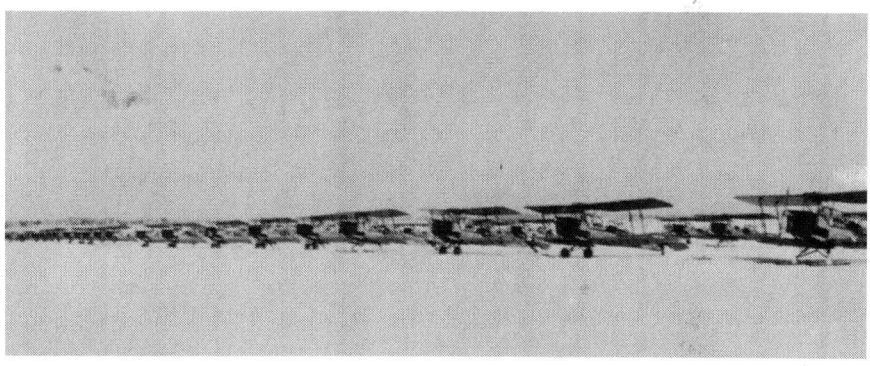

When I was at Pendleton there were about 45 Tiger Moths. In the photograph you can see the Tiger Moths are all lined up in a neat row sitting on the hard packed snow of the airfield. Most of the Tiger Moths have wheels and some have skis. The photograph is from the Bob Middleton Collection.

The skis could pose a hazard, however. In order that the tips of the skis did not dig into the snow upon landing, bungee type cords were connected to each ski tip and to a connection on the bottom of the fuselage just behind the engine. This kept the front tips of the skis always pointing up. The ground crew forgot to connect the bungee cords on a Tiger Moth one day. Just as it became airborne on takeoff the ski tips were pointing down. The ski tips dug into the snow, wiping out the landing gear and the Tiger Moth was flipped onto its back. Fortunately, the student pilot and the instructor were only shaken up and not injured.

I was assigned to D Flight and our Commanding Officer was Pilot Officer W. Godby. Initially we did a classroom training to supplement what we learned at No. 5 ITS. In February it was so cold with temperatures in the day at minus 2° Fahrenheit. We had just spent 10 weeks in Belleville, and I thought Belleville was cold but the day after day of sub-freezing temperatures at Pendleton were crazy. I had never experienced temperatures this cold in my entire life. On February 15, 1943 at night the temperature dropped to minus 33° Fahrenheit. All of the school's aircraft were kept inside heated hangers at all times as the straight 30 weight oil used in the engines would become so thick that the engines would not be able to turn over and start. The bush pilots in Northern Ontario would drain the oil from their engines when their aircraft were not running and would keep the oil in a heated building. Before the pilots would start the engines, the oil would be heated and then poured into the engine immediately before starting their engines. Because our aircraft were designed for Canada and the bitter cold weather the aircraft all had enclosed cockpits with sliding canopies and a tube that surrounded the engine exhaust pipe that brought heated air into the cockpit. The Canadian built Tiger Moth aircraft even had brakes but, most of the aircraft we were flying in were the British built Tiger Moths without brakes.

To endure the cold temperatures, we were wearing fur covered insulated flying coveralls that were affectionately nicknamed Teddies because we looked like bears when we were wearing them. I never wore a Teddy myself. Learning how to fly was a great deal of mental and physical effort I found that I would become hot without the Teddy. The Canadian built Tiger Moths had plenty of heat for me. I have always found that I get hot easily. Later in this book you will see photographs of me in just my shirt with the shirt sleeves rolled up while other folks have their jackets on.

Photograph of the Teddies that the guys were wearing. The photograph is from the June 1944 *Pendletonic* magazine.

I started my flight familiarization training with a flight in Tiger Moth number 8959 on Monday, March 1, 1943 with Flight Sargeant Tingey. I was actually sitting in the cockpit of a Tiger Moth, a real aircraft just like *Tailspin Tommy* and my other heroes. Up until today I had only been given instructions in the classroom about all the various controls in the cockpit of the Tiger Moth. I now familiarized myself with the aircraft and the controls. I learned how the stick or control column affected the ailerons on the wings which caused the aircraft to bank left or right. Holding the stick to the left made the aircraft bank to the left while pushing the stick to the right caused the aircraft to bank to the right. The aircraft elevator is the horizontal surface on the tail while the rudder is the vertical surface of the tail. Pulling the stick back caused the trailing edge of the elevator to go up which in turn makes the aircraft climb up into the sky. Pushing the stick forward caused the trailing edge of the elevator to go down which in turn makes the aircraft descend down to the ground. I learned how to operate the rudder bar with my feet to make the aircraft turn without banking. Pushing the right bar down turns the aircraft to the right while pushing the left bar turns the aircraft to the left.

I went over the operation of the instruments in front of me such as the altimeter and the airspeed indicator. The airspeed indicator was simply a flap attached to a spring that is mounted on the leading port wing strut. As the aircraft went through the air the wind pushed the flap and the numbers printed on the scale at the edge of this flap indicated the speed of the aircraft. Sargeant Tingey drilled into my head that the altimeter showed me the altitude above sea level and that the ground in the Pendleton area is 140 feet above sea level. "Remember the altimeter is not corrected to our location at Pendleton and you are 140 feet closer to the ground than what is indicated above sea level." Good thing that I could do the mental math in my head.

I learned the steps in starting the engine. The magneto switch that enabled the spark plugs to fire. Switch on, switch off. The Tiger Moth did not have a starter motor. To start the engine the propeller was turned by a member of the ground crew for the pilot. With switch off the propeller was turned through to clear any oil from the cylinders. Our Commanding Officer had given safety instructions to all personnel involved in starting the engines. The person turning the propeller always had to stand behind the propeller on the left side of the aircraft. The starter would pull down on the propeller and when it started you backed up to your left. When standing in front of the propeller when starting you had the risk of being sucked into the propeller or run down if the wheel chocks were not in place. We had no wheel brakes.

Sargeant Tingey called out to the starter, "Contact." The fellow starting the Tiger Moth pulled down on the propeller and the engine sputtered and chugged to life. Wow another milestone in my career of a Pilot. After the engine was started, I learned the use of the throttle lever to increase or reduce the speed of the engine. I learned to use the fuel level indicator attached to the fuel tank above my head in the middle of the upper wing. The gauge was a clear tube with a little plastic ball to indicate the fuel level. The tank held 86 litres of fuel which was enough for two hours of flying. The fuel to the engine was gravity fed from that upper wing tank so remember you cannot fly inverted for more than a few seconds at a time. First, I learned how to taxi down the runway using the rudder pedals to steer. Sargeant Tingey told me to put my feet on the pedals lightly so I could feel how he was moving the pedals.

We carried parachutes with us in the Tiger Moth in the form of a seat pack that you would sit on. Your parachute was your seat cushion. I do not remember anyone at Pendleton bailing out while I was there, but I do remember many crashes. It took a great deal of work to pack a parachute so there was a fine of $5 if you pulled the rip cord handle for no good reason. If you jumped out of a Tiger Moth while in the air and left your parachute behind, you would be fined $500. Sounded silly but that was the rule.

On March 2, 1943 we were going to be flying. Up to now I had never been airborne. Sargeant Tingey and I were flying for 40 whole minutes. Again, part of the training was to lightly touch all the controls and feel the motions that Sargeant Tingey was putting these through while he was flying the aircraft. We flew together for the rest of the week until Thursday, March 4, 1943. Using the aircraft Gosport tube communication intercom Sargeant Tingey constantly told me to do this and do not do that. He did it so much that after a week I could hear him in my head telling me how to fly the Tiger Moth. I could even hear Sargeant Tingey in my sleep.

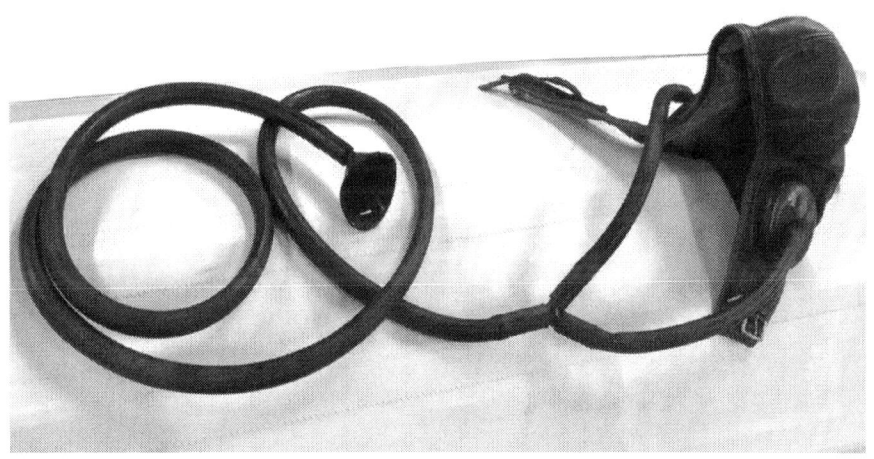

Photograph a one way Gosport tube set. The photograph was taken by Dan Middleton at the Tiger Boys Aeroplane Works Museum in Guelph, Ontario.

There were two sets of Gosport tubes, so the intercom was two way. The intercom in the Tiger Moth was extremely crude pneumatic hose type of affair with listening cups at the receiving end in the leather helmet and a funnel you spoke into on the speaking end. The funnel was supported under my chin by a cord attached to the helmet. It was similar to a ship intercom. How the intercom overcame the racket of the Tiger Moth engine I do not know but it did work well. The engine was extremely loud, and I had no hearing protection aside from the leather flying helmet.

On Saturday and Sunday, March 6 and 7, 1943 there was a spectacular blizzard that socked in all operations on the base for two days. The Base Manager had to send a telegram to the Air Officer Commanding, AOC. The Manager stated that the only transportation from the base, the railway station and the town of Pendleton was by freight sleds pulled by the crawler tractor. He estimated that there were enough supplies to last two weeks. The Manager stated that the flying operations would commence again in 48 hours.

The Manager requested a special Sicard snowblower plow to clear the roads by Saturday, March 20, 1943. Any urgent sick cases would be brought out by air by the Waco built aircraft. Lastly the Manager stated that the diesel electric generator has saved the heating situation at the school 4 times since it was installed.

The snowblower was invented by Arthur Sicard of Saint Leonard-de-Port-Maurice, Quebec. In 1925 after years of development work Arthur Sicard had the first working snowblower. The first commercial unit was sold to the town of Outremont on the Island of Montreal, Quebec in 1927.

I commenced flying with Sargeant Tingey again on Monday, March 8 to Friday, March 12, 1943. As spring approached the ice and snow on the runways was melting which was leaving great holes in the ice and snow. We now had to dodge these holes every time we took off, landed, or just taxied. Initially we were sticking flags in the holes to mark them. As the melting continued and we ran out of flags we were putting pine trees in the holes. The runways were quite a sight of flags, trees and holes. The graders and rollers would be out there attempting to keep the runways flat. There would still be weak spots in the top crust of solid looking ice and snow that the aircraft wheels would occasionally drop into.

In one week alone seven wooden propellers were wrecked from aircraft wheels being caught in the unmarked holes. While I was taxiing one time when I was returning from a flight my port wheel fell into one of these hidden holes in the snow. I was lucky as I was not travelling fast. The wheel dropped in and I just stopped. If I had been travelling faster the Tiger Moth would have flipped forward and jammed the rotating propeller into the snow and wrecked another propeller. I would have broken the eighth propeller that week. Two fellows from the ground crew came out and picked up the port side wing by hand and held it up while I gunned the engine to move the Tiger Moth forward. Thankfully, that was the only hole my Tiger Moth fell into that day. Eventually the Manager brought in scrappers to clear all the ice and snow off the runways. Once the runways were completely clear of ice and snow, we were able to practice flying at night. We had to put fire smudge pots out on both sides of the runway and then after we finished flying, we took them back to the hangers.

Vintage fire smudge pot. Photograph taken by and courtesy of Reg James.

C.A.P. 1 VOL.1
2nd Edition

SEQUENCE OF INSTRUCTION

1 A.	FAMILIARIZATION - GROUND
1 B.	FAMILIARIZATION - AIR (Including simple explanation of Flight)
1 C.	TARMAC CHECK - (Including starting up and handling of the engine)
2.	THE FLYING CONTROLS
3.	TAXIING
4.	STRAIGHT AND LEVEL FLIGHT
4 I.F.	STRAIGHT AND LEVEL FLIGHT ON INSTRUMENTS
5.	CLIMBING, DESCENDING, GLIDING
5 I.F.	CLIMBING, DESCENDING, GLIDING ON INSTRUMENTS
5 A.	STALLING
6.	TURNING
6 A.	CLIMBING TURNS
6 B.	DESCENDING TURNS
6 C.	GLIDING TURNS
6 I.F.	TURNING ON INSTRUMENTS
7.	THE TAKE OFF
7 A.	OUT OF WIND TAKE OFF
7 I.F.	TAKE OFF ON INSTRUMENTS
	THE CIRCUIT
8.	GLIDING, APPROACH AND LANDING
8 A.	OUT OF WIND LANDINGS
9.	ENGINE ASSISTED APPROACH
10.	SPINNING - (Including further demonstrations of stalling and incipient spinning)
10 I.F.	SPINNING ON INSTRUMENTS
11.	SOLO CHECK (Including overshoot and undershoot procedure)
12.	SIDE SLIPPING
13.	PRECAUTIONARY LANDINGS
14.	LOW FLYING
15.	STEEP TURNS
15 A.	STEEP DESCENDING AND GLIDING TURNS
16.	GLIDING TURNS - (See Sequence 6)
17.	FORCED LANDINGS
18.	ACTION IN EVENT OF FIRE
18 A.	ABANDONING AIRCRAFT
19.	INSTRUMENT FLYING (GENERAL)
20.	
21.	
22.	AEROBATICS
23.	
24.	
25.	NIGHT FLYING

No. 10 E.F.T.S.
Form No. C.F.I.3

The Pendleton practical flying course outline. Photograph from the Bob Middleton Collection.

I saw the results of the entire front of Tiger Moth 4043 falling through a weak spot in the icy crust. You can see in the photo that fortunately the pilot was unharmed. The photograph is from the Bob Middleton Collection.

There was one fellow on the base that seemed to take great pleasure in bullying me or teasing me by coming up behind me and flicking my ear. This would really hurt. My ears were still so very sensitive after being frozen walking back from the *Holiday Inn* movie in Belleville a few months ago. This one day I had had enough so I chased him around the outside of the operations hall until he fell down from exhaustion from running through the three-foot-deep snow. When I caught up with him, I jumped on him and gave him a snow job he would never forget. After that we had an understanding and became the best of friends for the rest of our time at Pendleton. After Pendleton I never saw or heard from him again. He was just another of the tens of thousands of airmen like me that came through the BCATP in the war years.

The weather between Saturday, March 13, 1943 and Thursday, March 18, 1943 was poor for flying and they can only teach so much ground school. This bunch of young fellows was becoming sort of rowdy and troublesome with nothing interesting to do. The Base Manager decided it would be great sport for all of us to do some marching. For a few days, our exercise was walking around the six mile perimeter of the base in the snow that was now four feet deep. The snow was so deep we were constantly pulling each other out of snow drifts. Each day we came back absolutely exhausted.

While I was at Pendleton I did not hear of anyone that was seriously injured or killed but learning how to fly is a risky business and many thousands of British Commonwealth flying students died in the process. The fellows flying in this Tiger Moth number 4098 were fortunate and walked away from this inverted crash landing. The photograph is from the Bob Middleton Collection.

On Saturday, March 20, 1943 I was training in a Link trainer for the first time at Pendleton. I was placed in the tiny, confined space and I had to fly a circuit completely by instruments. I could not see outside of the box. Generally, the object was to fly a square circuit and you needed to end up exactly where you started. Every week I had a trip in the Link trainer.

I was back in Tiger Moth number 9691 flying with Sargeant Tingey for 50 minutes Sunday, March 21, 1943. An hour after we landed both of us went up again for a 25 minute flight in Tiger Moth 8960. We landed and after I had taxied back, and I shut off the engine Sargeant Tingey got out. Sargeant Tingey told me to stay in the Tiger Moth and take it up for one takeoff and one landing all by myself for my Solo flight. This was a total surprise for me as no mention of me going for my Solo flight that day had been mentioned before we took off. The ground crew fellow tightened the Sutton harness in the empty front seat so that it would not tangle with the controls. This was another first for me, flying all by myself.

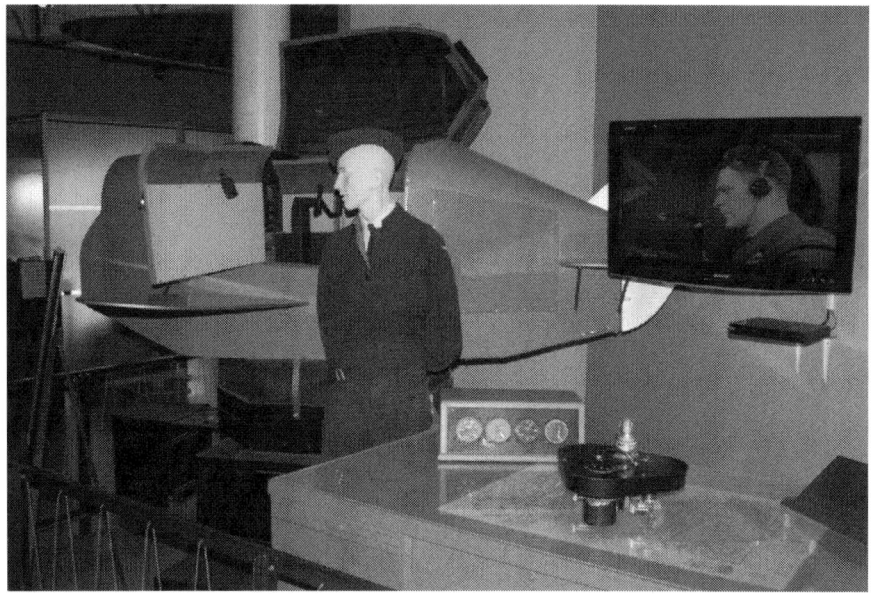

An example of the Link trainer located at the Canadian Warplane Heritage Museum at Hamilton, Ontario. The photograph is courtesy of the Canadian Warplane Heritage Museum.

Watch out *Tailspin Tommy* and Bill Barnes. I had so many things to remember and no one to help me should I get into difficulty. I must be able to do this by myself or Sargeant Tingey would not have told me to Solo. I started out on the runway and as my speed approached 45 miles per hour the tailwheel came up of the ground. I gave the Gipsy Major engine a bit more throttle and the ground just dropped away from under me and I became airborne. This was now the biggest thrill of my life, flying all by myself. I was also a bit scared because now that I was in the air I had to somehow get the Tiger Moth back on the ground again in one piece. There was no one to help me out or take over. The entire time I was in the air I could still hear Sargeant Tingey's voice inside my head telling me how to fly the Tiger Moth.

I came around for my Solo landing and as I approached, I still heard the instructor's voice in my head reminding me that, "You cannot make a good landing from a bad approach." "Yes. Sargeant Tingey." I felt that my first approach was rotten, so I took the Tiger Moth around again for a fresh approach. I managed to get the Tiger Moth back on the ground in one piece with a nice two-point landing. Wow! I flew an aircraft all by myself. I had been flying all by myself for a whole 15 minutes that I will never forget. I still remember that flight 77 years later. In the summer of 1945 when I was back in Toronto, Ontario working for the telephone company I sketched a picture of myself on my Solo flight in that Tiger Moth. I was on my way to being that Hurricane or Spitfire fighter pilot that I had dreamt about as a kid and signed up to be when I was a teenager, or so I thought.

Sketch of my Solo flight. From the Bob Middleton Collection.

I went into the mess and had lunch and when lunch was finished Sargeant Tingey, and I went up in Tiger Moth 5894 for a short 10 minute flight to point out some things and drill those points deeper into my head. I landed the Tiger Moth once again and after I had parked the aircraft Sargeant Tingey told me to take her back up again this time for a longer flight. "Be careful though and bring her back in one piece." There I was for my second flight by myself both on the same day. There is absolutely nothing in the world that is equal to flying an aircraft by yourself, floating in the air above the ground. By the time I had returned to the land of mortal beings I had been in the air for 45 minutes all by myself. This was going to call for some partying tonight with my pals. After these flights there were many flights with just me in total control of a Tiger Moth. The maneuvers were easy for me as I had been reading *BILL BARNES AIR TRAILS* for so many years. In his short stories, Bill Barnes would describe the use of the aircraft controls as he went through all his maneuvers. One of my favorite maneuvers was the falling leaf where you side slip the aircraft back and forth falling like a leaf from a tree. Thanks Bill Barnes.

A few days later on Tuesday, March 23, 1943 I went up in Tiger Moth 8865 to practice some slow rolls that I had never done by myself. I went up quite high to 9,000 feet to leave a good margin of safety between me and the ground should I experience difficulties. This was a medium height for a Tiger Moth that had a service ceiling of 13,000 feet. I started down and lost control for a while and I was in a dive going about 150 miles per hour. My airspeed indicator was in the red and I thought to myself, "What would Bill Barnes do?" I remembered to pull out of the dive slowly so as to not pull the wings off and regained control of the Tiger Moth. After I had recovered from this experience I fooled around in the sky for a while. I realized that my fuel was low as indicated by the little ball in the tube above my head and it was about lunch time according to my watch and my stomach. The fuel level indicator on the Tiger Moth was so simple. I side slipped off about 2,000 feet and came into land. "What the heck." I got a red Aldis lamp which informed me not to land so I pulled up to go around again. On my second approach I received a red flare. "What the heck!" And now there is another fellow in a Tiger Moth taking off while I have the red flare. The landing aircraft always has the right of way and this jerk is taking off.

On the downwind leg the most feared instructor on the base pulled in tight right beside me and motioned to pull up on my Sutton harness which I did. I figured I had something wrong with my aircraft and he wanted me held in securely. I just about had a fit when I saw who it was. He peeled away slowly and waved as he did so as you see in movies which left me very perplexed. There were no radios in the Tiger Moths so no one could communicate with me to say what was going on. As far as I could tell my Tiger Moth was performing perfectly well. Everything appeared to be working. I made a precautionary approach close to the ground using lots of power in case I needed to pull up at the last minute.

63

In this photograph you can see the Sutton harness, the control stick and the rudder pedals. The photograph was taken by Dan Middleton at the Tiger Boys Aeroplane Works Museum in Guelph, Ontario.

Oh, my goodness, as I came in, I saw the meat wagon, fire truck and what looked like the entire station personnel standing beside the runway. They were waiting for me to land, and I had absolutely no idea of what my problem was. I wondered, what is wrong? I touched down with my best landing ever and all seemed OK. Then the starboard wing began to drop, and I applied power to straighten out the ground loop that the Tiger Moth was trying to make. It was at this point that I realized the starboard wheel was somehow missing. The landing gear on the starboard side felt like it was coming through the floor. I managed to keep the aircraft straight and as I slowed the starboard wing tip just gently touched the ground and the Tiger Moth swung around 90 degrees and stopped. I quickly switched off the engine, noticed that there was no fire and said, "thank you." The handle under the wing tip was slightly scuffed. This was one of my best two wheel landings. It just happened to be on the port wheel and the tail wheel. Four people came over to the aircraft after I got out. Three fellows lifted up the starboard wing and then one fellow put the piston attached to the starboard wheel back into the oleo sleeve. I went back to the hanger in the crash truck. One of the ground crew members taxied the aircraft to one of the hangers for repairs. I believe a pin had fallen out of the oleo piston.

The School's Commanding Officer and Sargeant Tingey did not believe me when I told him that I had not been flying low and hit a tree or a fence. All of us young would-be pilots did love flying fast and extremely low. I think I descended too fast and the air going past the wheel pulled the Oleo apart and then the wheel was left dangling. I graduated from Pendleton No. 10 EFTS on March 23, 1943 with 26 hours and 30 minutes of Solo flying time. I was a certified Tiger Moth pilot.

When I landed on one wheel I was so happy that I did not land like this pilot that did a ground loop upon landing. From the Bob Middleton Collection.

It was now well into spring and I was off on leave in Toronto. I caught up with my friends, family and Pat. I spent more time making my aircraft recognition scrapbooks.

Chapter 6

UPLANDS AND THE HARVARD

In May 1943 after I graduated from Pendleton, I was posted to No. 2 Service Flying Training School (SFTS) at Uplands located just east of Ottawa, Ontario where they were flying Harvard trainers. This is the same flying school that the movie *Captains of the Clouds* starring James Cagney was filmed at on July 19 and 20, 1942. Just like James Cagney I was learning to fly the North American Aviation monoplane Harvard training aircraft. The aircraft was made of metal and the engine looked huge compared to the Tiger Moth engine. The airspeed indicator went up to 300 knots, about 330 miles per hour. Wow I could fly fast. It had a maximum speed of 280 miles per hour with a cruise speed of 145 miles per hour.

The Harvard trainer was built by North American Aviation in the USA. The Americans called it the T-6 Texan. In Canada and England, it was called the Harvard. The Harvard first flew in 1935 and a total of 15,495 aircraft were built. The T-6 or Harvard were used by all the USA Armed Forces and the RCAF and RAF. 1,173 Harvard trainers were supplied by purchase or lend-lease to the BCATP. Most of the Harvard aircraft were used in Canada. The Harvard weighed 5,600 pounds loaded and had one Pratt & Whitney 600 horsepower R-1340 Wasp nine cylinder radial engine. The Harvard ceiling at 24,000 feet was twice that of the Tiger Moth. The rate of climb of the Harvard at 1,200 feet per minute was twice that of the Tiger Moth.

It was such a thrill to fly the Harvard with the single wing which was almost three times faster than the de Havilland Tiger Moths I had been flying at Pendleton.

I thought the Harvard was such a beautiful aircraft. Only a year ago I was working in the tool room of the machine shop at the General Electric transformer factory on Lansdowne Avenue and Davenport Road in Toronto. Boy oh boy, this was living. After all those Bill Barnes airplane magazine's stories I read, model airplanes that I built, movies and matinee series like *Tailspin Tommy* I watched as a kid, I was going to be flying a real airplane.

A North American Aviation T-6 Harvard trainer. The photograph is courtesy of the Canadian Warplane Heritage Museum in Hamilton, Ontario, Canada.

While at Uplands I saw a Douglas C-47 for the first time in front of me. That aircraft goes by the names C-47 in the USA or Dakota in Canada and the UK. Until now I had only seen a C-47 in magazines and newsreels. The civilian version is called the DC-3. I was walking under the great huge wings and was thinking to myself, "How does it ever get off the ground with those tiny 1,200 horsepower R-1830 Pratt & Whitney engines?" Remember in April 1943 I was only a 19 year old kid and that Dakota really impressed me.

My first flight in a Harvard was with Instructor Pilot Officer Donohue in Harvard 3675 on Saturday, April 21, 1943. The engine crankshaft and propeller on the Harvard are huge and heavy compared to the Tiger Moth and has a serious gyroscopic affect. On that first flight as soon as the tailwheel came off the ground the aircraft made almost a 90 degree turn to the right as it shot across the runway. Wow, that was exciting. In my future flights I knew what was coming and I compensated with left rudder just as the tailwheel came off of the ground.

A picture of the recently restored Dakota FZ692 at the Canadian Warplane Heritage Museum. This Dakota actually saw service in France during and after D-Day. The photograph is courtesy of the Canadian Warplane Heritage Museum in Hamilton, Ontario, Canada.

I spent many hours flying in Link trainers where you used instruments only and no visual contact with the rest of the world. I trained with 6 different instructors. The landing speed of the Harvard is almost twice the landing speed of the Tiger Moth and I had one small problem landing it. When I was landing the Harvard, I usually found that I was landing 4 feet high or 4 feet low. 4 feet low was hard on the aircraft. Sometimes I got the landing right. The instructors tried and tried. After a while they told me that if this was not war time and there was more time to train me, they could eventually train me to land the Harvard correctly. When I was fifty years old an optometrist informed me that I was five percent cross-eyed and as it turns out therefore I could not land the Harvard at the higher speed. If you were more than 5 percent cross-eyed your depth perception is poor, and you cannot land an airplane properly and become a pilot.

I read in the book *The Fly by Nights* written by Donald Fessey, an RAF Navigator that had washed out landing Harvard trainers as well. It was due to his eyes not being able to adjust to rapid changes in reflected light between the grass and the concrete runway while landing at the higher speed.

After my last Harvard training flight on May 2, 1943, I was washed out as a pilot. I was devastated as I had dreamt about becoming a pilot and flying for so many years. "Lack of Flying Ability" really made me feel rotten. I was so close, but it was not to be. I would not get to fly Hurricanes or Spitfires just like my aviation heroes. I have always said however that becoming a Navigator probably saved my life.

Flying time	England	hrs.	Service Schools Attended	Time to Solo
	U.S.	hrs.	No. 5 I.T.S.Belleville,Ont.	EFTS: 9:25 hours.
	Canada 65	hrs.	No.10 EFTS, Pendleton, Ont.	SFTS: 8:35 hours.
			No. 2 SFTS, Uplands, Ont.	did not solo

Unit by which eliminated: No. 2 S.F.T.S.,Uplands.

Reason for Elimination: Lack of Flying Ability

Medical Category: A1B , A3B

Decision of Reselection Board: NAVIGATOR

	V.G.	Good	Average	Poor
Temperament		X		
Personality		X		
Keenness	X			
Intelligence	X			
Service Spirit	X			
Determination	X			

I.T.S. Remarks: A hard worker, very pleasant and anxious to get ahead, aggressive, keen, good mixer. Sincere, dependable, co-operative and willing.

EFTS Remarks: Average pilot, good air sense. Should do well in service school. Aerobatics are good. Instruments are fair. Showed good progress during course. Inclined to be careless.

SFTS Remarks: Training discontinued due to lack of flying ability. This pupil was very keen to fly and put forth a commendable effort. His general flying, other than the landings, was very good. However, his approach to land was very inconsistent and his judgment on landing was poor, and he was unable to go solo.

T.91 Remarks: Training discontinued due to lack of flying ability. Pupil's flying was good average with the exception of his landings which were very inconsistent and unsafe. This pupil was keen to fly. He has a good personality and disposition and is recommended for further aircrew training as Navigator.

My final report card from Belleville, Pendleton and Uplands recommending me for training as a navigator. From the Bob Middleton Collection.

May. 5/43.

Darling Bob:

I'm sorry about the disappoint you had, but don't you think its just as nice to be a Navigator any old day.

I'm sure that Navigators course will be awfully hard, because it has an awful lot of figuring to it.

It wouldn't have made any difference to me what your in, because I like you just the way you are.

Part of the letter that Pat sent to me after she learned that I had been washed out of pilot training at Uplands SFTS. The picture is from the Bob Middleton Collection.

Chapter 7

LEARNING TO NAVIGATE

After I washed out from No. 2 SFTS at Uplands I was shipped off to the No. 5 Manning Depot at Lachine, Quebec where someone would figure out what to do with me. Once I arrived, I discovered I was part of a group of 30 washed out pilots. You never saw such a gang of dejected souls in your life. All of us had so badly wanted to be Hurricane or Spitfire pilots and now we found ourselves doing menial jobs while we were waiting to find out what we were going to do for the rest of World War II. The bunch of us were wandering around just goofing off and hiding out of sight behind the barracks. We were all feeling quite rotten.

One day our Corporal Instructor told us that the higher ups had noticed our lollygagging attitude and he told us it would not do. He told us it was making him look bad being in command of a bunch of misfits. I am sure he was just pretending he would be in trouble so that we would want to help him out. The Corporal made us a deal and he told us that if we would drill in a sharp fashion for fifteen minutes out of each hour on the parade ground we could slack off behind the barracks for the rest of the hour. We did as he asked for a few days. A few days later we were marching around that parade square for a few minutes when we noticed that all the new recruits were standing on the side watching our display. We stepped up our performance some more and you never saw such a sharp drill team in all your life. We all did such a great parade square performance that the same day we were shipped off to No. 4 Air Observer School (AOS) in London, Ontario for Navigator training. You never saw such a happy gang of misfits in your life. I am sure that the 6 week mathematics course I took in Quebec City in September and October of 1942 put me in the good books for navigator training. It was my good luck that I flunked the mathematics at Basic Training in Toronto, and I was then sent to Quebec City for the mathematics training. Someone must have seen the ability in me. In all I was only at No. 5 Manning Depot at Lachine for less than 10 days. I am sure the powers that be knew what they were doing and they knew how to get the morale of 30 washed out pilots back up and ready to go.

Monday, May 17, 1943 was the day of the amazing Dam Busters raid by Wing Commander Guy Gibson and 617 Squadron bursting the Möhne and Eder Dams in the Ruhr Valley of Germany. This had been achieved with only 18 Lancaster bombers and crews with a top-secret bomb designed by Barnes Wallis. This was marvelous news for everyone in England and it gave a great boost in morale. It was a big win for Bomber Command.

No. 4 Air Observer School in London, Ontario in 1943. In this photograph you can see the two story school buildings that were arranged in the shape of an H. The link between the buildings held the showers and washrooms. Photograph from the Bob Middleton Collection.

As another case of my very good luck, I have always figured that I am still alive because I became a Navigator. I became a very good navigator and I always navigated us back home alive.

In June 1943 I started Navigator training at No. 4 AOS in London, Ontario. The two letter code for the London aerodrome was XU. I was enrolled in course No. 77. The head instructor for the course was Flight Officer Findley. He was a great teacher and a real nice guy who had been a hard rock miner before he became an RCAF Navigator and Instructor. The first two weeks we had lots more ground school where we learned how to plot a course, find your wind, find compass error, and use a sextant to shoot the stars. Compass error applies to the variation or deviation of a true course vs. the magnetic course. I was taught how to read the stars, locate the stars, know the star names, and know what to do with the information. I learned to read the clouds and name the clouds and position lines. A position line is a line that can be identified on an aeronautical chart and by observation on the surface of the earth. The intersection of two position lines we call a fix. I learned that weather forecasting was as much an art as it was science. The training aircraft at this aerodrome in 1943 was the twin engine British built Avro Anson Mk. 1. The Anson being used in Canada were all wood construction. The wings were all plywood while the fuselage framing was wood which was covered with fabric. The Anson had the distinction of being the first aircraft of the RCAF and RAF to have retractable landing gear.

The twin engine Avro Anson Mk. 1 aircraft 6365 from No. 4 London AOS. Photograph from the Bob Middleton Collection.

The Anson first introduced in 1936 was designed and built by Avro in England. Between 1936 and 1952 about 8,138 Anson aircraft were built in England and 2,882 Anson Mk. II and Mk. V were built in Canada at Victory Aircraft in Malton, Ontario. This is the same factory where the Canadian Avro Lancaster Mk. X was built. While I was at London AOS, we were flying the British built Anson Mk. 1 that had the hand cranked manually operated landing gear. The Anson Mk. 1 was powered by two 350 horsepower Armstrong Siddeley Cheetah engines.

My first trip out in an Anson number 874 was on Tuesday, June 22, 1943 at 13:30 in the afternoon. We left London and flew 190 miles to St. Marys, Drumbo, Tillsonburg, Port Stanley, Strathroy and back to London all in one and a half hours. This trip is shown on the map on page 78. The Anson was being flown by Mr. Bond who was a contracted pilot from Trans-Canada Air Lines working for the RCAF. Once trained an RCAF pilot was too valuable to fly navigation training aircraft so private contractors flew our trainers. On this flight I was the second navigator. RAF trainee, Peter Parnham was the first navigator on this flight and some others I was on. I really did not like this fellow, and we did not get along well. He was from England and had a bossy attitude towards some people. The second navigator did a great deal of observation work, calculating and doing fixes for the first navigator which allowed him to concentrate on directing the pilot. The second navigator also had the rotten job of raising and lowering the manual landing gear on the Anson. Operating the landing gear at London AOS was by a hand crank that required 149 revolutions to raise or lower the landing gear.

I was the first navigator for a trip on Wednesday, June 30, 1943 in Anson 6748 flown by Mr. Carne at 14:00 in the afternoon. We flew from London to Delhi, Glencow, Kellys and back to London on a 180 mile trip that lasted 2 hours and 45 minutes. Trip is shown on the map on page 78.

Monday, July 26, 1943 I went out as first navigator in Anson 169 with Mr. Dillobough for a 640 mile 3 hour and 30 minute trip. We flew from London to Point Clark, Collingwood, Oakville, past London to Grand Bend and back to London. This trip is shown on the map on page 78.

Head Instructor Flight Officer Findley.
Photograph from the Bob Middleton Collection.

I was the first navigator for a trip on Wednesday, June 30, 1943 in Anson 6748 flown by Mr. Carne at 14:00 in the afternoon. We flew from London to Delhi, Glencow, Kellys and back to London on a 180 mile trip that lasted 2 hours and 45 minutes. Trip is shown on the map on page 78.

Monday, July 26, 1943 I went out as first navigator in Anson 169 with Mr. Dillobough for a 640 mile 3 hour and 30 minute trip. We flew from London to Point Clark, Collingwood, Oakville, past London to Grand Bend and back to London. This trip is shown on the map on page 78.

On July 30, 1943 I was flying with Pilot Mr. Alexander as first navigator in Anson 6171 with sealed orders. So exciting as it was almost like a real operation. The flight lasted 2 hours and 40 minutes. On July 31, 1943 I was the first navigator on my first navigation exercise at night with Mr. Brunelle in Anson 6895. We took off at 21:15. We were flying to Goderich via various cities and back to London. Goderich is on the east shore of Lake Huron. As the navigator I am the person that gives the pilot all the course, altitude and speed information. Our speed was to be 100 miles per hour, a standard cruising speed. I had noticed since we set course that the engines of this Anson were very noisy and were vibrating a great deal more than usual.

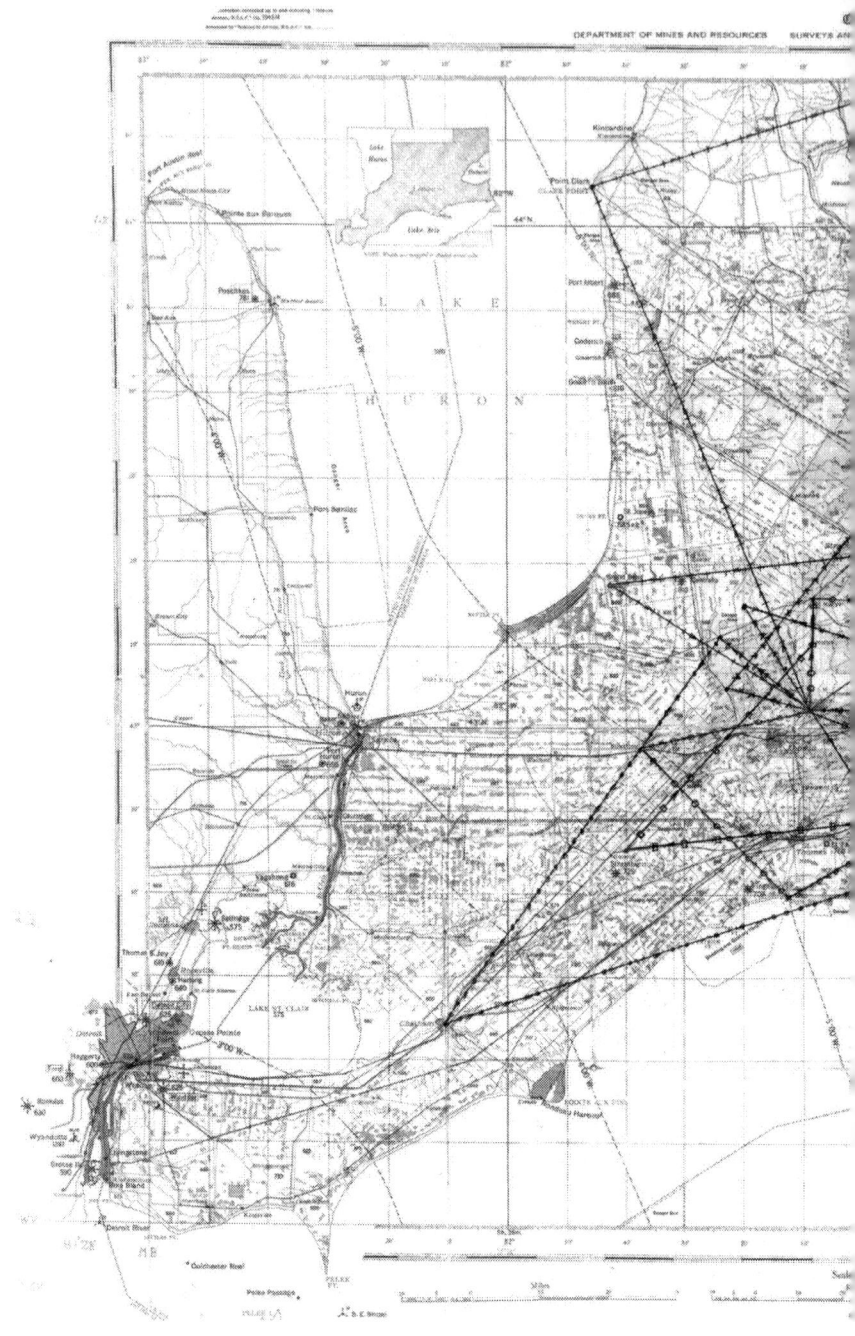

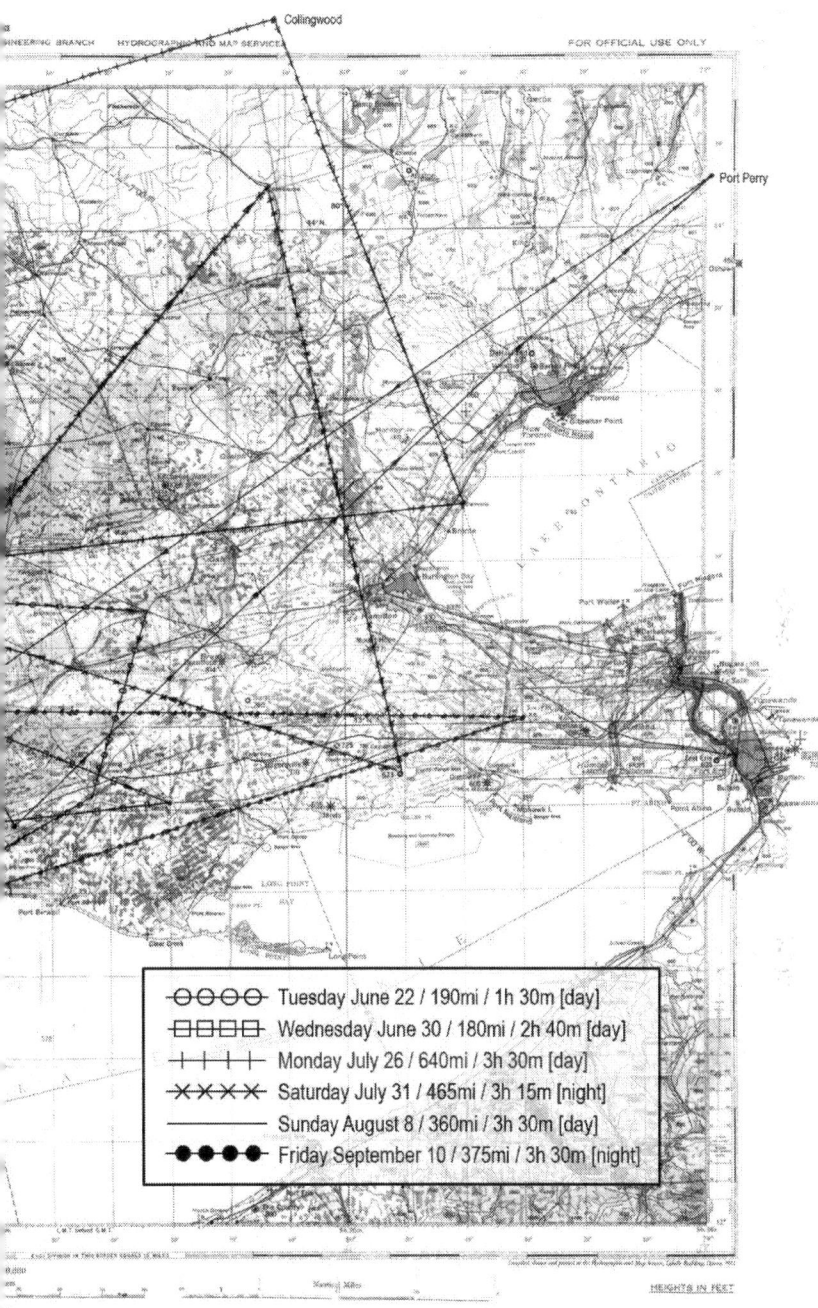

The actual map that I took with me while flying in the Anson aircraft at London AOS. Some of my routes are marked and labeled.

After a while I had the sneaky feeling, we were somehow lost as we should have passed over Goderich ten minutes earlier. It turned out that we were somewhere out over Lake Huron. I went up to consult with Mr. Brunelle the pilot. When I was up front, I asked him what speed we were flying, and he told me we were flying at 100 knots just as I had asked. I had only told him 100 as up to now all the Anson trainers we had flown in had miles per hour air speed indicators. It happened that this Anson had an air speed indicator calibrated in knots. We were actually flying about 115 miles per hour. It was no wonder the engines were objecting so strenuously. Mr. Brunelle proceeded to reduce our speed to 87 knots and the noise and vibration ceased. I now had to figure out exactly where we were so I could get us safely back to London, Ontario. I did not know it then, but this would be good practice figuring out where we are in the black of night for future real bomber operations.

One foggy day we were having difficulty finding London and the pilot gave me some attitude. I must have ticked him off because when we finally found London, he flipped the Anson on its side in a steep turn so I could see out the window better. He flipped it so rapidly I ended up on my tail end. He thought it was hilarious. When we arrived back at London the Anson ran out of fuel just after he parked the aircraft. The joke was now on him being rather surprised and embarrassed. The assistant to Flight Officer Findley called a group of us to the second floor of one of the school buildings and told us that he needed us to move a huge, wooden map table with map drawers to the ground floor. This table was 8 feet long, $3^{1/2}$ feet wide and must have weighed hundreds of pounds. It could not be disassembled before moving it. It would not fit through the door, so we removed the door, the complete door frame and one stud on one side. Once we had the opening prepared, we stood there looking down the stairs wondering how we were going to get it down the stairs without injuring ourselves. Officer Findley's assistant said to us, "It's just a matter of time." We did manage to get the map table moved downstairs without injury.

As Navigator, Air Observer trainees we had to learn to use huge, heavy cameras to take F24 pictures of the ground. The negative produced by the camera is 5 inches by 5 inches square. The negative had to be large in order to enlarge the picture and still have sufficient detail to make the picture useful. This was the same type of camera used in the bombers to take the photographs of the bombed target from 18,000 feet in the air. I was using the camera only a few thousand feet above the ground to take single pictures like the picture of London AOS. We would also take a series of in-line photographs. For these the pilot would fly the Anson straight, level and at a constant speed while I took a series of photographs. After these photographs were printed, I would staple the pictures together to create one very long picture. The exercise was called short line overlaps. This helped us understand aerial reconnaissance and how maps of targets are produced from aerial photographs. My first experience with this practice was in Anson 9600 at 15:30 on Thursday, August 26, 1943. I had to hang out of a window of the Anson while holding onto the camera and taking my photographs. I would kneel on the floor of the Anson with my legs tight against the inside of the fuselage and everything above my belly button was hanging outside of the aircraft. There was a safety rope attached to the camera to catch it in case I let go of it. There was not any rope attached to me in case I fell out of the Anson. I do not recall hearing about any trainees falling out of an aircraft. That flight lasted 1 hour and 15 minutes. Over a 3 week period I did two more short line overlap photography flights.

The type of camera I was using to take the short line overlap photographs. The camera weighed about 25 pounds. This photograph was taken at the National Aviation Museum in Ottawa, Ontario by Dan Middleton.

These photographs show the aerial reconnaissance made up from the short line overlaps. You can see that the pilot flew in quite a straight line. The photograph is from the Bob Middleton Collection.

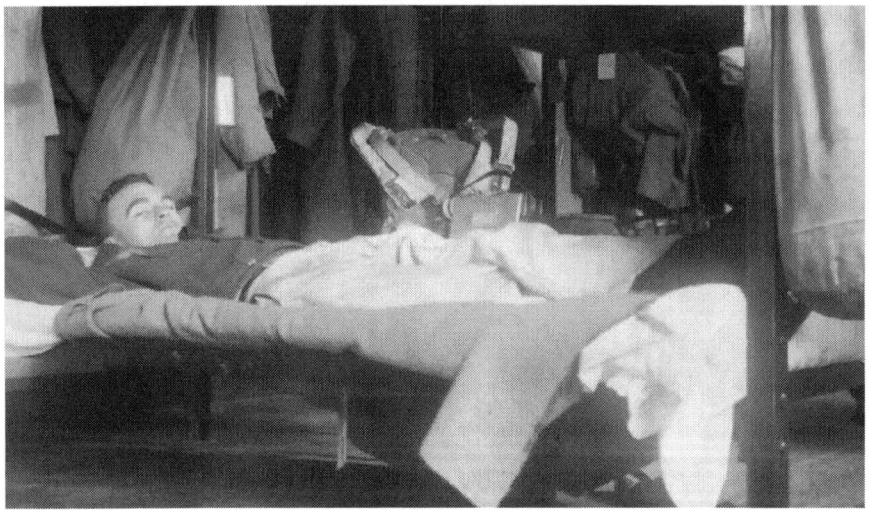

Dan Monahan, aka Horizontal Monahan. Photograph from the Bob Middleton Collection.

Dan Monahan was quite a character and quite memorable. He was not lazy at all but if the situation at hand allowed him to sit down, he would sit down and if the situation at hand offered him a chance to lie down Dan would lie down. We would find Dan in the lying down position so often we all nicknamed him Horizontal Monahan.

We had a great time all piling into this old jalopy. I am the fellow behind the driver in the white shirt with the shirt sleeves rolled up. I was always hot. You will notice everyone else except for Lowry and another fellow have their jackets on. Lowry is the fellow with his hand on his cap. The fellow sitting on the running board in front with the white pants is Dan Monahan. I forget the name of the fellow beside Dan. The fellow on my left side is Charlie Ryans. The fellow just above my left shoulder is Jack Kelly. Some of these folks you will read about later in my story. The photograph is from the Bob Middleton Collection.

I graduated from Navigation School on October 15, 1943 with my Navigator Officer half-wing. The ceremony was attended by His Worship Mayor Heaman the Mayor of London. Mayor Heaman addressed the gathering. Our wings were presented to us by Wing Commander W. R. Kingsland the Commanding Officer of the school. At end of the ceremony, we all made our Ceremonial March Past. I was now Sergeant Middleton. My new identity disc number was J37180.

There was a huge banquet for all the graduating RCAF and RAF officers. There was plenty of beer and alcohol involved, in fact way too much so we all partied like crazy after the official ceremony. The next day after graduation the instructors told all of us that we still had 3 more exercises to complete our training. We only had 33 of the 36 trips that were required to complete the course. The morning after the party we had to make up these 3 trips. I had to do square end search practice at only 1,500 hundred feet. The air was very turbulent and bumpy.

Some graduates of No. 4 Air Observer School, RCAF at London, Ontario. These are Toronto men that received their Navigator wing at the school. We did not have our commissioned officer uniforms yet. This photograph was taken by the Toronto Telegram and appeared in the evening newspaper on October 19, 1943. This is a photograph of the print that the newspaper gave us. From left to right, standing are Sergeants Robert Joyner, John Page, Robert Burton, Jack Kelly, Robert Middleton, Jim Dowell, Charles Ryans, and Wally Henderson. Left to right, sitting are Sergeants Anthony Orchard, Herbert Galloway and Arthur Matthews. The photograph is from the Bob Middleton Collection.

It was an extremely hot, humid day so we were all very damp. I certainly wished I had not drunk so much the night before, but I managed to hold it in and not throw up. For square end practice you fly an ever-expanding square. To start you divide the visibility by 2 and fly in a straight line to that distance and make a 90 degree turn and fly the half visibility distance. For the next two sides you add half the visibility distance and repeat in an ever expanding square until you find what you are looking for. You can see one of these on the map. I had to make 2 squares that morning.

After the square end search practice, I had to navigate a cross-country trip at 9,000 feet from London to Toronto and back to London. It was so pleasant up at 9,000 feet in the cooler temperature and very smooth flying. Normally we would have flown at 5,000 feet but after the morning in the heat and humidity the pilot decided to fly in the smoother cooler air. For the return trip the pilot let me fly the Anson all the way back to London. This was such a thrill for me as I thought I would never get to fly any aircraft again and here I was flying a twin engine job. By the time, my Navigator training was complete I had 60 flying hours in the daylight and 35 flying hours at night.

The Canadian RCAF Navigators were all made Commissioned Officers. The RAF Navigators that were in the same course as I remained as Non-Commissioned Sergeants (NCO's). The RAF Navigators had to gain their commissioned status through a recommendation from their crew Captain. The school gave $200 to a local tailor to make each of us our Officer uniforms. We thought this was rather fishy, but we did not complain. That tailor also threw that huge banquet for all the graduating RAF and RCAF Navigators. It was curious that we became Officers right away because graduating Pilots did not automatically become Commissioned Officers. As a Commissioned Officer I would now be paid an extra $6.00 per day flying pay on top of my regular pay. An NCO was only paid 75 cents per day flying pay on top of their regular pay. We would earn this flying pay once we were in the UK at a training unit that involved flying or an operational squadron. The flying pay would continue for 6 months after your last flight. This was a good incentive to Commanding Officers to go on operations with the crews. This pay difference between an NCO and a Commissioned Officer always bothered me once we were on operations as we were all putting our lives on the same line and we all depended on each other to do our jobs perfectly. Any member of the crew not doing his job perfectly could get us all killed.

All the British Commonwealth airmen were at minimum non-commissioned Sergeant Officers. In a Luftwaffe managed German Prisoner of War camp all Allied flying officers were treated well and did not have to do forced manual labor. In the United States Army Air Force, USAAF only Pilots, Copilots, Bomb Aimers and Navigators were Commissioned Officers. Everyone else in a USAAF bomber crew was an Enlisted Man. In the German Prisoner of War camps the enlisted men were not treated as well as the officers and they had to do forced manual labor. The USAAF enlisted men were sent to different camps than the USAAF Commissioned Officers.

It was now halfway through October 1943 and I was given two weeks leave back home a posting for more training in England and a one-way railway ticket to Halifax. I took the train back to Toronto from London and spent the next two weeks with friends, family and Pat McIntyre my fiancée. We said we would write every day while I was in England. I still have some of Pat's letters that I saved. All my letters that I mailed disappeared except for one to my parents.

The No. 77 AOS Graduating Class picture at London AOS. This was before we received our Commissioned Officer uniforms. I am standing in the back row directly under the Anson aircraft number 6143. My friend George Lewthwaite is in the back row fourth from the right. Lowry wearing sunglasses is in the back row 12th from the right. Photograph from the Bob Middleton Collection.

After I returned home in 1945, I placed an X beside the names of 8 men on the graduation program that I had heard were Killed in Action. It is very haunting many years later to see the service numbers of these men killed in action above and below my J37180 service number. Somehow, I was spared.

7 men from London No. 4 AOS No. 77 course that were Killed in Action.

F/O George Lewthwaite, J37164 died on July 24, 1944 in a training accident at Tholthorpe 1666 HCU. The Halifax they were flying in was observed to have exploded in the air and all members of the crew were lost. George Lewthwaite and the crew are buried at the Cemetery at Harrogate, Yorkshire, UK.

F/O Anthony Orchard, J37160 died on November 2, 1944 while flying with RCAF 415 Squadron on an operation to Dusseldorf, Germany. Anthony Orchard and the crew except for the Flight Engineer who survived are buried at the Rheinberg War Cemetery, Germany.

F/O Joseph Hong, J37185 died May 23, 1944 while flying with Honeybourne 24 OTU in Whitney AD701 on a leaflet operation to Alencon, France. Joseph Hong and crew are buried at the Bretteville-sur-Laize Canadian War Cemetery, France.

F/O Jack A. Kelly, J37186 died on August 4, 1944 while flying with RCAF 434 Squadron in Halifax LW436 on an operation to Bois de Cassan, France. Jack Kelly and 4 crew members are buried at the Drosay Churchyard Cemetery, France. and is buried in France. Two crew members survived.

F/O Harold F. Le Noury, J37183 died November 2, 1944 while flying with RAF 77 Squadron in Halifax MZ829 on an operation to Dusseldorf, Germany. Harold Le Noury and crew are buried at the Hutton War Cemetery, Belgium.

F/O James Fraser, J37166 died November 1, 1944 while flying with RCAF 424 Squadron on an operation to Oberhausen, Germany. James Fraser and crew are buried at the Nederweert War Cemetery, Netherlands.

F/O Arthur Mathews, J37178 died September 13, 1944 while flying with RAF Riccall 1658 HCU in Halifax JD380 on bullseye operation and a diversionary training operation over the North Sea. Arthur Mathews and crew are remembered at the Runnymede Memorial, Surrey, UK.

GRADUATION CEREMONY

and

PRESENTATION OF WINGS

TO

AIR NAVIGATORS and AIR BOMBERS

OF

No. 4 AIR OBSERVER SCHOOL, R.C.A.F.

BY

WING COMMANDER W. R. KINGSLAND

Friday, October 15th, 1943

•

OFFICIALS

Chief Supervisory Officer	General Manager
Wing Commander W. R. KINGSLAND	MR. C. R. LEAVENS
No. 4 Air Observer School, R.C.A.F.	Leavens Bros. (Training) Ltd.
London - Ontario	No. 4 Air Observer School, R.C.A.F.
	London - Ontario

Front page of our graduation program. Photograph from the Bob Middleton Collection.

Ed. Kelly.

Jim Dowell

AIR NAVIGATORS - COURSE 77

Rank	Name	Home Address
x LAC	Bennett, Leonard W.	London, Eng.
LAC	Berry, Clarence D.	Hamilton, Ont.
LAC	Brouillett, Gerald C.	Montreal, P.Q.
LAC	Burton, Robert S.	Toronto, Ont.
x LAC	Cook, Orlando	Hamilton Beach, Ont.
LAC	Cutt, Kenneth H.	Goderich, Ont.
LAC	Dilley, Jack D.	Stanmore, Middlesex, Eng.
LAC	Dowell, James H.	Toronto, Ont.
LAC	Elie, Joseph W.	Montreal, P.Q.
LAC	Fraser, James	Clinton, Ont.
LAC	Galloway, Herbert K.	Toronto, Ont.
LAC	Glover, William V.	Peterborough, Ont.
LAC	Henderson, Wallace G.	Toronto, Ont.
x LAC	Hong, Joseph	Windsor, Ont.
LAC	Hunter, Herald E.	Kingston, Ont.
LAC	Hyland, Frank E.	Windsor, Ont.
LAC	Joyner, Robert C.	Toronto, Ont.
LAC	Kamin, Sockley	Windsor, Ont.
LAC	Keith, Bruce A.	London, Ont.
LAC	Kelly, Edgar J.	Montreal, P.Q.
x LAC	Kelly, Jack A.	Toronto, Ont.
x LAC	Le Noury, Harold F.	Hamilton, Ont.
x LAC	Lewiewaite, George A.	Montreal, P.Q.
LAC	Manning, Frank R.	Reston, Man.
LAC	Mathews, Arthur G.	Toronto, Ont.
LAC	McVey, Edward B.	South Porcupine, Ont.
LAC	Middleton, Robert J.	Toronto, Ont.
LAC	Mitchell, Gideon G.	Edinburgh, Scot.
LAC	Monahan, Almas W.	Berlin, New Hampshire, U.S.A.
LAC	Nairn, Lawrence D.	Montreal, P.Q.
x LAC	Orchard, Anthony B.	Toronto, Ont
LAC	Page, John M.	Toronto, Ont
LAC	Parnham, Peter J.	Boston, Lincolnshire, Eng.
LAC	Ryans, Charles A.	Toronto, Ont.
x LAC	Salisbury, Herbert F.	Rivers, Man.
LAC	Scammell, John G.	Fredericton, N.B.
LAC	Sinnamon, Albert W.	Catford, Eng.
LAC	Talbot, John E.	Wirral, Cheshire, Eng.
LAC	Teeple, William G.	Timmins, Ont.
LAC	Thorpe, Kenneth W.	Hucknall, Notts., Eng.
LAC	Tucker, Arthur W.	London, Eng.
LAC	Turner, David R.	Glace Bay, N.S.
LAC	Walsh, James	Manchester, Eng.
Cpl.	Wright, Ellwood S.	Wallington, Surrey, Eng.
LAC	Zolty, Peter S.	Birmingham, Eng.

The first page inside the graduation program. After I returned to Toronto in 1945 I placed an **X** beside the names of the fellows that I had heard did not survive the Second World War. Photograph from the Bob Middleton Collection.

89

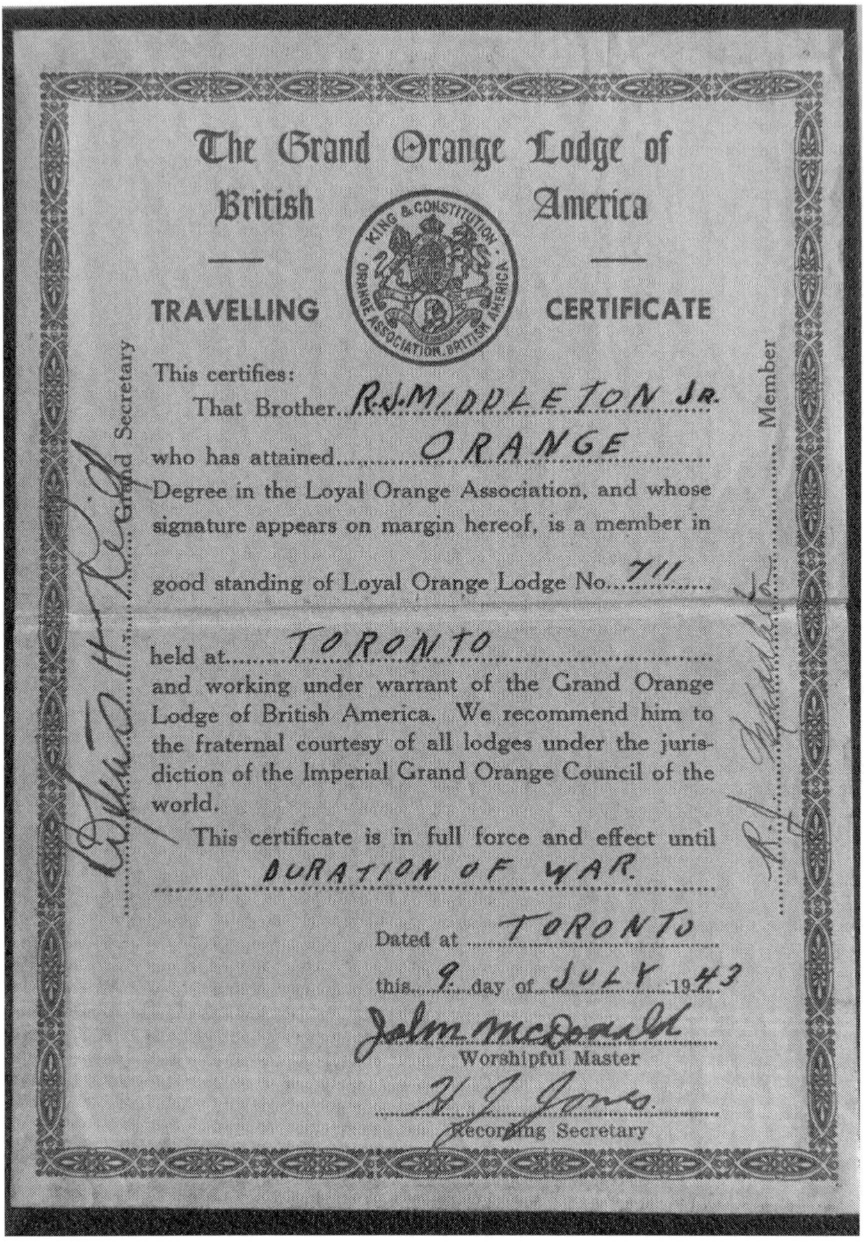

The Grand Orange Lodge of British America

KING & CONSTITUTION · ORANGE ASSOCIATION, BRITISH AMERICA

TRAVELLING CERTIFICATE

This certifies:

That Brother R. J. MIDDLETON JR.

who has attained ORANGE

Degree in the Loyal Orange Association, and whose signature appears on margin hereof, is a member in good standing of Loyal Orange Lodge No. 711

held at TORONTO

and working under warrant of the Grand Orange Lodge of British America. We recommend him to the fraternal courtesy of all lodges under the jurisdiction of the Imperial Grand Orange Council of the world.

This certificate is in full force and effect until

DURATION OF WAR

Dated at TORONTO

this 9 day of JULY 1943

John McDonald
Worshipful Master

H. J. Jones
Recording Secretary

Grand Secretary

Member

During the summer, before I left for England Dad convinced me that I should obtain from the Orange Lodge a travelling certificate if I should need some assistance from the Orange brotherhood while overseas. I was now known as Brother R. J. Middleton Jr. Photograph from the Bob Middleton Collection.

My London AOS Navigator School graduation picture. In this photograph I am a Commissioned Officer. Photograph is from the Bob Middleton Collection.

Chapter 8

BOUND FOR ENGLAND

On Monday, October 18, 1943 at Union Station in Toronto I boarded the train to Montreal, Quebec. In Montreal I boarded the *Ocean Limited* which was an overnight train with real berths that ran from Montreal to Halifax, Nova Scotia. Tuesday night we arrived at the Halifax train station where we were put on buses going to the Y Manning Depot in Halifax. We arrived at the Y Manning Depot at three in the morning and they gave us all a bunk. Generally, when folks arrived in Halifax, they hung around for a few weeks waiting for a ship bound for England and we were eager for a good time partying and enjoying ourselves in Halifax. This did not happen in our case and I never saw Halifax except from the ship when we were leaving. It appears we arrived just hours before a ship bound for England was about to sail. We were woken up at 06:00 in the morning and by 08:30 we had been fed breakfast and we were on our way to the RMS *Mauretania*. By 09:00 we were walking up the gang plank of the RMS *Mauretania* for our new adventure. At 11:00 on Wednesday, October 20, 1943 we had weighed anchor and we were on our way to England on board the almost new, previous luxury liner, the *Mauretania*.

The *Mauretania* had first sailed as a luxury liner on June 17, 1939 and supplemented the *Britannic* and the *Georgic* on the London to New York route. In August 1939, the *Mauretania* was requisitioned by the British government for use as a troop ship. At the end of December 1939, the *Mauretania* sailed to New York City and then on to Sydney,

Australia to be converted to a troop ship. It was much safer to do the conversion work there, away from the threat of Goering's Luftwaffe bombers at home in England. At the end of May 1940, the *Mauretania* sailed in a convoy along with the *Queen Mary*, the *Queen Elizabeth* and the *Aquitania* carrying 2,000 troops from Australia to South Africa. From South Africa the *Mauretania* sailed for Britain to continue her career as a troop ship.

One of the postcards of the RMS *Mauretania* as the luxury liner that I bought while on board the ship but I did not send this one home. When I sailed on the *Mauretania* it was painted an ugly battleship gray. The picture is from the Bob Middleton Collection.

On my trip over to England the *Mauretania* carried about 4,000 troops. After we came on board, we were given the usual instructions about the dos and don'ts while on board. We were assigned cabins that had been each fitted with real bunk beds. We did not have to sleep in hammocks. We were told that there were 11 fellows in each cabin and there were beds for all. I should have been in more of a hurry to claim a bed because when I arrived at my assigned cabin there were no more beds left. It appeared there were beds for 10 fellows. When it was time to go to sleep, I decided to make the bathtub my bed. That worked alright for the first night. Sometime during the second night some rotten so and so turned on the saltwater shower while I was sleeping in the bathtub. Everyone thought that it was a hilarious practical joke on me. That was probably an inevitable outcome of sleeping in a bathtub while sharing a cabin with 10 other 20 year old fellows. For the rest of the trip, I slept on the floor of our cabin. And it is quite amazing how you get used to adverse conditions when you have no other choice. What could I have done? Gone up to the Captain and complained! He probably would have laughed at me as well.

The daylight hours were great. We were served a marvelous full breakfast at 06:00 and dinner at 18:00. We were served by the original stewards and all the plates and cutlery and white tablecloths were still being used. We felt like kings on a luxury liner. We had a snack of beef soup and hard tack at noon. There was only one canteen on the ship where we could by candy bars, cigarettes, or anything else we needed. There was always a long lineup at the canteen, and wouldn't you know that almost every time I got up to the counter there was the lifeboat drill. We had one lifeboat drill each day at varying times of the day. The *Mauretania* cruised at 25 to 30 knots and there were no other ships to keep up with her, so we sailed alone. To avoid German U-boats in the Atlantic we sailed south close to the coast of the United States and then proceeded eastward somewhere around a Caribbean latitude. The weather and sun were so nice while we were heading east that many of us were sunning ourselves with our shirts off lying in deck chairs. Once we had crossed the Atlantic Ocean and had reached the Azores we sailed north along the coast of Spain and then to Liverpool, England. The entire trip had taken 15 days. The entire time we were on board the bath and shower only had salt water. The day before we arrived in England the water was switched to fresh water and I had a freshwater bath. We were now much more presentable Colonials.

Chapter 9

<u>WE ARRIVED IN ENGLAND</u>

On November 3, 1943 we arrived in Liverpool and while we were waiting around for the tugs to bring the *Mauretania* into dock, we were entertained watching two Fairey Swordfish torpedo bombers practicing imaginary torpedo runs to broadside the *Mauretania*. The Fairey Swordfish was a biplane torpedo bomber with a crew of 3 that was designed in 1933.

One of the fellows watching beside me had a telescope that I borrowed to watch the Swordfish torpedo bomber action. I looked at the gunner with his Vickers 0.303 caliber gas operated machine gun and the observer sitting behind the pilot. The Wireless Operator/Gunners and the Observers in the two Swordfish looked like they were bored to tears as neither had anything to do. The training was all about the pilots torpedoing the *Mauretania*. There is a picture of this machine gun on page 155.

The Fairey Swordfish biplanes were the torpedo bombers launched from the British aircraft carrier *Ark Royal* that attacked and crippled the German battleship *Bismarck* on May 26, 1941. The torpedoes from the Swordfish damaged the rudder of the *Bismarck* causing it to be jammed at 12 degrees to port. The *Bismarck* was unable to flee to a safe German occupied port in France as it could only steam in a large circle to port. The crew of the *Bismarck* had opened the watertight doors below the water line and set explosive charges in order to scuttle the ship. Within 12 hours on May 27, 1941 the British battleships *King George V* and

Rodney had caught up with *Bismarck* and opened fire. The cruiser *Dorsetshire* finished off Bismarck with torpedoes and sunk her.

Postcard of the Fairey Swordfish biplane torpedo bomber. Postcard from the Bob Middleton Collection.

The German battleship *Bismarck*. Photograph from the Dan Middleton Collection.

German battleship *Bismarck* took 4 years to build and was commissioned in August 1940. The *Bismarck* and the sister ship *Tirpitz* were the two largest ships ever built by any European country up to that time. The *Bismarck* was 823 feet long, had a beam or width of 118 feet, displaced 50,000 tons and could steam at 34 miles per hour. The armor belt around the ship was 13 inches thick, the deck was 4 inches thick, and the cannon turrets were 14 inches thick. The main cannons were comprised of eight 14 inch cannons, twelve 6 inch cannons and 40 assorted other size cannons.

After we disembarked, we were all loaded into a train and travelled to Bournemouth, England. Bournemouth is a coastal resort town on the south coast of England on the English Channel. The train cabins had no heat and I had packed my greatcoat into my bag that was not with me. All I had to wear was my thin gas cape and I froze for the entire trip. We were billeted in the barracks that turned out to be the swanky Bournemouth Inn. The accommodations were quite nice. It was quite pleasant to sleep in a real bed again and not the floor. While there we learned to use the crazy English money. There were pounds, shillings, crowns, half-crowns, half-pennies, and the giant size pennies. The food was good while there. There were plenty of pubs in the town and all of us future airmen took full advantage of the opportunities to enjoy the British beers.

After a week we were sent to the Monarch Hotel that was a mile northwest of the Bournemouth Inn. The accommodations there were quite nice as well. We ate our meals in the place next door. It was great being in England and I only had to pay for beer. On Sunday our day off a bunch of us would go to the movie theater that was only a ten minute walk from the Monarch Hotel. One fellow introduced me to the Topper series of paperback novels written by Thorne Smith. These were hilarious stories about Topper, a banker, who is helped out in life by the ghosts of a husband and wife that died in an automobile that he purchased. I entertained myself for many hours reading Thorne Smith novels in the lobby of the hotel.

We had so many training courses in naval warship recognition we were all thinking we were going off to North Africa. Aircraft recognition with the use of the flash cards also continued. If a Luftwaffe aircraft was approaching you needed to take evasive action or shoot it down. If it was a friendly aircraft, you did not want to shoot it down. I still have all those flash cards and I totally amazed my sons Dan and Dave at Christmas 2019 as I can still correctly name 95 percent of the aircraft within a few seconds. Back then aircraft recognition was life or death.

BLEMHEIM   **LIBERATOR**   **TYPHOON**   **HAMPDEN**

CORSAIR   **HURRICANE**   **HEINKEL 111**   **LANCASTER**

Some of the flash cards of aircraft that we were given to memorize. The photograph is from the Bob Middleton Collection.

My report card from London No. 4 AOS indicating my aircraft recognition was 50 out of 50. The photograph is from the Bob Middleton Collection.

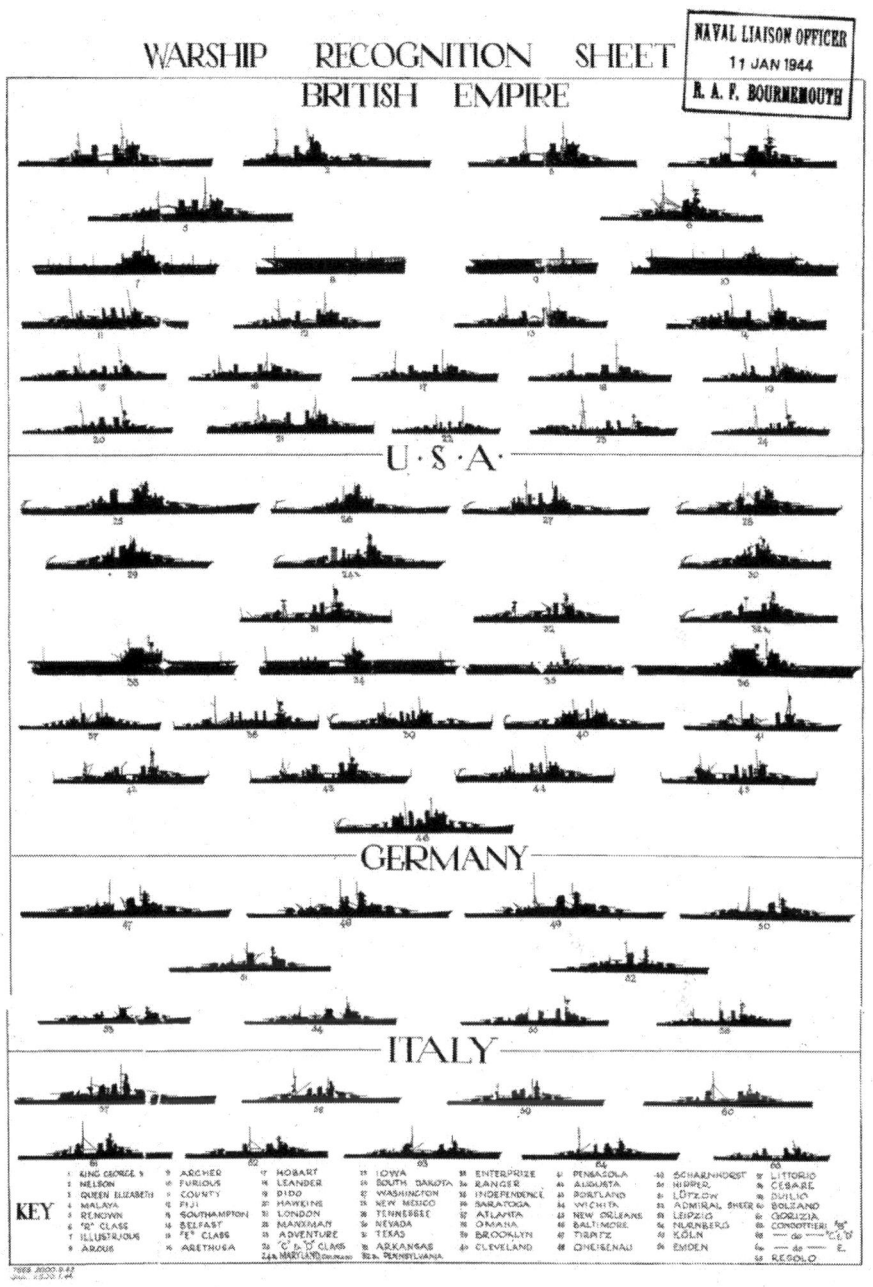

One of the actual Warship Recognition Sheets I kept with me. From the Bob Middleton Collection.

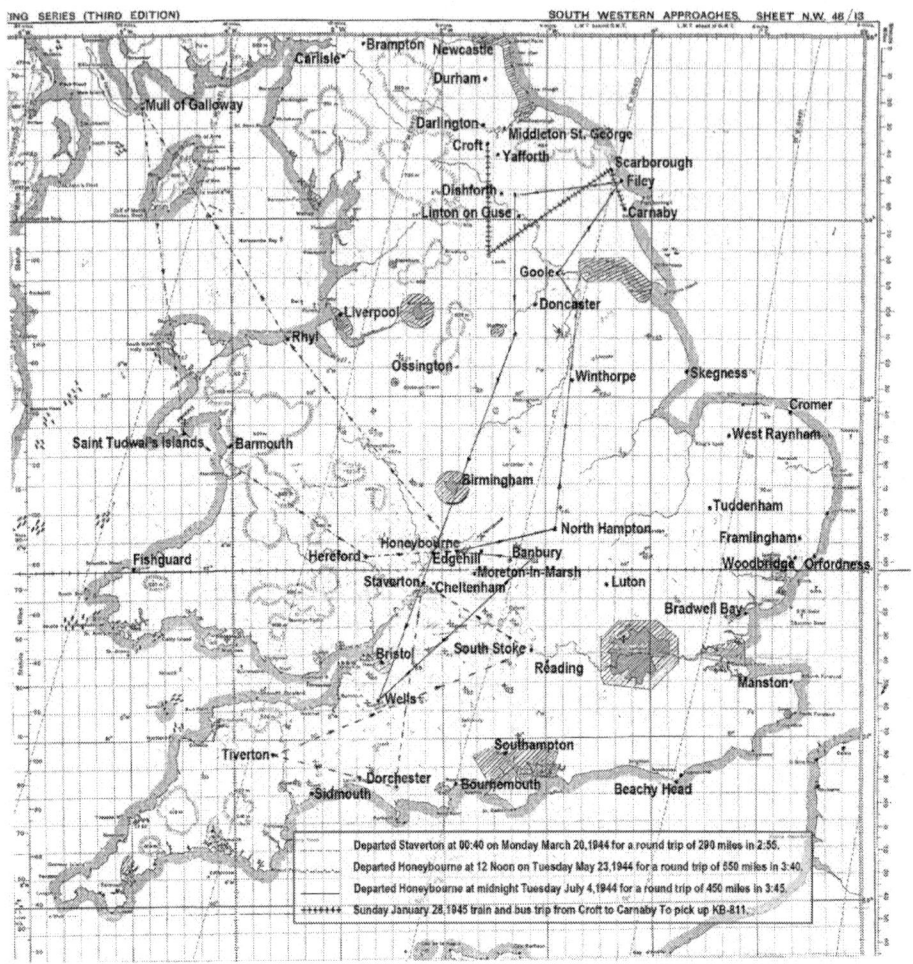

My map of the Occults and Pundits located in England. My legend book with the Morse code letters for each Occult was lost over the past 75 years. This map which I still have went in every aircraft that I flew in while overseas. This map flew with me over enemy occupied Europe. The map has been marked up showing the locations of some operational aerodromes, training aerodromes and turning points. The areas marked with the hash marks were "No Fly Zones." If you flew over these areas they would shoot first and ask questions later. The map is from the Bob Middleton Collection.

One day I went off with my London AOS pal Lowry, another navigator, to the town of Salisbury. Lowry played the organ, and he was invited to play the pipe organ in the Salisbury Cathedral by the organist. This was quite an exceptional honor for him. Lowry was pretty good at playing the organ. While Lowry was playing the organ, I wandered around the very impressive cathedral for quite some time. The cathedral had bodies entombed in the walls. I had never seen anything like this in Toronto.

Lowry took this picture of me in front of Salisbury Cathedral. The photograph is from the Bob Middleton Collection.

Before our hosts at the cathedral sent us away, we asked them where we should have dinner. We were told to go to the Salisbury Restaurant. We had time before the bus would arrive so off, we went for dinner at the Salisbury Restaurant. The restaurant had Salisbury steak on the menu. This was absolutely great. We had not seen steak for some time and that is what we ordered. When dinner arrived, the steaks turned out to be large hamburger patties. Puzzled we asked what these were because we had ordered steaks. The waitress told us we ordered Salisbury steaks and that is what these are. Anyways the steaks tasted very good. J. Wellington Wimpy would have been very pleased. I will speak more about J. Wellington Wimpy later.

We left Salisbury in a double decker bus that was towing a trailer. The trailer was generating coal gas fuel from coal which powered the bus. In the time of fuel shortages, the British sure were resourceful. The Military had priority for gasoline and diesel fuel so the civilians had to work around the situation as best they could.

This is a picture of that coal gas burning bus in Salisbury. The photograph is from the Bob Middleton Collection.

We were in Bournemouth for Christmas 1943. The war still seemed far away for us and we were having a marvelous time during our time off. Our group of Canadian Navigators was in a pub and we were celebrating with a group of telegram delivery ladies as it was a few nights before Christmas. Sometime about 9:00 PM they told us they had to leave and continue delivering telegrams. The telegrams they were delivering were not bad ones informing people of men missing or killed in action. Those were delivered by the military. We had been having such a great time in the pub singing Christmas carols and popular tunes and we did not want it to end. We told them we would tag along with them and while they were delivering the telegrams we would sing to the recipients. We all piled into their delivery van. The recipients thought the singing telegrams were marvelous. A good time was had by all until both tires on the left side of their van went flat. During the war in England all steel of any sort that would not be missed was taken for the war effort. At one time the road we were travelling on had a long steel railing beside it. It had been removed and there were stubs of steel poking out of the road that could not be seen in the dark. There were no streetlights illuminated in England during WWII. The ladies drove over the sharp stubs. We told the ladies we would stay with them until help came to fix the flats but, they told us to take off as both groups might get in some kind of trouble with the authorities.

For an entire month we practiced ground school navigation. We all spent some very good times in the pubs in Bournemouth. A number of great photographs were taken. You must remember we were only 20 years old. The beds in the Monarch Hotel were quite an upgrade after sleeping on the floor of the cabin in the *Mauretania*.

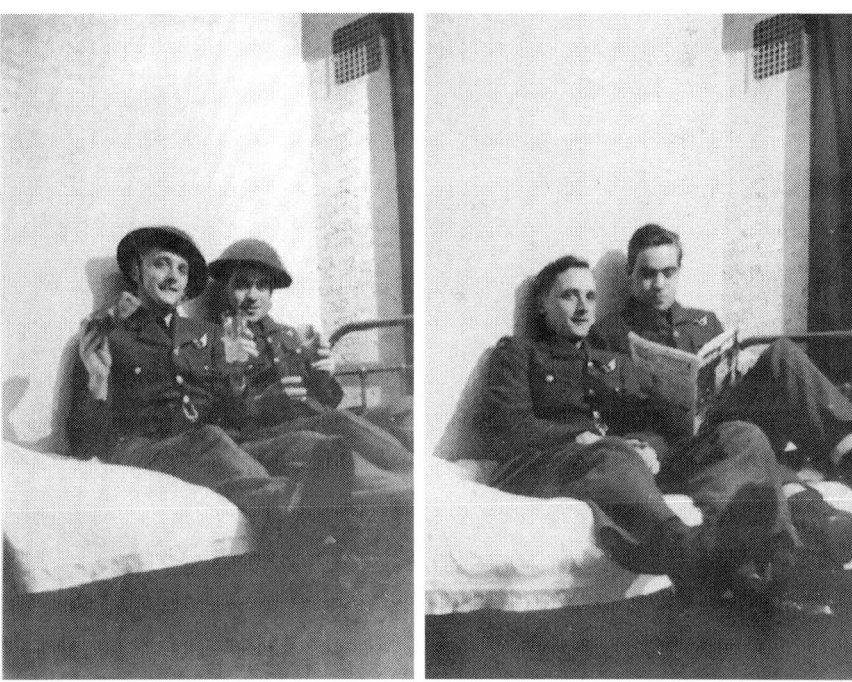

Relaxing in the Monarch Hotel after a pub crawl in Bournemouth. Photographs are from the Bob Middleton Collection.

Chapter 10

COMMANDO AND SURVIVAL TRAINING

In January of 1944 we were sent about 70 miles west of Bournemouth to Sidmouth for a month. Sidmouth is another coastal resort town in the South West Region of England on the English Channel in Devon. At Sidmouth we were given commando training that could come in very handy if we were shot down in some unfriendly European territory. Maybe we could help the resistance trying to help us evade capture. After 6 weeks in Bournemouth, we had become a little bit physically soft. This was about to change. The first day after lunch I was issued used boots, used khaki overalls and an Enfield rifle with a bayonet attached. The boots must have been worn by 400 fellows before me. The Sargeant told us to charge up the hill in front of us with our rifles with the bayonets attached. Then we charged down the backside of the hill and charged up another hill. When we got to the top of the second hill we dropped to the ground on our stomachs and then proceeded to fire our rifles with no ammunition loaded. After we had practiced shooting for a while we were told to repeat the operation from the other direction. We dropped down on the ground and pretended shooting again. Then up and away we went in the other direction again. By the time we reversed again and dropped down for the fourth operation I barely had enough strength to pull back the bolt and cock the rifle. After we had dinner that day, we had no problems falling asleep.

A few days later we were training on the use of Smith & Wesson six shooter revolvers. They taught us to hold the revolver low by our side and fire the gun from the hip. The result of my efforts for a while was to shoot the dirt about 6 feet in front of me. Eventually, I improved at firing the revolver just like a cowboy in a Western movie. This pistol practice must have been intended to help us if we were given a weapon by a resistance fighter. It is very interesting to note that no one in Bomber Command actually flew with any sort of sidearm. We were not issued any personal weapons and there were no firearms in the bombers. Possibly, this was safer for a downed Bomber Command airman as the German soldiers knew we could not fire back. Possibly Bomber Command was saving money by not issuing firearms to bomber crews. If we were cornered after landing in German occupied territory you would simply put your hands up, step out and surrender. You hoped a German soldier captured you versus an enraged villager with a pitchfork. The USAAF bomber aircrews on the other hand did all carry sidearms into combat. I have read that if a USAAF aircrew member was downed in enemy territory some would throw away the sidearm in order to avoid being shot by a German soldier. If there were 3 or 4 German soldiers to one Allied flyer the odds of avoiding getting killed would not have been particularly good. The USAAF aircrew members were issued with 0.38 or 0.45 caliber pistols.

A photograph of a Sten machine gun. Photograph taken by Dan Middleton at the Ontario Regiment RCAC Museum in Oshawa, Ontario.

Photograph of a Smith & Wesson revolver taken by Dan Middleton at the Ontario Regiment RCAC Museum in Oshawa, Ontario.

A couple of days later we were introduced to the fully automatic Sten gun. The STEN acronym comes from the names of the weapons designers Major Reginald V. **S**hepherd and Harold **T**urpin and the **EN** is for Enfield. This was a cheaply built submachine gun designed and built in Britain and later manufactured in many Allied countries. It served its purpose and could fire 400 to 500 rounds per minute. It used a clip that held thirty-two 9 mm rounds. The Sten gun was considered a scatter gun and it was only used at close range as it was only accurate for about 100 yards. It had a tendency to jam and had a tendency to fire by itself if set down too hard or dropped. If dropped on the metal butt it could start firing in the automatic mode and it would not stop until it ran out of rounds. Needless to say, you could be horribly injured by this gun if you were not careful with it. Fortunately, our group of trainees had no accidents with the Sten guns.

They gave us these machine guns with live ammunition, and we practiced firing at block walls with sandbags stacked in front of the walls. When you are only 20 years old it was quite a thrill firing away with a submachine gun. We just tore into those sandbags with all the 9 mm rounds we could find.

The next day we were trained in throwing Mk. 2 fragmentation hand grenades that looked like a pineapple. We learned that you lobbed the grenade.

We were wearing these Brodie style tin hats to protect our heads. We were also trained in the use of the gas masks. Photograph taken by Dan Middleton at the Ontario Regiment RCAC Museum in Oshawa, Ontario.

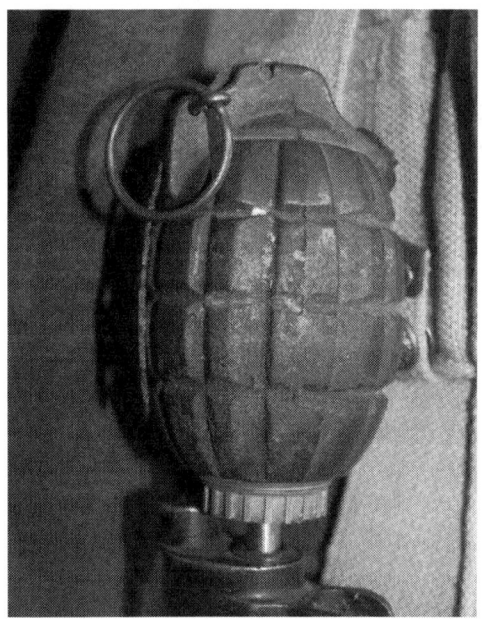

Fragmentation Grenade. Photograph taken by Dan Middleton at the Ontario Regiment RCAC Museum in Oshawa, Ontario.

If you threw these like a baseball you could throw out your shoulder or worse still, throw it into the ground just a few feet in front of you and blow yourself up. To throw a grenade you also had to stand up whereas by lobbing the grenade you could do it almost lying on your side. This way you were much less of a target for someone that was shooting at you. We were wearing the Brodie type tin hats again to protect us from any shrapnel that may come towards our heads. For this practice we were standing just below the crest of a small rise. That day we all lobbed many dummy grenades down the hill. We each lobbed one live grenade down the hill and ducked. It was great fun blowing holes in the ground. One fellow was so very fortunate that day. He was wearing his Brodie tin hat in the very dashing Errol Flynn fashion with his tin hat pulled down almost covering his face.

Normally when you pull the pin and remove the handle from the grenade a very strong spring drives a pin down to the fuse which sits ahead of a lead plug in the bottom of the grenade. On this occasion when the pin went down somehow it blew the lead plug out of the bottom of the grenade and the plug struck the front of his tin hat with quite a force. If he had been wearing the tin hat in a normal fashion the plug would have hit him in the face seriously injuring him. I picked up that lead plug and brought it home with me.

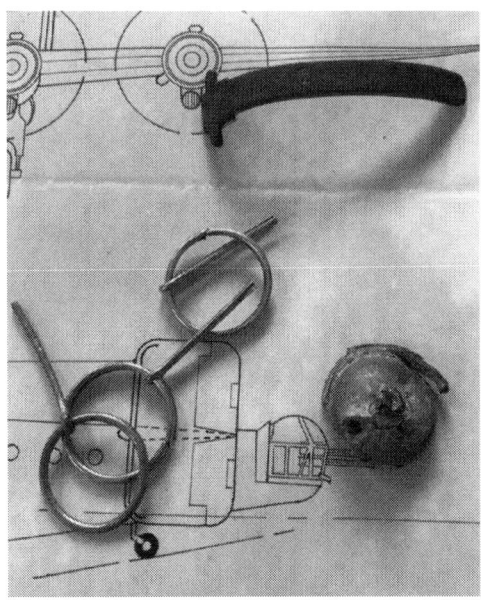

The lead plug that hit him in the head along with three pull pins and a handle. From the Bob Middleton Collection.

111

For a few days we had to climb up a large diameter rope attached to a 30 foot high pole. The rope was at about a 45 degree angle. We wrapped our legs around the rope, hung on with our hands and inched our way along the rope while hanging upside down. There was nothing besides rocks to catch us if we let go. No safety net. This was a good incentive to hang on and get to the top of the pole. The pole had ladder rungs that we climbed down on once we arrived at the top.

On a rainy day or two we had great adventures playing Lookers and Evaders. Half of the trainees were the Lookers team, and they were playing the part of the German soldiers looking for downed airmen. The Evaders team, playing the part of the downed airmen, were trying their best not to get caught or shot. We were each given Lee Enfield rifles with 5 blanks. The Evaders were dropped off in a part of the English countryside that none of the Canadians were familiar with. We were given a map and the pretend safe house of the resistance was at a pub. The Evaders had to get there without being shot. The Lookers were wandering about the same countryside searching for Evaders.

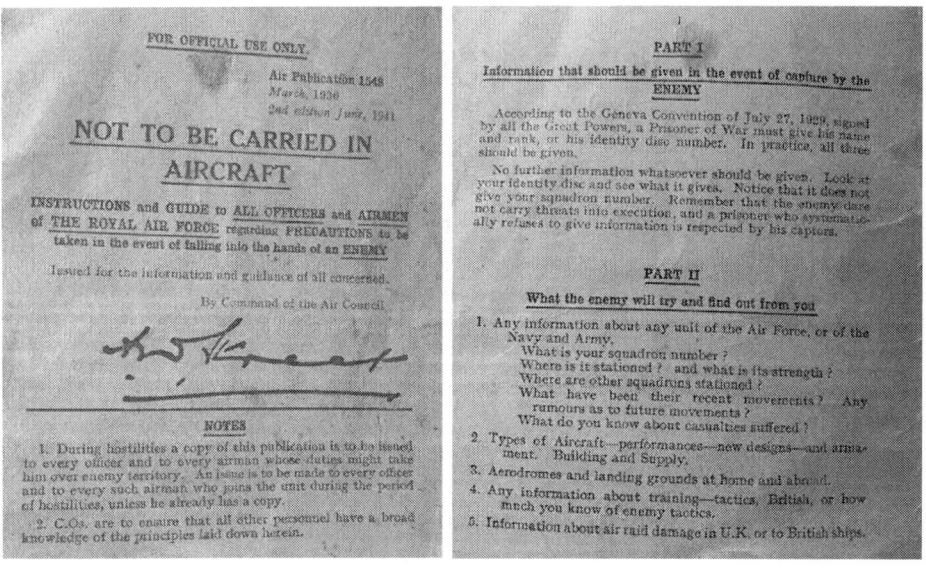

These are photographs of my own "If Captured" training booklet that I was issued. The photographs are from the Bob Middleton Collection.

This all ended up as fun with each other claiming they shot and killed the other so you must stay down. The person being shot of course would say, "You missed me." The fellow who did the shooting would argue. "I shot you dead so stay down." We were just like a bunch of big kids playing Cops and Robbers.

While at Sidmouth we were trained on what to do and what not to do if you were captured by the enemy. I was given a little training booklet with ten pages. We were never to carry this booklet with us on a real operation.

These were great days we had at Sidmouth and I think I have never been in such good physical shape. One day at the end of February they told us we were finished training and tomorrow we would be leaving for Air Observer School. That is how rapidly things seemed to happen for me in the RCAF.

While I was in England, I had to get used to the adjustments in the time that increased the useful daylight hours after 18:00. Before the Second World War England had used Daylight Savings Time the same as in Canada but they called it British Savings Time, BST. In England during the Second World War Daylight Savings Time started on Sunday, February 25, 1940 and did not change back to standard Greenwich Mean Time, (GMT) for five years until Sunday, October 7, 1945.

The Graduation photograph from the Sidmouth Commando School. These fellows are all RCAF Navigators. I am fourth from the left in the bottom row. George Lewthwaite is second row from the back on the far right. Photograph from the Bob Middleton Collection.

In 1963 GMT was changed to UTC, Coordinated Universal Time. UTC the acronym for Coordinated Universal Time is a compromise between the English speaking and French speaking people. The English wanted CUT and the French wanted TUC, so they settled on UTC. GMT is now a time zone and UTC is primary time standard by which the world regulates clocks and time.

GMT is at the 0 degree of longitude line called the Prime Meridian. It passes through the courtyard of the Royal Observatory in Greenwich, England. There is a Prime Meridian plate in the ground. If you straddle it one foot is in the west and the other foot is in the east. While I was in England during the early spring and summer the clocks were turned ahead another hour for British Double Summer Time or BDST. Sunday, April 2, 1944 the Daylight Savings Time was doubled and later went back to Daylight Savings Time on Sunday, September 17, 1944. On Sunday, April 2, 1945 the Daylight Savings Time was doubled and went back to Daylight Savings Time on Sunday, October 7, 1945. This British Double Summer Time allowed residents to work and go about their business later into the night without artificial lighting. That reduced the use of coal which was needed for the vital war manufacturing industries.

Goodness, while I was at Croft the sun did not go down until 23:00. On the bases all our operations and all our logs used Standard GMT time. When we were off the base, we had to be very careful that we did not look at the local clocks in the pubs or stores or train stations as we could potentially be one or two hours late getting back to the base. This would get you reprimanded by your Wing Commander.

During the Second World War throughout Europe including Germany single Daylight Saving Time was used only in the early spring and summer months with the time being set back to Standard time in the fall. I suppose the German government did not see a need to reduce the waste of the daylight hours and the coal used for lighting.

Chapter 11

MORE NAVIGATOR TRAINING

At the end of February 1944, I arrived at Staverton No. 6 Air Observer School (AOS) for a refresher navigation course. This was also an experimental aerodrome which was across from the Dowty Rotol propeller factory in Staverton. I saw a few experimental aircraft while I was there.

Staverton was a permanent RAF station, and the food was really good except for the hard toast smeared with grease that was served at breakfast. I hated hard toast. In the afternoon of Monday, February 28, 1944 I went up as the second navigator in an Anson with Pilot Flight Sargeant Remington for a 2 hour and 20 minute trip. We made many turning points on the way to the target. After a couple more flights as second navigator I was the first navigator for the rest of my time at Staverton. The British Avro Anson aircraft were different than the Anson aircraft in Canada. These Anson aircraft had hydraulically operated landing gear. This was such a treat. The second navigator did not have to hand crank the gear up after takeoff and then down to land.

On Thursday, March 9, 1944 I was flying with Pilot Flight Sargeant Ashton. We were testing a new experimental blind landing aid called OGU. I cannot remember what the acronym stands for however, but I do remember what we did. The station would take a bearing on our aircraft and then send it to the Wireless Operator in Morse code, and he would give me the bearings back to the station. I would draw a line on a special map, and I would give the pilot the altered course and we would circle into the runway. It worked very well from what we experienced but we never used it again. Flying over England was marvelous as it was spring, and everything was so green.

On Tuesday, March 14, 1944 I went on my first navigation night training flight with Pilot Flight Officer Stapleton in an Anson. The weather was rotten, so we did not complete the trip. We were out for 1 hour and 30 minutes. On Monday, March 20, 1944 I went on a three hour 290 mile night trip with Pilot Flight Sargeant Lalonge. The route we took on this training trip is shown on page 102. We flew from Staverton to Dorchester and Tiverton both in the south of England, to South Stoke in the Midlands and then returned to Staverton. My last flight as a Navigator trainee at Staverton was a night trip with Pilot Flight Sargeant McCarthy on Friday, March 31, 1944. All together I had been on 19 flights and had accumulated another 42 hours of flying time.

One day a friend and I went off for a day trip to Bristol. We had a great time there and eventually we arrived at the train station to return back to Staverton, but we had miscalculated. This was late spring and at that time England was on British Summer Time (BST) or Daylight Savings Time. All of our RCAF wrist watches were set to Greenwich Mean Time (GMT) which was one hour later than BST. We missed our train by one hour. The next train would not be leaving until 06:00 the next day. "OH shit!" We were going to be AWOL (Absent Without Official Leave). There could be painful consequences when we got back. Where were we going to stay for the night? In the Short Guide to Bristol that I had we were able to find the address of a local YMCA Hostel. There was nothing we could do to get back, so we found the local YMCA Hostel and paid for two beds. We left to find a place to eat dinner and have a beer since we were staying overnight. When we returned to the YMCA, I discovered that someone had thrown up all over my bed. I went to the front reception desk and I was assigned to a new bed. We got up early and made it to the train on time. We arrived back at Staverton and slipped into the classroom at 10:00 and sat down. To our complete amazement no one said a word about us being missing or late. Just luck again. We could have been sent to the Glass House at Sheffield.

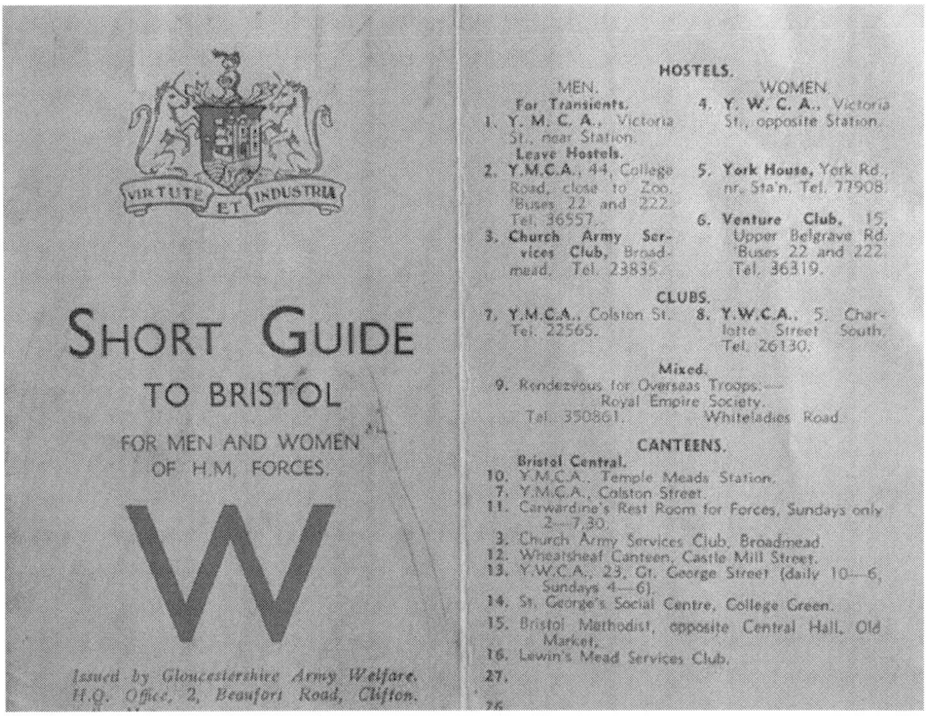

VIRTUTE ET INDUSTRIA

SHORT GUIDE
TO BRISTOL
FOR MEN AND WOMEN
OF H.M. FORCES.

W

Issued by Gloucestershire Army Welfare, H.Q. Office, 2, Beaufort Road, Clifton.

HOSTELS.

MEN.

For Transients.
1. **Y. M. C. A.**, Victoria St., near Station.

Leave Hostels.
2. **Y.M.C.A.**, 44, College Road, close to Zoo. 'Buses 22 and 222. Tel. 36557.
3. **Church Army Services Club,** Broadmead. Tel. 23835.

WOMEN.

4. **Y. W. C. A.**, Victoria St., opposite Station.
5. **York House,** York Rd., nr. Sta'n. Tel. 77908.
6. **Venture Club,** 15, Upper Belgrave Rd. 'Buses 22 and 222. Tel. 36319.

CLUBS.

7. **Y.M.C.A.**, Colston St. Tel. 22565.
8. **Y.W.C.A.**, 5, Charlotte Street South. Tel. 26130.

Mixed.

9. Rendezvous for Overseas Troops:— Royal Empire Society. Tel. 350861. Whiteladies Road.

CANTEENS.

Bristol Central.

10. Y.M.C.A., Temple Meads Station.
7. Y.M.C.A., Colston Street.
11. Carwardine's Rest Room for Forces, Sundays only 2—7.30.
3. Church Army Services Club, Broadmead.
12. Wheatsheaf Canteen, Castle Mill Street.
13. Y.W.C.A., 23, Gt. George Street (daily 10—6, Sundays 4—6).
14. St. George's Social Centre, College Green.
15. Bristol Methodist, opposite Central Hall, Old Market.
16. Lewin's Mead Services Club.
27.

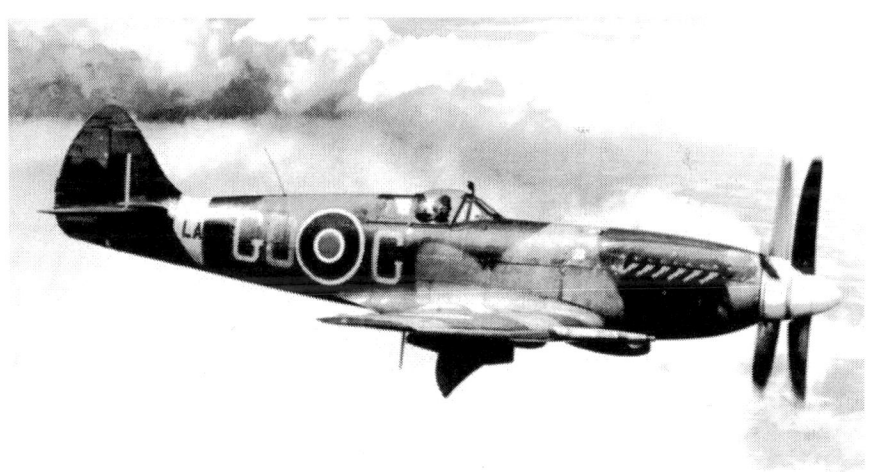

The Short Guide to Bristol that I had. From the Bob Middleton Collection.

Spitfire with the counter rotating propellers. Photograph is courtesy of Phil Listemann at RAF-in-Combat.com.

At Staverton one day I saw a Spitfire with counter rotating propellers take off. It was so incredibly fast. The pilot opened the throttle and in about four lengths of the aircraft the tail wheel came off of the ground and in another length, it was airborne and then rose practically vertically like a rocket. This was such an amazing sight. Oh, I did wish I was the lucky pilot taking that Spitfire into the wild blue yonder. That Spitfire was endowed with a 37 liter 12 cylinder Rolls-Royce Griffon engine that turned out greater than 2,000 horsepower with high octane fuel. Some Griffon engines developed 2,400 horsepower. That engine is so powerful that one large diameter or two counter rotating propellers were needed to take full advantage of the awesome power. Because the aircraft used counter rotating propellers the aircraft did not want to turn to the left or right when the tail wheel came off the ground as in a single propeller aircraft. That Spitfire had a top speed of 450 miles per hour. The power plant and propeller on that Spitfire made a very loud and distinctive sound I had never heard before and I have never heard again. It turns out from what I have read counter rotating propellers produce a loud high-pitched sound.

Experimental Wellington Mk. VI with the high altitude test chamber. The photograph is courtesy of the Brooklands Museum, Weybridge, Surrey, UK.

There was an experimental high altitude Wellington Mk. VI at the aerodrome. It looked like a Wellington with a huge propane tank stuck in the front with a tiny spherical canopy on the top for the pilot. This

Wellington was using Rolls-Royce V-12 Merlin 60 engines instead of the usual Bristol Pegasus or Hercules radial engines. The RAF was experimenting with pressured cabins to eliminate the crew having to wear oxygen masks. With this Wellington the engineers were experimenting with creating a bomber that could fly as high as 38,000 feet.

While we were walking across the field one afternoon an experimental aircraft and four escort motorcycles with sidecars came out of a hanger. There were soldiers with machine guns sitting in the sidecars. The aircraft was escorted out to the end of the runway. From there it took off like a regular propeller driven aircraft possibly to fool people that were watching. The group of us continued on foot to the town of Cheltenham to find The Bishop's Cave Pub. While we were walking down the street that experimental plane flew overhead. As I was the expert in aircraft recognition one of the guys asked me what it was. I told him it looked like the Westland Whirlwind with a T-type tail. A 12 year old boy walking beside us said, "No, that's the new jet." It was the Gloucester Meteor jet fighter. A 12 year old kid knew we had a top-secret jet fighter but, we did not know. This was the first time any of us had ever seen a jet. Wow! Jet engine powered aircraft was the makings of a Buck Rogers science fiction movie serial.

A Westland Whirlwind picture from my scrapbook. Picture from the Bob Middleton Collection.

A postcard of the Gloucester Meteor. Picture from the Bob Middleton Collection.

At the beginning of April 1944 our group of Navigator Trainees were finished Navigation School at Staverton and we were ready to move on to applying our trade in a medium 2 engine bomber as Navigators.

Chapter 12

HONEYBOURNE OTU AND WELLINGTONS

In the middle of April 1944, we were all transferred to No. 24 Operational Training Unit (OTU) at Honeybourne in Worcestershire, England. Honeybourne is about 25 miles south of Birmingham in England's West Midlands County. The first thing we had to do was to crew up with the other fellows to form a bomber crew. The process was called "Crewing Up" and it was unique to Bomber Command.

The American USAAF administration selected the members for each bomber crew. You were assigned your crewmates like being in a high school home room. You flew with crew members you were assigned to fly with, and you were stuck with them.

For the two engine medium bomber we were now going to be training in, there was required 5 crew members all with a different trade or skill. A two engine medium bomber crew was made up of a Pilot, a Navigator, a Wireless Operator/Air Gunner, an Air Gunner, and a Bomb Aimer. The bomber aircraft used in Bomber Command sometime after 1942 all had a Pilot and no Copilot. There is not a second set of controls in Bomber Command Mosquito, Lancaster, or Halifax bombers. American bombers all had dual controls with Pilots and Copilots. In Bomber Command bombers if something happened to your Pilot you hoped that some washed out Pilot who became a Navigator or Bomb Aimer could remember something about flying until everyone had bailed out. Pilots were valuable and a scarce commodity by the end of 1942 and I suppose in the eyes of British aircraft designers having a second pilot was wasteful. After all the folks up in the air were just soldiers. At the beginning of May about 75 to 80 fellows all with different qualifications or as it was called trades, were put inside a huge hall at Honeybourne. This would be enough to make up at least 15 crews. We were told to go find ourselves crew partners. Bomber Command "Crewing Up" felt like we were at a high school dance and you were looking for an attractive girl to ask to dance with you. All of the fellows in the hall either had a full wing Pilot brevet or half-wing brevet on their jacket that signified what trade you were.

None of us had ever done anything like this before we entered the hall. We had been told that there was the correct number of members of each of trade in the hall to make up many full crews with no one left out. I casually went about looking for people to team up with. I finally saw a fellow that had a B on his brevet. I looked him up and down and asked him if he was in a crew yet. He told me he was not. His name was Jack. I really did not care much for this guy, but he was the only person I could find who was not crewed up yet. I asked him if he wanted to crew up with me. He looked me up and down and said "Sure, why not." I said, "Let's go find ourselves a Pilot and the rest of a crew." Somehow, we did not find ourselves a Pilot or any other crew members to team up with. At that point, the hall seemed to be shy of one Pilot, one Wireless/Gunner and one Air Gunner to make up complete crews. We had been too slow choosing crewmates. At this point Jack and I felt like orphans with nothing to do.

Jack the Bomb Aimer and I hung around waiting for the next "Crewing Up" assembly. We thought we were going to be added to another crew but that did not happen. Jack really liked drinking at the local pubs. One night in the dark he was coming back from a pub on his bicycle, and he saw two headlights coming towards him. He thought these lights were from two motorcycles. Jack decided to ride between the two headlights and really scare the two fellows on the two motorcycles. As it turned out those two headlights were from one truck. He ended up badly injured and landed in the hospital. Jack was a write-off as far as a future part of my crew. As I was by myself now, I waited for the next course to start. I had more ground school training but there was no parade ground drill practicing at OTS.

WAG = Wireless / Air Gunner
AG = Air Gunner
E = Engineer
B = Bomb Aimer
N = Navigator
At bottom = Pilot

Photograph of the RCAF bomber crew brevets from the Bob Middleton Collection.

123

The next "Crewing Up" day arrived about 2 weeks later. Again, about 75 fellows entered the same huge hall. This time I really knew how this "Crewing Up" thing worked, and I was bolder and quicker in looking for other crew members. I may have been a bit shy the last time. I walked up to Ray Rose a fellow with a B brevet who was looking rather lost and forlorn. I looked him up and down and asked if he needed a Navigator. Ray looked me up and down and I suppose he liked what he saw so Ray said "Sure." Ray and I went off to find three more crew members. Ray and I walked up to a very tall Don Rombough who had a Pilot brevet on his jacket and asked him if he needed a Bomb Aimer and a Navigator. Ray and I looked Don up and down. Don looked us up and down and then Don said "OK." Don had already found Ken Smith a Wireless/Air Gunner. Those two fellows now looked Ray and I up and down and they both said "Sure." Ray and I looked Ken up and down and we both said "Sure." The four of us said "Let's go find ourselves an Air Gunner for the rear turret." We walked up to Jack Cornock an Air Gunner who had an AG brevet on his jacket. We all looked Jack up and down and asked him if he wanted to join us four. Jack looked the four of us up and down and said, "Sure." We were now a bomber crew of five. The "Crewing Up" process had only taken 5 minutes. The 5 of us in only 5 minutes had chosen who we wanted to spend the rest of the war or our lives with. As far as we were concerned, we now had the best Bomber Command crew in the RCAF. This is really the way it happened. We were assigned to D Flight at Honeybourne. When finished our two engine bomber training we would go on to the 4 engine bomber Heavy Conversion Unit (HCU) where another Air Gunner and a Flight Engineer would be assigned to our crew of 5.

Up to now Honeybourne No. 24 OTU was training crews on old beat-up Armstrong Whitworth Whitley 2 engine medium bombers. To us the old beat-up Whitley bombers looked like junk. In the air the Whitley looked odd. When in level flight it appeared to be descending due to the angle that the wings were set at. By 1944 these bombers had been relegated to mostly OTU training, Coastal Command and glider towing. There were about 1,800 Whitley bombers built. There are no complete Whitley bombers in existence today. There is part of a Whitley bomber fuselage and some Whitley bomber parts at the Midlands Aircraft

Museum in Baginton, UK. The Whitley was used on the first night of the war to drop propaganda leaflets over Germany. This gave the Whitley bomber the distinction to be the first Allied bomber to penetrate into Germany and to bomb Berlin. The result of that first raid on Berlin changed the course of the Battle of Britain because Hitler was so infuriated, he ordered the Luftwaffe to cease attacking RAF airfields and attack London instead. This allowed the RAF to rebuild its strength and was probably decisive in the Battle of Britain.

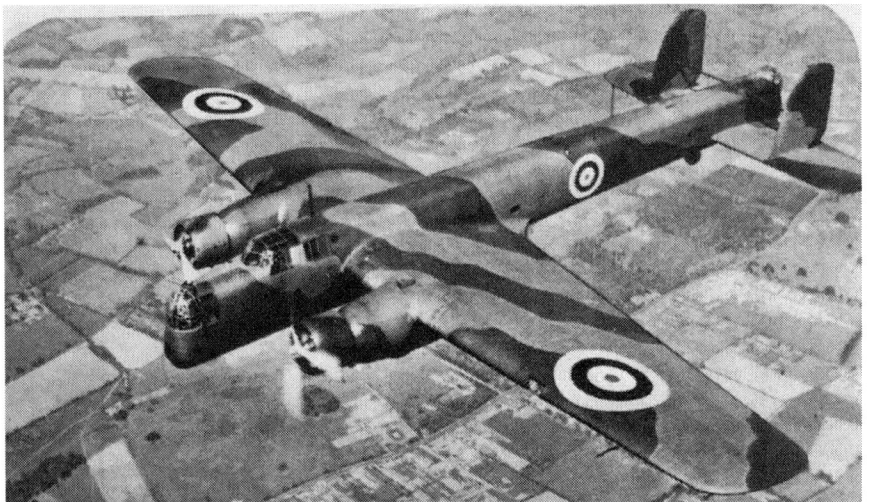

The Armstrong Whitworth Whitley bomber picture from my scrapbook. From the Bob Middleton Collection.

One morning I went outside, and all the old Whitley bombers were gone and brand spanking new Vickers Wellington Mk. X bombers were sitting in the dispersal areas. This was fabulous. More good luck for me and our crew. For me that 2 weeks wait turned out to be a blessing. We would be training in brand new Wellingtons. One of the Wellington bombers we were flying in had only 7 hours on the hour meter. That 2 weeks wait for a next "Crew Up" was such great luck, again. We were flying in these great bombers designed by Vickers' chief designer, Rex K. Pierson using geodetics adapted by Barnes Wallis, the same fellow who had designed the huge R100 airship I saw flying over Toronto when I was a kid. Remember earlier in the book I said we would hear about Barnes Wallis again.

The Vickers Wellington Bomber. The painting WELLINGTON by Robert Taylor ©
The Military Gallery. Courtesy of Robert Taylor © The Military Gallery.

My 1945 sketch of a Wellington Mk. X Bomber designated as TY-X or X-RAY that
we were flying in at Honeybourne. The sketch is from the Bob Middleton Collection.

The front starboard side of the Wellington fuselage showing the geodetic design. The picture is of Wellington N2980 R for Robert at the Brooklands Museum in the UK. The photograph is courtesy of the Brooklands Museum, Weybridge, Surrey, UK.

The geodesic dome is the Cinesphere at Ontario Place in Toronto, Ontario. Photograph taken by Dan Middleton.

The Wellington bomber was designed in 1936 with a unique geodetic airframe. The entire skeleton of the aircraft looked like a basket weave or a diamond pattern. The same geodesic design is used at the Cinesphere at Ontario Place. The geodetic design made the aircraft lighter, very strong and tough. The entire outer skin of the Wellington was covered with doped Irish linen. There is no aluminum skin covering the frame. Small holes in the fabric were much easier to repair than aluminum skinned aircraft. The repair mechanic simply had to sew a patch in place and then apply aircraft dope.

Aircraft dope is a lacquer that has been plasticized so it can be applied to fabric to cover aircraft. This tightens and stiffens the fabric which is stretched over the framing. It makes the aircraft both airtight and weatherproof.

Many Wellington bombers would return from operations with severe battle damage that would have destroyed aircraft with conventional aluminum skin air frames. The geodetic frame however made the Wellington unable to tow gliders as it was feared that the geodetic frame would stretch causing the control surfaces to lose full range of control. The Mk. X Wellingtons we were flying in had the huge 1,600 horsepower Bristol Hercules Mk. VI 14 cylinder sleeve valve radial engines. Out of the 14,641 Wellington bombers that were built there are only two in existence in UK museums. More Wellington bombers were built for Bomber Command than any other bomber. The Wellington bomber also has the distinction of being the only bomber that Bomber Command used from before the beginning of World War II to the end of the war. Many of the other early bombers were obsolete by 1943. The Halifax bomber did not enter service until November 1940 and the Lancaster bomber did not enter service until February 1942.

The Vickers Wellington bomber was affectionately nicknamed "Wimpy" after the cartoon character J. Wellington Wimpy who appeared in the Popeye cartoon series. Wimpy was the very polite and very proper character that was always mooching something and always eating hamburgers. Wimpy's classic line was "I'd gladly pay you Tuesday for a hamburger today." Of course, Wimpy never showed up on Tuesdays to pay for that hamburger.

For a week we were all learning our individual trades in the Wellington bomber in ground school. On Tuesday, May 5, 1944 I went out on a daylight cross-country flight three hours long with Pilot Officer Ward in an Anson to introduce me to the English countryside. Just like at Staverton it was such a beautiful sight flying over England in May. The squadron designation for all the aircraft at Honeybourne OTU was TY. I started training on Wellington Mk. X bombers on Thursday, May 11, 1944 with various pilots while Don was receiving inflight pilot instructions on flying the twin engine Wellington Bomber. The weather in May of 1944 was glorious, with beautiful blue skies and warm weather. It was so warm that one day I was sweating with my mask and helmet on while at lower altitudes. Once we were up at 10,000 feet my pencil kept getting stuck and was jumping over little lumps on the chart. The little lumps were frozen sweat droplets that had dripped from my mask and froze when they landed on my charts. From Tuesday, May 16, 1944 to the end of May 1944 we were out flying every day except for 2 days off.

Tuesday, May 23, 1944 found Ray and I taking off at 12:00 noon on navigation and bombing training trip in Wellington TY-TOM with Flight Officer Thompson. The trip was a 550 mile, cross-country ride of 3 hours and 40 minutes. This trip can be found on the map on page 102. We flew from Honeybourne north to Rhyl, and to the Mull of Galloway in Scotland then south to Saint Tudwal's Islands. From there we flew to Hereford then to the target and back to Honeybourne.

Through the months of May and June 1944 we did dry dinghy drills and parachute drills, once a week, twice each day. We needed to be ready for any disaster in the air that required us leaving the aircraft before it crashed into the ground or ditched in the water. I recorded a dozen dry dinghy drills in my logbook that we did at Honeybourne but I do not remember them so I cannot tell anybody about them. I have been told that we may have done these in an old, grounded Wellington. We would have climbed out of the Wellington and then jumped into a dinghy on the grass. To escape from the Wellington, when ditched or belly landed, there was a hatch above the pilot and the astrodome could also be removed.

In a true emergency ditching we would have to sit with our backs to the front of the aircraft and hold on. The only person in the Wellington that had a seat harness during a ditching was the pilot. The seat I sat on was on a slide so that it could be stored under my bench. That was not very secure. Any evasive action that Don performed meant we all had to hang on. In a true emergency just before we jumped or swam out of the emergency exit, we would pull the cords on our Mae West floatation vest to inflate the vest with co^2 from two small gas cylinders. Without the Mae West you sink very quickly due to the weight of all the clothes and gear you had on.

The dinghy was stored at the back of the starboard engine nacelle on top of the wing and the panel covering it would open automatically when a water sensor on the bottom of the wing detected water. The cover would come off and the dinghy was ejected while at the same time being automatically inflated by co^2 from small cylinders. The dinghy had a tether attached to the wing and the dinghy would be waiting in the water for the crew members to climb aboard.

We did dry dinghy drills the same days that we did parachute drills. Parachute drills took place inside a hanger with a high ceiling. There was a large version of what looked like a kiddie slide. Above the slide was a track that had a cable attached and to that a harness that we would wear. We put on the harness that was similar to a parachute harness and climbed onto the top of the slide. Then we went down the slide. The end of the slide ended 10 feet above the floor. On the floor there were tumbling mats that we would land on. After we came off of the slide the harness controlled our fall to the ground similar to falling by parachute. Just before I hit the mats, I would curl up into a fetal style position and just as I hit the mats I would try to land on my side and shoulder and then roll. If you tried to land on your feet, you had a real good chance of breaking something.

The normal way to climb in and out of the Wellington was by a ladder through the 20 inch by 37 inch hatch directly underneath the pilot's position. This hatch would be used to leave the aircraft in an emergency while in the air. The tail gunner could leave his turret by rotating it 90 degrees to starboard and then jumping or climbing out. There was also a diamond shaped panel on the starboard side near the tail that could be kicked out in an emergency.

We did wet dinghy drills on Tuesday, May 29 and Saturday, July 7, 1944. Wet dinghy drills required a swimming pool and we had to travel about 50 miles south to Cheltenham to a swimming pool located there. At the pool we were wearing our full battle dress and our Mae West life preserver. On the front cover of this book, we are wearing our Mae West. The J-type dinghy used by Bomber Command was about 8 feet in diameter and could hold at least 7 fellows. The dinghy was already in the water and we had to swim to it. We pulled the two cords to inflate our Mae West and then we jumped into the water. We then swam for the dinghy and climbed in. It was like one crazy pool party. We jumped in many times each practice day. We also had to learn how to flip over an upside down dinghy before we could climb into the dinghy. The dinghy is quite heavy and large, so this requires some team work to get the dinghy right side up. The last time we went into the pool on the second day we were all sitting on the edge of the dinghy with our backs pointing outward. To get into the water from the dinghy you sat facing inward and then flipped backward into the water like a scuba diver. You slipped in this way to avoid smacking your face on the dinghy or getting things like your parachute attachments stuck on the dinghy. On this particular practice little did I know that Ray as a practical joke had bled the inflation gas out of my Mae West. All the gear and battle dress weigh so much that when I went into the water with my deflated Mae West, I dropped straight to the bottom of the pool like a rock. I was really scared as I had no idea what happened. I pushed off from the bottom of the pool with all the strength my legs could muster. I struggled my way to the dinghy and then swam to the edge of the pool while hanging onto the dinghy. When I made it back to the edge of the deck Ray was laughing hysterically and then the rest of the crew joined in laughing. Even the instructor thought it was hilarious. Everybody had a great time at my expense and eventually I had to laugh as well.

A portion of the Honeybourne section in my logbook. Everyone in the bomber had to acknowledge that they understood how to operate the fuel cocks and how to pump oil into the engine oil tanks. The photograph is from the Bob Middleton Collection.

There is no Flight Engineer on the Wellington so that meant that all of the crew members needed to know how to operate the fuel cocks to balance the fuel tanks in the wings and fuselage. You could run out of fuel in one or both engines if this balancing was not done when required. All of our trips were short, so we never actually had to fiddle with the fuel cocks.

The Hercules engines were very thirsty for lubricating oil so there was a 15 gallon oil overload tank located in the fuselage. When the low oil level warning light for an engine illuminated in the cockpit it was the task of a crew member to operate a hand pump to top up the engine oil tanks. Ray was closest to the overload tank, so he generally operated the pump if needed.

The engine oil overload tank and hand pump. The picture is of inside Wellington N2980 R for Robert at the Brooklands Museum in the UK. The photograph is courtesy of the Brooklands Museum, Weybridge, Surrey, UK.

All through May and June 1944 we were flying circuits and bumps. Circuits and bumps are when the pilot flies a predetermined square course and lands and takes off many times on one trip. This is for the pilot practicing takeoffs and landings in the Wimpy. Don must get it right every time for all of our sakes. We did high level bombing practice for Ray the Bomb Aimer and the Pilot. We did many cross-country trips for my Navigation practice. Ken the Wireless Operator got lots of practice as he was in constant contact with base on all of our exercises. Jack the Tail Gunner must have been bored to tears as he did not get any practice as there was nothing to shoot at. He did get a grand view of England from the rear of the aircraft, however. Jack, being Tail-End Charlie, always saw where we had been.

On Monday, June 5, 1944 just before midnight we all went out for a night cross-country practice in Wellington TY-Y-YOKE. Once we were up in the sky, we realized that we were surrounded by hundreds of aircraft with the navigation lights on. There were extra navigation Occults and Pundits lit up that night as well. About 20 minutes after 01:00 in the morning we were recalled back to base with no explanation. The next morning one of the fellows in my hut woke me up and said, "It's D-Day." It was Tuesday, June 6, 1944. There had been a betting pool on what day D-Day would be. We were betting on the day D-Day would happen because we all knew it was going to happen. We just did not know what day it would be and where in France it would take place. Neither did the German High Command. I won a half-crown from another guy as I had bet that D-Day would be June 6. I went outside of our hut and watched all the C-47s returning with the parachute static lines trailing behind. While looking up at those returning C-47s I wondered to myself how many of those brave soldiers were dead. With this operation happening overhead I realized that the war was getting closer to me. It would not be long before we were flying on real operations. Monday, June 13 all of our crew went off on leave for a few days to Glasgow, Scotland for a short break. One of Ray's cousins in the Navy was stationed there and that seemed like a good reason to go there. The train trip from Honeybourne to Glasgow was about 8 hours. The marvelous perk of being in the armed forces in England during WWII was free train and bus transport any time you wanted it. It just had to be authorized by the base Commanding Officer. We hung around with Ray's cousin for a day and then we were on our own as he had to report back for duty. We were staying at a nice bed and breakfast run by two elderly ladies. These ladies were quite strict, and they had a 22:00 curfew to be back. For the entire time I was in

England this was the only curfew. All the other places we visited in England had no curfew. We were waiting outside of a very popular pub for dinner in a very long line up one night. When the owner happened to wander outside and saw five men dressed in RCAF uniforms he took kindly to us and sent us to the head of the line. Ray's cousin was not with us that night. We left Scotland and were back on June 18, 1944.

My practice route forecast for June 6, 1944. The form is from the Bob Middleton Collection.

On Saturday, July 3, 1944 we went out on a High Level Bombing practice in Wellington TY-Z-ZEBRA but the ceiling was 15,000 feet and Ray could not see the ground so we could not proceed. We asked for permission to return and Don was told to circle at 1,500 feet. We had to constantly keep an eye out for other aircraft because the visibility stunk.

134

That is me in the shirt and tie with rolled up sleeves hanging around at the tail of Wellington HE633 designated TY-X-X-RAY in the dispersal area at Honeybourne. This Wellington crashed at Honeybourne on January 6, 1945 when one of the engines failed during takeoff. Luckily, everyone on board walked away unharmed from the crash on that occasion. The bomb bay doors are open in this picture. This photograph is from the Bob Middleton Collection.

We stooged around flying in a circle for about an hour and had not received any message to land. We finally decided, maybe if we go lower the R/T, Radio Telephone would work better. The R/T worked when we got below 500 feet. The Honeybourne base controller asked us, "Where have you been?" We were told that a Wellington had crashed at the base and, "You need to divert to Moreton-in-Marsh aerodrome on QE183 magnetic." We had seen a big fire burning while we were circling. Away we went at just about zero feet since there was almost no visibility. In 20 minutes, we should have found Moreton-in-Marsh, but we had not. It was decided we would land at the first aerodrome we came to. The visibility was so bad, and we were so low that we were all looking out for other aircraft, trees and hedges. About ten minutes later we found an airfield. Don landed there and taxied up to the control tower. Don called the tower and asked where we were. In a very British accent, the fellow in the tower asked us, "Where do you think you are?" Don answered, "Is this Moreton-in-Marsh?" The fellow said, "Oh! I'm afraid you boob old boy. This is Edge Hill." Edge Hill was a satellite aerodrome of Moreton-in-Marsh about ten miles away. It was late so we stayed the night.

We were all listening to their wireless that night. That night I heard the radio announcer in Germany named Lord Haw-Haw on the radio for the first and last time. I never listened to his show again as it was so much crap attempting to demoralize British and European citizens. At the beginning of the war people found Lord Haw-Haw somewhat entertaining. It was estimated that eight million people listened to him each night. By the time the German Luftwaffe was bombing England the broadcasts by Lord Haw-Haw had become extremely unsettling to the British. The show was all talk by a traitor. Lord Haw-Haw generally started the show saying, "Germany Calling, Germany Calling."

Pictures of William Joyce, Lord Haw-Haw and his wife Margaret Joyce, Lady Haw-Haw. Photographs from the Dan Middleton Collection.

Lord Haw-Haw was born an American, William Joyce, who had lived in the UK since he was 15 years old. In order to get a British passport in 1933 he falsely claimed to be a British National. This was ultimately his undoing. In August of 1939 William Joyce moved to Germany and later in 1940 became a naturalized citizen of Germany and started his infamous broadcasts originating in Berlin. A few months after the war ended in 1945, he was captured by the British MI-5 Military Intelligence Service and the British Army. William Joyce held that fraudulently obtained British passport and was tried as a traitor to the British Empire. On January 3, 1946 William Joyce was hanged as a British traitor in his Majesty's Prison at Wandsworth. During WWII traitors were hanged. Lord Haw-Haw was the last person in England to be hanged for treason. Late in 1946 Margaret Joyce, Lady Haw-Haw was spared the noose and was banished to Germany and interned as a security risk.

The next morning after the horses were herded off of the airfield we returned to Honeybourne. The reason we were diverted that night was because the Wellington BK251 from Honeybourne had crashed into the bomb dump while landing. There was an instructor on board the aircraft and the pilot was practicing landing with a dead engine. When the engine was shut off the pilot turned into the side with the dead engine which is the last thing you want to do. If your starboard engine is the only engine running it is only safe to make a turn to starboard. If you turn to port the extra lift from the starboard side with the working engine will cause the port side to dip down and the starboard side to lift up causing the aircraft to spin into the ground. If you are close to the ground the pilot may not be able to recover before hitting the ground. On this night the pilot spun the Wellington into the bomb dump and everyone on board was killed. There were seven men on board the aircraft that night instead of the usual five men. I cannot remember how many times Don shut down a starboard engine or a port engine and then restarted them. Don practiced dead engine landings by shutting down an engine at a critical time. The five of us always managed to walk away from all of Don's single engine landings.

It certainly was not safe in flight training. About the time I was at Honeybourne there were four crashes involving aircraft and crews and aircraft based at Honeybourne.

The first crash was on Sunday, May 14, 1944 when a Whitley NI436 stalled on an overshoot from Honeybourne. No one was injured.

Fifteen days later on Monday, May 29, 1944 an Anson R9805 overshot a landing at the Leamington aerodrome. The pilot was unharmed, but the Anson was wrecked.

On Tuesday, July 4, 1944 Wellington BK251 crashed into the bomb dump at Honeybourne while the pilot was practicing landing with a dead engine. The aircraft was destroyed and all seven RCAF crew members were killed. The crew members are all buried at Brookwood Military Cemetery Surrey, UK. This was the first major accident at Honeybourne OTU since converting to Wellingtons.

Sadly, on Friday, July 14, 1944 a Wellington HE381 designated TY-G-GEORGE spun into the ground at the village of Long Compton. Three RCAF crew members, one RAF pilot from No. 19 OTU and the RAF Wireless Operator was killed. The 3 RCAF crew members are buried at Brookwood Military Cemetery Surrey, UK. The RAF Pilot is buried at St. John The Baptist Cemetery Surrey, UK. The RAF Wireless Operator is buried at Wellogate Cemetery Hawick, UK.

While we were at Croft, on Sunday, January 6, 1945 Wellington HE633 TY-X-X-RAY that we had flown in many times crashed on takeoff at Honeybourne. There were no injuries.

Midnight, Tuesday, July 4, 1944 found Ray and I taking off on night navigation and bombing training trip in Wellington TY-Z-ZEBRA with Flight Officer Bendall. The trip was a 450 mile, cross-country ride of 3 hours and 45 minutes. This trip can be found on the map on page 102. From Honeybourne we flew east to North Hampton and from there flying north passing over Occult 16, Goole and Filey. From Filey we flew west to coordinates 53° 55' N, 02° 00' E, west to coordinates 53° 25' N, 01° 30' E and southwest passing over Honeybourne to Wells. From Wells we flew northeast to Occult 22, then to two targets and back to Honeybourne. This trip had so many turning points for me to navigate I was exhausted by the time we returned to Honeybourne.

Thursday, July 6, 1944 at 15:00 found us flying with Don in Wellington TY-P-PETER. We were out on a High-Level Bombing, HLB practice with eight real live bombs. Fighter affiliation was also included on this trip, so Don received practice on making the corkscrew maneuvers and the rest of us received practice in hanging on. Fighter affiliation is when one of our own fighters pretends to attack our bomber and then tries to follow that bomber as the bomber pilot tries to avoid being shot up.

Generally, Jack had little to do on our training exercises. Jack was even bored with watching the beautiful English countryside passing away from him.

Our five man Wellington Bomber crew at a dance in Birmingham in July 1944. Names in order from left to right: Ken Smith, Wireless Operator. Ray Rose, Bomb Aimer. Don Rombough, Pilot. Bob Middleton, Navigator. Jack Cornock, Tail Gunner. In this picture our pilot Don was still a non-commissioned officer. Photograph from the Bob Middleton Collection.

Jack was tired and he did not feel like climbing into the rear turret and asked me if I wanted to ride in the rear turret before we took off. I was delighted. Someone had to be in the rear turret as it was necessary to swing the turret to the port side on taking off. This compensated for the engine torque just as the Wellington tail wheel came off the runway. For me it was a marvelous thrill riding in the rear turret watching the English countryside passing away from me because in my position in the aircraft I had no window and I never saw anything. I was playing with the turret in all different directions and raising the guns up and down. The guns were in safe mode, but it was still entertaining. After ten minutes I got out of the rear turret and Jack took his usual place. I directed us to where we had to fly and Ray planted the 8 bombs on the target.

The first time we did fighter affiliation in the Wellington it was a bit terrifying. It's interesting that I don't remember much about the first corkscrew. Sitting in the Navigator's position in the Wellington I could not see outside. All I could do was hold on tight to anything I could find. Jack the tail gunner would call out corkscrew port or starboard and Don would flip the Wellington onto its side and then dive the Wellington bomber so that we were heading straight down. I was in my position with no window wondering how the fabric covering the bomber could stay on. The g-forces were tremendous, and anything not tied down in the bomber for a few moments was floating weightless in the air. Once Don dove the Wellington straight down as far as he felt necessary to escape the attacker, he reversed the controls and headed up with the 2 mighty Hercules engines going full bore. Now all the g-forces were reversed, and the gravity was making everything fall towards the rear of the bomber. Wow! And we would practice this maneuver more than once during the day. I am fortunate that I do not get airsick or seasick. We were out for 2 hours and 45 minutes on this trip.

Saturday, July 15, 1944 was my 21st birthday and the crew had a small party for me that day. No alcohol of course. We all made that decision early on that before we went out for any flying there would be no drinking beforehand. We took off from Honeybourne at 23:20 that night in Wellington TY-X-X-RAY. We were out for 4 hours and 30 minutes on a 644 mile trip. This trip is shown on the map on page 102.

It was quite an adventure and a great deal of navigation practice for me. I believe that was the intention. We flew to Southwold on the east coast then to coordinates 53° 55' N, 02° 00' E and then the target coordinates 53° 00' N, 03° 00' E out in the North Sea halfway between England and the Netherlands. From the target we flew to Skegness then to a spot a bit north of Ossington then way up north to Newcastle on the northeast coast and back to Ossington.

Don and I are standing at the front of Wellington HE633, TY-X-X-RAY. Don always liked to hang on to the propellers. In this picture you can clearly see the ribs under the doped linen fabric covering and the ladder that we used to climb in and out of the Wellington. It helped to be young, strong and slim. The photograph is from the Bob Middleton Collection.

By the time we were approaching Ossington it was 04:00 in the morning and we landed at Ossington and stayed there the rest of the night. I'm not exactly sure why we landed at Ossington besides being late. It may have been to get the crew accustomed to being diverted at the end of an operation. While we were out over the North Sea the entire crew sang Happy Birthday to me over the intercom. This was a very special birthday I have remembered my entire life. How many people know exactly what they were doing and where they were on their 21st birthday 76 years later? The next day it was a short 45 minute daylight flight from Ossington back to Honeybourne.

We were such a motley looking crew having just come back from some flying practice. There is Don hanging onto that propeller. Left to right: Ralph, Ken, Bob, Ray, and Don. The guns in the front turret have been removed and the openings covered over. The photograph is from the Bob Middleton Collection.

On Monday, July 17, 1944 we went out on a daylight High Level Bombing practice with 8 live bombs in Wellington TY-O-OBOE. Later that night we practiced fighter affiliation and high level bombing in the dark of night. We were practicing what we soon were going to encounter during real combat.

Front view of Wellington HE633 and the Instructor, Jack, Ray, Ken and Bob. The photograph is from the Bob Middleton Collection.

Ralph Hamel is seen hanging out of the hatch for the rear turret. If the tail gunner had to bail out he would use the hydraulics if it was working or the hand crank to manually rotate the turret to this position. On the ground it was much easier to get in and out this way as well. Ralph turned out to be the mid-upper gunner that went with us to Dishforth and then Croft after we graduated from Honeybourne. The photograph is from the Bob Middleton Collection.

My Honeybourne logbook pages from June 12, 1944 to July 16, 1944. From the Bob Middleton Collection.

Our crew finished flying at Honeybourne No. 24 OTU on Tuesday, July 18, 1944. I had been on 37 training flights in 2 engine Wellingtons since May 5, 1944. Since I joined the RCAF in August of 1942 I had accumulated 153 daylight flying hours and 92 nighttime flying hours. While at Honeybourne I had been on a total of 47 training trips with 29 of those flown by Don.

After we graduated from training on 2 engine Wellington Mk. X bombers at No. 24 Honeybourne OTU we spent the last week of July 1944 on leave in London.

Chapter 13

JULY IN LONDON AND V-1 MISSILES

Ray and I feeding pigeons in Trafalgar Square London, England. These pigeons were very tame and would sit on your hand. From the Bob Middleton Collection.

We were in London in the last week of July 1944 during the peak of the attacks by the German V-1 missiles. These were the world's very first cruise missiles called flying bombs, buzz bombs and doodlebugs. This was one of Hitler's many vengeance weapons that were created by the German scientists and engineers at the secret facility at Peenemünde to exact vengeance on England, the country that was bombing German cities. About 30,000 of the weapons were built by slave labor at a massive, secret underground facility at Mittelwerk, Germany. Peenemünde and Mittelwerk are shown on the map on page 230. The rocket engine of the V-1 was a simple pulse engine that fired about 400 to 800 times per minute, and it made a very distinctive loud buzzing or humming sound as it flew along. The V-1 contained about 1,700 pounds of high explosive that exploded when the bomb crashed to the ground. The V-1 had a gyro-controlled guidance system that kept the bomb running in a straight and level course at a 2,500 to 3,000 foot altitude.

The V-1 flew at 350 to 400 miles per hour which was the top speed of British fighter aircraft. The bomb was launched from a ramp that was aimed in the direction of the target many miles away. The V-1 had a little propeller on the nose that spun as the missile flew through the air. The propeller was connected to a clock work mechanism that tripped the rudder and elevator at the predetermined distance that had been set before launch. The V-1 then started down in a dive that disrupted the fuel supply to the engine causing the engine to stop and become silent. Over the target the V-1 would crash down into whatever was below it. The buzz bombs that were landing in England had a range of about 150 miles and were all launched from catapult launching ramps in France. While the engine was running it made a putt, putt type of sound and when the engine went silent you knew it was coming down somewhere close by.

While in London I heard and saw one buzz bomb as we were standing in Trafalgar Square. I heard it coming from behind us and I kept saying to myself keep going, keep going. The buzz bomb passed us by. "OH good." The engine cut out a short while later and came down. I never wanted to hear the sound of the engine cut out before the bomb went past me. These were terrifying to the people in England. The V-1 bombs started landing in England on Tuesday, June 13, 1944.

As the British and Allies advanced after D-Day all of the launching sites in France were destroyed. By the end of March 1945 V-1 missiles stopped falling on England. As the launch sites in France were being destroyed the V-1 missiles were carried airborne and launched from Me 111 aircraft for a short while. There were about 9,500 launched towards England.

F-bombs shot down

Flying bombs launched over the North Sea last night were met by fierce gunfire as they approached the coast.

Two bombs were shot into the sea and one exploded over a village in Southern England, causing damage but no casualties. London had a brief Alert.

October 15, 1944 newspaper clipping from a British newspaper. From the Bob Middleton Collection.

About 6,000 of these buzz bombs were destroyed before they reached their targets by fighter aircraft, balloon cables and anti-aircraft guns. These were quite a challenge for the fighter pilots due to the high speed and the huge amount of explosives in the bombs. By the time a fighter pilot got close enough to shoot it down he was also close enough to be caught in the blast and the shrapnel from the explosion. It took great skill and daring. Another way that the fighter pilots learned to destroy the buzz bomb was to fly up alongside it and then move over close enough so the fighter's wing tip would be under a wing of the buzz bomb. The fighter aircraft wing tip would cause disturbance to the air under the wing tip of the buzz bomb. That disturbance caused the wing of the bomb to move upwards, and the gyro controller of the bomb would lose control of the bomb and it would crash to the ground or water. This tipping of the buzz bombs was done over the channel or over open fields to reduce the loss of life when the bomb landed and exploded. This precision maneuver was all done while flying at 400 miles per hour. This was a job for the Spitfire and especially for the de Havilland twin engine Mosquito fighter which had speed to spare.

The famous RCAF Fighter Ace, Russell Bannock flying in de Havilland Mosquito fighters, downed 20 V-1 missiles in 1944 and 1945. Russell once told me he downed 8 of the V-1s by tipping them. On one operation Russell shot down 4 V-1s in one hour. Russell became Chief Test Pilot for de Havilland in 1946 and became Vice President and President of de Havilland from 1976 to 1978. My son Dan and I were sitting beside Russell at our Air Crew Association Christmas lunch in December 2019 a month after his 100th birthday. Sadly Russell Bannock left us on January 4, 2020.

Painting of a fast Spitfire fighter aircraft tipping a V-1 missile. This painting is called "Tipping Point" and is courtesy of artist Mark Donoghue at Mark Donoghue@hangar7art.

Chapter 14

HEAVY CONVERSION TRAINING IN THE HALIFAX

At the beginning of August 1944, the 5 of us were posted to Dishforth No. 1664 Heavy Conversion Unit (HCU) where we all learned to fly in 4 engine bombers. Dishforth was about 40 miles away south of the RCAF aerodrome at Croft in Yorkshire. The aircraft designation prefix for aircraft at Dishforth was DH. The morning we first arrived at Dishforth we heard the loud noise of a Halifax bomber flying low over our heads while it was landing. Without looking up we all started to run for the ditches thinking it was a buzz bomb. After we realized that it was one of ours, we hoped we did not look too stupid to our new mates at Dishforth.

The first 2 days at Dishforth was spent in ground school learning all about the Halifax Mk. V bomber and flying in such a huge beast compared to the Wellington Mk. X. At this point in our training Don was not a Commissioned Officer but he was our "Skipper" and what he said goes. There was never any saluting or calling me Sir between Don and myself. Don was the boss of the aircraft and crew. Don received his commission about September 20, 1944. While at Honeybourne OTU we had picked up Ralph Hamel the Mid-Upper Gunner. He was the fellow in in the photo hanging out of the rear turret of the Wellington at Honeybourne. At Dishforth HCU we also picked up Art Morency the Flight Engineer. The Wellington bomber did not have these two positions. Now we were a crew of 7. This is the course where Don learned to fly a 4 engine bomber with the assistance of Art the Flight Engineer. In the twin engine Wellington Don had to do everything but a four engine bomber is too much for one pilot to operate all by himself. In 4 engine bombers the pilot concentrated on flying the aircraft. The Flight Engineer would operate the throttles at all times, ensure that the fuel in the fuselage and wings was balanced, and monitor the condition of all the engines. The Flight Engineer worked with the ground crew to ensure our aircraft was always in top condition and if there were any issues Art would work with the ground crew to get things right. Art performed many more functions as well to free up Don to just fly the bomber. Everyone else got more practice at their own trade. The gunners are the only fellows that do not get much practice. It was rather boring for them.

At Dishforth No. 1664 we were flying in the older Halifax Mk. V with the 1,280 horsepower Rolls-Royce V-12 Merlin Mk. XX engines and the arrow shaped tail rudders and short squared off wing tips. The Halifax Mk. V at twice the size and weight of the Wellington was rather underpowered using the Merlin Mk. XX engines and was not a spectacular performer. The Merlin Mk. XX engines were excellent engines but 4 of them were not powerful enough for the Halifax.

Besides the lack of power, the Halifax Mk. V had 2 other major faults. The arrow shaped tail fin was subject to becoming stuck in the full rudder position. This was called rudder lock-over which caused the rudder to overpower the ailerons and put the aircraft into a spiral dive. To recover from this the pilot had to remove the opposite aileron, move the control column forward until the speed had increased to 150 mph, centralize the rudder, and then recover from the dive. During this recovery, the aircraft would lose about 4,000 feet. Hopefully when this happened you had 4,000 feet to spare between you and the ground. Many aircraft and crews were lost due to the rudder lock-over in training and combat before the problem was solved by Aeroplane and Armament Experimental Establishment, A&AEE Boscombe Down and Royal Aircraft Establishment, RAE Farnborough. The fix for this problem was to increase the fin and rudder area by 40 percent. The leading edges of the improved vertical fins were now straight and had a backward facing D shape instead of the forward-facing arrow shape.

All of the Halifax bombers with the Merlin engines also had a serious problem with vibration due to the Handley Page designed engine mounts and engine nacelles. Handley Page had designed and used engine mounts that were riveted together instead of using the welded together engine mounts designed and recommended by Rolls-Royce. The riveted together engine mounts allowed excessive vibrations at various engine speeds which caused fatigue of many engine related components. Oil coolers, radiators, air intakes, reduction gear casings, engine mountings and other components all failed due to excessive vibration. Many times, these failures were fatal to aircrews in combat. All forms of patches were done to try to compensate for the riveted engine mountings which were the cause of failures. They were never replaced with welded engine mounts. Eventually all of the Merlin powered Halifax bombers were withdrawn from operations into Germany as the loss of aircraft and lives was too high. The vibration issue and lack of power was solved when Handley Page began building Halifax Mk. III bombers with the Bristol Hercules engines. Of course, at the time while we were training in the Halifax Mk. V bombers, we had no idea how dangerous they actually were. This stuff was all top-secret at that time.

Later when we were posted to Croft, we were operating Halifax B Mk. III bombers with the mighty 1,650 horsepower Bristol Hercules Mk. XVI sleeve valve radial engines and the D shaped rudders that did not lock up. The Halifax Mk. III was a much better performer than the older Halifax Mk. V and so much closer an equal to the Lancaster. Those beginnings of the Halifax had spoiled the aircraft's reputation however and it was always thought of as inferior to the Lancaster. The Halifax could not carry as much as the Lancaster and the Lancaster was more adaptable for more roles with the long bomb bay. I liked both aircraft just the same.

The Lancaster and the Halifax both had two sets of aerials. There were aerials running from just behind the canopy to the top of each vertical tail plane. This aerial was mostly for short distance voice communication over the target and close to your base aerodrome. The voice communication was the Radio Telephone or R/T for short. For long distance communication we used Morse code and we called this the Wireless. For the long distance communication to our base in England the aircraft had a 150 foot long trailing aerial that had lead weights on the end. The transmitter was not especially powerful but having a 150 foot long aerial 18,000 feet high in the air certainly helped make up for the low power. This aerial would be let out by the wireless operator once we were in the air and clear of other aircraft. Before we would land the wireless operator would reel the aerial back in.

A Halifax Mk. V Series 1 bomber with the arrow shaped rudders and Merlin engines. The nose of this model was different than the ones we flew in. Photograph is courtesy of the Imperial War Museum. © IWM Image ATP-10962C.

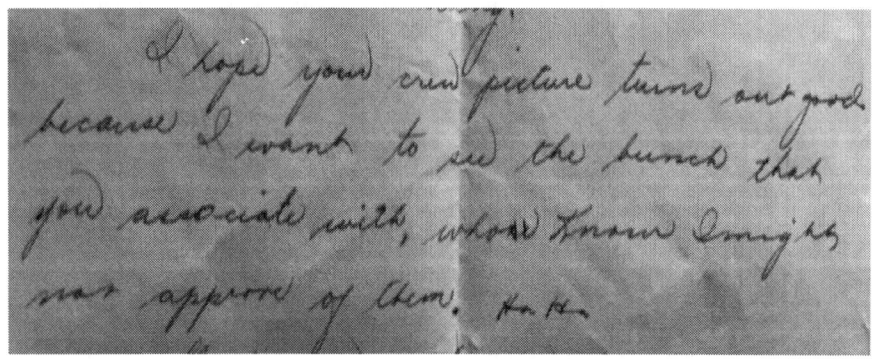

This a part of a letter from Patricia that she sent on December 15, 1944 telling me she was looking forward to seeing the formal picture of what the crew looked like that I was hanging around with. "I hope your crew picture turns out good because I want to see the bunch that you associate with, who knows I might not approve of them. Ha, Ha." The photograph is from the Bob Middleton Collection.

Our seven man Halifax and Lancaster Bomber crew. Names in order from left to right. Front row. Ray Rose, Bomb Aimer. Don Rombough, Pilot. Bob Middleton, Navigator. Rear row: Jack Cornock, Rear Gunner. Ralph Hamel, Mid-Upper Gunner. Ken Smith, Wireless Operator. Art Morency, Flight Engineer. We all felt we were the best aircrew in the RCAF. This photograph was taken in December of 1944 after we had done eighteen operations. Our pilot Don had been a Commissioned Officer since September 20, 1944. Ray was not a Commissioned Officer yet. Don was still working on Ray's commission. The photograph is from the Bob Middleton Collection.

Ray Rose, our 24-year-old Bomb Aimer was from Victoria, British Columbia where he worked with his father in the family jewelry store, Rose's Jewelers.

Don Rombough our Pilot was from Gananoque, Ontario.

Jack Cornock was our Rear Gunner who came from Toronto and was about the same age as I was.

Ralph Hamel our Mid-Upper Gunner was a 37 year old wheat farmer with a wife and five children from Saskatchewan. I have no idea how he managed to get into the RCAF. As a wheat farmer he must have been working in an essential service. This demonstrates how willing many people were to put their lives on the line to stop the evil tyrant in

Germany and his gangsters from taking over the world.

Ken Smith our Wireless Operator came from Windsor, Ontario.

Art Morency our Flight Engineer was a remustered aero engineer from Montreal, Quebec. A Canadian, let alone a French Canadian, Flight Engineer was not very common over in England. Most Flight Engineers even in RCAF crews came from England. The Flight Engineer sat or stood beside the Pilot and saw everything that he saw.

On Friday, August 18, 19 and 21, 1944 we did air to air and bombing practice in the daylight.

We did more fighter affiliation on Thursday August 25, 1944 in Halifax DU-S-SUGAR. The corkscrew maneuver is a huge stress on a large bomber, especially a fully loaded bomber.

Fighter affiliation in the Halifax was an amazing new experience when Don did the corkscrew maneuver. The Halifax had a marvelous clear dome at the nose. The view in the daylight was stupendous. When Jack or Ralph spotted the attacking fighter that was making the fake attack on us they would call out "Corkscrew" either port or starboard. I would stand with my feet straddling the bottom of the nose and my arms and hands straddled the top of the dome. I would be standing over Ray who was lying down in his position. In real a combat operation I would have hung on to something else near my position. On a real combat operation all of my instruments on my table would start to rise up and I had to quickly grab and hang onto all my instruments and my circular calculator while hanging onto something solid attached to the aircraft. I usually had a 1 or 2 second warning over the intercom to prepare myself. Don would turn the control wheel in the direction the gunner told him and then kick the rudder in the same direction until we were heading straight down. By the time we reached the bottom of that mad dive we were traveling over 250 miles per hour straight down. Once Don had dove the Halifax straight down as far as he felt necessary to escape the enemy fighter, he reversed the controls and headed up with the 4 Merlin engines going full bore. The 4 Merlin's were complaining about the treatment. Now all the g-forces were reversed, and the gravity wanted to pull me from the nose blister. Ultimately the airspeed of the bomber drops to 145 miles per hour during the climb which is continued at full power until the bomber regains the original operational altitude. It was hoped that on the initial dive the bomber would be well below the fighter. Once the bomber started to climb steeply it was hoped the fighter would not be able to maintain a distance behind the slow moving bomber without stalling. The fighter therefore would end up passing by the bomber. Ultimately the German fighter would go find another victim. At one point the aircraft is almost upside down and everything not tied down is flying about the inside of the aircraft. I was always amazed that the wings always stayed on the bombers during the corkscrew maneuver. I have always been blessed with a stomach that could withstand a gyrating aircraft and riding on ships across the rolling ocean. This was certainly more exciting in the big Halifax versus the smaller Wellington, and I could see where we were going straight down standing in the nose blister. After we had dropped a few thousand feet I was asking myself, "When will this be over?" No amusement park ride that drops a mere few hundred feet by gravity can match a 2,000 foot dive at over 250 miles per hour and corkscrewing down while standing in the nose of a Halifax.

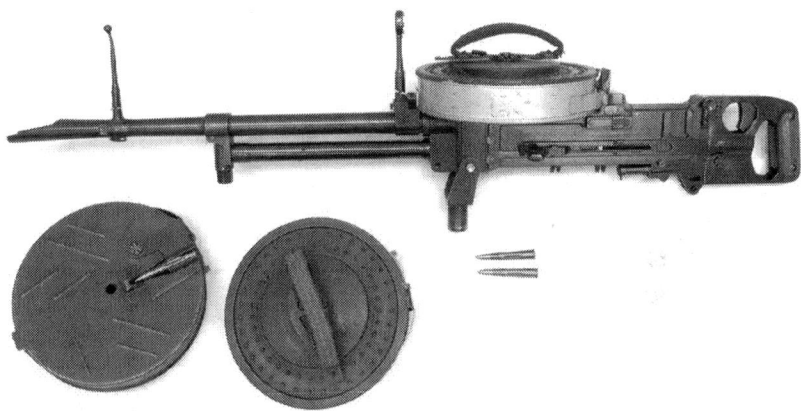

The Vickers type K gas operated machine gun with the ammunition pans and the shells. The photograph is courtesy of John Hipwell at Wolverine Supplies in Virden, Manitoba.

There was a Vickers K type gas operated 0.303 caliber machine gun that poked out through a round hole in the centre of the blister. It was tied back to one side by something similar to a bungee cord. Ray had a real hate for that gun and the pans of ammunition. He was always bumping into the gun and the round pans of ammunition that were not secured were always sliding about on the floor. When we practiced the corkscrew, the pans were everywhere. In all our operations in training and combat Ray never fired that gun once.

The spectacular window on the world through the nose of the Halifax Mk. VII at the National Air Force Museum of Canada at Trenton, Ontario. The Bomb Aimers panel is on the right of the side. The Vickers K type machine gun poked through the round hole in the centre. Photograph was taken by Dan Middleton.

One of the times after Don had performed the corkscrew that day the controls locked in the straight and level position heading out to the North Sea that was only about 15 minutes away. We were very lucky that the controls did not lock into the dive position. As I said earlier the Halifax Mk. V bombers with the arrow shaped rudders were infamous for the rudder locking up. It was also called rudder stall. We did not want to get wet so Ray, the Bomb Aimer and I opened the trap door in the bottom of the aircraft and had our legs dangling in the air ready to bail out but, we did not throw the trap door out.

Me sitting beside the lower hatch in the Halifax Mk. VII, NA337 at the National Air Force Museum in Trenton, Ontario May 17, 2019. The Halifax I was sitting in is one of only three complete Halifax bombers currently in existence in the world. Photograph taken by Dan Middleton.

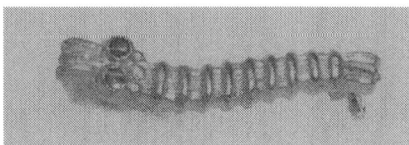

Replica of a caterpillar pin that we did not earn. The pin is only 1 inch long. The photograph is from the Bob Middleton Collection.

We were looking forward to joining the Caterpillar Club and receiving a caterpillar gold pin for bailing out. This was an exclusive club sponsored by the parachute manufacturers for airmen that had bailed out of their aircraft due to an emergency. Bailing out as a paratrooper in a normal operation did not count towards a caterpillar pin. Don got on the R/T with the base, and they gave him instructions on how to free the controls. Don was successful, regained control and turned the aircraft around. We put the escape hatch back in place. Luckily, we had not thrown the hatch out.

Originally all parachutes were made from silk. Silk is made by silk caterpillars so by wearing a caterpillar pin it showed that your life had been saved by silk caterpillars that supplied the material for the Irvin parachute. The club was founded by the Irvin Parachute Company in 1922. "Life depends on a silken thread" is the club's motto. By the end of WWII, the Irvin Parachute Company had given out 34,000 pins. To claim a caterpillar pin, you had to mail in a description of your bail out in an emergency and the written proof. It is estimated that over 100,000 airmen had bailed out in an emergency situation during WWII. There were other parachute manufactures besides the Irvin Parachute Company and these companies had Caterpillar Clubs as well.

Ray and I were so disappointed not to qualify for the caterpillar pin that day. Just before landing back at Dishforth that day, the controls locked on Don again. He brought the Halifax in fast and hard. We must have bounced about 30 feet into the air when we hit the ground and somehow within seconds Don managed to get the aircraft under control. We ended up about 40 feet off the runway on the grass. A landing like that with locked up controls could get everyone killed as the aircraft had a good possibility of one wing dipping and smashing into the ground. Don was such an excellent pilot, and we owed our lives to Don for his amazing flying skills many times over. Ray was interviewed in November 2013 by Richard Watts of the Times Colonist newspaper in British Columbia and Ray commented on Don's abilities. Ray said, "We had a marvelous pilot, absolutely fantastic. He did everything he was supposed to do and that is why we were all still alive at the end."

While we were training at Dishforth on Monday, July 24, 1944 Halifax JD372 from 1666 HCU, Wombleton just blew up in the air according to a Dishforth crew that was flying close to it at the time. The official report in the squadron log was that it was flying at 7,000 feet when the starboard outer engine caught fire and it spun into the ground. We did not hear why it happened. The crew had been doing fighter affiliation which involves the stressful corkscrew maneuver. Possibly it had an engine mount vibration related failure. It was war time, and the results of the investigation were top-secret. It was another 7 lost soldiers in a training accident. The Navigator in that Halifax was George Lewthwaite, the same fellow that taught me how to play chess at Honeybourne, OTU and had lifted my pay book out of my pocket while we were training in the decompression chamber at Belleville ITS. George and I were in all the same training classes up to and including Honeybourne and the trip across the Atlantic. He is in the Sidmouth graduation picture on page 113. George Lewthwaite and 4 other crew members are buried at Stonefall Cemetery Harrogate, UK. The Wireless Operator is buried at St. Pancras Cemetery London, UK and the Flight Engineer is buried at Pennyfuir Cemetery Oban, UK.

Training accidents involving airmen within the British Commonwealth during WWII claimed the lives of about 10,000 men. Training is risky business. Between July 2, 1944 and September 23, 1944 7 Halifax aircraft based at Dishforth HCU crashed during training operations.

Friday, July 7, 1944 Halifax EB156 crashed with no loss of life.

Thursday, July 20, 1944 Halifax DG348 crashed with no loss of life.

Tuesday, July 25, 1944 Halifax LK694 crashed with no loss of life.

Monday, August 7, 1944 Halifax DG363 crashed into the North Sea with the loss of all 7 crew members. The Navigator is buried at Stonefall Cemetery Harrogate, UK. Six crew members are remembered at the Runnymede Memorial Surrey, UK.

Friday, August 25, 1944 Halifax ZU-U crashed with no loss of life.

Thursday, August 31, 1944 Halifax LL283 crashed with 6 survivors. The Pilot is buried at Blacon Cemetery Chester, UK and the Flight Engineer is buried at the Hertford Road Cemetery, Enfield, UK.

September 23, 1944 Halifax DK143 crashed with only 2 survivors. The Flight Engineer is buried at St. Peter-In-Thanet Churchyard Cemetery Kent, UK. The other 4 crew members are buried at Stonefall Cemetery Harrogate, UK.

Did I mention that those old Halifax Mk. V aircraft we were flying in were worn out?

On Saturday night, August 25, 1944 we went on an 828 mile spoof raid that took us just 30 miles from the enemy occupied Dutch coast in Halifax DH-Y-YOKE. We flew from Dishforth to Cromer and then out across the North Sea to the spoof target at coordinate 53° 00' N, 04° 00' E and then returned passing over Luton, England. We continued on and did many turns and targets before returning to Dishforth that night. We were out for 5 hours. Some flak was seen coming up from the Dutch coast but there were no fighters. The route we took on this training trip is shown on page 230.

The purpose of a spoof raid is to draw up the German fighter force and then turn around and leave before they can reach you. This wasted the efforts of the Luftwaffe fighter crews chasing a fake attack and meant that the fighters would have to land and refuel before they could go after the real main bomber force that was travelling to some other target. This saved the real bomber force from some fighter harassment on the way to the target. The return trips were more risky as the Luftwaffe fighter force knew we were going back home to England.

On Monday, August 28, 1944 we did a cross-country flight at night in Halifax DH-H-HARRY. This was a disaster. Our aircraft did not have H2S ground scanning radar nor GEE radio navigation and there was 10/10ths cloud cover so we could not see the ground. I really had no idea where we were. I had to use dead reckoning and I managed to make a 40 mile error in my air plot. Needless to say, we were lost up in the air until there was a break in the cloud cover and I got a fix from an Occult that was flashing the code letters for Ispwich. I had made a book and map with all the Morse code letters for all the Occults in England. The book disappeared years ago but I still have that map. That map is on page 102. Once I had a fix on that Occult, I was able to tell Don a course to steer to get back to Dishforth. An Occult is a bright light located at many locations around England that flash a unique code in Morse code. The next morning our Commanding Officer had all 10 crews in for a serious talk. The Commanding Officer of Dishforth was so angry with the bunch of us that he told us if we performed that poorly on our next trip, we would all be cleaning the toilets or digging ditches. It appeared I was not the only navigator who got lost that night.

The next night, Tuesday August 29, 1944 we were so surprised that we were all going on a nighttime spoof raid on the northern Dutch coast. We left at 21:15 in Halifax DH-L-LARRY for an 851 mile, 5 hour and 50 minute round trip. On this training operation there were 9 turning points. This was a great deal of navigation practice for me and the navigators of the other crews. We flew way out over the North Sea and approached to within 30 miles of the Dutch coast and then turned back. We were 200 miles from England and only 100 miles northwest of Wilhelmshaven, Germany. Looking at the plot of that trip from 76 years ago we sure were close to being in harm's way that night. The route we took on this training trip is shown on page 230.

During our trip we did see a great deal of flak coming from the Dutch coast and from ship based flak batteries but it was far enough away not to bother us.

Before we landed Ken started to reel in the 150 foot long trailing aerial but it was only about 10 feet long. 140 feet of aerial wire was wrapped around something somewhere. We did not remember flying low enough to hit trees or buildings with the aerial. Sometime during the trip in the dark another aircraft must have come within 150 feet of our aircraft and clipped our aerial. Luckily, we all returned safely that night. The operation was a great success, and the Commanding Officer was very pleased with the results of our spoof raid. This turned out to be our last training flight at Dishforth. We had been at Dishforth only 3 weeks and made 9 training flights in Halifax Mk. V aircraft. Just like that the next day we were graduated and ready for combat operations. I received an assessment of Average for my Navigation training at Dishforth No. 1664 HCU. I had accumulated 169 hours of Navigation flying in the daylight and 109 hours of Navigation flying at night. All the graduated crews received their posting to RCAF aerodromes, and we would all be going onto real combat operations.

Chapter 15

NAVIGATING ELECTRONICALLY WITH H2S AND GEE

Saturday, August 27, 1944 found me on a 4 hour flight with an instructor in a Halifax Mk. V learning how to use the H2S ground radar while actually airborne. Up until now I had only had H2S theory in ground school. H2S ground scanning radar was one of those electronic marvels that started development in 1941 and began to be used in early 1943 that allowed us to see the ground through clouds and the dark of night. The H2S forward facing scanning antenna was hidden behind the teardrop shaped radome blister on the underside of our bombers. The H2S radar gave a rather crude image of the ground that I did not find especially useful. The image on my screen was often not very clear. I had to have an outline picture or a map of the area we were bombing that I could compare the H2S image to. I had to know ahead of time what image I was looking for. With H2S I could tell the difference between water and land or water and a city. A built-up area of a city or a city surrounded by open field all looked the same on the H2S screen. During a bombing run using H2S I would give the target information to Ray and he would release the bombs accordingly. A major downside of the H2S radar was that the German fighters could track our aircraft by the signal that our H2S radar sent out in front of our aircraft. In Berlin the Germans were able to make the radar image confusing by mounting metal radar reflectors on buildings around Berlin. In the paintings by Mike Steele-Morgan you can see the H2S unit at the navigation station of the Halifax on page 201 and the Lancaster on page 252.

There was another wireless navigation aid that we were using called GEE that I learned how to use while training at Dishforth. The Wellington bombers at Honeybourne were not equipped with GEE.

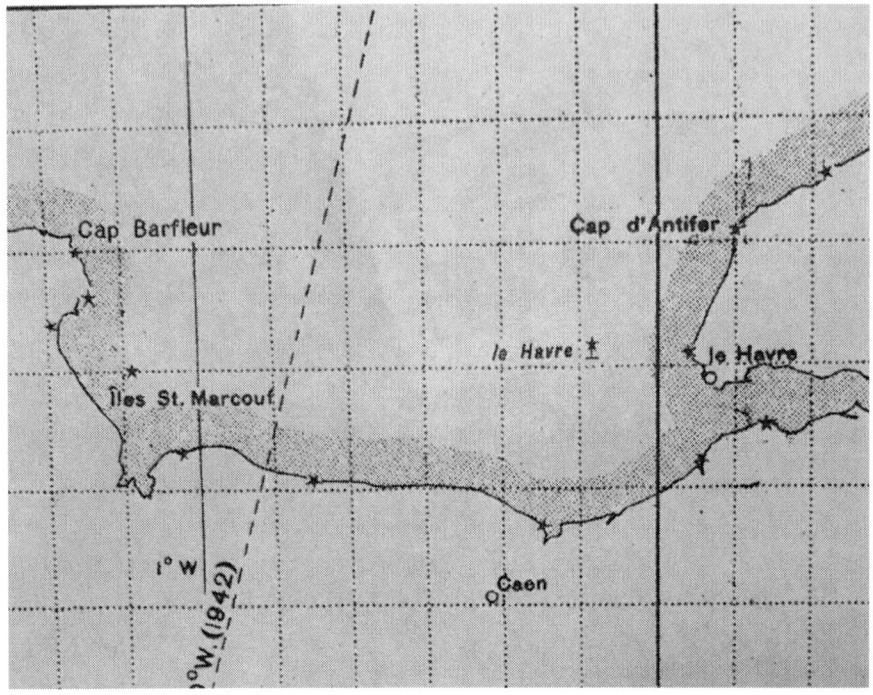

This map shows the Navigator the shapes of what he is looking for on his H2S radar screen. The map is from the Bob Middleton Collection.

GEE radio navigation had been in development by British scientists and engineers since 1939 and was installed in some operational bombers starting in March 1942. These brilliant British scientists and engineers were affectionately called boffins. GEE was a precursor of the Loran navigation system developed by the Americans. By 1943 all of Bomber Commands aircraft had GEE installed. The system was based upon using three transmitting stations about 100 miles apart from each other that transmitted a series of pulses. One station was the master and the other 2 were repeaters. The repeater stations broadcast a signal pulse that was time delayed from the original master signal pulses. The delay was a very short time, a few microseconds.

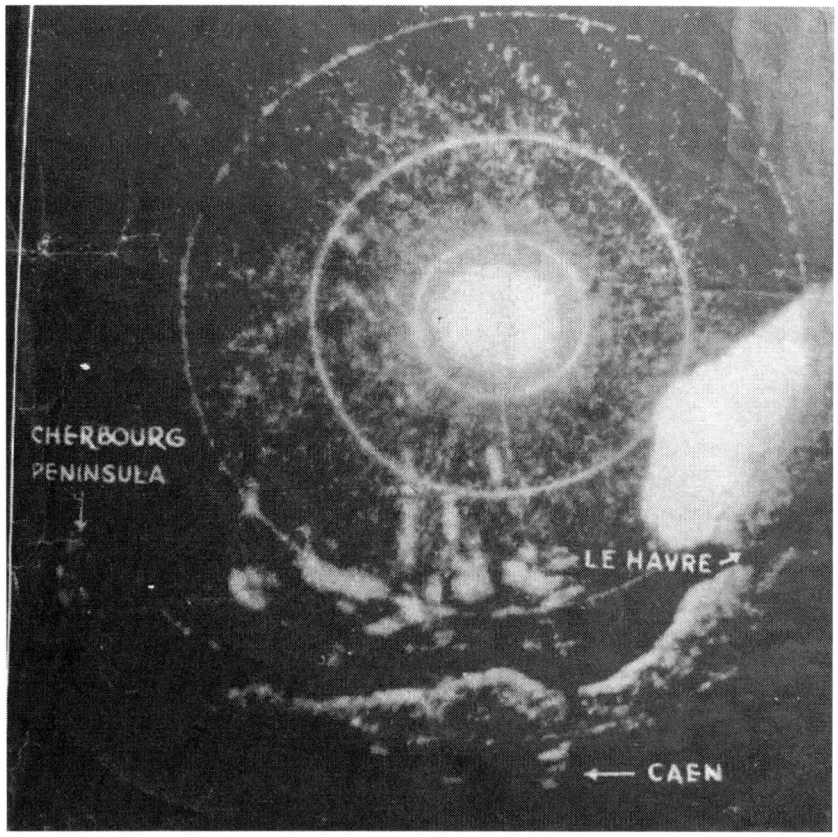

This picture is an image of an H2S picture of the coast of France on D-Day, Tuesday, June 6, 1945. Many of the spots in the English Channel in this image are the ships of the Invasion Fleet. You can see from this photograph how I needed to know what the target looked like. If the target was on the shore you could find it. You can see locating Caen inland would be difficult. The picture is from the Bob Middleton Collection.

Over Germany GEE was accurate to about two miles. As we were closer to the transmitting sites the accuracy became greater. The transmitters were originally only in England but after D-Day there were transmitting stations in France as well. As the Allied armies moved closer to Germany the GEE stations were moved closer to Germany as well. This helped to increase the accuracy over Germany. I was able to use GEE to find the runway at Croft on our return trips. At the receiving end of the signal was a very short stub aerial mounted on the bomber. You can see the location of the GEE aerial on my drawing of the Halifax on page 178. The radio signal went to the GEE box receiver and then to the GEE box. In the paintings by Mike Steele-Morgan you can see the GEE box at the navigation station of the Halifax on page 201 and the Lancaster on page 252. There were three different receivers for the GEE box that were pre-tuned to three different frequencies and different GEE transmitter groups.

The biggest downfall of GEE was that it could be jammed by German radio signals. By the time we were over Germany the GEE signal originating in England or France was not very strong and the signal could be swamped by very strong local German transmitters. Navigators would use the receiver box that worked best with their location and the frequencies that had the least amount of intentional jamming by those German transmitting sites.

If the GEE was jammed, I would shoot the stars with my astro sextant. The Germans could not jam the stars. The most important task for me was to do my dead reckoning as accurately as possible. Our lives depended upon it. I learned how to use GEE in a 4 hour training session while at Dishforth.

On the next two pages are my sketches of the GEE box and the images on the screen that I would observe. I drew these sketches in 1945, once I was back home in Toronto.

The readout for the GEE was a 5 inch round oscilloscope display. The trace on the screen was green in color. The GEE box had 6 controls that I fiddled with to obtain the image I needed. Referring to the 4 sketches of the screen I made I will explain how I used GEE. On screen one I would line up above each other the master pulses on the upper and lower traces. You can see there are actually 4 traces on the screen. I had to know what I was looking for to start the process and all the way through. This was the same as using a slide rule. Once these pulses were aligned, I used the magnification control to expand the image to what is shown on screen two. The 2 lower traces have the positive and negative pulses lined up under the positive pulse of the upper trace. I now flipped a switch, and I would have the set of traces you see in screen 4. I would line up the tall lines on the left so that the traces start at the same spot. The top and bottom pair of traces each shows a graticule line that I would read off by counting the lines on each. The negative pulse was the marker that was used to count the positive pulses. Each positive line was counted and, that number corresponded to curved lines on a map that were numbered according to what transmitter sites you were receiving. In my example the top trace is 10 and the lower trace is 14. Looking at the map where the curves with those numbers intersected is where you were plus or minus 2 miles. The map I sketched shows the runway at Croft. Screen 3 is one example of what I would see when the Germans were jamming the GEE frequencies. The image was scrambled and was useless. The German scientists and engineers had captured GEE units from crashed aircraft and had figured out how to jam the GEE signals.

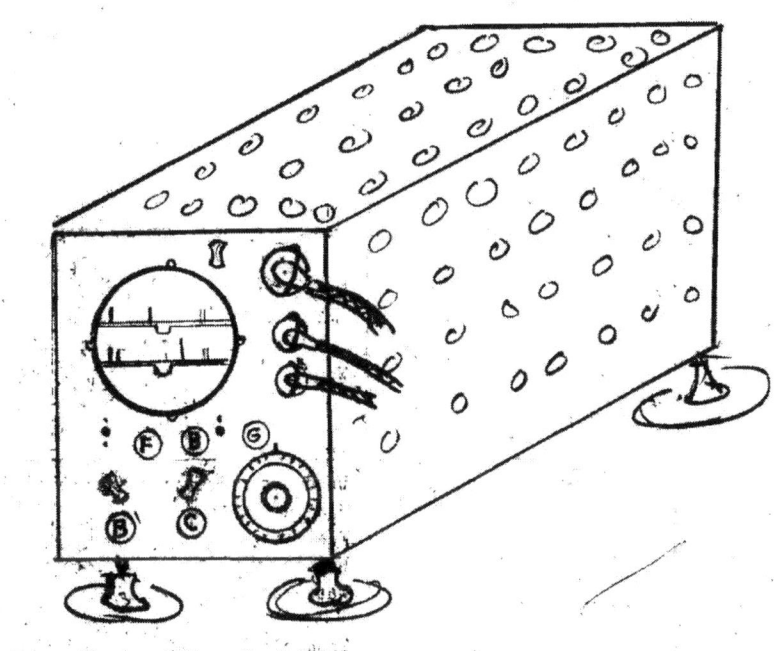

My sketch of the GEE Box. Sketches from the Bob Middleton Collection.

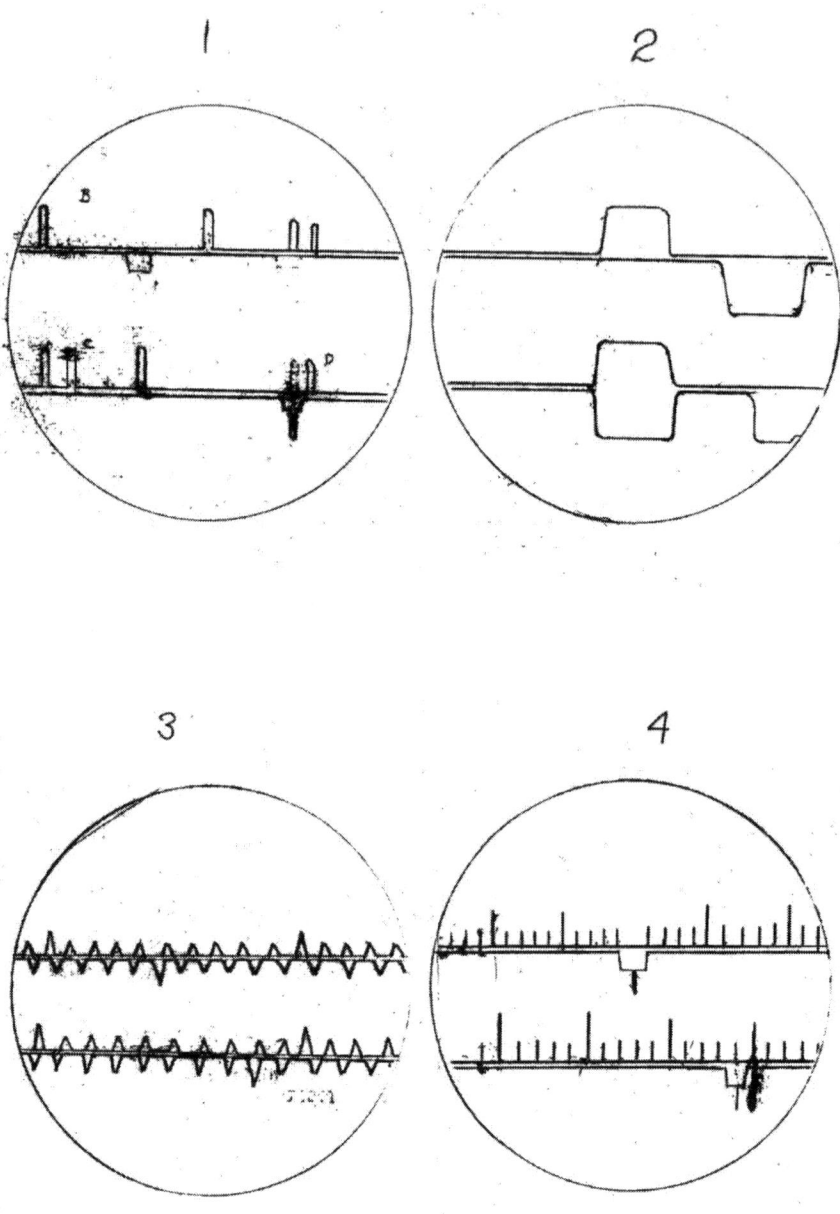

Traces that I would see on the GEE box screen. From the Bob Middleton Collection.

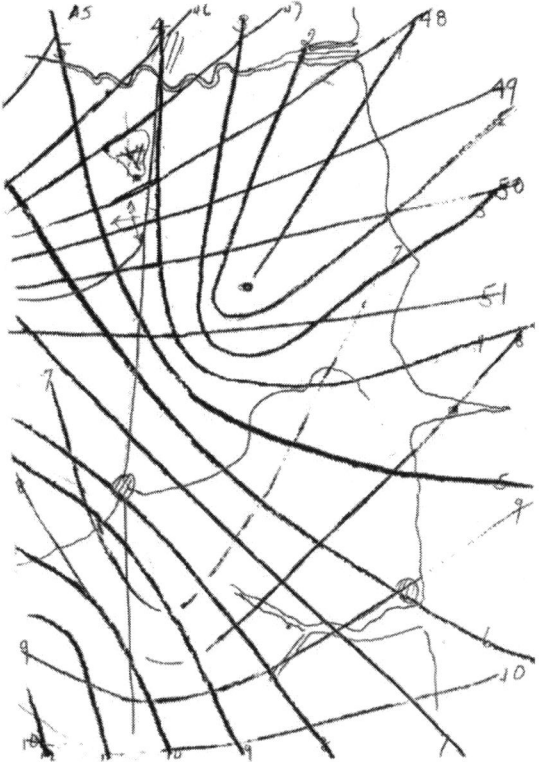

My hand drawn GEE map. Near the top of this map the triangle is the location of the 3 runways at Croft.

A Lancaster bomber from RAF Bardney 189 Squadron showing the H2S radome under the belly just below the CA. I cannot recall where I took the photograph. It may have been a Lancaster diverted to our aerodrome or it was a Lancaster at an aerodrome we had been diverted to. The photograph is from the Bob Middleton Collection.

Chapter 16

CROFT AND THE CHOP SQUADRON

The Croft aerodrome was opened by the RAF in 1941 for use by the RAF No. 4 Group. In 1943 Croft became a satellite aerodrome of Middleton St. George which had been taken over by the RCAF No. 6 Group and initially was used as the RCAF 1664 Heavy Conversion Unit. On December 10, 1943 431 Iroquois Squadron moved to Croft from the aerodrome at Tholthorpe. One day later the 434 Bluenose Squadron also moved to Croft from the aerodrome at Tholthorpe. The Croft aerodrome is shown on the map on page 102.

On Friday, September 1, 1944 our crew from our Dishforth No. 1664 HCU course was the only crew posted to 431 Iroquois Squadron located at Croft in Yorkshire. Our squadron had the honor of being named after the fierce and brave Iroquois warriors. The squadron's motto is "Warriors of the Air." While at Croft we were all immensely proud to be in an RCAF Squadron named after the fierce fighting and courageous Iroquois warriors.

When we were assigned to 431 Iroquois Squadron many of our mates at Dishforth wished us good luck and jokingly told us it was nice knowing us as we were going to the Chop Squadron. The chop is what happened when you were killed or Failed to Return, FTR during an operation. 431 Pilot, Reg Harrison who has spoken with my son said that the folks at the Dishforth Heavy Conversion Unit told him, "We should hope we didn't get posted to Croft as it is the "JINX" Squadron." Reg and his crew were assigned to Croft about three months before our crew arrived. Everyone knew that Croft had a bad reputation for crews failing to return at that time.

Before our crew arrived at Croft and our crew started on operations the 431 Iroquois Squadron at Croft was having a very hard go of it.

The Wing Commander and flight commanders while I was stationed at Croft. The picture was taken at one end of the briefing room. The tall fellow at the centre is Wing Commander Eric Mitchell. The fellow to his left is our B Flight Commander Frank Guillevin. The photograph, PL 32028 is courtesy of Library and Archives Canada.

172

During the months of July and August of 1944 the squadron had lost 16 aircraft and crews. Five of Iroquois Squadron aircraft and crews were lost during an operation to Hamburg on the night of July 28/29, 1944.

When we started our tour at Croft the 431 Wing Commander was Eric Mitchell and our B Flight Commander was Frank Guillevin.

Crest of the RCAF 431 Iroquois Squadron. In English, the motto is "Warriors of the Air"

The Croft 431, 434 Squadron Airman Memorial. The photograph was taken by and is courtesy of Nick Ager in the UK.

173

There is a Memorial erected at Dalton-on-Tees beside the Northallerton Road, about one mile from Croft. On top is an bronze Airman looking across the road towards Croft with his left arm raised above his face as if looking out for returning aircrews. The inscription on the bottom reads, "Dedicated to 78 Squadron RAF, 1664 HCU, 419, 427, 431 and 434 Squadrons RCAF. 1941 to 1945." The inscription on top reads, "In memory of and to honor those who served at Croft during World War II. Dedicated by the members of 431 Iroquois and 434 Bluenose RCAF Squadrons. 6 Group Bomber Command. 26 September 1987."

Aerial view of RCAF Croft in the north of England. Aircraft can be seen sitting in the paved round dispersal areas. The photograph is courtesy of Richard Koval.

RCAF Croft was the home to the Canadian 434 Bluenose Squadron and the Canadian 431 Iroquois Squadron. The curvy track around the runways was the perimeter track. Off of the perimeter track are the round dispersal areas that the bombers sit on. Some pads were paved and some were not. Our bombers were dispersed or kept away from each other so that if one bomber blew up during an attack or an accident there was less of a chance of a chain reaction blowing up all of the bombers if the bombers had been neatly lined up close together. The Americans found out the hard way at Pearl Harbor when they lost so many neatly lined up aircraft when the Japanese attacked on Sunday, December 7, 1941.

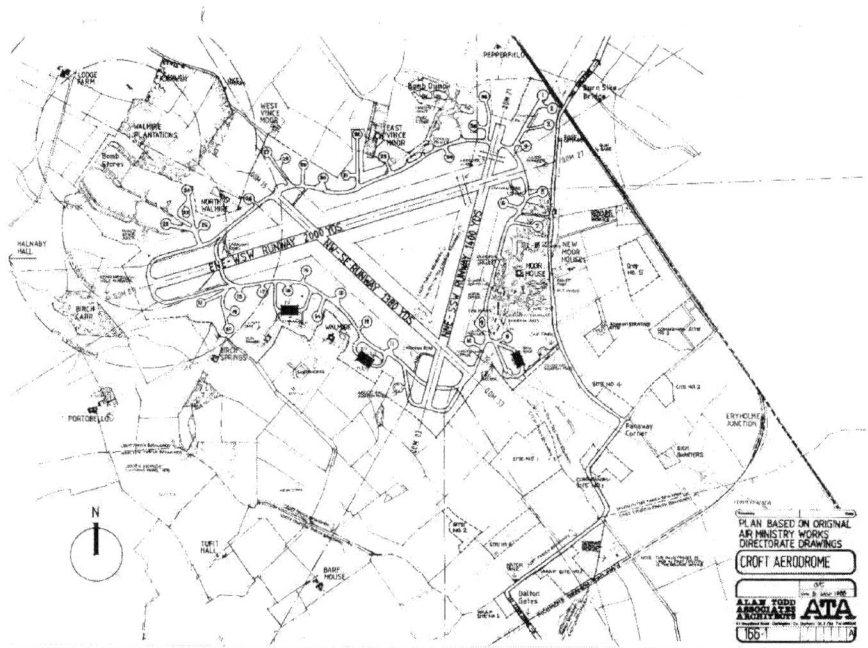

The Engineer's drawing of the Croft Aerodrome. The picture is courtesy of Richard Koval.

The pilots used to say the Halifax Mk. III climbed like a homesick angel with its mighty engines but it had the glide angle of a brick. The Halifax was a very solid aircraft built like a brick outhouse. The Halifax Mk. III used the mighty 1,650 horsepower Hercules XVI 14-cylinder radial sleeve valve engine built by Bristol. I felt safe inside the Halifax and it was very roomy inside. I especially liked the Halifax for the marvelous view through the front perspex. It was 6 feet high and 3.5 feet wide. Ray Rose learned to use the marvelous Mk. XIV bomb sight. I learned more about the GEE navigation aid and how to fiddle with the H2S ground radar. Now our very survival depended on how well I could use these pieces of advanced equipment. We did more fighter affiliation and more corkscrews. In the Halifax Mk. III when

Don did his climb from the bottom of the corkscrew those Hercules Mk. XVI engines lifted the bomber like nobody's business. These engines were 29 percent more powerful than the 1280 horsepower Rolls-Royce Merlin Mk. XX engines used in the Halifax Mk. V.

The beautifully restored Halifax B Mk. VII bomber, NA337 at the Air Force Museum of Canada in Trenton, Ontario, Canada. There are only three fully restored Halifax aircraft in the world. The photograph was taken by the Museum Public Relations photographer, Theo Czerny-Holownia and is courtesy of Air Force Museum of Canada at Trenton, Ontario.

The mighty Bristol Hercules XVI engine on display at the Bomber Command Museum at Nanton, Alberta. Lovingly nicknamed, "The Monster". The photograph is courtesy of Karl Kjarsgaard of the Halifax 57 Rescue Project.

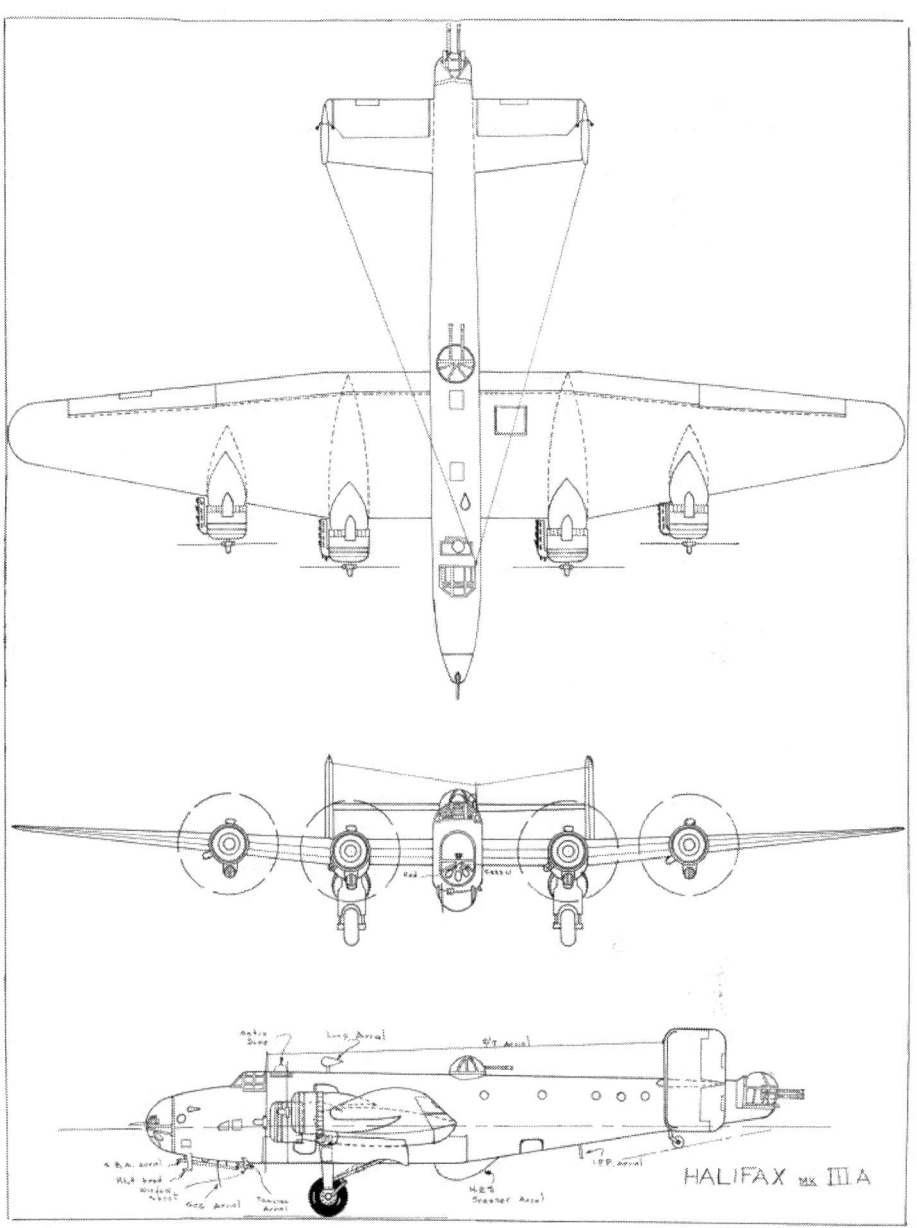

Drawing I made in the summer of 1945 of the Halifax Mk. III, A. This is the bomber that we were flying at Croft on our first 10 operations. Drawing is from the Bob Middleton Collection.

177

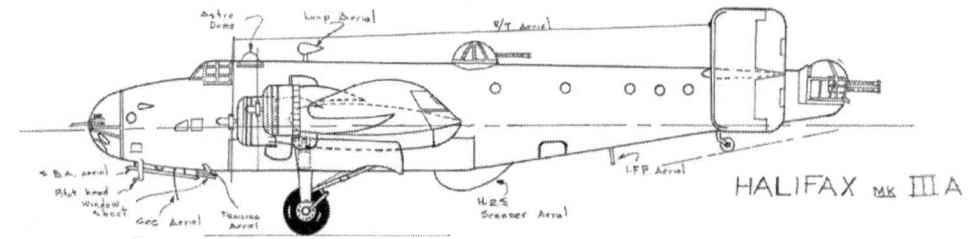

In 1945 I made this drawing showing all the various aerials on the Halifax Mk. III, A. The drawing is from the Bob Middleton Collection.

Once I became a Navigator on the Halifax and the Lancaster, I had all sorts of 1944 state of the art electronic equipment so I became quite fascinated by electronics. The H2S radar and the GEE navigation aid had only been in existence for two years. And these were being continually refined all the time. In 1945 I made a drawing showing all the various aerials on the Halifax Mk. III, A.

The SBA or Standard Beam Approach aerial and associated electronics was used to guide the pilot landing the aircraft at night or in poor visibility. The SBA was similar to the modern Instrument Landing System, ILS. Beacons on the airfields were picked up by the aircraft receivers on the landing approach. The main beacon with a narrow beam was at the end of the runway. When lined up correctly with the runway the pilot received a steady tone. If the aircraft was off to the left or right the pilot heard a series of tones in dots or dashes. There was also a visual indicator on the dash.

The aerial for the GEE navigation system was about 3 feet in length which was the quarter wavelength for the 70 to 90 Megahertz frequencies used.

The trailing aerial was about 150 feet long and was used with the lower frequency continuous wave (CW) Morse code communication. This was our long range communication between our base in England and our aircraft while over Fortress Europe.

The Loop Aerial was used in conjunction with the main radio receiver as a direction finding aerial. It gave you a general idea of which way you were pointing if you knew where the transmitting station was that you were receiving.

The Radio Telephone (R/T) aerial was used for local aircraft to aircraft or aircraft to base voice communications and was only useful for about 30 miles. Over the target it was generally only used by the Master Bomber to give directions to the bomber force.

The H2S radome was on the underside of the aircraft. Under the dome was a microwave dish aerial pointing down at the ground. It swept from side to side to scan the ground. The H2S radar painted a somewhat useful picture of the ground.

The IFF aerial was used by the Identification Friend or Foe identification radar system.

The Pitot head was connected to the Indicated Air Speed Indicator, IAS gauge. This was not an aerial. Indicated Air Speed, IAS is the speed that is indicated on the aircraft air speed indicator, but it is not your True Air Speed, TAS. True air speed is affected by altitude and temperature. As you fly higher the air becomes thinner and the indicated airspeed is lower than your true air speed. As the air becomes colder the air is denser and the IAS will be higher than true air speed. I had a circular calculator to calculate our true air speed from all these variables. Your speed over the ground called ground speed is determined by the speed of the wind you are flying in. If you have a head wind your ground speed is your true air speed minus the wind speed. If you have a tailwind your ground speed is your true air speed plus the wind speed. If the wind is blowing at an angle across your path, then there are a whole other set of calculations to determine your ground speed as it will be a vector of the true air speed and the wind speed. I had to know our ground speed in order to know where we were, how to arrive at the target on time and get back home again. This took a great deal of work making constant calculations.

The chute for the release of Window was under the navigator's position.

On Monday, September 4, 1944 we did an all up war load test so Don could feel how a fully loaded Halifax handled. The Halifax Mk. III bomb load test involved flying with 16,000 pounds of fuel and 11,000 pounds of bombs. The bombs did not have fuses or tail fins and were theoretically safe. Don managed to get the Halifax to stager up to 24,000 feet. I do not know how he got it up so high. It was such a marvelous feeling to be up so high in that cold stark blue sky. Never

179

had any of us been that high in the sky to see our little world from so far away. We never ventured that high again in any bomber after that flight. This made me think of the 1937 Frank Capra movie *Lost Horizon* about Shangri-La, starring Ronald Colman. During a few scenes when the DC-3 aircraft was climbing higher and higher over the Himalayas the altimeter was shown many times until it showed 21,000 feet. The folks in the movie were feeling very cold and were having some difficulty breathing as the DC-3 was not pressurized. As we know from my experience in the depressurization chamber at Belleville the folks in the DC-3 would all have been passed out from the lack of oxygen and very cold or frozen by the lack of heating. But it made a really good suspenseful movie scene.

The tricky task for Don was to land the fully loaded Halifax bomber back on the ground without busting it. In a normal round trip operation Don would be landing the bomber just about 25,000 pounds lighter than when we took off. Altogether that day we took off and landed fully loaded 4 times. Landing fully loaded was a good exercise for future operations. A Halifax bomb load is seen in the photograph on page 226.

Chapter 17

<u>BOMBS</u>

On our operations we used various sizes and types of bombs.

General Purpose bombs or GP bombs had thick walls containing 35 percent explosives by weight. The GP bomb was used to penetrate trucks and tanks and also fragment into many pieces to do maximum harm to personnel from the flying shrapnel.

Semi-Armor Piercing or SAP bombs had thick walls containing 35 percent explosives by weight and strong tips designed to penetrate through steel armor and concrete.

Medium Capacity or MC bombs had thin walls containing 50 percent explosives by weight. The MC bomb was designed to blow buildings apart.

High Capacity or HC bombs had very thin walls containing 75 percent explosives by weight. These were blast bombs and were designed to blow buildings apart. In almost every operation we flew in our Lancasters, a 4,000 pound HC blast bomb called a cookie was used. The cookie had a very thin wall casing that contained 3,000 pounds of high explosives and looked like a 10 foot long oil drum. The cookie was designed to blow everything apart.

All of these types of bombs could be used with time delays as short as 0.025 seconds or as long as hours or days in the case of Long Delay, LD fuses. The short delay was designed to blow a building apart only after it had passed through the roof and/or a couple of floors. We wanted to do more than just blow roofs off of buildings. The bomb hitting an object like a roof only initiated the delay timer. The much longer LD time delays were designed to explode a bomb hours after it had buried itself in the ground or a building. The purpose of this was to harass and terrorize rescue workers after the raid had ceased. This discouraged firefighting and cleanup operations as personnel on the ground never knew if there were time delay bombs buried in the rubble. The rescue workers knew these could explode at any time. There could be any number of these LD bombs in a load of bombs. These types of bombs were used by both the Axis Air Force and the Allied Air Force.

Incendiaries were used on almost all of our later operations in Lancasters. Incendiaries were hexagonal units 18 inches long weighing 4 pounds made from a magnesium casing that burned extremely hot. The purpose of the incendiaries was to set everything combustible on fire after we had blown things to pieces. Because the incendiaries contained magnesium putting water on these made them burn more violently. The only thing that could extinguish an incendiary was sand. All about towns in England at this time there were buckets of sand outside the entrances to every building. The individual incendiaries were packaged into Small Bomb Containers, SBC. The SBC was 5 feet long and was designed to release the individual incendiary sticks in as wide a pattern as possible.

All of these types of bombs were used by both sides during the Second World War. Many of the techniques used in the German bombings of England were copied and used by Bomber Command to bomb German occupied areas.

An SBC loaded with magnesium incendiaries. © IWM image CH 6272.

This is a photograph of a replica Cookie blast bomb at the Canadian Warplane Heritage Museum in Hamilton, Ontario. The section from the back end with the fuses to the line around the drum is hollow. This made the cylinder front end heavier than the back end so that it would travel straight down and not tumble. If the bomb does not land on the front end it just splits open without exploding. This was determined through experience. The photograph is courtesy of the Canadian Warplane Heritage Museum.

500 pound bombs at the Canada Aviation and Space Museum in Ottawa, Ontario. The photograph was taken by Dan Middleton

183

Chapter 18

WINDOW AND GERMAN RADAR

Early on in the Second World War the German scientists and engineers had developed extremely accurate and deadly radar. On the German radar screens our bombers would show up as individual bombers or groups of bombers as we came into the range of the radar as we crossed the French coast. There were also radar stations along our routes all the way to Germany and the German towns. The radar operators were able to accurately judge the number of bombers, the altitude, and the direction the bombers were heading. From this information the radar operators would guess where we were heading. The German radar worked very well. The radar operators directed the Luftwaffe fighter pilots where to find us and the direction we were heading. With that information the Luftwaffe fighter pilots would set an intercept course and shoot us out of the sky.

In the early 1940s British scientists developed a method named Window to create a confusing image on the German radar screens. Window is made up of varying lengths of black paper with a foil backing 5/8″ wide packaged in bundles with 2,200 strips about 3″ in diameter. The foil reflected the German radar signals that were beamed into the sky looking for the bomber stream. The length of the strips was selected according to the frequency of the radar signal that was being used to find us. Window was not used until July 24, 1943 as it was feared the German bombers over England would start to use it as well to fool British radar operators. By July 1943 Bomber Command felt there would never be any German bomber forces attacking England again, so it was safe to start using Window without it being used against them. Window was an early form of chaff used to confuse the German radar operators.

When we were dropping Window into the sky the reflections from the thousands of strips of window would show up as a cluster of targets that would swamp their radar screens. It looked like there were huge formations of bombers instead of individual bombers. This made it difficult to guide the fighter pilots to exact locations of our bombers and the number of bombers. Even a small group of bombers would look like hundreds of bombers. The Window did help us when we were in the range of the radar controlled searchlights and flak guns. Our bombers would show up on the screens as large blobs instead of focused points. Window made the German flak gun and searchlight radar less accurate. Anyway, we convinced ourselves that the Window helped protect us. After any operation there were tens of thousands of strips of Window all over the target and the path to and from the target. It looked like Christmas decorations hanging from houses, hedges, trees and wires.

Window was used for the first time on the 728 bomber raid on Hamburg on the night of July 24, 1943. That night all the radar operators were so confused by all the blobs on their screens that the fighters were not dispatched to where the bombers were. That first night Window was a fabulous success for Bomber Command. Of the 728 bombers sent to Hamburg that night only 12 Failed to Return. After a few nights the German engineers began to counter the effects of our use of Window, and it was not as effective as on that first night.

During our briefings we were told at what point in our flight we should start dumping Window through the Window chute. As we came closer to the target Art our Flight Engineer was dumping a packet of Window down the chute every minute. I made sure he did. "Hey Art, are you dumping Window?" When we were really close to and over the target Art would put a bundle into the Window chute every 30 seconds. After one operation I picked up some strips of Window from our bomber and tucked it away in a safe place and brought it home. I found it very interesting as Window was such advanced cutting edge counter measures technology in 1944.

Photograph of me holding one strip of Window that I had picked up from the floor of a Lancaster bomber one morning. The strips are 5/8″ wide and 12″ long. One strip has a piece missing from it. This photograph was taken in November 2019. I had this strip folded 4 times and the short one folded 3 times tucked into the pages of my Danforth Tech machine shop handbook. There is also a thin strip I picked up as well. I probably placed it in that the book 73 years ago. I had been telling my son Dan about the Window I had and he found it in the book that was inside my metal trunk I had bought in England and brought home to Canada. The photograph is from the Bob Middleton Collection.

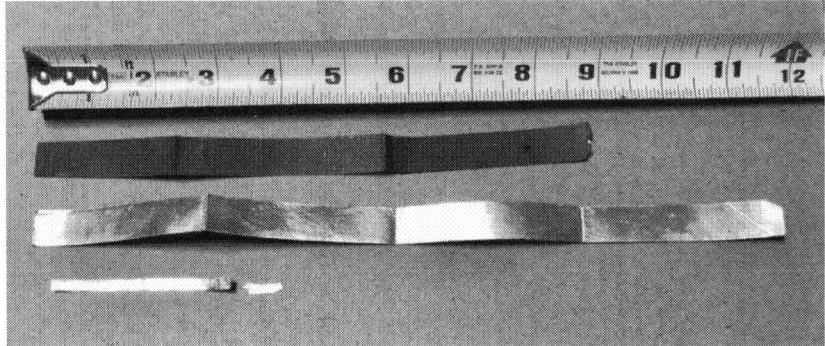

Chapter 19

FLAK

This is an 88 mm mobile German flak gun. The photograph was taken by Dan Middleton at the National Military Museum in Johannesburg, South Africa.

The name flak was an English shortened version of the German name **FL**ugzeug**A**bwehr**K**anone meaning "Aircraft Defense Cannon." The Germans developed some huge terrifying flak cannons that fired 88 mm shells weighing 20 pounds that could reach heights of 30,000 feet and higher at rates of 16 rounds per minute. The most common size was the 88 mm shell. In the cities of Berlin, Hamburg, Vienna and

Stuttgart there were huge flak towers that stood 140 feet high with even larger 128 mm flak guns mounted on the top. These guns fired 5 inch diameter projectiles weighing 57 pounds up to 48,000 feet into the sky. No bombers were safe from these guns. German engineers had to create these defensive guns as Germany and German occupied Europe were on the defensive from Bomber Command's relentless bomber attacks since 1941.

There were three types of flak that we experienced in our time in the hostile skies of Europe.

Barrier Barrage Flak was a curtain of steel that was thrown up randomly into the air in front of the bomber stream that we had to fly through. This flak did not use optical or radar sighting. It would surround a target.

Box Barrage Flak was in a form of a box hanging in the air. The flak gunners would create a box of flak in front of the bomber stream that was 3,000 feet across, 3,000 feet high and about 1 or 2 miles long. We had to fly through that flak as it was in line with our path to the target. It was like trying to fly through a three-dimensional mine field in the sky.

Predictive Flak was the most advanced type. This flak utilized radar-controlled guns to aim the flak in front of the aircraft. The radar would measure where a single aircraft was and then a mechanical computer would predict where the aircraft was going to be. This is when our use of Window confused the radar-controlled flak guns. The tail gunner had to keep a close watch for predictive flak. It would work like this. A flak shell would explode behind your aircraft and a second shell would come up right after that one but closer to your aircraft. A third and fourth one would come up even closer. By the time the fourth shell in a predictive flak series came up behind you the Tail Gunner should be yelling turn to port or to starboard or corkscrew to port or to starboard to escape from the fifth shell. The fifth shell would get you if the mid-upper gunner or the tail gunner were not paying attention. We escaped from predictive flak one time doing the corkscrew and another by changing course. We never came across predictive flak until we were on operations in Lancasters. We never saw any flak in our daylight operations over France in Halifax aircraft.

By the autumn of 1944 there were about 1.1 million flak gun

operators. About half of these were trained soldiers. There were about 128,000 young women operating these guns along with young boys.

The Third Reich was consuming 3.5 million heavy flak shells and 12.5 million light flak shells monthly by autumn 1944. Light flak shells were smaller than 37 mm. Heavy flak shells were larger than 37 mm. Statistics show 3,348 heavy flak shells were required to down one bomber while 4,940 light flak shells were required to down one bomber.

Defensive German flak over a German city during an Allied raid in WWII. These flak shells could be travelling up to 9 miles high into the sky. Sueddeutsche Zeitung Photo / Alamy Stock Photo CPM847.

Chapter 20

FLYING FOR KEEPS

Don flew as a second pilot or as it was nicknamed a "Second Dickey" with a seasoned crew twice to have some sort of idea of what he was in for when he took out his bomber and crew for their first Combat Operation together. The second pilot would stand or sit in the Engineer's position for the operation he was on and observe what was going on inside and outside of the aircraft. When Don returned after these trips, he gave us an idea of what we were in for. He did not tell us everything however as he was probably recovering from his experience and also did not want to terrify us. These 2 trips also helped Don know how to direct his crew on a real operation.

On Sunday, September 10, 1944, Don flew as second pilot in Halifax MZ-375 designated as U-UNCLE to the target Le Havre, France. Eric Mitchell, our Wing Commander was the pilot of the aircraft. They were up at 14:21, reached the target at 16:17 and were back down at 18:52. There were 18 of Iroquois Squadron aircraft in the operation. There was no cloud to 5/10ths cloud and good weather. Cloud tops at 7,000 to 8,000 feet. The bomb load was six 1,000 pound, three 1,000 pound General Purpose and four 500 pound bombs for a total of 11,000 pounds of bombs.

On Tuesday, September 12, 1944 the Iroquois Squadron put up 17 aircraft on an operation to bomb the railway lines in Wanne-Eickel, Germany. Most of the aircraft on this operation suffered flak damage. Our squadron was near the beginning of the attack. Defenses were intense with flak in barrage form and as predicted flak. Pilot R. R. Haw's aircraft was extensively holed, and the crew had some exciting moments. Navigator J. W. Abell of Pilot R. R. Haw's crew was hit in the leg by flak. He was given first aid during the operation. On return Navigator J. W. Abell was treated in hospital. The Flight Engineer M. G. Glue of Pilot Officer Quinlan's crew stopped a small piece of flack with his head. M. G. Glue was treated in hospital upon their return. Three aircraft had their H2S radar blisters shot away. The general opinion of all the crews was that the flak was so thick you could walk on it. The operation was considered successful, and all of our aircraft returned.

On Friday, September 15, 1944 the target was Kiel, Germany and Don flew as second pilot in Halifax MZ-416 designated as E-EDWARD. They were up at 21:48, reached the target at 00:01 and were back down at 04:44. Their bomb load was one 2,000 pound bomb and eleven 500 pound incendiary clusters.

When we first started flying on operations all the bomber crews had to fly 30 operations to complete a tour. After a crew completed a tour of operations they were screened, and the crew members would all be sent to various locations to become instructors in their trades. After about 6 to 10 months of being instructors all those fellows would be once again assigned to combat operations for a second tour of 30 operations. The chance of surviving a second tour of 30 operations was less than your first tour. If you and your crew survived that second tour of 30 operations, then you were all screened and went off to be instructors. And, yup after 6 to 10 months as instructors you were on operations again for a third tour of 30 operations or non-combat ground roles. Though flying operations was dangerous many men chose operations over a desk job. I believe the idea was that you flew in combat or served in other roles until you were killed, or the war was over. Again, I was lucky as the end of this war was 8 months away. I would go home after my first tour. The 30 operations we all had to fly included the 2 that Don had flown as a Second Dickey. For the rest of the crew that meant we only had to fly 28 operations. Thanks so very much Don!

My crew's first operation was in a Halifax Mk. III MZ-860 designated as P-PETER on Sunday, September 17, 1944. This was a 3 hour and 35 minute round trip to Boulogne-sur-Mer, France in the daylight. Don had just got back from Kiel, Germany at about 05:00 on Saturday morning and now he was flying his first operation Sunday morning. I suppose they did not want him to forget what he had just learned in the unfriendly skies of France. There was a force of about 800 heavy bombers in this operation with 200 of those aircraft supplied by the RCAF. We were number 1 in order of 9 Halifax bombers from 431 Squadron in this operation. We were up at 07:28 and reached the target at 09:14. We bombed the target from 9,000 feet at 170 mph Indicated Air Speed, IAS on the red Target Indicators, TI's. It was clear over the target but with heavy clouds of smoke. Many railway and road bridges were destroyed along with many small buildings.

A daylight aerial photograph of Boulogne-sur-Mer taken from the Halifax of Pilot Officer Pitzek taken 1 minute before we were over the target. The photograph is from the Bob Middleton Collection.

Our bomb load consisted of six 1,000 pound Semi-Armor Piercing, SAP bombs, three 1,000 pound General Purpose, GP bombs and six 500 pound Medium Capacity, MC bombs for a total of 12,000 pounds. All the bombs were set with a time delay of 0.025 seconds. All of our aircraft returned safely to Croft and we were back down at 11:20. It was determined that about 3,000 tons of bombs were delivered to enemy positions around the port. Shortly after the bombardment the Allied ground forces were able to advance and Boulogne-sur-Mer, France was in Allied hands within a week.

This is the daylight aerial photograph of Boulogne-sur-Mer taken from the Halifax of Pilot Officer Reesor one minute after we were over the target. You can see many bomb craters. The pilots all had first pick of the photographs when they were available. Don always grabbed our photographs from all of our operations. I imagine the photographs I collected were from aircraft where the pilots had no interest in keeping some memento to remind themselves of their operations. For many fellows when their tour was finished they never wanted to see a Halifax or Lancaster bomber again. Photograph from the Bob Middleton Collection.

Access was needed to the Belgium port of Antwerp, but it was blocked by German heavy gun emplacements on the island of Walcheren. The next operation to the area was to be Monday, September 18, 1944. The crews of A Flight went off on that operation which gave us a break.

During the month of September 1944 Bomber Command and the Canadian Army were hammering away at the huge cannons that could fire on England or shipping that was in the English Channel. Some of these guns fired 14 inch shells. These gun emplacements were at Le Havre, Calais, Boulogne-sur-Mer and Cap Gris-Nez in France.

Operation number 2 in Halifax MZ-681 designated as V-VICTOR on Monday September 18, 1944, was a 3 hour and 35 minute round trip to Domburg, Netherlands in daylight. On this operation we carried with us Sargeant Hubert Bishop as an extra air gunner. I had always thought that Herbert was younger than myself. He looked young and had a great eager attitude. In 2020 I was surprised to find out that he was 29 years old when he was flying with us. The Halifax bomber was originally designed with a lower ventral turret but somewhere along the design path of the Halifax the lower ventral turret was eliminated, and a plug was fitted in its place. On this and on five more operations the plug was removed, and we had a single 0.50 caliber machine gun mounted on a swivel attached to a steel crossbeam across the opening. Hubert manned this machine gun, and he was to fire at the German targets on the ground during the low altitude operations. I believe Hubert sat with his legs dangling out of the opening. He was listed as a Mid-Under Gunner on the battle order of the operations.

Photograph of Hubert Bishop after he had become a Commissioned Officer in November 1944. The photograph is courtesy of the aviation website, Aircrew Remembered.

We were number 11 in order of 15 431 Squadron Halifax bombers in this operation. We were up at 15:47 and reached the target at 17:45. The bombing altitude was 10,000 feet but the operation was aborted on instruction of the Master Bomber when we reached the target due to heavy 10/10ths cloud. The bomb load was nine 1,000 pound General Purpose and four 500 pound General Purpose bombs for a total of 11,000 pounds. All of our bombs were brought back. All of 431 Squadron's aircraft in the operation were diverted to land at Linton-on-Ouse and we were back down at 19:20.

During the afternoon briefing for that trip to Domburg we understood that if we could not bomb the primary target then we were to bomb the secondary target. If we could not bomb the secondary target, we should bring the bombs back. Over Germany there were times when the bombs would be dropped on a target of opportunity if they were not used. In this operation there were Allied forces everywhere on the ground and random dropping of our bombs would have killed our own troops. Our bombs should have been dumped unarmed in one of the designated English Channel bomb disposal areas, but we brought ours back to Linton-on-Ouse. After Don parked the aircraft in the dispersal area the ground crew technician removed the camera that takes the photograph of the bombing results from the aircraft. After the camera was removed the technicians generally tested the bomb release by running the rotary switch through all the bomb release positions. The switch is located within a few feet of where the camera is mounted in the nose of the Halifax bomber. The fellow did not know we had brought back 11,000 pounds of bombs because normally nobody does that.

Don had no problem bringing the bombs back and landing since he had done 4 fully loaded landings only 4 days earlier. When the technician operated the release mechanism all the bombs fell out of the aircraft rapidly one after the other making a horrible loud clanking sound as the bombs hit the asphalt. The Halifax jumped up in the air the landing gear oleos having been suddenly relieved of the weight of the bombs. You have never seen a ground crew move so fast. The poor fellow inside had to scramble back through the aircraft and out the door on the port side. The bombs were still in the safe mode and none of them exploded. Somehow nothing was said of the incident and no one was scolded. We considered ourselves lucky.

Even if the bombs were not in safe mode the little propeller in the back of the bomb must turn about ten times in the wind while descending to release the striker that allows it to strike the fuse when it hits the target. This is a safety measure to prevent a bomb from exploding if it falls on an aircraft flying at a lower level. The bomb in safe mode will pass through the aircraft without exploding giving the crew a chance of survival if it did not pass through something vital.

One time we did drop a safe bomb in the bomb disposal area of the English Channel on September 26, 1944. It exploded when it hit the water. We learned that a bomb in safe mode might not always be safe.

The bomb aimer's control panel showing the rotary switch for selecting which bombs will be released. This photograph was taken by Dan Middleton inside the Halifax Mk. VII at National Air Force Museum in Trenton, Ontario.

Our next operation number which should have been number 3, in Halifax MZ-681 designated as V-VICTOR on Tuesday, September 19, 1944 was a 2 hour and 5 minute abortive trip to Domburg, Netherlands in daylight. Sargeant Bishop was flying with us again this trip. We were number 10 in order of 15 431 Squadron Halifax bombers in this operation. We were up at 14:23 but were recalled due to heavy cloud at 14:50. This trip did not count towards our operations total as we never reached the target. At 8,000 feet and position 53° 26′ N, 01° 05′ W we jettisoned three 1,000 pound bombs and four 500 pound bombs. We brought back six 1,000 pound bombs that were hung up. This time Art or Don informed the ground crew that there were still bombs on board. All the aircraft in the flight returned home safe and we were back down at 16:28. Our next trip would count as trip 3.

Later on, October 3, 1944 the RAF visited Walcheren and Domburg in the Netherlands in 8 waves of 30 Lancasters each to breech the dikes and flood the German gun emplacements. The army was having a terrible time trying to chase the German troops out of the area, so the Allied army commanders decided to flood them out. Months later the Dutch were not exactly pleased with the sea water flooding even though it expedited them being freed from German occupation.

Me sitting at the Navigator's position in the Trenton Halifax Mk. VII with grandson Chris and Museum Director Kevin Windsor at the Trenton Air Force Museum of Canada on August 13, 2019. The GEE box is on my left. The photograph was taken by the Museum Public Relations photographer, Theo Czerny-Holownia and is courtesy of the National Air Force Museum of Canada at Trenton, Ontario.

© Copyright Art Prints Direct UK

This is an accurate painting of what the Navigator's position looked like and felt like in the Halifax during a night operation. The GEE box is at the left of the bench and the H2S ground scanning radar is the screen at the right above the bench. The single light above the bench was the sole illumination. The fellow to the left of the Navigator is the Wireless Operator. This is one of 4 of the artist's prints that hang in my dining room. The painting is by artist Mike Steele-Morgan and is courtesy of Art Prints Direct UK.

I have always considered myself to be a Nosy Navigator and sitting only a few feet from that tremendous transparent nose of the Halifax was a window on the world for me. I would watch the takeoff and landings and all the action on the ground on all the operations. Many men were terrified of all the action going on outside. I was not. It was a break from my navigation duties.

Operation number 3 in Halifax KA-498 designated as G-GEORGE on Wednesday, September 20, 1944 was a 3 hour and 20 minute round trip to Pas-de-Calais, France at night. The operation involved over 600 aircraft including 81 Halifax bombers and 26 Lancaster bombers from the RCAF. We were number 14 in order of 14 431 Squadron Halifax bombers in this operation. We were up at 16:10 and reached the target at 18:02. We bombed the target from 10,000 feet. The attack was very good, but it would require a few more visits to bring the enemy to submission. The bomb load was nine 1,000 pound bombs and six 500 pound bombs for a total of 12,000 pounds. All our aircraft were diverted and landed safely at RAF Silverstone. We landed at 19:30. On Thursday, September 21, 1944 we all returned from RAF Silverstone to Croft on a 1 hour flight. We arrived back at 17:00.

Our B Flight Commander, Frank Guillevin impressing Flight Officer Peggy Tynsdale as he illustrates a "line-shoot". Two of Guillevin's fellow pilots, Dave Borland and Norm McLeod grin at the display. Frank Guillivan and Peggy Tynsdale were both from Montreal. The Indian head behind them was the new version of the Iroquois figurehead. The photograph, PL 32729 is courtesy of Library and Archives Canada.

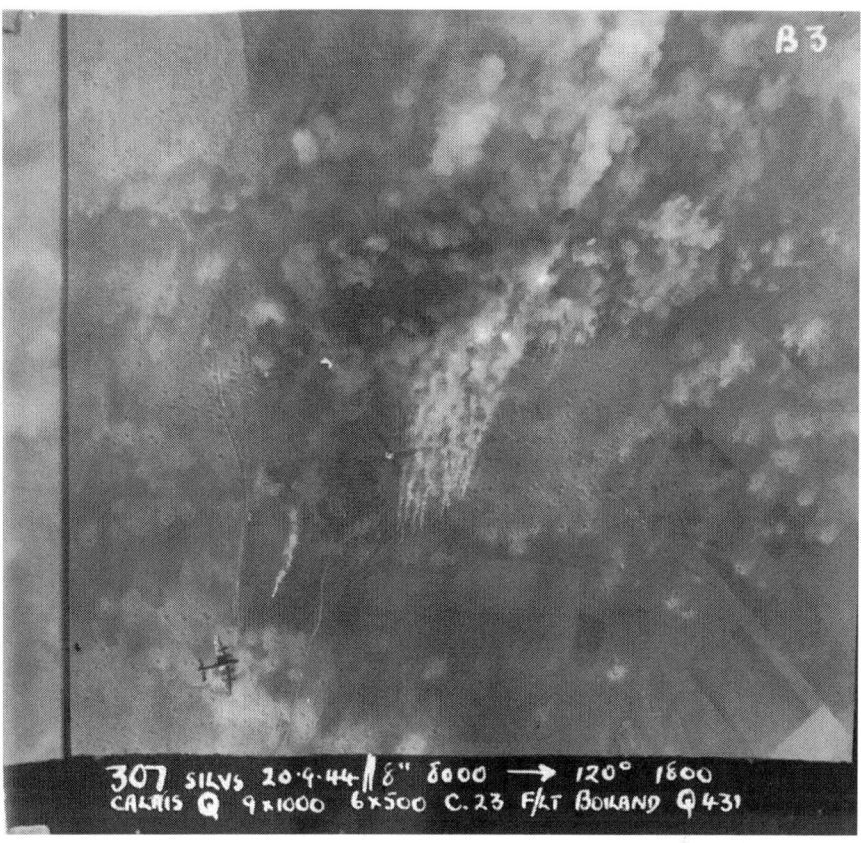

This picture is the photograph from the Halifax of Pilot Officer Boiland 2 minutes before we dropped our bombs over the target of Calais, France. There is another Halifax in the left corner of the picture under the Halifax flown by P/O Boiland. That was 60 seconds after Pilot Boiland's Halifax released its bombs. That is how close together we were and how important the Navigator was to keep each other out of harm's way. The trails of smoke rising in the air are from the target indicators. They dropped the same 12,000 pounds of bombs as we did. The photograph is from the Bob Middleton Collection.

Chapter 21

OUR OPERATION NUMBER FOUR

On Sunday afternoon September 24, 1944 we checked the Daily Routine Orders, DRO board outside the Mess Hall for operations for the next day. We knew of operations one day or less in advance. We found we were on for a morning departure on Monday, September 25, 1944 to somewhere. We knew what time the briefing was but did not know where we were going. We usually had a very good guess of what the operation was about. Information was tight to prevent word getting out about where you were heading to and what time we would be there. If the enemy found out ahead of time, they would be sitting there waiting to shoot you down. Our bomb loads, aircraft and equipment had no secrets. Enough of our bombers had been shot out of the sky that they knew all about our equipment that they recovered from the crash sites. Ray and I took photographs of bombs and bombers and took the film to be processed into prints by photography shops located off the base. The only secrets were where we were going and what time we would be there. Once we were all briefed, and everyone knew the time and where we were going the communications leaving the base was even tighter. No one knew who might be a Nazi spy. Someone with loose lips blabbing in a public place could be overheard by a Nazi spy or a Nazi informer being paid by the enemy. "Loose Lips Sink Ships" was the saying.

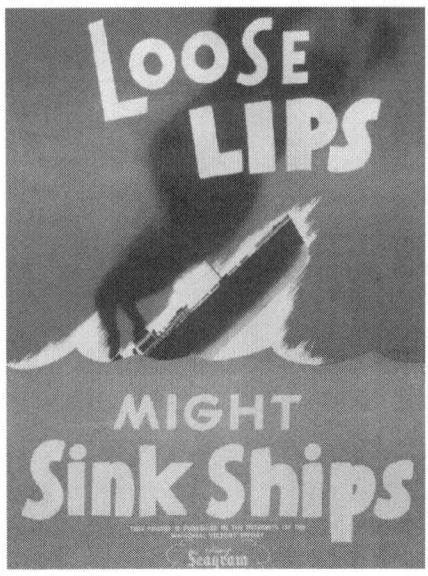

Posters warning people to not speak about anything they might know. Images CWM 19720038-009 and CWM 19710135-101 coutesy of the Canadian War Museum in Ottawa, Canada.

We did not do any drinking that night. We did no drinking at least 12 hours before any operation. Your life and the lives of the crew depended on every crew member being as sharp and alert as possible. A 1 second delay in your reaction time by anyone or a foggy miscalculation on my part could be disastrous. If the rear gunner missed a night fighter closing in on our aircraft or did not notice that predictive flak was homing in on our aircraft, we could all be goners and had the chop. If the call from the rear gunner to do a corkscrew was a second or two late and the pilot was a second or two slow putting his aircraft into the dive at the start of the corkscrew, we could be all dead. Don our Pilot never flew the aircraft using the Automatic Pilot, nicknamed George, as there was about a 1 to 2 second delay after it was disengaged before you regained control of the aircraft and could dive. Those 2 seconds could mean life or death. Don always said that when he wanted the aircraft controls, he wanted them immediately.

We hung about for a while that night and then hit the hay a bit early. I would have to be at the Navigator briefing about 06:00 in the morning. The Navigators' briefing always was 1 or 2 hours before the main briefing to give us time to prepare our charts and logs. The briefing which included all our calculating of individual routes took at least 1 hour. Walking up to the door of the briefing room I wondered where we were going. I had no idea where we were going up to this point. All the Navigators walked into the briefing room with our eyes glued to the big map of Europe. On the map was the red tape showing the route and the target. Thank goodness today it was a short 4 hour round trip across the English Channel to Calais, France and back to support the Canadian Army forces near Calais. I relaxed a bit. I only have to navigate to Doncaster, Reading, Beachy Head, the French coast and then back again.

There were not huge amounts of German defenses left at Calais, France by late September 1944. Bomber Command had been slamming the German defenses hard since D-Day. Whenever we saw the map and that red line of tape went deep into Germany your guts sank, you winced and became very tense. Some of the men's faces turned pale. We could be up there for 8 hours in the enemy occupied sky over Fortress Europe with so many unfriendly things up there that could kill you or bring you down to become a POW for the remainder of the war.

I sat down with my bag of tricks, a Mercator chart, and my logbook. Once we had all sat down, we were given our times over the target. Each crew had the same assigned times over the target and altitudes we were flying and bombing at. We were told our turning points and times and altitudes. Whenever possible we never flew in a straight line. We would make many course changes to confuse the German defense forces. We had to keep the German defenders guessing where we were going. Sending up their fighters to targets that we were not going to would waste their fighter resources and wasted the fighter's limited supply of fuel. The A Flight or B Flight Commander would be standing at the blackboard with the pointer in his hand just like teachers in Danforth Tech high school had been just 2 years ago. In high school maybe you would daydream or let your mind wander to more interesting subjects. In this classroom we all paid attention to every single piece of information and advice given to us. Remember boys if you are shot down and captured, name, rank and serial number only. I always sat down at the front so as to hear and see as much as possible. I knew my survival and my fellow crewmates survival depended on me performing my job perfectly. I had to get us over the target in the daylight or the dark of night by dead reckoning plus or minus 90 seconds in the cold weather or plus or minus 60 seconds in the warmer weather. The rule was later changed to 90 seconds in winter and summer. We bombed at 3 altitudes and if you were on one of the lower altitudes at the incorrect time you might be on the receiving end of a friendly bomb. If you were flying at the upper altitudes and arrived over the target and bombed at an incorrect time you had a chance that you could kill the crew members of an aircraft flying under you. We were given the currently known weather and the speed and direction of the winds at the various altitudes. I started to copy down the route to the target on my chart. So, then I was measuring angles and distances against those wind forecasts. As the time over the target was given to us, I worked out the time and the courses which gave me the time to Set Course. When this was all done which generally took 1 hour all of the Navigators entered their results beside their Pilots name on the board. Any Navigator that had an entry that was not very similar to the majority of the Navigators would have to sit down and find his error and correct his work. Any error had a chance of killing you and the 6 other crew members. By figuring out our route individually we all knew how to get there and back. Bomber Command Navigators did not follow a lead or master navigator like the American USAAF did.

All of our flying especially at night was by dead reckoning the same way that submarines would navigate. I had two advantages over the submarines, however. I could use the radio navigation aid called GEE to get a fix of our location. GEE however was regularly jammed by the Germans. If GEE was jammed, I would shoot the stars with my astro sextant to get fixes on where we were. The Germans could not jam the stars. Our Bomb Aimer Ray Rose would regularly do star fixes for me during a trip. Ray became quite good at it and was generally accurate to 3 miles. There was a great deal of stress on the Navigator. As a Navigator you never stopped and had a break as your Pilot required a course to fly every 6 minutes. I spent about 5 minutes of calculating in order to give Don our pilot that course every 6 minutes and I started my work for each operation 1 or 2 hours before any other crew member. Sometimes on the very long trips by the time we would get back over the English Channel or the North Sea it was possible to find me passed out from exhaustion. In Guy Gibson's book *Enemy Coast Ahead* he commented that after a long nighttime trip to Germany the next day his Navigator was practically useless.

Briefing of 431 and 434 crews at Croft for the operation to Essen, Germany on October 27, 1944. Group Captain, Bob Turnbull the Station Commanding Officer is sitting on the left front in the aisle. His cap has the gold "scrambled eggs." Photograph PL 33941 is courtesy of the Library and Archives Canada.

After the Navigators' briefing the rest of the crews would pile into the briefing room. On an operation involving 18 aircraft there would now be at least 126 crew members in the room. There were 7 crew members for each Halifax or Lancaster aircraft. Until everyone sat down and were settled this was an extremely noisy room. If the red tape on the map went all the way to Zeitz, Nürnberg, Munich or some other target deep into Germany the noise in the room settled rather quickly. The fear would set in quickly to the rest of the crew members. The members of my crew would come in and sit down around me and listen to the massive amount of information and instructions that the briefing involved. Everyone listened intently as we all knew our very lives depended upon us knowing as much as possible. Everyone knew we were playing for keeps. We were told about the weather over the target and on route, how much cloud and erratic winds we could expect, the bombing height and the type of target markers that the Pathfinder Force would be using. Then we would hear about the other less friendly items such as the areas to expect flak, the German fighter concentrations, any known special defenses such as master searchlights, fake cities, fake target indicators and jamming of our GEE.

The two white circles in the nose are the Z Equipment lights in the Bomb Aimers perspex of Lancaster NX-611, "JUST JANE". It is located at the Lincolnshire Aviation Centre in East Kirkby, United Kingdom. This Lancaster currently provides taxiing tours and the museum is very close to having "JUST JANE" airworthy. The photograph is courtesy of the Lincolnshire Aviation Heritage Centre at East Kirby, Spilsby, UK.

We were reminded to check the Z equipment every 15 minutes to verify it is sending out the visual infrared identification code of the day. The front of our Lancaster bombers had two infrared lamps mounted in the nose of the Bomb Aimers perspex. These lamps were used to flash those secret Morse code letters of the day to identify our bombers as friendly. The Luftwaffe pilots would like to fly along with us in our stream and shoot us down. The Luftwaffe fighter pilots would also follow the stream back to England to shoot up bombers coming in to land. In our bomber stream there would be our Mosquito aircraft looking for those enemy aircraft travelling with our stream. If your aircraft was not blinking the valid code of the day the Mosquito aircraft could shoot you down. The lights were operated by a motor driven cam that operated switches that energized the infrared lamps. It was Art's job every 15 minutes to go past me to where the operating mechanism was to ensure that it was working. I wrote in my logbook each time Art checked the mechanism. If Art forgot I would tell him he needed to go and check the Z equipment. Z equipment not working could get you killed by our own fighters. I believe the men in the Mosquito fighters wore special goggles in order to see the infrared lights. There is very little information available about the use of Z equipment. I do not remember hearing about any one being shot down because their equipment was not working.

Once we were deep into Germany the Flight Engineer would drop out packets of Window through the flare chute to confuse German radar operators. The gunners were told to keep a sharp lookout at all times and especially during the return trip and watch out for predicted flak. Pilots were told not to be put off by the harmless Scarecrow flak that looked like an aircraft exploding and to always be ready to execute the corkscrew evasive maneuver if ordered by the gunners. The predicted flak and the enemy fighters almost always came in from behind or underneath. Bomb aimers were told to follow the Master Bomber's instructions and if using Wanganui target indicators remember to take the wind compensation out of the Mark XIV bomb sight computer. The Flight Engineer was urged to keep careful track of which tanks the fuel is in, keeping the fuel supply balanced from side to side and keep track of the amount of fuel remaining at all times.

When a target was obscured by cloud and or smoke the Pathfinders would drop target indicators attached to parachutes called Wanganui. These would hang in the air above the target for a few minutes. When bombing using Wanganui the bomber aimer would not dial in the wind correction as the Wanganui would be drifting the same as the bombs would drift. These were various colors and looked like fireworks. From the ground the Wanganui looked like upside down Christmas trees. The Pathfinders would use H2S radar, GEE or OBOE to mark the target.

After the morning briefing spam sandwiches and tea were served. If we were going on a night operation, we would also be offered spam sandwiches. I do not remember our crew or any other crew eating anything after the briefing. I heard the No. 2 RAF groups would have a breakfast of a real egg and bacon before they left. Our crew always chose to have our bacon and the one real egg after the debriefing if we returned from the operation. On days when there was no operation on, we would have bacon and powdered scrambled eggs. The real egg was the reward for a job well done. Just about every one of us would make a couple of visits to the toilet before we picked up our flying gear. My digestive system would be so tied up in knots that I usually had to go to the toilet 2 or 3 times. Like how your stomach is twisted before an exam or a visit to the dentist only worse. You could be dead in a few hours, but you put that thought away in the back of your mind. We would go to the gear room where we picked up our parachutes, and a Mae West, the inflatable yellow life vest that we wore at all times. We would pick up our helmets with headphones, microphone and oxygen mask. Later in November we wore flying boots that were actually shoes with leggings sewn on.

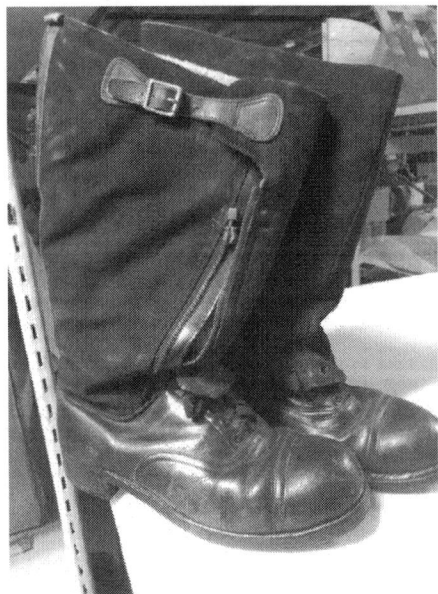

The shoes with sewn on leggings. The photograph is courtesy of Karl Kjarsgaard of The Bomber Command Museum in Nanton, Alberta.

If you found yourself on the ground in enemy territory you would tear the leggings off and you were left wearing what looked like black Oxford shoes. Walking around in German occupied territory with your flying boots on or with bare feet would give you away as being a downed airman.

As the Navigator I would have my personal bag of tricks with me already, but I would pick up an astro sextant. My navigation computer was in the bag. Once we had all our gear together the crews would climb into pickup trucks or buses which took us out to our kites in the dispersal area on the perimeter track. Sometimes we would catch a ride on the NAAFI wagon going out to the dispersal area. The NAAFI wagon was the food truck driven and operated by the Women's Auxiliary Air Force, WAAF officers that fed the ground crews.

1944 • LANCASTER BOMBER • YORKSHIRE ENGLAND • LINTON ON OUSE • THE 150 FEMALE STAFF MEMBERS

Compliments of:

RITZ & DUTES DIGITAL PHOTO RESTORATION • JEFF FREEMAN • ART DIRECTOR • 15423 YONGE ST. • AURORA • ONTARIO • 905 713 0954

Photograph of 150 WAAF Officers at Linton-on-Ouse. The Women's Auxiliary Air Force, or WAAF, was established in 1939. It had women signing up at a rate of 2,000 a week at its peak in 1943. The women did jobs from being clerks and kitchen workers, to drivers. They intercepted codes and ciphers and finally as the war progressed they did more masculine type jobs. They built weapons, built and fixed aircraft, became mechanics, engineers, electricians and fitters for airplanes. WAAFs with pilot licenses worked in the Air Transport Auxiliary and delivered aircraft around the UK. The war could not be won without women. The photograph is from the Bob Middleton Collection.

NAAFI stands for the Navy, Army and Air Force Institutes. It was started in 1920 by the British government to sell goods to the servicemen and their families. They ran clubs, restaurants, cafes and canteens. We could buy food or coffee from the NAAFI wagon before we left but then we would have the problem of having to go to the back of the bomber during flight and use the Elsen toilet to relieve ourselves.

If the operation was cancelled before we climbed on board we went back and turned in our charts, logs and all our gear. We were left alone to do whatever we pleased with the rest of the day or training that may have been planned before the operation was planned. This was great but we still had the same number of trips to complete.

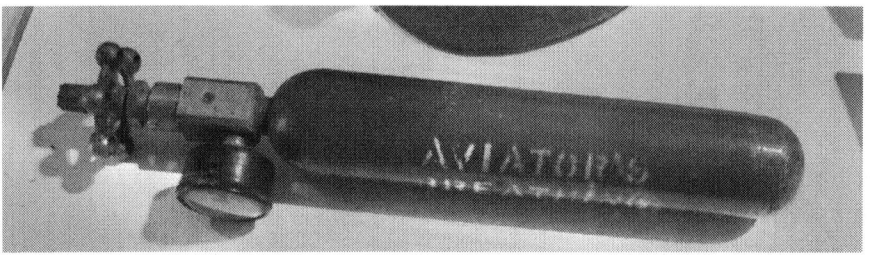

Photograph of the oxygen bottle you had to connect to the hose on your mask if you had to leave your position and your oxygen hose did not reach your new position. The photograph was taken at the Canadian Warplane Heritage Museum by Dan Middleton.

Once we got out to our assigned aircraft we milled around smoking, telling stories and making jokes. We were waiting for our time to climb aboard our aircraft. Depending on many factors we would leave from the dispersal area or we would taxi the aircraft onto the runway and the aircraft would be parked, lined up ready to go. If there was to be much of a wait the engines would be shut down and we would climb out and wait. If the Lancaster Merlin engines idled too long the engines would overheat. If the Halifax Hercules engines idled too long the spark plugs in the lower cylinders would foul and would need to be replaced before the aircraft could take off. Ground crews did have to change spark plugs while aircraft were sitting on the runway. And yes, we all hung around the aircraft smoking with 2,000 imperial gallons of high octane gasoline and 12,000 pounds of bombs on board. Crazy when I think of that now. Some crew members had a whiz on the tailwheel of a bomber for good luck. Art the Flight Engineer and Don our Pilot would converse with the ground crew about the serviceability of our aircraft and the starting procedures. Our aircraft was sitting there at the dispersal area with the trolley accumulator hooked up and ready to give the onboard batteries assistance in starting the engines. If it was cold this helped turn over those cold Merlin 224s or Hercules XVIs. Many times however the ground crew would have preflight tested the engines and warmed the engines up for the crews.

Photograph of the Elsen toilet in Halifax NA337 taken by Dan Middleton at the National Air Force Museum of Canada at Trenton, Ontario.

By the time we climbed on board the bomber our digestive systems were empty. The last remnants of the last coffee may have been deposited on the tailwheel for luck. Our crew at least did not take coffee or food with us. If you ate or drank anything you would have to leave your position to relieve yourself on the Elsen toilet. If you had to leave your position you also had to connect your oxygen hose to a small bottle of oxygen and carry that along with you.

Once in the aircraft everyone had to be at their position, totally aware and alert the entire time. If you were a gunner and you left your post for a moment and we were suddenly pounced upon by a German fighter there would be no one to spot the fighter and call out an evasive maneuver or to start firing back. If we did have to leave our post, we had to let Don know. The one time one of our crew members did go to use the Elsen chemical toilet Don said over the intercom "Ralph. Let me know when he gets back there." He He He! Once the poor fellow sat on the Elsen toilet Don started to practice evasive maneuvers. None of us bothered using the toilet after that. Our longest round trip to Nuremberg was almost 10 hours with no one using the toilet. In Halifax, Mosquito and Lancaster bombers the pilot had to stay in his seat constantly. There was not an extra set of controls or a Copilot to relieve the pilot when he was tired.

Halifax Mk. III bombers marshalled on the runway at Croft with the engines shut down ready to go on D-Day, June 6, 1944. Photograph PL 30123 is courtesy of the Library and Archives Canada.

As the time grew near for takeoff, we climbed onboard and settled in to our respective jobs and spent time getting all of our equipment ready. I tucked my parachute into its usual spot on the floor. Hopefully, if I ever needed it, I would find it where I left it as there was nothing to secure it in place.

All ready to go with all of our gear on. This was an operation in a Lancaster. Photograph from the Bob Middleton Collection.

The Wireless Operator, Navigator, Bomb Aimer, Mid-Upper Gunner and Flight Engineer did not wear their parachutes. They all used a clip-on chest pack that was stored close by. If you were in a bomber that was spiraling out of control you hoped, you could find your parachute in the dark with tremendous g-forces tossing you about. Once we were in the aircraft and settled into our positions and psyched up ready to go if the operation was cancelled, we were like a bunch of angry wet hens. Once ready to go you could not help thinking about whether you would be coming back. You pushed that thought into the back of your mind, but you did allow yourself to admit that IF you came back from this one you would have one less operation to do. You kept the remaining number of trips on your tour to yourself. If anyone in the crew ever mentioned the remaining trips the entire crew would have clobbered him in fear of him having jinxed all the remaining trips. Then the Merlin 224s would be started up. Each Pilot and Flight Engineer started the engines in their own preferred sequence. Don would start engine number 1, the outer port engine first. This was one of the two outer engines with a generator to charge the batteries and run electrical equipment. Number one was the only engine with the air compressor that operated the brakes and other equipment. After a few revolutions it would cough to life with a cloud of smoke. Don would let number 1 settle down and then continue to start number 2, number 3 and number 4. At this point Don and Art were very busy with preflight checks. Each engine had two magnetos and two spark plugs per cylinder. Art would turn off one magneto on each engine to ensure the engine RPMs did not drop by more than 150 RPM. Do those engines sound smooth and are all of the 48 cylinders firing correctly? Once the Merlin 224s were all up and running it was a tremendous racket. The helmet and plastic headphones did practically nothing to reduce the racket. In a Mynarski Lancaster flight I was on with my sons Dan and Dave on Victoria Day 2018 we measured the idling sound level to be 110 decibels sitting under the mid-upper turret. This is incredibly noisy. It is no wonder I require hearing aids today. I asked Don if he had his St. Christopher medal with him. Don is wearing it so we are good to go. Don never forgot to bring the medal. A girlfriend in England had given Don the St. Christopher medal. I had placed my cap on top of the fuselage just behind the pilot and the R/T radio gear as I always did. It never seemed to move from there. It was kept in place by the set of R/T gear located at that spot. To place my cap elsewhere would be unlucky and tempting fate. Don and Art continued doing their preflight checks. Are all the controls working correctly? Art was getting good engine readings on the 4 engines. Yes. Everything appears OK so the wheel chocks are pulled away and the ground crew was waved away. Don nudges the throttles open and starts to taxi out onto the runway. We are number 19 on this operation today. The ground crew, the administration personnel, and the men not on this operation are standing beside the runway waving the crews off. There were always people waving at us as we took off on an operation. No more thoughts about survival now, it was time for me to get to work. The GEE box was working OK and the correct Radio Frequency, RF receiver was in place. H2S is on and it looks OK for now. There is nothing to see yet with the H2S as we are on the ground still. All my navigation equipment is here, and my parachute is put out of the way. My Officers cap is sitting in its usual place behind the R/T set on top of the fuselage under the canopy. The bayonet connector for my oxygen line is plugged in. When we were on a daylight operation, we did not put on our oxygen masks until we reached 10,000 feet. When we were on an operation in the dark, we wore our oxygen masks before we left the ground. I am all ready at my end, so I go and stand behind Art our Flight Engineer and watch the takeoff. I always stood there watching every takeoff. At this point Art is sitting on his folding seat beside Don our Pilot. We receive the green Aldis light signal from the end of the runway, so it is our turn to depart. Ourselves on board are all waving to the well-wishers at the end of the runway as the 4 mighty 1,640 horsepower Merlin 224s roar to life. The sound from the engines is music but it is so loud. On our flight on Victoria Day 2018 my son Dan measured 120 decibels back sitting under the mid-upper turret on takeoff with no wartime load on board. By the end of the 2,000 foot runway Don has to get about 65,000 pounds off the ground. A Lancaster bomber which weighs about 32,000 pounds carries 12,000 pounds of bombs, 2,154 imperial gallons of high octane gasoline and lots of ammunition. Oh! Good we made it off the ground, we have cleared the trees and bushes and we are climbing so there is no going back. The fully loaded Lancaster Mk. X could gain 600 feet per minute, but we had lots of time, so Don never had to push it. As Croft was so far north in England, we would be at altitude well before we crossed the south coast of England at Beachy Head. Croft was 275 miles from Beachy Head. All the RCAF squadron aerodromes were up in Yorkshire in the north of England. The RCAF crews had to fly $1^{1/2}$ hours longer in each direction than RAF crews for flights that took the southerly route to Happy Valley and beyond. We could not fly in a straight route to Beachy Head as we would pass over Sheffield which was in a no fly-zone and that could get you shot down. Our route was south to Doncaster, to Reading and then Beachy Head.

It is time for me to get to work now. We are circling around Croft while we are waiting for the other aircraft and crews that are taking off after us and by the time, we are all gathered we have gained some more height. We were usually near the end of the takeoff order, so we did not have to wait more than ten minutes. We have gained height of 5,000 feet and I am ready to set our course and the navigation lights are turned off. The navigation lights were only used for takeoff and landing. It was always a nervous time when the navigation lights were turned on as the lights made us a perfect target for any enemy aircraft that may have made it past the home front defenses.

This real threat actually never materialized in a serious fashion until just after midnight on Sunday, March 4, 1945 when a group of Junkers Ju 88 fighters were able to penetrate the British defenses flying low under the radar in an enemy operation called Gisela. There were Bomber Command night operations to Dortmund and Kamen in Germany on the night of Saturday, March 3, 1945. The Luftwaffe Ju 88 fighter units stationed in Belgium were watching for the return leg of the operation and at the right time departed and flew just 50 feet above the English Channel all the way to the coast of England just behind the returning bombers. Just after the returning RAF bombers arrived back over England with the navigation lights turned on the Ju 88 fighters pounced on the RAF bombers and were able to down 33 bombers. 23 bombers were destroyed completely. 10 bombers were damaged. Of our bombers damaged or destroyed there were 6 aircraft and crews in training from heavy conversion units. The Luftwaffe fighters attacked aircraft as far north as Croft. The fighters came down and strafed Croft but luckily no one was injured. I was away on a leave on that night and missed the action.

Photograph of the German Junkers Ju 88 fighter aircraft from my scrapbook. From the Bob Middleton Collection.

When I returned one of the fellows in another Nissen hut showed me a bullet hole in his bed post. The enemy lost 34 aircraft in their attack. 12 aircraft were damaged and 22 were destroyed or failed to return.

Our operation number 4 in Halifax KA-656 designated as X-X-RAY on Monday, September 25, 1944 was a 4 hour and 10 minute round trip to Calais, France in the daylight. We were number 14 in order of 19 of 431 Squadron Halifax bombers taking part in this operation. There were 575 bombers on this raid. We were up at 09:52 and reached the target at 11:36. The cloud cover was 4/10ths to 7/10ths in the target area. We bombed from 6,000 feet at an IAS of 166 mph 150 yards starboard of the red TIs plus 3.5 seconds. There was plenty of dust and smoke in the target area.

That day we had Hubert Bishop flying with us again as a Mid-Under Gunner. He was a really nice guy who flew with us 6 times to targets in France. I had always thought that he was the same age as me but as it turns out he was 29 years old. During this second trip with us I asked what he was shooting at since we were only 6,000 feet above the ground. He told me there was not much he could see but he had fired off all the rounds. He was a very eager fellow and I think he was having fun. We were bombing the Germans about 10 miles inland from the beachhead. We were bombing so close to our own army that our aircraft were fitted with a switch operated by the Navigator that would inhibit dropping of the bombs by the Bomb Aimer. On earlier operations the spot we were not to drop bombs on was marked with yellow smoke or tape. We never saw any of these markings and other crews missed the markers as well. I do not know how close we came to bombing our own troops. Our troops were close to the beach and we had to pass over them. The German army was about 90 seconds inland after we passed the coast of France. I was given a stopwatch and my job was to leave the bomb drop enable switch off until we reached a time that would give us the correct distance inland past our own troops. After the 90 seconds I would flip the switch on, and Ray could then release the bombs when he was on target. I suppose Command came up with the scheme as some Bomb Aimers had been bombing our own troops. Everyone looks the same from a mile or two high in the sky.

Our bomb load was nine 1,000 pound and four 500 pound bombs for a total of 11,000 pounds. One 1,000 pound bomb hung up and was brought back to Croft. Due to the heavy cloud cover results were not seen but the effort was considered to be fair. All of 431 Squadron's aircraft returned safely and we were back down at 13:57.

An RAF and RCAF Bomber Command issue Mark IX astro sextant. This picture is courtesy of the Canadian Warplane Heritage Museum at Hamilton, Ontario.

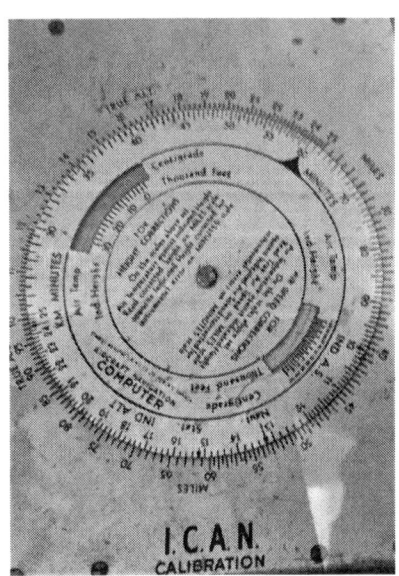

A dead roconking navigation computer the same as the one I had in my bag of tricks. I had to return mine when we finished our operations. The photograph is courtesy of the Canadian Warplane Heritage Museum.

Chapter 22

MORE HALIFAX OPERATIONS

My 1945 sketch of Halifax Mk. III KA-656, SE-X-X-RAY flying over the cliffs of Scarborough, England. From the Bob Middleton Collection.

We flew 4 times in Halifax KA-656 SE-X-X-RAY. In 2018 some people pointed out to me that the designation on the aircraft spells SEX. I had never noticed that. I was asked if we thought anything about flying in an aircraft named SEX or did others make rude comments about it. At the time none of us ever noticed. I suppose we had so many other things to be concerned about than flying in a bomber named SEX. In present times flying a military designated SEX would probably be a dumb and distracting national controversy. The only aircraft in all of

Bomber Command that could have this designation was 431 Squadron as the Squadron's designation letters were SE.

431 Iroquois wall art. *Smoke Signals*. Photograph from the Bob Middleton Collection.

Operation number 5 in Halifax KA-656 designated as X-X-RAY on Tuesday, September 26, 1944 was a 4 hour round trip to Calais, France in the daylight. Hubert Bishop is riding with us again shooting up German troops and their equipment from his mid-under gunner position. We were number 12 in order of 16 431 Squadron Halifax bombers taking part in this operation. The operation had a total force of 750 bombers including 170 RCAF bombers. We were up at 09:13 and reached the target at 10:44. We bombed the target from 6,500 feet flying at an IAS of 165 mph. We had good weather and visibility and identified the red TIs. As per instructions from the Master Bomb Aimer we overshot the target TIs by 4 seconds. This was another operation where I had to use the bomb drop enable switch and stopwatch to disable the dropping of the bombs. This operation of the switch was a bit different on this operation as there was a pocket of German soldiers with our boy's west of the German troops and east of them. I had to inhibit the bombs for 2 minutes after the coast. Then after 60 seconds with the bomb switch enabled, I had to flip the switch off again. As a result, we had only dropped part of our bomb load. There was only negligible flak and no fighter aircraft in the area, so Don circled around to repeat the operation and then Ray deposited the rest of the bombs on the target. One bomb was hung up. After this operation we all agreed that we would never take a second go at any target in Germany. That would just be utter madness. The force was bombing strong points around the town of Calais. Our bomb load on this operation was nine 1,000 pound bombs and four 500 pound bombs for a total of 11,000 pounds. One 1,000 pound bomb was jettisoned safe at 50° 26' N, 00° 57' E. When this bomb hit the water, it exploded. So much for a bomb being safe that is in safe mode! This attack was considered to be fair. All of our aircraft and crews returned safely to Croft and we were back down at 13:12.

Two days later Calais and Cap Gris-Nez were visited again by 500 bombers of Bomber Command. On Saturday, September 30, 1944 Calais was surrendered to the Canadian Second Corps. The Canadian Army General H. D. Crerar sent this message to Sir Arthur Harris, Commanding in Chief of Bomber Command in recognition of the part that Bomber Command had played.

"Our total casualties in the capture of Calais and Gris-Nez were under 300 and over 12,000 German prisoners were captured. Considering the strength of the German defenses such a success would have been impossible but for the accurate, consistent, and timely effort of Bomber Command. I hope you will accept my sincere appreciation of all you did for us and pass on to your staff and aircrews and ground staff my thanks for their indispensable share in this very satisfactory operation. I hope your casualties were light."

One of the Halifax Bombers we were flying in being loaded up. The photograph is from the Bob Middleton Collection.

Every day at 13:00 I would set my watch to the precise second by the BBC Greenwich Mean Time (GMT) broadcast. My watch always seemed to be ahead or behind a few seconds every day when I would set my watch. Our head Navigator told me that wasn't possible for my watch to gain or lose 2 seconds over a day. Whenever we went on an operation, we all set our watches to the correct GMT time. The seconds were critical as my astro charts were all calculated to the minute and the second. If your time when you took your astro fix was off by 2 seconds your position would be incorrect by 2 miles. I had to get our bomber over the target plus or minus 90 seconds at night during the winter. Being off course a mile or two could get you out of the bomber stream all by yourself and you would be easy pickings for any lurking German fighters. For the German Luftwaffe fighter pilot, it was so much easier and safer to pick off a straggling bomber that did not have the protective guns of the neighboring bombers in the stream. They picked off bombers the same way that a wolf would pick off a stray lamb from a flock.

2153.CRT. 26·9·44// 8"7000' →150°T·1042.8
CALAIS AIP 10 ·W·9ₓ1000 6ₓ500 c2ᵢₛₑcₛ KERCHER W·431.

This picture is the photograph from the Halifax of Pilot Officer Kercher one minute before we dropped our bombs over the target of Calais, France. This is how close together we were and how important the Navigator was if only to stay out of harm's way. They had two more five hundred pound bombs than we dropped. In the photograph you can see all the bomb craters inside the Citadel. The photograph is from the Bob Middleton collection.

Operation number 6 in Halifax KA-656 designated as X-X-RAY on Wednesday, September 27, 1944 was a 5 hour and 45 minute round trip to Sterkrade, Germany in daylight. We were 14 in order of 21 431 Squadron Halifax bombers taking part in this operation. We were up at 07:38 and reached the target at 10:00. Over the target area we were at 17,000 feet flying at an IAS of 160 mph. The cloud cover was 9/10ths, the tops were at 9,000 feet and no TIs were seen and Ray could not identify the target. For a while, the flak was heavy to moderate and then became heavy. The compass packed it in so the operation for our crew was aborted. This was considered a poor effort. We brought back our sixteen 500 pound bombs. There was rather confusing and constantly changing targeting information. A few pilots felt it to be a wasted effort and an endangerment to the entire bomber stream. The Master Bomber's Halifax was damaged by flak and the Navigator of that aircraft was injured. Other aircraft were bombing a factory through slits in the clouds. Heavy explosions were seen by the other crews. K. K. Davis the Navigator in Halifax MZ-882 SE-B flown by Pilot Officer B. A. Mawhinney had his hands badly hurt by flak. Despite his injury he continued to perform his duties, though blood marred his maps and charts. Light flak damage was sustained by a few crews. We all returned to Croft and we were back down at 13:21.

My logbook details for our trip to Sterkrade September 27, 1944 showing all our turning points. From the Bob Middleton Collection.

There was a pilot called Crash who was unlucky when he was operating an aircraft. Late in September Crash was taxiing his aircraft onto a runway from the perimeter track and he misjudged where the tailwheel was and the tailwheel came off of the hard surface onto the grass and the wheel was stuck. Instead of getting help from the ground crew to put the tailwheel back on the asphalt he throttled up the engine power and the stress broke the back of the bomber just where the mid-upper turret and the lower hatch is. This is a weak spot in the Halifax fuselage. The aircraft became scrap.

At this point in my story, I am including the acting 431 Squadron Wing Commander's daily comments from the squadron log. On the dates when aircraft and crews were never seen again you will see FTR, Failed to Return.

Crews leaving the briefing room after their briefing for the September 28, 1944 operation on Cap Gris-Nez. The photograph, PL 33509 is courtesy of Library and Archives Canada.

Operation number 7 in Halifax KA-656 designated as X-X-RAY on Thursday, September 28, 1944 was a 4 hour and 5 minute round trip to Cap Gris-Nez on the coast of France at night under three quarters moonlight illumination. This is the last flight that Sargent Bishop flew with us shooting up machines and troops on the ground. We were number 4 in order of 15 431 Squadron Halifax bombers taking part in this army cooperative operation. We were bombing the German coastal guns and the Germans inland from the beachhead. We were up at 17:16 and reached the target at 19:19. Over the target area we were at 9,000 feet flying at an IAS of 170 mph. There was no cloud but a bit of light ground haze over the target. There was no flak. The red and green TIs were identified with no problems. We bombed the centre of the concentration of green TIs. The Master Bomb Aimer was difficult to hear as there was a lot of chattering going on the R/T. It was considered a good attack, well concentrated. Our bomb load was nine 1,000 pound GP bombs with 0.025 seconds time delay and four 500 pound MC bombs with a 0.025 seconds time delay. All of 431 Squadron aircraft returned safely and we were back down at 21:20.

Friday, September 29, 1944 Pilot Officer H. C. Vicar and his crew were screened today after completing their tour of operations.

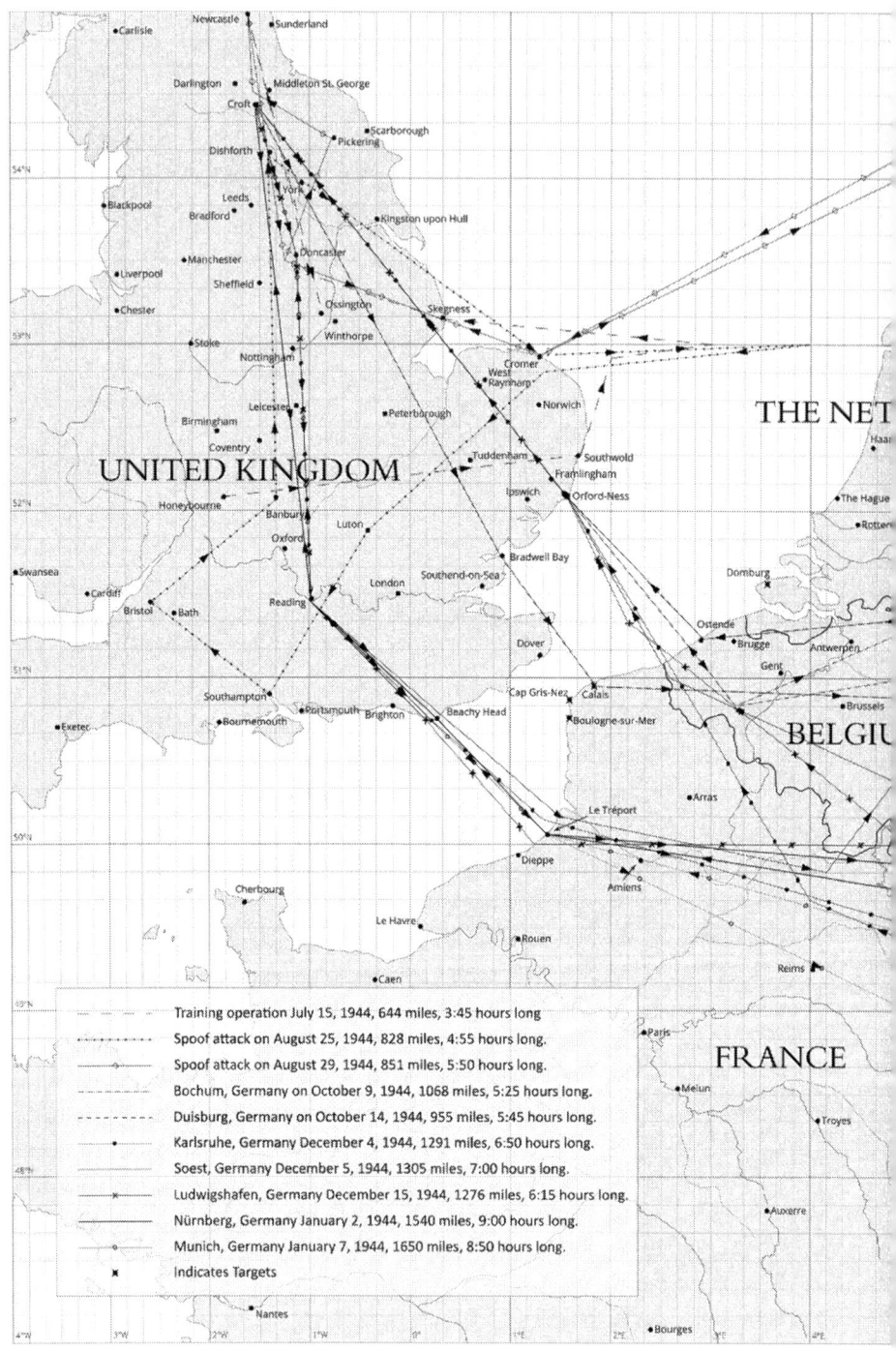

Training operation July 15, 1944, 644 miles, 3:45 hours long

Spoof attack on August 25, 1944, 828 miles, 4:55 hours long.

Spoof attack on August 29, 1944, 851 miles, 5:50 hours long.

Bochum, Germany on October 9, 1944, 1068 miles, 5:25 hours long.

Duisburg, Germany on October 14, 1944, 955 miles, 5:45 hours long.

Karlsruhe, Germany December 4, 1944, 1291 miles, 6:50 hours long.

Soest, Germany December 5, 1944, 1305 miles, 7:00 hours long.

Ludwigshafen, Germany December 15, 1944, 1276 miles, 6:15 hours long.

Nürnberg, Germany January 2, 1944, 1540 miles, 9:00 hours long.

Munich, Germany January 7, 1944, 1650 miles, 8:50 hours long.

x   Indicates Targets

This map shows routes on 3 training trips and 7 operational trips.

The next day, Saturday, September 30, 1944 we had good weather and extensive training was carried out day and night.

Monday, October 2, 1944 there were no operations. We were on standby however and carried out limited training. Pilot Officer J. Coates and crew were screened today after completion of their tour of operations. All the squadron aircraft are now equipped with H2S ground radar.

Tuesday, October 3, 1944 we were already for standby operations, but only limited training could be carried out as all our aircraft were fueled up and bombed up. You do not want to be training with fully loaded aircraft. Dropping a bomber back on the tarmac fully loaded is very hard on the undercarriage.

The very next morning, Wednesday, October 4, 1944 15 aircraft in A Flight took off on raid to Bergen, Germany. The crews reported only light flak and the weather over the target was clear, with good visibility. The attack was very concentrated and two large explosions were seen. Pilot Officer J. A. Bruce and crew were screened today on completion of a complete tour of operations.

On Thursday, October 5, 1944 there were no operations, but extensive training was carried out.

One day later, on Friday, October 6, 1944 operations were called for a night trip. However, further word came through that a maximum effort was being asked for a much earlier time. Through heroic efforts on the part of everyone in the Squadron we managed to get 20 A flight aircraft off. Two others that were pledged could not be fueled and bombed up in time for the operation. One crew returned early. Crews reported it was a good raid and the target was well pranged.

On Saturday, October 7, 1944 Pilot Officer M. C. MacLeod and crew were screened after an outstanding performance. An operation involving 21 aircraft was called today but the operation was scrubbed before the briefing.

By Sunday, October 8, 1944 the weather was so poor that there were no operations or training. The seventh Victory Bond drive at Croft started today with a bang and we reached well over 50 percent of our quota the first day. The money that was raised by Victory Bond drives was used to buy equipment to wage war against the enemy. The Victory Bonds paid three percent interest on maturity. The rate was comparable to a good savings account. Some of the Victory Bond posters would send shivers up your spine.

Image CWM 19750317-183 courtesy of the Canadian War Museum in Ottawa, Canada.

During WWII an American radio bond drive promotional ad stated, "Tell your boss to deduct 10 cents from every dollar he pays you and lend it to Uncle Sam. Sign up for this simple savings plan today, and when victory comes , you,ll have war bonds in in your pockets instead of Axis bonds on your wrists."

Image CWM 19920108-012 courtesy of the Canadian War Museum in Ottawa, Canada.

Chapter 23

BOCHUM, GERMANY

Operation number 8 in Halifax MZ-375 designated as U-UNCLE on Monday, October 9, 1944 was a 5 hour and 45-minute round trip of 1,068 miles to Bochum, Germany at night under a half moon illumination. The route we took on this operation is shown on page 230. This was another important target of coal and iron industries in Happy Valley. We were number 12 in order of 15 431 Squadron Halifax bombers taking part in this operation. There were 200 RCAF bombers taking part in this operation of 440 bombers. During the briefing, the Meteorology Officer had informed us that the winds on the way to Bochum were blowing from the north at about 70 miles per hour. Many of our operations to Happy Valley involved flying east across France or Belgium and then flying north to the targets in Happy Valley. We were up at 17:19 and we crossed at Calais, France. While flying south east before we reached Germany, I discovered that we were off our course farther south of where we should have been when Don told me that the rest of the stream was off to our starboard. At this point I calculated that we were in the jet stream and the winds were 130 miles per hour from the north. I had Don make three corrections and we were back on course. Eventually we had to turn north just south of Bonn and head straight up north to Bochum with an IAS somewhere around 200 mph. With the Bristol Hercules engines working as hard as they could without damage and using up too much fuel, we were only travelling over the ground at 80 miles per hour. That turning point was

95 miles south of Bochum. Goodness, we were hardly moving, and we were just like sitting ducks flying at that ground speed for a little longer than an hour in the moonlight. The flak that night was very heavy and scary. We saw two enemy Messerschmitt Me 109 fighter aircraft that night but neither fighter bothered with us. So, luck was with us that night. 3 RCAF bombers from other squadrons did not return from Bochum that night. We finally reached the target at 20:32. Over the target area we were at 18,000 feet flying at an IAS of 165 mph. There was 8/10ths cloud with breaks over the target. The red and green TIs and Wanganui Target Indicators were identified with no problems. Wanganui was a target indicator that dropped slowly through the clouds on a parachute. It looked like fireworks and it drifted with the wind, so Ray did not need to make a wind correction in the bomb sight. This blind target marking was done by the Pathfinders guided by OBOE and H2S radar.

REMARKS
(Including results of bombing, gunnery, exercises, etc.)

BASE- BRADWELL BAY- CALAIS-
0725- 5050 - BOCHUM- OSTENDE
- ORFORDNESS - POS'N A - BASE
TARGET PARTIALLY OBSCURED BUT
BOMBED T.I.'S - TWO ENEMY A/C
SEEN BUT DID NOT ATTACK -FLAK
HEAVY - GOOD ATTACK (RUHR)

My logbook details for our trip to Bochum October 9, 1944 showing all our turning points. From the Bob Middleton Collection.

We bombed the red TIs with a 2 second overshoot as per the Master Bomber's instructions. We dropped 8 clusters of 400 pound incendiary sticks along with six 500 pound No. 14 incendiary clusters. Incendiaries were seen in a concentrated area followed by fires after we bombed. The Pathfinder Force was scattered. The damage we inflicted that night on the target was mostly in the south west part of Bochum and was considered only moderate. On the way back we flew north from Bochum and turned west crossing the Belgium coast at Ostend and across the English Channel to Orford Ness. We all felt it was a good attack in Happy Valley that night. We were back down at 23:04 and all of our aircraft returned safely to Croft.

Every 2 weeks we had to do practice dingy drills at Croft. If we had to ditch in the English Channel or the North Sea, it would be very good to get out quickly and into the dingy. An Instructor would come to our aircraft to test the crew. We would all be in the aircraft at our usual positions. Don would announce on the intercom that we were preparing to ditch. Don would then call out "Hit" once and then "Hit" a second time. To land a bomber in the water you try to put the tail down in the water on the first hit. This drags the rear of the aircraft and then the front of the aircraft should just flop down on the water. If you hit the water with the front of the aircraft first the aircraft will dig into the water violently and possibly flip over or submerge. On Don's second call out of "Hit" the Instructor would start his stopwatch and we would begin to get out of the aircraft and walk out on the wing to where the dingy would be sitting. We usually did this in 20 seconds which was a time that pleased the Instructor. There was no wet dinghy or parachute practice at Croft.

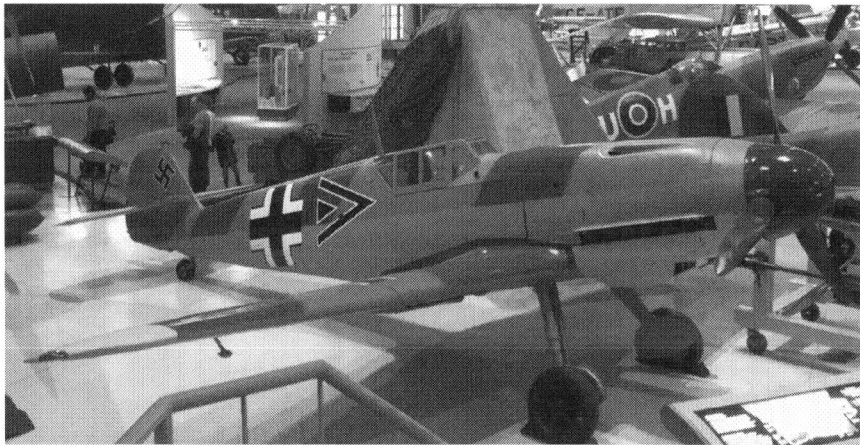

A restored Messerschmitt Me 109 fighter. The Me 109 used a twelve cylinder inverted diesel engine built by Daimler-Benz. It had a top speed of 370 miles per hour and a range of about 90 minutes. About 37,000 Me 109 fighters were built in various configurations. The photograph was taken by Dan Middleton at the Canada Aviation and Space Museum in Ottawa, Ontario.

237

Chapter 24

OPERATION HURRICANE AND DUISBURG

In October 1944 Duisburg, Germany became the main target of Operation Hurricane. This was a joint operation with Bomber Command and the USAAF Eighth Air Force. The plan was created by Air Chief Marshal, Sir Arthur Harris. The Allied air forces wanted to demonstrate to the German High Command the overwhelming superiority of the Allied air forces. This was an attempt to convince the German High Command to consider surrendering before more German people were killed. It did not work however, and the German people continued fighting their losing fight driven by their leader, Adolf Hitler.

Operation number 9 in Halifax MZ-378 designated as H-HARRY on Saturday, October 14, 1944 was a 5 hour and 45 minute round trip of 955 miles to Duisburg, in the Ruhr Valley of Germany during the early morning. The route we took on this operation is shown on page 230. Allied aircrews nicknamed the Ruhr Valley as Happy Valley as the German defenses there were terrible for us. It was anything but happy for Bomber Command or USAAF aircrews. This daylight operation involved 1,000 bombers. We had a large RAF fighter escort for the operation. I do not remember seeing the fighters as the fighters must have been flying much higher above the bomber stream. Duisburg at the junction of the Ruhr and Rhine rivers was the logistic centre of the Ruhr Valley and the largest inland port in the world in 1944. The targeted subjects for this operation were the sprawling conglomeration of chemical and steel factories in the area.

I woke up at 01:00 to attend the Navigator briefing. We were number 11 in order of 20 431 Squadron Halifax bombers taking part in the operation and we were up at 06:33 and reached the target at 08:53. Over the target area we were at 20,000 feet flying at an IAS of 150 mph. The visibility was poor with 8/10ths cloud and lots of smoke. We identified the target visually and bombed the centre of the town. The flak was intense barrage flak. I saw 2 of our aircraft shot down by the flak. Don said he saw 5 bursts of Scarecrow flak. There is some contention as to whether or not Scarecrow flak actually existed. This was flak that was rather harmless fireworks that was supposed to look like a bomber exploding. When it exploded it made a great deal of sparks in colors of red and orange. The Scarecrow was supposed to scare the bomber aircrews. It did work as it was scary looking. Since it was relatively harmless why would the Germans have used all those resources on something that could not shoot down a bomber? Bomber Command's Commanding Officers told us it did not exist. To this day no one really knows. Recently, I have read that by the fall of 1944 there were shortages of the chemicals used in the manufacture of the explosives for the flak shells. Some shells contained fillers which may have been the ones that we called Scarecrow.

It was a good operation, and I made a note in my log that the target was real hot. By hot I mean there was lots of flak going up and exploding all around us. In the daylight flak was much more terrifying as the black cloud, after the flak exploded, hung in the air for a long time. The black smoke from the flak burst is like the thunder that comes after the lightning. The thunder won't hurt you, but it is scary. In daylight we thought to ourselves "Oh Shit we have to fly through all that flak!" At night you saw the flash and then the flak burst was gone. It was no less dangerous at night, but you only saw the flash for a short moment, and it was gone. In the 2019 movie *Midway* the producers got the daylight flak exactly as it was.

During this morning operation 3,960 tons of bombs and 900 tons of incendiaries were dropped on the target. Our bomb load was seven 1,000 pound SAP bombs and six 500 pound MC bombs with a 0.025 seconds time delay. At 10:02 we jettisoned one hung up 1,000 pound bomb in a safe mode from 5,000 feet at 51° 20′ N, 02° 75′ E. This was a bomb disposal location in the English Channel. The bomb was in safe mode, but the bomb exploded when it landed in the English Channel. All our aircraft returned safely to Croft and we were back down at 08:53.

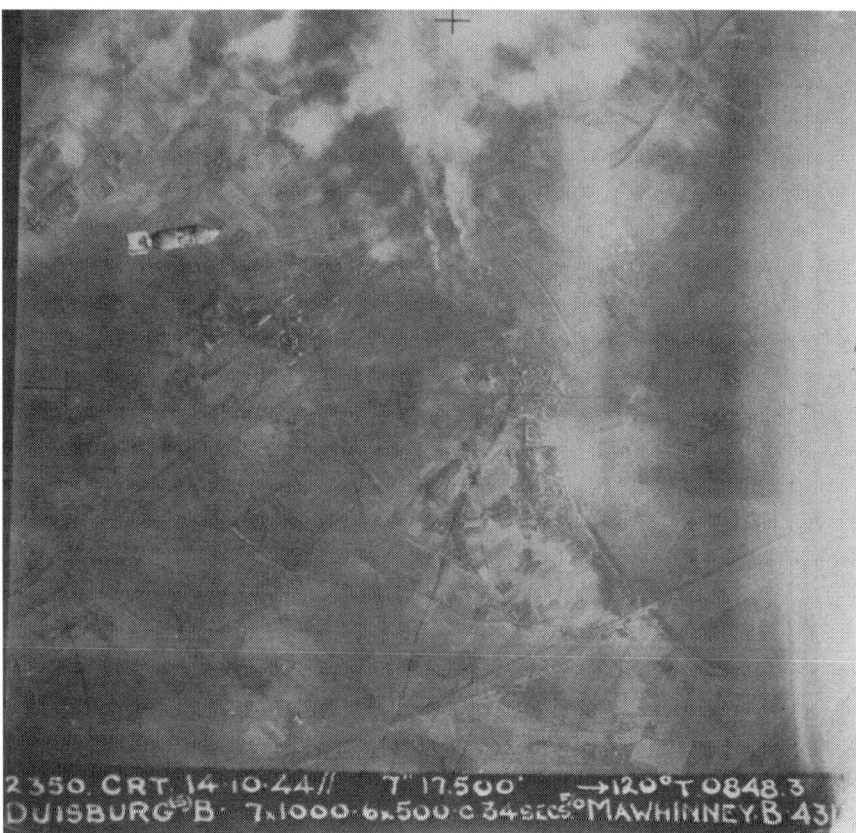

BASE - ORFORDNESS - 5050 0315E - 5123
0520E - DUISBERG - 5106 0600E
5050 0315E - ORFORDNESS - BASE
VERY HEAVY BARRAGE FLAK - SAW TWO
AIRCRAFT SHOT DOWN BY FLAK - FIVE BURSTS
OF 3 SCARECROW SEEN - ATTACK SCATTERED
BUILT UP AREA HIT (RUHR)

My logbook details for our daylight trip to Duisburg October 14, 1944 showing all our turning points. From the Bob Middleton Collection.

2350 CRT 14 10 44// T 17.500' →120°T 0848.3
DUISBURG B 7x1000 6x500 c 34sec 50°MAWHINNEY B 43

This is the daylight photograph of Duisburg taken from the Lancaster flown by of Pilot Officer Mawhinney five minutes before we arrived above Duisburg. That is a 500 pound bomb seen falling in the photograph. The photograph is from the Bob Middleton Collection.

Shortly after we had returned and had been debriefed and I had my one real egg and bacon we were informed that we would be going back out the same day on a late night operation to Duisburg, Germany. I went to bed about noon and managed to fall asleep. I must have been very tired.

Operation number 10 in Halifax, MZ-434 designated as O-OBOE on Saturday, October 14, 1944 was another 5 hour and 55 minute round trip to Duisburg, Germany at night this time under the illumination of a three quarters moon. This operation again involved about 1,000 Allied bombers. There were two waves of 500 bombers each with the waves 2 hours apart. We were number 10 in order of 17 431 Squadron Halifax bombers taking part in this operation. We were up at 22:30 and reached the target at 01:40.

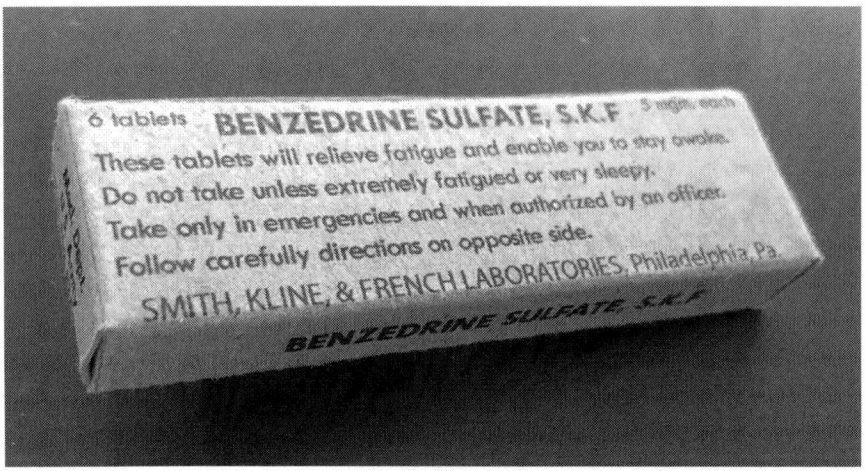

A replica of a USAAF issue Wakey-Wakey tablet package. We never saw the packages. The Medical Officer handed out two pills to each fellow that was flying. The photograph was taken by Dan Middleton and is courtesy of WWII Soldier.Com Products.

Before we left the Medical Officer gave us all two 5 mg amphetamine pills or as we called them Wakey-Wakey pills to keep us awake and alert. A 10 mg dose would help keep you awake and alert for about 5 hours. I did not want the effects of the drug to wear off until after we were on our way home and close to home, so I took mine just after we crossed the French coast about an hour after midnight. I was beginning to feel drowsy about then and the last thing anyone wanted was a snoozing Navigator. A few minutes after I took those Wakey-Wakey pills everything lit up around me like daylight. I suddenly felt like a Superman. Wow it must have been really good stuff. No wonder so many people can become addicted to amphetamines. It was estimated that Bomber Command went through 72 million 5 mg Benzedrine tablets during the war. This was the only time these pills were issued to me.

Over the target area we were at 21,000 feet flying at an IAS of 150 mph. The visibility was poor with 8/10ths cloud and lots of smoke. We identified the target visually and bombed the centre of the town. The flak was heavy and there were many searchlights. It was a good operation, and the target was well hit with many fires seen. The entire area was ablaze. Our bomb load was seven 1,000 pound SAP bombs and six 500 pound MC bombs with a 0.025 second time delay. At 02:02 we jettisoned one 1,000 bomb in a safe unarmed state from 5,000 feet at 51° 20′ N, 02° 75′ E. In this operation 4,400 tons of bombs and 550 tons of incendiaries were dropped on Duisburg and the surrounding area. All of our aircraft returned safely to Croft and we were back down at 04:19 October 15, 1944. On this trip to Duisburg our crew was the last crew to fly in O-OBOE and return alive.

The result of the two raids on Duisburg was devastating and many factories in the area never fully recovered before the end of the war. Bomber Command had dropped about 9,800 tons of bombs and incendiaries on Duisburg in one 19 hour period. About 2,500 people were killed on the ground. Nearly half of the most important industrial plants had been destroyed. The railway yards were extremely damaged and the next day no rail activity was seen. The nearby airfield was cratered by over 90 bombs.

In comparison the Operation Gomorrah raid on Hamburg on July 27, 1943 that caused a huge firestorm used 2,326 tons of bombs.

After I had been in England for a while, I wrote letters to Pat every day. I sent letters to my Mom about once a week. My Dad got his own letter about once a month. I could not say much about operations. Any newspaper clippings about operations were removed. Only personal stories and photographs were allowed by the censors.

A letter that Pat mailed to me, postmarked December 7, 1943. This letter caught up with me while at Commando training at Sidmouth. In this letter Pat wrote, "Gee! I didn't know that time could be so long when you're waiting for a letter from you. Thanks an awful lot for the cable. It was quite a surprise, I nearly lost ten years growth. It's about the nicest thing you've ever said and it made me think you were back home with me for a couple of days anyway."

Only one letter that I sent to Canada exists today. Pat wrote to me about once or twice per week. I still have about a dozen of Pat's letters.

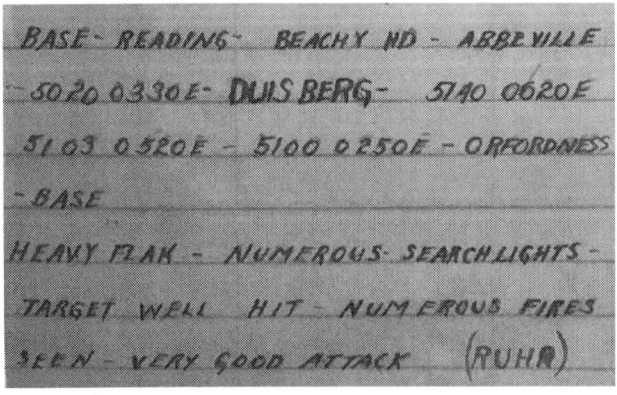

My logbook details for our night trip to Duisburg October 14, 1944 showing all our turning points. From the Bob Middleton Collection.

A letter that I had written to my Mom and Dad after the Duisburg operations. I had not included any newspaper clippings with the letter as it seemed the clippings were removed by censors after our letters were mailed. Photograph from the Bob Middleton Collection.

On Sunday, October 15, 1944 we were briefed to go off to attack the great naval base at Wilhelmshaven, Germany about 17:00 that night as a spare crew if we were needed. Wow! This would be three operations in less than thirty hours. We had only returned at 04:17 that morning. This was going to require some more Wakey, Wakey pills.

While we were waiting in Halifax MZ-434 designated as O-OBOE with the engines already running our Wing Commander Eric Mitchell came over to our aircraft and asked if everything was working OK in our bomber, O-OBOE. Don told him that all was fine. Commander Eric Mitchell told us that the Navigator that was sitting in G-GEORGE was having difficulty with the GEE box so he was sending that crew over to take O-OBOE on this operation. He told me to climb into G-GEORGE and check out the GEE box and then standby.

Our crew and the crew of Arthur M. Park swapped aircraft and we wished each other good luck as we passed each other. Once in the aircraft Don fired up one of the engines that has a generator so I could check out the GEE box and the H2S. I could find no problems with the GEE box or the H2S in G-GEORGE. Our crew could stand down and have a rest as there was no other standby crew required.

Pilot Officer Arthur M. Park and his crew took off in O-OBOE at 17:21. Pilot Arthur M. Park and crew only had two trips together and this would be their number three trip. There were 8 Iroquois Squadron crews that went off to Wilhelmshaven, Germany that night. Pilot Officer Arthur M. Park and his crew that left in O-OBOE that night were never heard from again. Seven more empty bunks that morning. You try not to think about it. We had exchanged greetings with the 7 fellows in that crew just hours ago as we traded aircraft. They were in the aircraft you were sitting in just a few hours ago. Earlier the same day we were the last crew to fly in O-OBOE and safely return. I think this novice crew had become lost somewhere over the North Sea. The route they took was probably close to what we had flown on our Tuesday, August 29, 1944 spoof raid to nowhere, 100 miles northwest of Wilhelmshaven, Germany while training at Dishforth No. 1664 HCU. This training trip is shown on the map on page 230. We made it back that night. That night of Sunday, October 15, 1944 the weather was very poor, and many crews had reported severe icing conditions over the North Sea. The Lancaster bomber had no deicing equipment except for the glycol deicing windshield spray. It was also reported that there was a great deal of predicted flak on the way to Wilhelmshaven that night. For a new crew there may have been just too many challenges working against them. The relatively fresh Navigator may have been lost. After the briefings for all of our trips Don would copy the details of the trip from my Navigator's chart such as compass headings, routes, altitudes, times, turning points and winds. If anything happened to me Don would have some kind of chance to get back home. From what I understand many Pilots did not do that. Flying without your Navigator in the dark would be like having your GPS stop giving you directions partway through a road trip and having no map for backup.

If we had not already been out two times that day, would we have been sent out in O-OBOE as the spare crew when the radar in G-GEORGE was not working? You wonder, is luck with the crew, the aircraft or is luck just a roll the dice chance? Did O-OBOE have no more trips left in her? Was that crew unlucky or was that aircraft unlucky? Boy we felt like that was a real close one. You don't think or dwell on this for very long as you would drive yourself nuts. We had at least 20 to 25 more trips to go. While I was at Croft for six months, I heard of only one or two fellows that were taken off to the hospital for being unable to cope with the fear of flying any longer. The term "Lack of Moral Fibre" was used by the RAF to shame and brand men that could not mentally take the stress any longer and refused to fly. If you let it, the fear could prevent you from doing what you had signed up for.

After an operation it was never announced who did not return. There was no board that showed missing crews that we had access to. The air crews were not privy to the Wing Commander's Log. We only knew that in an Officers' Nissen hut there were empty beds. Our hut only had Commissioned Officers in it. The missing men in a Commissioned Officers' hut could be a Pilot, a Navigator and possibly a Bomb Aimer. We did not associate very much with the members of the other crews in our hut or any other hut as there was no point getting involved in their lives as they might not be there tomorrow. You would have to deal with that ache in your gut for your missing pal. I would only chum around occasionally with one or two of the other crews Navigators.

Fortunately, over the 6 months that I was at Croft there were never any empty beds in my Nissen hut. If you did not return after an operation the base Adjutant would clear out your belongings and go through them before they were sent home to the next of kin. The Adjutant would remove articles from your kit that would only upset the folks at home and cause them to think less of their lost loved one.

The accommodations at Skipton-on-Swale in Yorkshire. Home of the RCAF 424 and 433 Squadrons. The accommodations at Croft were similar. Croft did not have a swimming pool however. We lived in the curved roof corrugated metal Nissen huts. Some of the wooden buildings were the washrooms. Photograph PL 45597 is courtesy of the Library and Archives Canada.

FTR   The aircraft and crew of Halifax MZ-434 designated as SE-O for OBOE flown by Pilot Officer Arthur M. Park failed to return from the operation to Wilhelmshaven and they are all listed as missing. Prior to this operation Pilot Arthur M. Park had four operations and the crew had only two operations. Pilot Arthur M. Park and 5 crew members are remembered at the Runnymede Memorial Surrey, UK. The wireless operator is buried at the Kiel War Cemetery, Germany. This was the first 431 aircraft and crew that had Failed to Return, FTR in the six weeks since we had joined the 431 Squadron at Croft. It appeared the luck of the squadron had improved.

Chapter 25

CANADIAN MK. X LANCASTERS ARRIVED AT CROFT

Lancaster KB-726 Mk. X VR-A flown regularly by the Canadian Warplane Heritage Museum. Lancaster VR-A is dedicated to the memory of Andrew Mynarski a Canadian airman that was awarded the Victoria Cross. The picture is courtesy of the Canadian Warplane Heritage Museum at Hamilton, Ontario.

On Tuesday, October 17, 1944 the first 10 Canadian built Lancaster Mk. X bombers were flown to our squadron. In readiness for a quick conversion there were no operations or training today. We had heard that the Lancaster was a marvelous aircraft and the Lancaster Mk. X aircraft we received that day were all built in Canada. We were going to be flying in these great modern marvels that were built in my hometown. The Lancaster was a first-class technical marvel of the time. Being designed in only 1940 it was the newest and most advanced bomber in any air force.

The AVRO Lancaster is a 4 engine heavy bomber created from the unsuccessful AVRO Manchester a two engine medium bomber. The Manchester bomber shown on page 46 used two 1780 horsepower 24-cylinder Rolls-Royce Vulture engines in the X configuration. The X configuration looks like two V12 engine banks 180 degrees opposite each other sharing a common crankshaft. The crankshaft of the Vulture was very prone to disastrous failures. The Manchester was underpowered, and the Rolls-Royce Vulture engines were not reliable. Many aircraft loses were the result of mid-air engine failure. In early 1940 AVRO Engineer Roy Chadwick the designer of the Manchester redesigned the Manchester with longer wings and 4 reliable Rolls-Royce Merlin V-12 engines turning it into the Lancaster. Rolls-Royce named all of their aircraft engines after birds of prey. The Merlin was a small bird of prey. The Lancaster was able to carry the heaviest bomb load of any aircraft built in the era. There were 7,377 Lancaster bombers built. Of those, 430 Lancaster Mk. X bombers were built by Victory Aircraft in Malton, just northwest of Toronto, Canada.

The Lancaster had an unobstructed bomb bay that was 33 feet long and 10 feet wide that could be configured to carry 22,000 pounds. The heaviest and longest bomb the Lancaster could lift off the ground and deliver to a target was the 22,000 pound Grand Slam earthquake bomb. The Grand Slam earthquake bomb was developed by Barnes Wallis in 1943. They were used to destroy viaducts, bridges, U-Boat shelters and coastal batteries because they could penetrate reinforced concrete 20 feet thick. 42 were used against German targets in 1943.

The Lancaster regularly carried on operations one 4,000 pound High Capacity blast bomb nicknamed a cookie plus thousands of pounds of other bombs and incendiaries. Pilots found the Lancaster wonderful to fly and many commented that the aircraft floated in the air and did not want to land. The wing main spar was very tall and strong which gave the aircraft its great strength. This great strength contributed to the aircrafts ability to sustain great damage and bring its crew back home. However, the tall main spar was a challenge to climb over at any time but, in a gyrating out of control aircraft in the dark of night it could prevent crew members from escaping a doomed aircraft. A photograph of the main spar is on page 299.

Unlike the Halifax Mk. III with the single Vickers gas powered scatter gun in the nose, the Lancaster had a proper hydraulic operated

Fraser Nash 5A turret with dual 0.303 caliber Browning machine guns that were intended to be operated by the Bomb Aimer. There was no seat for Ray. He just had to stand if he was operating the turret. The turret looked very impressive but, it is interesting to note that I do not remember Ray ever being in the nose turret. I know he never fired the guns. Except for one night there were never any German fighters that came within range of the front turret guns.

The RCAF Bomber Command squadrons all flew the marvelous Lancaster Mk. X with the 1,640 horsepower American Packard built Merlin Mk. 224 engines. The first Lancaster Mk. X built in Canada was KB-700, nicknamed the Ruhr Express. The Ruhr Express flew in 49 operations but sadly on return from the last operation it ran into a ditch digging machine that had been left at the end of the runway at Middleton St. George after landing and it burned completely. The plan for the Ruhr Express had been to bring it back to Canada after the 50th operation to raise money in a Victory War Bond drive.

The crew positions at the front of a Lancaster. 1, Pilot, 2, Navigator, 3, Flight Engineer, 4, Bomb Aimer, 5, Wireless Operator. The photograph was taken by Dan Middleton at Canada Aviation and Space Museum in Ottawa, Ontario.

This is an accurate painting of what the Navigator's position looked like and felt like in the Lancaster during a night operation. The GEE box is in front of the Navigator on the bench, the H2S ground scanning radar is the screen at the right above the bench and on the desk by the navigator's left hand is the circular computer. The single light above the bench was the sole illumination. The Wireless Operator was to my left in his compartment. This is one of 4 of the artist's prints that hang in my dining room. The painting is by artist Mike Steele-Morgan and is courtesy of Art Prints Direct UK.

On Wednesday, October 18, 1944 Wing Commander, Eric Mitchell announced that B Flight, that I belonged to, would be the first to train on the new Lancaster bombers and A Flight would continue operations in our Halifax bombers. Six more Lancaster Mk. X bombers arrived the same day. That afternoon while I was standing in the office doorway of Jack Sisman, Navigation Officer I let out a loud grown of dismay. One of those new Lancasters that just rolled by was KB-741 and it was designated as SE-Y-YOKE. "Another bad luck Y-YOKE Kite!" Jack was not really impressed with my comments. Ray took a photograph of KB-741 after it arrived. That photograph is on page 337. Jack's dad was the owner of the T. Sisman Shoe Company in Aurora, Ontario, the manufacturer of the famous Scampers, the shoe with a layer of cork.

Eight A Flight Halifax aircraft were detailed for an operation that night, but that operation was later called off. A dance was held in the Officers' mess that night and it was considered, by all that attended, to be a great success. There were no operations, and the entire Squadron was able to go to the dance.

Thursday, October 19, 1944 an operation was detailed for an early morning raid, but it was cancelled during the briefing. Training flying continued with the members of B Flight flying our new Lancaster bombers.

The weather was so bad on Friday, October 20, 1944 there were no operations called for and there was no flying. Today we spent the entire day in Lancaster ground school.

On Sunday, October 22, 1944 we did two cross-countries in our new Lancasters while some new crews did cross-country training in our old Halifax bombers.

FTR   On Wednesday, October 25, 1944 while on a training flight brand new Lancaster KB-813 designated as SE-S-SUGAR flown by Pilot Officer Gordon Wrigley crashed for unknown reasons 40 miles northwest of London near the village of Tingrith. The entire crew was killed in the accident. The crew had just joined our squadron and had not been on any operations. They are buried at the Brookwood Military Cemetery in Surrey, UK.

We were training in Lancaster KB-859 designated U-UNCLE for 3 hours in the morning and 30 minutes in the afternoon doing circuits and bumps. The Lancaster was so marvelous to fly in. The 4 Merlin engines were certainly loud, however. We were up in the morning and the afternoon.

I don't think we realized it back then that the engines were so loud that they drowned out the sound of machine gun fire and exploding flak. The fellows with a view could see the flak, the searchlights and the bombs exploding on the ground 18,000 feet below us but none of us could hear the explosions. This was great for me and Ken, as we were sitting behind the blackout curtain and we did not see or hear anything. Until I turned out my light, pulled back the curtain and looked outside I did not really know what was going on outside our aircraft. The weather was good on Friday, October 27, 1944 and there was extensive training in Lancaster and Halifax bombers. Five Lancasters went on a bullseye at night when the target was lit by an infrared light.

Saturday, October 28, 1944 the weather was good and again intensive training continued. We were flying in Lancaster KB-741 designated as Y-YOKE. We did a two hour cross-country training trip from Croft to the Mull of Galloway, the most southern point in Scotland then on to Saint Tudwal's Islands off the north of Wales and then back to Croft.

The final Victory Loan total was $42,000 from 251 bond sales. It was a really good response from all of the folks in 431 Squadron.

As of Sunday, October 29, 1944 there were 9 Lancaster bombers all in B Flight. No operations were on. The weather was great so we in B Flight were continuing our training while A Flight had started Lancaster ground school training. Our B Flight was devoting all our time on training in our new Lancasters. Each Flight had 9 aircraft to make up the squadron total of 18 aircraft.

A Packard built Merlin 224 engine. Photograph was taken at the Canadian Warplane Heritage Museum in Hamilton, Ontario by Dan Middleton.

Chapter 26

Y-YOKE CHOP KITE STATISTICS

We were again flying in Lancaster KB-741 designated as Y-YOKE for some local flying and bombing practice. We were very concerned about flying in this brand new Lancaster designated as Y-YOKE. In 1944 and 1945 most of the 431 Squadron and 434 Squadron Halifax and Lancaster bombers at Croft with the Y-YOKE designation eventually Failed to Return from an operation. The Y-YOKE aircraft at Croft were also known as the "Chop Kites." Yes, we were all very superstitious.

These are the statistics on the Y-YOKE bombers stationed at Croft. Even though we nicknamed these bombers "Chop Kites" we still climbed into them and went off on our operations. When I joined the RCAF on July 12, 1942 I signed for the mortgage on the dotted line and my signature was my word and my bond. It was my sworn duty to carry out my orders. It was like playing Russian roulette in Y-YOKE because we all knew that eventually 7 men would not return. We learned to put this at the back of our thoughts.

Y-YOKE aircraft in Croft 431 Squadron:
Wellington HE-440 designated as SE-Y Failed to Return from Duisburg, Germany on May 12, 1944.
Halifax MZ-628, designated as SE-Y Failed to Return from Vaires, France on July 18, 1944.
Halifax MZ-858, designated as SE-Y Failed to Return from Stuttgart, Germany on July 28/29, 1944.

Halifax MZ-372, designated as SE-Y Failed to Return from Kiel, Germany on August 15/16, 1944.

Halifax NR-122, designated as SE-Y was received from 433 Squadron and was then sent to 415 Squadron where NR-122 survived the war.

Halifax LL-233, designated as SE-Y was sent to 434 Squadron and then sent to 1659 HCU, 1664 HCU and eventually SOC, Struck Off Charge.

Halifax LK-708, designated as SE-Y was sent to 434 Squadron and then sent to 1659 HCU, 1669 HCU and eventually SOC, Struck Off Charge.

Lancaster KB-741, originally designated as SE-Y was designated SE-C-CHARLIE a few days after January 8, 1945. Possibly, our Commander thought the luck of the aircraft would be better by changing the name or he thought we would not know we were still flying in Y-YOKE.

Lancaster KB-741 SE-C was loaned to 434 Squadron and kept the SE-C-CHARLIE designation.

Lancaster KB-808, designated as SE-Y Failed to Return from Hildesheim on March 22, 1945. The Lancaster was flown by Pilot Officer Jack Duggan and crew with 32 trips, 121 points and 220 hours. These men were caught in the change from the 120 points system to 35 operations for a complete tour. Their aircraft was hit in the bomb bay by flak on the run in to the target. The cookie, along with 8,000 pounds of assorted bombs, fuel and aircraft exploded instantly. I would have thought that after the designation of Lancaster KB-741 was changed sometime after January 8, 1945, the squadron would have scratched the use of the bad luck Y-YOKE designation for any future aircraft.

Y-YOKE aircraft in Croft 434 Squadron:

Halifax LK-971, designated as WL-Y Failed to Return from Berlin, Germany on February 15/16, 1944.

Halifax LW-437, designated as WL-Y Failed to Return from Hamburg, Germany on July 28/29, 1944.

Halifax LW-436, designated as WL-Y Failed to Return from Bois de Cassan, France on August 4, 1944.

Halifax MZ-876, designated WL-Y was transferred to Bomber Command Instructors School.

Lancaster KB-834, designated as WL-Y Failed to Return from Essen, Germany on March 11, 1945.

Lancaster KB-741 SE-C was loaned to 434 Squadron and kept the 431 Squadron SE-C-CHARLIE designation. While Lancaster KB-741 SE-C was on loan to 434 Squadron it Failed to Return from Chemnitz, Germany on Wednesday February 14, 1945. This was the only operation when KB-741 was used by 434 Squadron and this was the first and last operation by new Pilot Douglas Magrath and his crew. No one was heard from again. They are buried at the Berlin 1939-1945 War Cemetery, Germany in the Commonwealth War Graves.

The only Croft Y-YOKE bombers to survive were the Halifax bombers that were transferred out of Croft when converting from Halifax Mk. V to Halifax Mk. III or converting from Halifax Mk. III to Lancasters.

On Monday, October 30, 1944 in Lancaster KB-806 designated as SE-X-X-RAY we did a three hour cross-country trip to the Mull of Galloway in southern Scotland then to the Isle of Saint Tudwal's Islands in Wales and back again to Croft. Later on, the same day we did a longer four hour nighttime cross-country trip in Lancaster KB-803 designated N-NAN. This was our first of our many flights in KB-803 N-NAN. We flew from Croft to Cambridge in the south England to Fishguard on the north coast of Wales then on to the Mull of Galloway in southern Scotland and then back to Croft. We were the first crew to fly in N-NAN with her brand new Packard built Merlin engines. This Lancaster had brand new engines as a previous pilot after completing his tour had flown the aircraft for quite some time with the throttles pushed through the gates and then buzzed a tower. That pilot ruined the engines. He ended up in the Officers' prison called the Glasshouse in Sheffield. This Lancaster became our favorite as we did so many operations in N-NAN, we felt it was ours. We treated the ground crew with many nights at the local pubs as thanks for taking such good care of N-NAN. Each ground crew took care of one aircraft.

Tuesday, October 31, 1944 we spent an hour practicing daylight bombing in Lancaster KB-806 designated SE-X-XRAY. Later that night in Lancaster KB-817 designated SE-P-PETER we spent 1 hour and 20 minutes doing some local nighttime flying.

The Town of Simcoe, Ontario had been looking after us folks very well. Lots of Christmas parcels showed up and everyone was anxious to open them up.

Minnie Simcoe the mascot appeared this day. Minnie Simcoe was a doll that was made for the 431 Iroquois Squadron modeled after Princess Pocahontas. She was made by the Simcoe chapter of the Imperial Order Daughters of the Empire, IODE. Minnie travelled with crews as a second pilot on at least 18 operations as a good luck charm. Her first operation was to Dusseldorf on November 2, 1944. The operations she flew on are recorded in the Squadron logs. Minnie Simcoe never flew on any operation in our aircraft. When Wing Commander Eric Mitchell was screened from operations at Croft, he was given Minnie Simcoe as a gift. Minnie Simcoe was stored away in a Mitchell family trunk for about 50 years. In 2008 Minnie Simcoe was donated to the Bomber Command Museum of Canada at Nanton, Alberta where she is on display. Minnie went on one last 431 Snowbirds Squadron operation with Major Chris Bard at the Lethbridge Air Show July 25-26, 2009.

Commanding Officer Wing Commander Eric Mitchell with Minnie Simcoe. The official ID tag number on battle orders for Minnie Simcoe was V.431-W02. Photograph is courtesy of the Bomber Command Museum of Canada at Nanton, Alberta.

Chapter 27

NIGHT MUSIC

The Bomber Command aircraft all had one big defensive weakness. None of the bombers had a lower ventral turret for protection against attack from below. The Wellington was designed without a ventral turret. The Halifax was originally designed with a ventral turret but these were never installed. The hole in the bottom of the Halifax was filled with a plug. The bottom opening in the Halifax Mk. VII displayed in Trenton had plywood doors that could be opened. This was for dropping supplies to resistance fighters in France and for dropping spies into France. It was much safer dropping out of the bottom of the aircraft as you were less likely to run into the elevator or rudder as these passed by you when you bailed out through the side door.

The Lancaster had such a long bomb bay that a turret would have been way at the rear of the aircraft. By having no lower ventral turret these bombers could carry an extra 2,000 pounds of bombs. The purpose of the British designed bomber was to carry as many bombs as possible to the target. Sometime during the design process of the British bombers Bomber Command did not include the lower turret. All the American bombers had a huge number of defensive guns and were built of heavier gauge aluminum. The skin of the Lancaster was slightly thinner than the thickness of a credit card. The American bombers all carried 10 men versus our 7 men. The American bombers all had the lower ventral turret and a single gun on both sides of the bomber. The result of all this was that the American bombers were heavier and could only carry 4,000 to 5,000 pounds of bombs to Germany. The Lancaster regularly carried 12,000 pounds of bombs to targets in Germany. The 7 men in one lighter and less armed Lancaster did the same damage as 20 men in 2 American bombers.

The German Luftwaffe took full advantage of this weak spot in the defense of our bombers. The German Bf 110 and Ju 88 fighters were equipped with radar to search out our bombers and a pair of 20 mm cannons mounted on top of the fuselage at a 60-to-70-degree forward facing angle behind the cockpit. The Germans called this Schräge Musik which translates to slanted music. We called it Night Music. To shoot down a bomber the Bf 110 or Ju 88 fighter would simply approach the target bomber from the rear and below. The pilot would line up his angled cannons below the wing on one side. Then in just the correct place the pilot would fire a few 20 mm rounds into the fuel tanks and then break away from the bomber quickly. The gunners in the bomber could do nothing as they could not see the fighter approaching in the dark. The first time the crew realized the fighter was there was when they were on already fire. Once a fuel tank was ignited the rest of the bomber caught fire and blew up in the air or became uncontrollable and crashed into the ground. Our bombers were defenseless to this form of attack. It was many months before Bomber Command determined the Luftwaffe had these slanted cannons and was using this technique.

A Junkers Ju 88 showing the two 20 mm forward angled cannons on top of the fuselage. Photograph from the Bob Middleton Collection.

Chapter 28

SEARCHLIGHTS, RADAR AND FLAK

The German army had searchlights that were radar controlled and could zero in on one bomber flying at 20,000 feet. Once the radar locked onto that one bomber a 200 millimeter master searchlight would be aimed at it. Once the 200 millimeter master searchlight had you then another ten or twelve 150 millimeter searchlights would join in to play on your bomber. Your bomber was at the apex of the beams eighteen thousand feet high in the sky. The 200 millimeter master searchlight was a very intense light with a blue tint. The coning looked like an upside down ice cream cone. We called the effect "coning." Once all those lights converged on our bomber we were lit up like daylight and were easy pickings for any Luftwaffe fighters or radar controlled anti-aircraft guns. Once you were coned it became many times brighter than daylight inside the aircraft. Don was blinded by the light and would lose his night vision and be almost blind in the dark skies. As soon as we were coned Don would yell over the intercom "corkscrew" and we would make that crazy dive straight down in the black of the night. I had to frantically grab all my instruments and then hang on for dear life. We would drop a few thousand feet in just seconds. Don corkscrewed the aircraft straight down in the dark for a few thousand feet without knowing if anything was below us. At the bottom of the dive Don would then fly with full power back up again without knowing if any other aircraft were above us. Lucky for us Don escaped the coning twice. This was an almost unbelievable feat. The odds of escaping being coned were lousy.

This is a mobile 150 mm German searchlight. This photograph was taken by Dan Middleton in 2014 at the South African National Museum of Military History in Johannesburg, South Africa.

At the Father's Day airshow at the Canadian Warplane Heritage Museum in 2014 I was talking to Heinz Horman who had been a volunteer at the Canadian Warplane Heritage Museum for 25 years. Heinz was a 16 year old anti-aircraft gunner in Nuremberg, Germany. We had bombed Nuremburg on January 2, 1945 and Heinz was there on the ground. Heinz and I were talking about our bomber and crew being coned twice and escaping both times. Heinz commented that no one ever escaped being coned and said he felt sorry for "You poor Slobs up there in the sky." I told him, "We felt sorry for you poor Slobs on the ground," at the receiving end of the bombing. Heinz told me that when they sent up box barrage flak, they would say to each other. "WE dare you bastards to fly through this!" We both commented that we wondered what the war was all about. "For guys like you or me what the hell was the whole thing about?" Heinz was only a 16-year-old boy carrying shells and loading an 88 mm flak gun 16 times a minute. Heinz would have been told since he was 12 years old that the British and Americans started the war, and they were all evil enemies. Just like me he was doing a job. He probably would have been shot or sent to a concentration camp if he had refused to fight.

Heinz and I were speaking together in 2014 like we were long lost friends that had not seen each other for years. The photograph was taken under the restored de Havilland Mosquito KA114 that was visiting from Virginia Beach, USA at the Canadian Warplane Heritage Museum. Photograph taken by Dan Middleton.

Chapter 29

STARTING ENGINES AND TROLLEY ACCUMULATORS

The trolley accumulator or Trolley ACC was an auxiliary power unit used to charge the batteries of an aircraft before flight and also supplement the starting power for the engines. In the UK lead acid rechargeable batteries were called accumulators. The trolley accumulator had a small gasoline engine and a 24 volt generator connected to a set of batteries. The use of the trolley accumulator took the stress off of the bomber's internal batteries during the engine starting process and also reduced the stress on the aircraft engine generators having to recharge the heavily discharged internal aircraft batteries just before and during takeoff. The internal engine generators of the aircraft were needed to drive all of the electrical gear on board the bomber. There is an electrically powered hydraulic pump in the engine oil tank that was used to feather the propeller of a dead engine. A takeoff with insufficient electrical power to feather a propeller from fine pitch should that be necessary during a full load takeoff could cause enough drag to prevent an aircraft from gaining sufficient height to clear the obstacles at the end of the runway.

On these variable pitch propellers, the blade pitch could be increased to the point where the chord line of the blade was almost parallel to the on-coming flow of air. This prevented drag on the dead engine propeller. This change of blade pitch is called feathering.

In cold weather the oil in the engines becomes thicker and a great deal more electrical energy is required to start these cold engines. To reduce the energy required to turn over very cold engines with thickened oil there were 4 "Dilution Control" buttons on the Engineer's panel. There was one button for each engine of a Lancaster. Pressing these buttons injected fuel into the engine crankcase. The fuel thinned the oil thus reducing the resistance of the cold and thick oil. You had to be careful however because if too much fuel went in an engine crankcase you could end up with an engine fire. To make matters tougher all lead acid rechargeable batteries lose 3 percent of the rated capacity for every one-degree Celsius drop below 22 degrees Celsius. In the winter in the north of England when the outside temperature is around freezing the aircraft internal batteries only have 30 percent of rated starting capacity left. This is why you will notice problems starting your vehicle when temperatures drop to freezing.

This is a photograph of a Trolley Accumulator at the Canadian Aviation and Space Museum in Ottawa, Ontario. This unit does not have a generator and would have been used with single engine fighters. It would have to be charged from utility power before use. The photograph was taken by Dan Middleton.

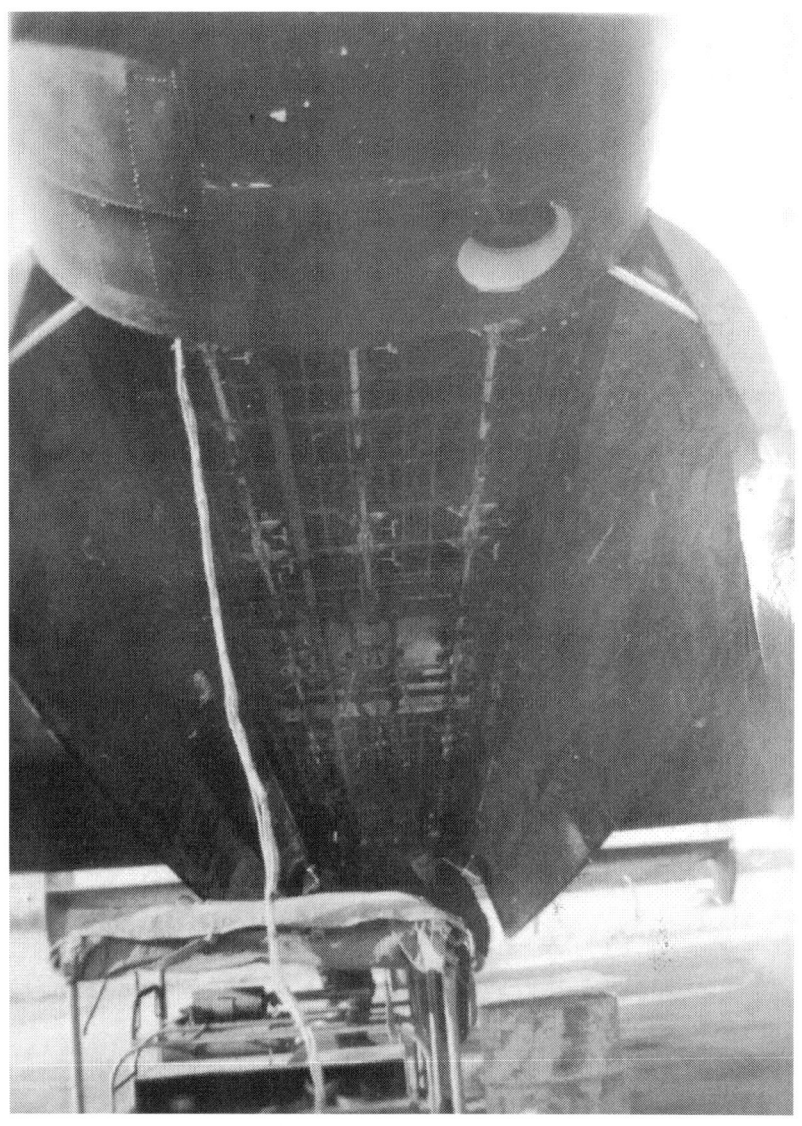

This picture shows a Trolley Accumulator, Trolley ACC sitting under the empty 33 foot long bomb bay of the Lancaster. This Trolley ACC is a battery, generator combination. Just in front of the bomb bay you can see the round opening for the reconnaissance camera used to take the bombing result photograph. The photograph is from the Bob Middleton Collection.

Chapter 30

NOVEMBER AND OPERATIONS IN LANCASTERS

Our first operation in a Lancaster was operation number 11 in Lancaster KB-741, designated as Y-YOKE on Wednesday, November 1, 1944. It was a 6 hour and 30 minute round trip to Oberhausen, Germany at night under the illumination of a full moon. I had complained about the new Lancaster designated Y-YOKE when it arrived and now, we had the honor to be the first crew to fly the latest "Chop Kite" on an operation and in full moon light. We were number 4 in order of 10 431 Squadron Lancaster crews taking part in this operation. A Flight was continuing training in their Lancasters and would soon be joining us.

We were up at 17:00 and reached the target at 20:33. Over the target area we were at 19,000 feet flying at an IAS of 160 mph. The visibility was poor with 9/10ths cloud. There were many searchlights. The flak was moderate and at times heavy. There was also some predicted flak. Ralph yelled out corkscrew. I can't remember which direction but as soon as I heard corkscrew, I grabbed my instruments and found something to hang on to. Away we went straight down but not as far as when we were coned. We saw one Me 109 fighter and we saw our first Me 262 jet fighter that night. The target was marked by Wanganui sky markers in red, yellow and green. We bombed on the red markers in the centre area. The target was well carpeted with incendiaries and many large bomb bursts. If the markers were on target this was a really good prang. Our bomb load was one 4,000 pound HC cookie and fourteen 500 pound No. 14 Mk. 1 cluster incendiaries. This was our first operation carrying a 4,000 pound cookie. Heavy damage was inflicted upon the iron and steel works. After the attack, the night fighters harassed all our bombers on the way home and shot down at least 3 aircraft while 3 other aircraft were lost to flak.

A photograph of the Messerschmitt Me 262 Jet Fighter at the South African National Museum of Military History in Johannesburg, South Africa. This was the first jet fighter aircraft of the Luftwaffe. The Me 262 had four 30 mm cannons in the nose and had a top speed of 560 miles per hour. Me 262 pilots claimed to have shot down 542 aircraft. Luckily for the Allied air forces the Me 262 was only introduced in April of 1944 and the Me 262 had serious issues with engine reliability and lack of fuel supplies to power them. Our best defense against these jet fighters was our P-51 Mustang fighters attacking them during takeoff or landing when they were defenseless. The picture was taken by Dan Middleton.

A typical bomb load with our Lancasters would have one 4,000 pound cookie, up to 8,000 pounds of 500 pound bombs with time delay fuses and canisters of incendiaries. We used the cookie to blow buildings apart and knock things over or weaken the structures. The 500 pound bombs with the time delay would go through the roofs and walls without exploding and bury themselves deep into the buildings and then blow the buildings apart from the insides. The incendiaries would ignite just above the ground and land upon the previous destruction and set everything on fire that could burn. This worked very well at causing massive destruction. The bomb aimers were given a sequence to release each type of bomb using the Mark XIV bomb sight. We all returned safely to Croft except for one crew. We were back down at 23:38.

FTR   One of our Lancasters and crew piloted by Pilot Officer Donald Conner in P-PETER, KB-817 was up at 17:10 but was never seen again. Pilot Officer Donald Conner the pilot had 30 trips and 130 hours. The Bomb Aimer had 29 trips, Wireless Operator had 28 trips, Mid-Upper Gunner had 30 trips, Rear Gunner had 30 trips and the Flight Engineer had 27 trips. These fellows were so close to the end of their tour. We later learned that Pilot Officer Donald Conner and the Flight Engineer were killed but four other crew members became guests of the Luftwaffe for the last few months of the war. Crew member J. M. Campbell landed in Holland and successfully evaded capture and made his way back to England. J. B. Ogg the Navigator reported that they were attacked by a night fighter on the return trip. The port engine and wing caught fire and extinguishing the flames was not successful and the pilot Donald Connor gave the order to bail out. He was awarded a DFC. He was buried in the Linne Roman Catholic Churchyard in the Netherlands beside his Flight Engineer R. C. Joiner.

The Lancaster bomber had a much smaller Bomb Aimer's transparent nose than the Halifax Mk. III and it was much further from my position and more difficult to get to. There was much less room at the nose so it would be crowded with Ray and I in the nose. Being the Nosy Navigator that I was I would go forward the few steps to go stand in the cockpit behind Art, the Flight Engineer and look out through the fantastic Lancaster canopy. On our few daylight operations in Lancasters I went up to look out very often to see what was going on and look at the gaggle of hundreds of our bombers in the sky. I was always happy to see all 4 of those propellers spinning happily. It made me feel good. I always came up to look at the target once we had arrived. I have always said that "I wasn't going to come all this way and not look out to see what we had done." We were proud of our work to defeat a cruel enemy. I have read in books about other Navigators who went up just one time while over the target to see what was happening and never did it again as it was too frightening. They would stay behind the blackout curtain for the entire flight. Ken our Wireless

Operator never came out from his safe secure spot just behind me. I know he did not because he would have had to go past me to get to the cockpit. He may have looked out through the astrodome that was directly over his position in the Lancaster.

Operation number 12 was in Lancaster KB-741 designated as Y-YOKE on Thursday, November 2, 1944. It was a 6 hour and 25 minute round trip to Dusseldorf, Germany at night under the illumination of an almost full moon. We were up flying in that "Chop Kite" again, number 4 in order of 8 431 Squadron Lancaster crews taking part in this operation. We were part of an operation that directed 990 bombers to Germany's third largest inland port and transportation centre. We were up at 16:18 and reached the target at 19:34. Over the target area we were at 20,000 feet flying at an IAS of 160 mph. The flak was a moderate to heavy barrage type using many searchlights to coordinate the flak batteries. There was never any shaking or a rough ride that I remember in either the Halifax or Lancaster bomber while the flak was exploding all around us on any of our trips. The extremely loud noise of the four engines drowned out the sound of the flak exploding so well that I did not hear it. On night operations while I was sitting in my blacked-out Navigator position constantly calculating our route I was practically oblivious to what was happening outside of our bomber. It may sound strange but, I really felt quite safe in my spot in the aircraft. We were attacked by one Focke-Wulf Fw 190, but it did not open fire. Possibly his guns jammed, and we were lucky again. We never saw the fighter return. The visibility was good with just a slight haze and some cloud. The targets were the marshalling yards and armament factories that were identified by red and green TIs. We bombed on the red and green TIs in the centre of the fires. The target was ablaze with at least five fires of orange color. It was a good well concentrated operation. We could see the fires from 60 miles away coming and going. All of our aircraft returned safely to Croft and we returned at 22:16. We carried one 4,000 pound cookie on this trip. It was estimated that the city was 70 percent destroyed in the built-up areas and about 50 factories were put out of commission. Some of these factories were out of commission for the remainder of the war.

On November 3, 1944 there were no operations, so we trained all day and four Lancaster crews practiced bombing bullseyes at night.

Operation number 13 was in Lancaster KB-803 designated as N-NAN on Saturday, November 4, 1944 was a 5 hour and 25 minute round trip to Bochum, Germany at night under a three quarter moon illumination. We had our meal at a regular time today before noon. My Navigator briefing was at 12:45 and the main briefing was at 13:45. We were number 5 in order of 9 431 Squadron Lancaster crews taking part in this operation. The RCAF supplied 220 bombers out of the force of 750 bombers to attack iron and coal centres, marshalling yards and other important industrial facilities.

Photograph of a Focke-Wulf Fw 190 at the South African National Museum of Military History in Johannesburg, South Africa. Photograph was taken by Julie Middleton.

We were up at 17:10 and reached the target at 19:42. Over the target area we were at 18,300 feet flying at IAS of 160 mph. On this trip to Bochum, we crossed the English Channel at Orford Ness and then flew east in a straight line and turned south about 50 miles from Bochum. On this trip to Bochum, we approached from the west and we did not have to fight those terrible headwinds like the previous trip to Bochum. There were numerous searchlights, moderate to heavy flak and many enemy fighters in the sky. We were chased by predictive flak that night. Jack had been watching the bursts of flak creeping up on the tail of the aircraft getting closer and he called out, "Prepare to corkscrew port or starboard." I had a moment to gather up my instruments and find something to hang on to. Maybe, 5 seconds later Jack cried out, "Port. Go. Now!" Away we went twisting away diving like mad down into the dark sky and when we came back up to the previous altitude, we were clear. We were some lucky folks that night. The sky was clear over the target area and we identified the green TIs. There was indication that some of the bombing was going on to the north-west of the target area. The target was a mass of flame with one particularly large orange flame. We dropped one 4,000 pound cookie and fourteen 500 pound No. 14 Mk. 1 incendiary clusters for a total of 11,000 pounds. We all returned unscathed and we were back down at 22:15.

A Lancaster being fueled by a Bowser. A full load of aviation fuel for a Lancaster was 2,154 imperial gallons. The photograph is from the Bob Middleton Collection.

Operation number 14 in Lancaster KB-802 designated as V-VICTOR on Monday, November 6, 1944 was a 5 hour and 15 minute round trip to Gelsenkirchen, Germany in the daylight. We were number 6 in order of 9 431 Squadron Lancasters taking part in this operation. The bomber force was about the same size as the attack on Bochum 2 nights ago. Our targets were the coking facilities, hydrogenation plants which process oils, so they do not go rancid in food processing, and synthetic

274

oil plants. We were up at 11:55 and reached the target at 14:11. Over the target area we were at 19,000 feet flying at an IAS of 160 mph. The visibility was 7/10ths cloud with tops at 8,000 feet. There were many fighters and exceptionally light flak. We bombed parallel to the marshalling yards visually on smoke and bomb bursts. Nothing was heard from the Master Bomber. The attack was rather scattered. We dropped one 4,000 pound cookie, six 1,000 pound Medium Capacity bombs with 0.025 seconds time delay fuses and six 500 pound Medium Capacity bombs with 0.025 seconds time delay fuses for a total of 13,000 pounds of bombs.

My logbook details for our trip to Gelsenkirchen November 6, 1944 showing all our turning points. From the Bob Middleton Collection.

While we were returning over the English Channel that morning Ralph asked me if I wanted to have a go in his mid-upper turret. "Well sure." I could not get in the turret quick enough. I climbed inside the turret and the view from the turret was marvelous. The mid-upper turret of the Canadian built Lancaster Mk. X is the Martin turret with the big double 0.50 caliber machine guns. British built Lancaster bombers only had the Browning 0.303 caliber pea shooters. The Luftwaffe fighter pilots were shooting at us with 20 mm cannon shells. The Martin turret also had a self-contained electrically powered hydraulic pump and did not depend upon hydraulics supplied by the port inner engine as in all other Lancaster bombers. If the port inner engine quit the turret would still operate. I had a ball swinging the guns up and down and rotating the turret all around the sky. The sky that afternoon was beautiful with big anvil shaped thunder heads. Coming out of those clouds in the distance I saw a huge American Republic P-47 Thunderbolt fighter appear. As the P-47 fighter came closer to us it appeared the pilot was going to line us up and practice shooting us down. At that close range in the air the P-47 was a huge aircraft. We were almost home, and I do not think Don felt like doing fighter affiliation at this point. No one called out to corkscrew. I decided that two could play so I swung my guns around and lined up the P-47 in my sights and I squeezed the trigger. To my surprise and the surprise of the P-47 pilot I squeezed off about six rounds. Ralph had not put the guns in safe mode before I climbed in. You never saw a fighter pull a turn in the sky so fast and bugger off. Nothing was ever said of the incident. I do not know if Ralph had to explain why there were a few rounds fired. In all our flights I do not recall Ralph or Jack ever firing their guns for testing or defense. At night the flash from our guns was a bright beacon that would give away your position. If a bomber gunner spotted a Luftwaffe fighter before being seen he would yell, "corkscrew," and the bomber would dive thousands of feet to hide under the cover of darkness.

All our aircraft returned safely to Croft that morning and we were back down at 17:10.

A Republic P-47 Thunderbolt fighter photo from my scrap book. The P-47 Thunderbolt was powered by a 2,300 horsepower Pratt & Whitney R-2800, twin bank, 18 cylinder radial engine. The engine spun a 12 foot diameter four blade propeller. This fighter weighed in at up to 16,000 pounds fully loaded and had a top speed of 430 mph. Republic built 15,000 of these fighters. The photograph is from the Bob Middleton Collection.

A Martin mid-upper turret from a Lancaster Mk. X with the twin 0.50 caliber machine guns at the Canadian Aviation and Space Museum in Ottawa, Ontario. The photograph was taken by Dan Middleton.

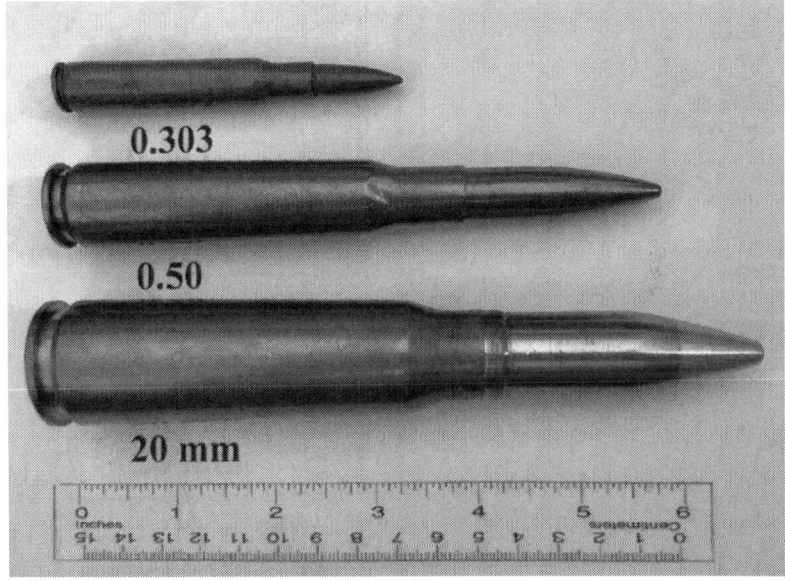

20 mm cannon shell and 0.50 caliber machine gun shell compared to a 0.303 caliber machine gun shell. The 20 mm cannon shell is 6.5 inches long. The 0.303 shell is one I brought back from Croft. Photograph from the Bob Middleton Collection.

After we returned from operation 14 on November 6, 1944 we went on leave for a week in London. While there I was woken up suddenly at 03:00 one morning while I was lying in bed. I heard and felt an almighty terrific explosion nearby and about 7 seconds later I heard the whistling noise and roar of a huge bomb going past very fast. I had just heard the V-2 ballistic guided missile, the latest vengeance weapon of Nazi Germany. The V-2 missile was designed and built at the same facilities as the V-1 missile. The V-2 was the world's first ballistic missile, and these were being launched from mobile sites in German occupied Netherlands and Belgium. There were 6,100 V-2 missiles produced by slave labor at the underground facility at Mittelwerk that also produced the V-1. It has been estimated that 15,000 slaves died during the 20 months that V-2 missiles were being produced. The first V-2 missile to hit London was launched from The Hague, Netherlands on September 6, 1944. The last V-2 landed in Kent, England on March 27, 1945. The V-2 with a range of 220 miles carrying 2,200 pounds of explosive travels up about 50 miles high and then comes down at a speed 3 to 4 times faster than the 1,125 feet per second speed of sound. Because it travelled faster than the speed of sound you heard it go by 7 seconds after it had gone past you or in my case hit the ground and exploded. This weapon was very scary as you did not hear it coming and you had no time to take cover. Suddenly, you were dead if it landed close to you. This is similar to being shot dead by a sniper a thousand yards from you. You would never hear the shot that killed you as the sound from the gun would reach you about 3 seconds after the bullet struck you. The V-2 was a true weapon of terror. Due to the high speed none of the V-2 missiles launched against England were intercepted. Out of 1,300 V-2 missiles launched towards England 1,115 reached the target. While we were in London there were air raid sirens going off all the time whenever one of the V weapons were detected. The idea was that when you heard a siren you should take cover in an underground air raid shelter. By this time, many Londoners did not bother to go underground for protection. We spent our time while the sirens were going off, when possible, in the pub that was in the basement of the Continental Hotel.

Saturday, November 11, 1944 while we were away in London there were no operations. Most of the afternoon at Croft was spent taking pictures with the press. Our unofficial mascot Minnie Simcoe was everywhere. Supported by girls from the RCAF Blackouts show and our attractive nursing sister Louise Dawson, suitable pictures were obtained for the Canadian press. It sounded like we missed a good show.

We returned to Croft on Sunday, November 19, 1944 and were ready to go again after our break.

Artist's depiction of the V-2 ballistic missile, launching stand and support equipment. Picture is from the Bob Middleton Collection.

The RCAF squadrons had hockey teams that played at the Durham Ice Rink in Durham located about 30 miles north of Croft. I was told our Batman was a great goalie and a favorite of Group Captain Bob

Turnbull, the Station Commanding Officer. He disappeared on various occasions to play hockey with the other Canadian Squadrons. I never made it to Durham to watch any of their games. There was only one Batman for every Officers' Nissen hut.

This photograph of our Batman and I was taken at the same occasion of our crew professional photograph. I do not remember his name. Photograph is from the Bob Middleton Collection.

Operation number 15 was in Lancaster KB-803 designated as N-NAN on Tuesday, November 21, 1944. It was a 6 hour and 25 minute round trip to Castrop-Rauxel, Germany at night under the illumination of a one quarter moon. We were number 10 in order of 16 431 Squadron Lancasters taking part in this operation. Our target was the coking plant and the synthetic oil manufacturing plant. We had a meal at 11:30. The Navigator briefing was at 12:30 and the main briefing was at 13:30. The winds that day were quite gusty. The aircraft was being buffeted about while we were sitting on the ground. I was standing behind Art while taking off as per usual. Art was calling out the speed. We were at 110 mph and things felt a bit tense when Don said he needed ten more to get off the ground.

Photograph of our crew before an operation. Yes, we flew with our ties on. Front row left to right, Flight Engineer Art Morency, Pilot Don Rombough. Back row left to right, Rear Gunner Jack Cornock, Wireless Operator Ken Smith, Navigator Bob Middleton, Mid-Upper Gunner Ralph Hamel, Bomb Aimer Ray Rose. This photograph is on the front cover. The photograph is from the Bob Middleton Collection.

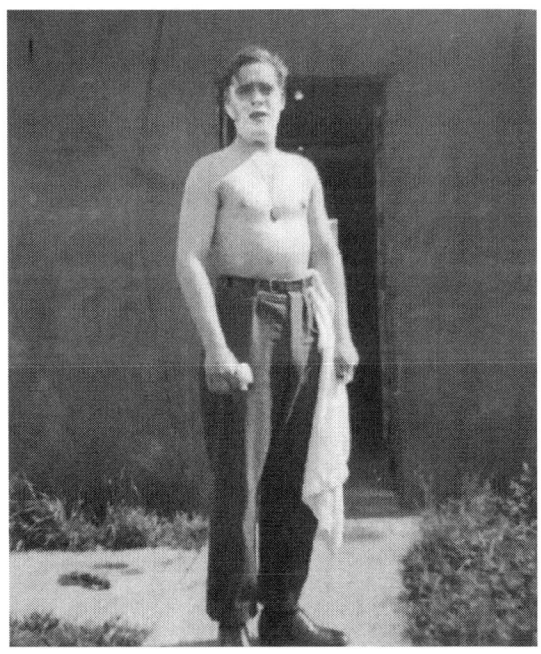

The washrooms and showers were in separate buildings from our Nissen huts. I was shaving one morning and Ray said. "Bob, go outside with the shaving cream on your face and I'll take your picture." I did not look very impressed. The photograph is from the Bob Middleton Collection.

Art pushed the throttles forward a bit more and we managed to just clear everything at the end of the runway. For a while, until we were clear of the gusts, I could see the ends of the wings bending up and down about three feet. We were up at 15:27 and reached the target at 19:05. Over the target area we were at 18,000 feet flying at an IAS of 160 mph. The visibility was good with just thin clouds and there were red and green TIs. We bombed the centre of the red TIs. There was a large explosion at 19:04 with a gigantic orange flame just before we dropped our bombs. The markers were well concentrated but with some dummies to the south of the target area. It was a good, concentrated attack. The damage was severe with most of the buildings destroyed including all the equipment inside and outside of the buildings. We dropped eighteen 500 pound bombs for a total of 9,000 pounds of bombs. All of our aircraft returned safely to Croft and we were back down at 21:54.

This sketch is my impression of a real HOT daylight operation over a target in our Lancaster KB-803 N-NAN. I switched the order of SE and N. Below us is a Croft 434 Bluenose squadron Lancaster marked WL. The picture is from the Bob Middleton Collection.

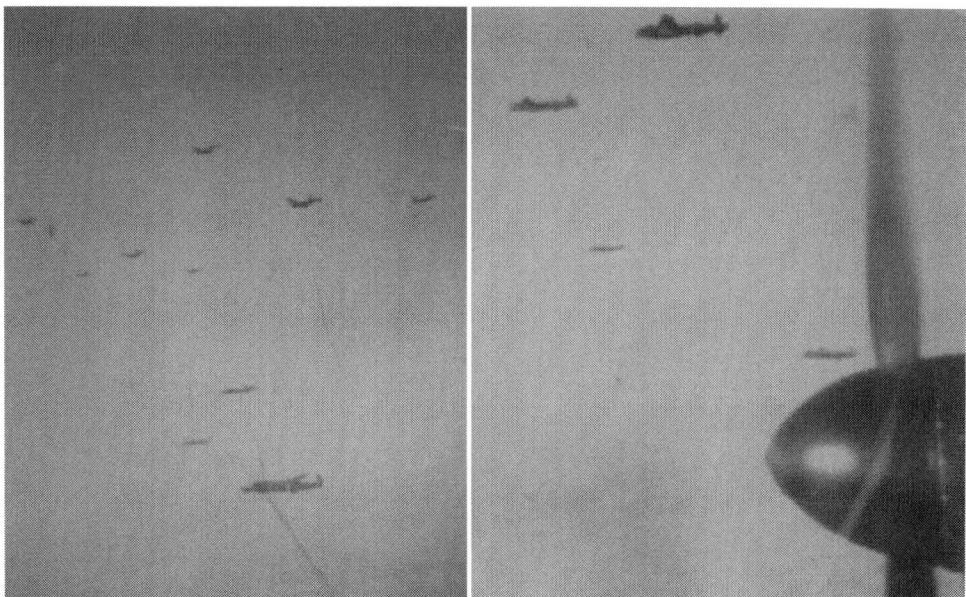

Two photographs I took of actual bomber gaggles in the daylight with no opposition present. What I would see on a daylight operation standing beside the pilot on the way outbound hours before reaching the target. These photographs I took while being the Nosy Navigator. You will notice that the view in my sketch is from the same aspect as the photograph showing the starboard inboard Merlin engine and propeller. Notice, I even show the fasteners at the front of the engine cowling. Whenever I went up to look at the scene through the cockpit canopy I was always pleased to see all four of those marvelous propellers spinning. The photographs are from the Bob Middleton Collection.

Operation number 16 in Lancaster KB-796 designated as R-ROGER on Monday, November 27, 1944 was a 6 hour and 20 minute round trip to Neuss, Germany at night under the illumination a little less than a full moon. Neuss was an important inland port and largest manufacturer of nuts and bolts in Germany. We were number 3 in order of 17 431 Squadron Lancasters taking part in this operation. That night the RCAF supplied 225 aircraft of the total force of 290. We were up at 16:34 and reached the target at 20:26. Over the target area we were at 18,200 feet flying at an IAS of 160 mph. The visibility was poor with 10/10ths cloud. There were red and green TIs. We bombed the centre of the red TIs. There was a large explosion at 19:04 with a gigantic orange flame just before we dropped our bombs. The TIs were well concentrated but with some enemy dummy markers to the south of the target area. It was a good, concentrated attack that caused a moderate amount of damage in the eastern parts of Neuss. Our bomb load was one 4,000 pound cookie, six American made 1,000 pound AN-M59 SAP bombs with 0.025 seconds time delay and five 500 pound GP bombs with 0.025 seconds time delay for a total of 12,500 pounds.

When we were on our return leg of the operation, we were informed that the weather had closed in and the fog in particular over most of England was as thick as pea soup that night. In England up until sometime in the 1950s the air was very dirty as the primary energy source of heating, electricity generation and factory mechanical power was burning coal. In the 1940's the fog was so thick that if you held out your hand in front of you at arm's length you could not see your hand. The fog that night was just that sort of pea soup fog.

A picture of FIDO employed at the RAF aerodrome at Gravely, England. Flames can be seen on both sides of the runway. The photograph is from the Imperial War Museum collection. © IWM Image CH15271.

We were advised to land at the aerodrome at RAF Tuddenham which was equipped with Fog Intense Dispersal Operation or FIDO for short.

The FIDO system used to get crews back safely when the runway was invisible under fog was an incredible sight. Before the use of FIDO if visibility was so poor that you could not reach any aerodrome that was not fogged in with the fuel you had remaining on board, the pilot would head the aircraft towards the English Channel. Before the aircraft reached the English Channel the crew would all bail out leaving the aircraft to eventually crash into the English Channel. This was done as an aircraft crashing on land could kill the crew and anyone on the ground where the aircraft came down.

FIDO consisted of pipes with nozzles on both sides running the length and width of the runway with fuel pumped into them and then set on fire. As the pipes heated up the fuel was vaporized and burnt extremely hot and bright. On both sides and both ends of the runway there was a raging inferno of flame. The heat from the flames was so intense that the heat would evaporate the suspended fog droplets so that the area directly over the runway for a height of 500 feet was clear of fog. The area over the runway was now clear and the flames provided a beacon for the returning bomber crews. The flames were seen by us for 100 miles from an altitude of 18,000 feet. Enemy intruder aircraft could also see the beacon and could use it as a guide to shoot down our returning aircraft while we were landing.

That night while we were returning the GEE signal was turning off and on which was the signal to watch out for enemy intruder aircraft over England. I told Don and the crew. FIDO was only used during severe pea soup fog conditions, so we had never seen it before. While we were still over France Don said that there was a huge fire burning somewhere in England. Before we were over the English Channel Don was told to divert to RAF Tuddenham. Landing using FIDO was a challenge for Don as the heated air created a huge updraft at the boundary we had to fly through. Don had to increase the landing speed by 5 mph to punch through the boundary between the cold air and the heated air to avoid being tossed higher. Any faster than that and we may run off the end of the runway. We landed a bit harder than usual.

When we landed at Tuddenham that night the runway was lit up like it was daylight. Don quickly moved the Lancaster to a dispersal area away from the flaming runway. When I got out the flames were so intense, they looked to me like an image of Hell. I sure wish I had my camera with me that night. FIDO consumed about 100,000 imperial gallons of fuel per hour. To light the flames required a flaming torch to be attached to a jeep or a bicycle which then drove fast down beside the pipes filled with fuel. I have read it is estimated that FIDO possibly saved the lives of 10,000 aircrew members which would have had to bail out or crash land with near zero visibility after being completely lost. A typical operation involving 400 aircraft would involve 2,800 crew members all returning in dense fog conditions. There always seemed to be a great deal of fog in England. All of our aircraft returned safely that night to RAF Tuddenham except for N-NAN that landed at Upwood and we were back down at 22:55.

I do not remember much about RAF Tuddenham. We had a late breakfast. At 14:25 on November 28, 1944 we flew back to Croft from Tuddenham for a 160 mile, 1 hour and 5 minute flight.

Operation number 17 in Lancaster KB-796 designated as R-ROGER on Thursday, November 30, 1944 was a 6 hour and 40 minute round trip to Duisburg, Germany at night under the illumination of a full moon. We had our breakfast at 05:30. The Navigator briefing was at 06:00 and the main briefing was at 07:00. We had quite some time to wait after the briefing before we left that afternoon. We were number 8 in order of 17 431 Squadron Lancaster crews taking part in this operation. The RCAF contributed 240 aircraft of the total 550 aircraft in this operation. We were up at 16:25. On many flights Ray would save me some work by doing astro fixes for me while I was calculating. Ray was quite good at doing the astro fixes, he enjoyed doing them and it gave him something to occupy his time when he was not on the bomb run. Regularly he would ask me if I needed an astro fix. I would always tell him, "Sure Ray. What do you have?" Until we were close to the target Ray really did not have much to do. Ray's fixes were usually accurate to three miles. He was usually sitting beside me on my Navigator's bench. The Bomb Aimer had a padded bench he would lay on during the bombing run that converted to a very small seat but, Ray liked sitting beside me.

Jack, our Tail Gunner would give me the wind drift information when I asked for it or whenever he was looking for something to do. He would line his guns to be parallel with any feature on the ground and then read off from the ring gear of the turret the number of degrees. If there was no side winds the guns would be pointed straight back. This only worked in daylight or a night with some moonlight and little cloud.

Don standing in front of the original Iroquois Indian Head on the end of the Briefing building. Photograph from the Bob Middleton Collection.

Those four marvelous Merlin engines were so noisy that the only way anybody on board could talk to each other was through the intercom. The entire time Ray sat there beside me during a trip we never said anything to each other unless it was for me asking him to help me with a GEE fix or an astro fix. We only talked business. No one on board chatted with unnecessary chatter. It was one common intercom system, and everyone heard each other. If we were all busy talking on the intercom, we would be distracted listening to each other's stories. At any moment, your full attention could be needed and if you were busy talking that could be the end for the entire crew. Movies you see of aircrews in action always show crews chatting away. I probably did the most talking of anyone, asking Ray for fixes, and giving Don fresh headings every 6 minutes.

Somewhere over Germany this night I asked Ray to give me a fix. Ray handed me the fix and after I looked at it I asked him. "What's wrong with you Ray? That fix is no good. It shows us being over the North Sea and we are over Germany. Go get me another fix." Ray came back with another fix that was not much better. "Get out of here Ray. What's wrong with you? I'll get it myself." Then, I noticed that the oxygen hose bayonet connector for his oxygen mask hose had come disconnected. He was suffering from lack of oxygen and was slightly intoxicated. After Ray was hooked up to oxygen again, he came back with a good fix but I told him I had already done it myself. Before we were at the bomb run Ray had recovered with no problems and was fine for the rest of the flight.

Shortly before we reached the target at 20:10 we were coned by at least a dozen searchlights. The inside of the aircraft was lit up brighter than day. It is a frightening experience as you know at any moment the night fighters will attack you or the radar assisted flak will zero in on you. Don yelled corkscrew, I grabbed my instruments and found something to hold onto as the floor dropped out from under me. Don dropped the bomber out of the sky. All I thought to myself was "When will this crazy ride in the dark stop and will we be alive when it stops?" After dropping thousands of feet in a few seconds Don started the climb back up and had those marvelous Merlins roaring away at full power. When Don had the aircraft back up close to our previous height the searchlights were gone. We were safe and we continued our bomb run. You did not know when all the searchlights would converge on your aircraft. It would happen in an instant with no warning. Don always kept full manual control of the aircraft at all times just for that reason. Over the target area we were at 18,000 feet flying at an IAS of 160 mph. The visibility was poor with 10/10ths cloud. The target was marked with Wanganui sky markers because you could not see the ground. The flak this night was light. We identified the target by red flares and yellow stars and bombed the same. It was considered a good attack, but nothing could be seen of the target due to the cloud cover. Even bombing through total cloud cover it was determined that more than 500 houses and many industrial facilities were destroyed. The primary target, a tar distillation plant was heavily damaged. We dropped one 4,000 pound cookie, ten 500 pound Medium Capacity bombs with a 0.025 seconds time delay and six 500 pound General Purpose bombs with 0.025 seconds time delay for a total of 12,000 pounds of bombs. All our aircraft returned to Croft except KB-788 piloted by Reginald Harrison. It was diverted to Carnaby due to loss of hydraulics caused by friendly fire from a Halifax. KB-788 belly landed at Carnaby. KB-788 was a write off and struck off charge. The crew only had minor injuries. We were back down at 23:04.

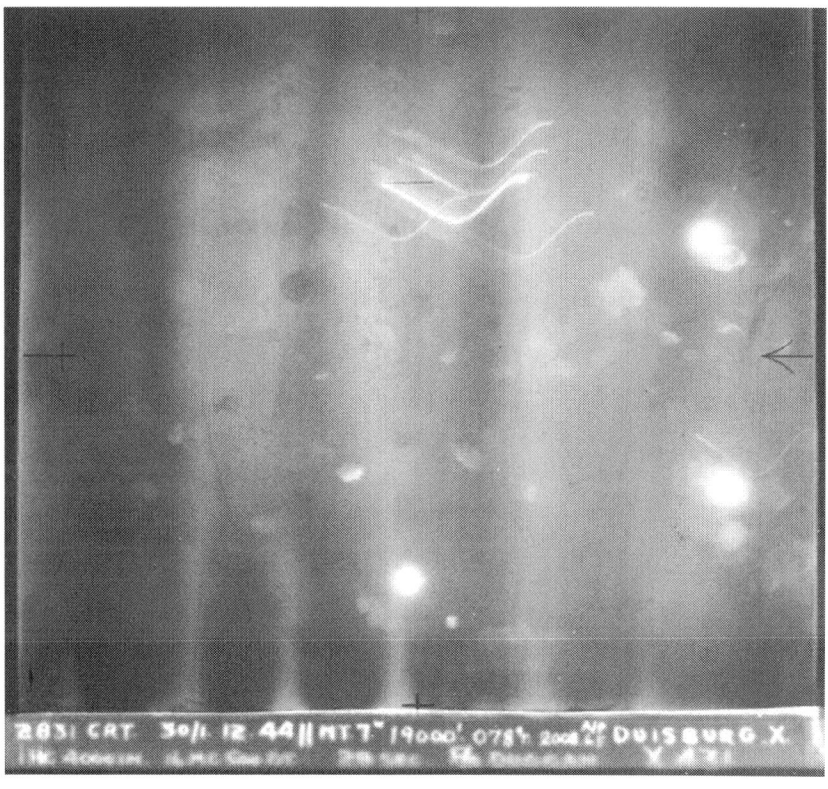

A photoflash photograph of Duisburg on November 30, 1944 taken from the Lancaster of F/O Jack Duggan and crew two minutes before we were over the target. Photograph from the Bob Middleton Collection.

Chapter 31

ROCKET FIGHTERS

On the operation to Duisburg in the daylight we saw a Messerschmitt Me 163 Komet rocket fighter for the first and last time. That aircraft was so incredibly fast. Lucky for us it was attacking other bombers that day. The Me 163 had a liquid chemical rocket engine that combined two violently incompatible chemicals together in a combustion chamber. This was a defense weapon of desperation of the Luftwaffe. It was their secret weapon that could reach the higher 30,000 foot altitudes that the B-17G Flying Fortresses of the American USAAF flew at. The regular piston engine powered Luftwaffe fighters could not easily reach that altitude. That altitude stretched their capabilities and took another five minutes to reach that altitude. Our Lancaster bombers loaded up could fly as high as 20,000 feet that could be easily reached by the Luftwaffe piston engine fighters.

The Komet fighter was extremely dangerous to fly. It had no landing gear and had to land on a skid. The fighter took off on a dolly with wheels that dropped off the bottom of the fighter once it was off of the ground. The rocket fighter could climb to 39,000 feet in a mere $3^{1/2}$ minutes. While climbing it could achieve 430 miles per hour. The Komet had 7 minutes of fuel which left only $3^{1/2}$ minutes to shoot down bombers. The rocket engine would propel the Komet fighter almost straight up through a bomber stream to 39,000 feet and then the pilot would then head downward at 500 miles per hour to fly back through a bomber stream. Because it flew so fast the pilot only had seconds to fire on a target bomber with his short range 30 mm cannon before he passed by the bombers going up and then down. The Komet pilot would be lucky to shoot at more than two bombers going up and two bombers coming down. In all the operations by the Me 163 Komet only 10 to 20 Allied bombers were shot down.

Once the Merlin engine powered P-51 Mustang aircraft using drop tanks had the range to escort our bomber streams to Germany and back the P-51 Mustang pilots would shoot up the Me 163 Komet while they were defenseless taking off or landing. This is the technique the P-51 Mustang pilots also used to destroy the Messerschmitt Me 262 jet fighters.

Photograph of a Red Tail Tuskegee P-51 Mustang from the Commemorative Air Force Collection at Mesa, Arizona, USA. The photograph was taken by photographer John Desramaux at a Brantford Air Show.

The P-51 Mustang was designed and built for the RAF by North American Aviation in the USA. With the original 1,200 horsepower Allison V12 engine without a supercharger the P-51 did not have great performance above 15,000 feet. The RAF opinion of the Allison powered Mustang was. "A bloody good airplane, only it needs a bit more poke." Ultimately at the request of the RAF, Mustang fighters were built with the 1,620 and 1,695 horsepower Packard built Merlin V-1650 series V-12 engine with two stage superchargers. There were 14,501 Mustangs built in various configurations.

This photograph is of an Me 163 Komet rocket fighter on display at the Canada Aviation and Space Museum in Ottawa, Ontario, Canada. The example of the Komet sits beside and under a Lancaster Mk. X bomber. The little propeller in the nose turned a generator for running the onboard electronics. The two wheel takeoff dolly and the landing skid can be clearly seen. The photograph was taken by Dan Middleton.

Photograph of a high flying B-17G Flying Fortress from Bob Middleton's aircraft recognition scrapbook. The picture is from the Bob Middleton Collection.

My son, Dan and I after our flight in the Commemorative Air Force B-17G Sentimental Journey at the Canadian Warplane Heritage Museum on Tuesday, July 8, 2013. The ride was for my 90th Birthday. The photograph is from the Bob Middleton Collection.

Manning a 0.50 caliber waist gun in the B-17G. Photograph by Dan Middleton.

294

Chapter 32

DECEMBER 1944

Operation number 18 in Lancaster KB-796 designated as R-ROGER on Saturday, December 2, 1944 was a 7 hour and 35 minute round trip to Hagen, Germany at night under the illumination of a full moon. We were number 2 in order of 16 431 Squadron Lancaster crews taking part in this operation. It was rare for our crew to be near the beginning of our B Flight stream. In this 500 aircraft operation there were 214 RCAF aircraft taking part. We were up at 17:21 and reached the target at 21:02. Over the target area we were at 18,000 feet flying at an IAS of 155 mph. The visibility was poor with 10/10ths cloud and tops at 16,000 feet. On route to the target there was moderate flak but over the target there was no flak. By the time we reached the target all the flak guns may have been destroyed. The target was identified by using GEE. Through the clouds large flashes of orange and yellow could be seen. We could not see the results at the time due to the cloud cover. It was estimated from photographs that over 1,600 houses and 90 industrial buildings were destroyed or seriously damaged. We dropped one 4,000 pound cookie, and sixteen 500 pound General Purpose (GP) bombs with 0.025 seconds time delay for a total of 12,000 pounds of bombs. All of our aircraft returned safely to Croft and we were back down at 00:55.

Operation number 19 was in Lancaster KB-803 designated as N-NAN on Monday, December 4, 1944 and was a 6 hour and 50 minute, 1,291 mile round trip to Karlsruhe, Germany at night. The route we took on this operation is shown on page 230. We were number 12 in order of 16 431 Squadron Lancaster crews taking part in this operation. We were up at 16:39. People have asked me how we managed to fly in the dark, by dead reckoning, radio silence, without modern navigation aids and not crash into each other. Mid-air collisions did happen. On the way to Karlsruhe that night I had gone up into the astrodome for a star shot and I saw a big flash in the clouds behind us. I figured two aircraft must have collided in the dark because at this point on the trip there was no flak or fighters. We reached the target at 19:29. Over the target area we were at 18,000 feet flying at an IAS of 160 mph. The visibility was poor with 10/10ths cloud and tops at 14,000 feet. We identified and bombed on red and green TIs. The area was well carpeted with incendiaries. The city was heavily damaged. We dropped one 4,000 pound cookie, and sixteen 500 pound Medium Capacity (MC) bombs with a 0.025 seconds time delay for a total of 12,000 pounds of bombs. All of our aircraft returned safely to Croft and we were back down at 23:32.

Operation number 20 in Lancaster KB-812 designated as F-FREDDIE on Tuesday, December 5, 1944 was a 7 hour, 1,305 mile round trip to Soest, Germany at night under a three quarter moon illumination. The route we took on this operation is shown on page 230. We were number 11 in order of 14 431 Squadron Lancaster crews taking part in this operation. This night the RCAF supplied 195 aircraft of the total bomber force of 485 aircraft. Ralph, our mid-upper gunner was not allowed to fly with us this night. He went the see the Medical Officer because he had a bad cold and was very congested. The Medical Officer grounded him until the cold cleared. Being congested and descending in a non-pressurized aircraft can cause your ears extreme pain and or cause your ear drums to burst. Ralph was so upset that he would not be going with us on that 7 hour trip to Soest that night that he was crying. I believe that sometime in our experiences together as a team we had become a Band of Brothers. That night our replacement mid-upper gunner was from A Flight.

We were up at 16:39 and reached the target at 21:29. Over the target area we were at 18,000 feet flying at an IAS of 160 mph. The visibility over the target was poor with 10/10ths cloud. We bombed using GEE as the red TIs and green TIs were obscured by cloud.

Ralph our mid-upper gunner on the left and Jack our rear gunner on the right standing in front of a Lancaster rear turret. The photograph is from the Bob Middleton Collection.

Don noted that there was a large explosion at 21:28. The attack was well concentrated, and the area was very well carpeted with incendiaries causing a great deal of damage to the railway lines and the railway buildings. We dropped one 4,000 pound cookie, and twelve 360 pound small bomb containers, SBC, of 4 pound incendiaries for a total of 8,320 pounds of bombs. All of our aircraft returned safely to Croft and we were back down at 23:32.

The entire time we were away I think Ralph was feeling incredibly guilty that he could not go with us and was worried that we may not come back. You never saw a Mid-Upper Gunner so happy to see the rest of his crewmates arrive back at base still alive.

BASE- POS'N A- READING- 5047 0018E- 5010 0130E
4950 0410E -5110 0550E- 5200 0650E-
SOEST- 5130 0810E-5035 0715E
5035 0610E 5015 0520 -5106 0235E
ORFORDNESS - POS'N A- BASE
10/10 CLOUD OVER TARGET -BOMBED ON GEE -MODERATE
HEAVY FLAK OVER TARGET. BIG EXPLOSIONS SEEN
VERY GOOD ATTACK   (RUHR)

My logbook details for our trip to Soest December 5, 1944 showing all our turning points. From the Bob Middleton Collection.

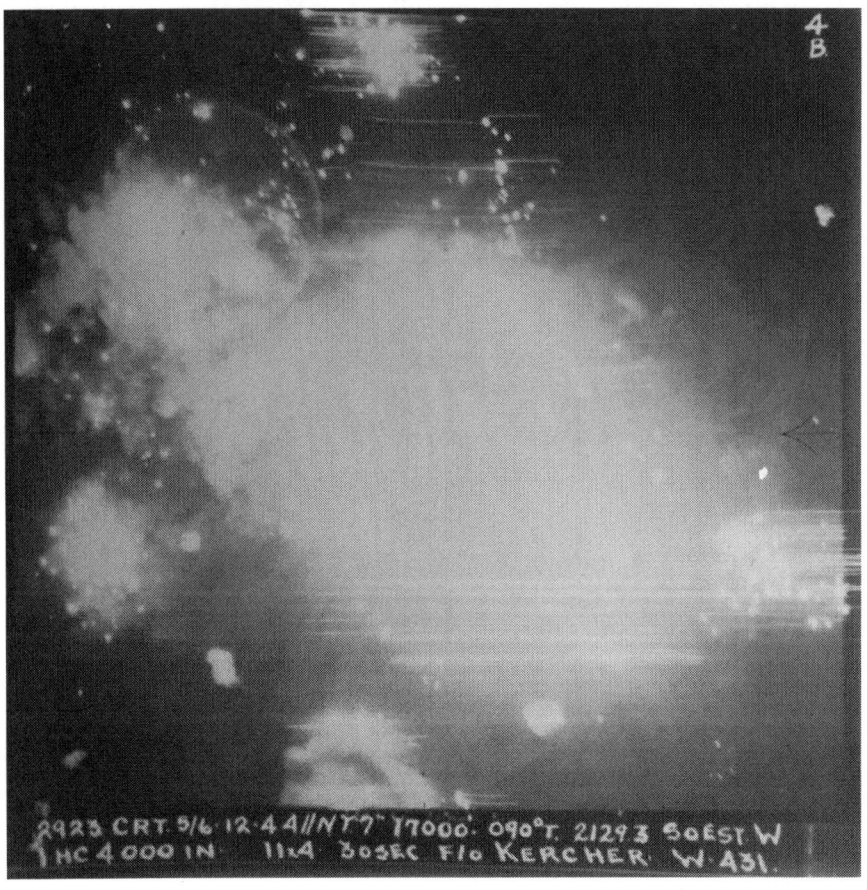

Photoflash photograph of Soest from the bomber of Pilot George E. Kercher. This is all smoke and bomb blasts. We dropped our bombs 2 seconds later at 21:29:5. The photograph is from the Bob Middleton Collection.

Operation number 21 in Lancaster KB-821 designated as P-PETER on Wednesday, December 6, 1944 was a 6 hour and 45 minute round trip to Osnabrück, Germany at night under the illumination of a half moon. This night Bomber Command sent 1,269 aircraft to bomb Osnabrück, Merseburg and Giessen. The RCAF supplied 200 aircraft to our target that night. We were number 3 in order of 12 431 Squadron Lancaster crews taking part in this operation. We were up at 16:17 and reached the target at 19:44. Over the target area we were at 20,000 feet flying at an IAS of 160 mph. We were really high up this night.

This is a photograph looking back from the Navigator's position showing the Wireless Operator's bench seat and the main spar. The main spar is about 3 feet high and is a formidable obstacle. I would have to climb over it in the dark while the aircraft was gyrating out of control if I had to bail out. The photograph was taken by Karl Kjarsgaard inside the Canadian Lancaster FM-159 at the Bomber Command Museum in Nanton, Alberta.

The visibility was poor with 10/10ths cloud and tops above 21,000 feet. We identified and bombed using GEE on the run in. The bombing was scattered and not much was seen through the clouds. Explosions were seen under the clouds. A good glow was seen with one large explosion at 19:43 lasting ten seconds. There was not a great deal of fighter activity as the Luftwaffe fighter force was spread out over the three targets. We dropped twenty 500 pound MC bombs with 0.025 seconds time delay for a total of 10,000 pounds of bombs. During the return leg of this trip I noticed a small flash of light just to my left. When I turned to look, I saw Ken Smith our Wireless Operator crumpled up lying on the floor against the corner of the main spar and the starboard side of the fuselage. He had been changing a transmitter tube in the Collins ART-13 transmitter and it gave him a jolt that sent him flying. Ken picked himself off the floor and once he recovered continued working on the wireless transmitter. All of our aircraft returned safely to Croft and we were back down at 22:31.

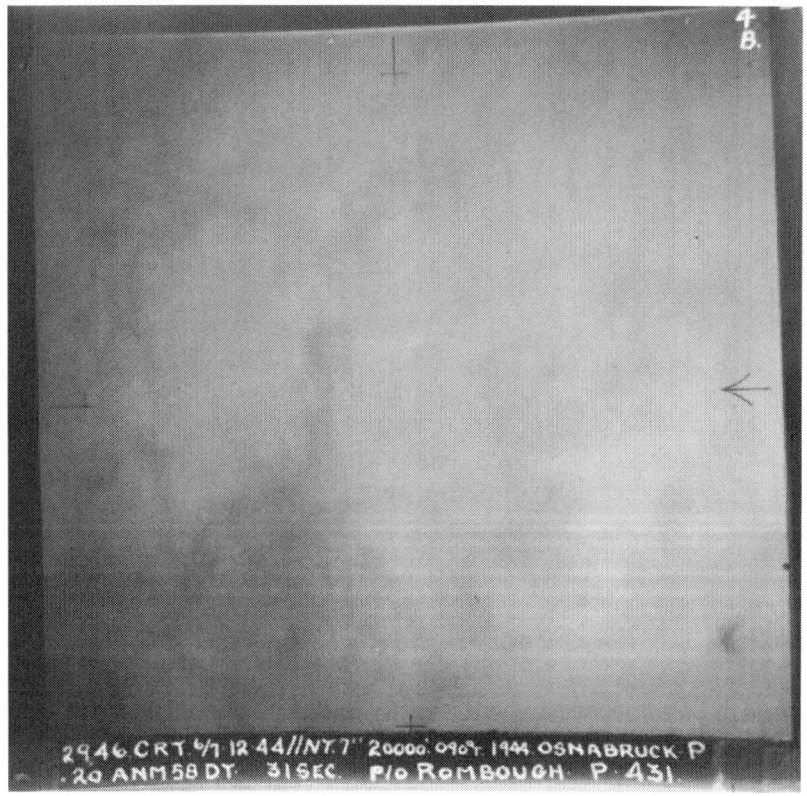

Photoflash photograph from our Lancaster N-NAN. This is what 10/10ths cloud and smoke looked like from 20,000 feet at night. This is the only photograph that Don had not picked up before me. I suppose Don had no interest in collecting a picture of cloud and smoke. The photograph is from the Bob Middleton Collection.

At 14:30 on Tuesday, December 12, 1944 we went out in Lancaster KB-803, N-NAN as part of a group gaggle exercise for a 4 hour and 30 minute cross-country trip practicing bombing using the H2S radar.

Operation number 22 in Lancaster KB-803 designated as N-NAN on Friday, December 15, 1944 was a 6 hour and 15 minute, 1,276 mile round trip to bomb a chemical factory at Ludwigshafen, Germany at night with no moonlight. The route we took on this operation is shown on page 230. We were number 8 in order of 17 431 Squadron Lancaster crews taking part in this operation. We were up at 14:30 and reached the target at 18:36. Shortly after we crossed the coast of France the sky was pitch black with no moon. Up until now we had never flown at night without some moonlight. It was incredible to look down at the ground and see absolutely nothing. There was only darkness and not a single speck of light anywhere. While flying over Europe since the blackout it was hard to imagine none of the lights from the ground being there. The view of the stars was incredible looking through the astrodome while flying above the clouds in the crystal clear sky 4 miles closer to the heavens without any light pollution from the ground. Over the target area we were at 19,000 feet flying at an IAS of 160 mph. The visibility was good with 4/10ths patchy cloud. There was moderate and heavy flak and some searchlights over the target area. We identified the red and green TIs and bombed on the green TIs. There were 15 very large well grouped red and orange explosions. Very large fires were seen. We dropped one 4,000 pound cookie, and fourteen 500 pound SBC incendiary clusters for a total of 11,000 pounds of bombs.

As we were leaving the target area we saw one Lancaster hit by something. In the dark it was hard to see if it was flak or a fighter. There were some flames from one engine. We were all yelling through the intercom "Push the Graviner button." Their Flight Engineer must have operated the Graviner engine fire extinguisher for the flames started to settle down. After a few moments however the flames started up again and the aircraft began to leave a trail of smoke and sparks that looked like fireworks. We were all yelling at them to get out. It felt surreal like we were an audience watching and cheering on our team at some extreme sporting event. We were heading home, and they were on their way to the target, and we never did see if they managed to put out the flames or bail out. We counted our lucky stars that we had escaped their fate.

All our aircraft returned safely to England but were diverted to the USAAF base at Framlingham. We got back down at 20:50 in time for a late dinner. We had always heard that the USAAF bases had great food and good accommodations. The food was not much better than Croft but at least they did not serve mutton. However, they did have really good fresh orange juice. I believe I had hamburgers along with my egg. The barracks we stayed in were worse than Croft and the conditions were poor. The entire place was not very well taken care of. At 13:30 on December 16, 1944 we flew 190 miles back to Croft from Framlingham in Lancaster KB-803 N-NAN for a one hour trip.

Before we left Framlingham one of our Croft pilots who had just finished his tour of operations buzzed the tower, runway and passed just a few feet above our Lancaster as he was leaving. We were sitting in our Lancaster third in line for takeoff watching the show. He was so low that his starboard wingtip looked to be only 3 feet above the ground at one point. When he got back to Croft he buzzed the tower there as well. That pilot ended up going to the Commissioned Officers' jail called the Glass House at Sheffield for the rest of his time in England. I was told that the jailed Commissioned Officers took great pleasure in catching their non-commissioned Jailers not saluting them. Their punishment would be ditch digging or a similar manual labor. That pilot was probably so happy that he was finished flying in the terrifying skies over occupied Europe that he momentarily lost his sense of reason. For a pilot to make it all the way to the end of a tour took incredible courage, fortitude and a sense of duty. During WWII RCAF Bomber Command Pilots that completed a full tour were awarded the Distinguished Flying Cross, DFC. I believe the pilot had the most terrifying seat in the aircraft. The pilot sat in his seat and saw fighters, flak, searchlights, our aircraft exploding or going down in the sky around his aircraft and the target burning. He had to fly the aircraft and could not go anywhere to hide from the terror all around him. The Flight Engineer had the same view as the pilot but, he had other duties such as shoving Window out of the aircraft that would take him away from the cockpit for short periods. I would go out and look at the scene for short periods and then go back to the imagined safety of my position in the aircraft to do my navigation duties. Ken, our Wireless Operator never went past me to venture up front to look out to see what was going on outside our aircraft. I do not know but he may have looked out through the astro dome that was above his position to see some of the action. At the Remembrance Day ceremony at the Canadian Warplane Heritage Museum in 2015 a group of 14 Lancaster crew members was assembled. There was one WWII Lancaster pilot in that reenacted Lancaster crew that told my son that he had never seen a Lancaster since 1945. Up until then for 70 years he had not been interested to see one.

© Copyright Art Prints Direct UK

This is an accurate painting of the scene of searchlights, flak and a burning target through the canopy of a Lancaster. The Pilot and the Flight Engineer would have to look at a scene like this until the aircraft left the target area. This painting is exactly what I saw as a Nosy Navigator while standing behind the Flight Engineer. In the print you can see the steel armor plate behind the Pilot's head. The Bomb Aimer is in the front nose looking out through his perspex at the scene below him. The painting is by artist Mike Steele-Morgan and is courtesy of Art Prints Direct UK.

The Distinguished Flying Cross, DFC. "The cross is awarded to officers and Warrant Officers for an act or acts of valour, courage or devotion to duty performed whist flying in active operations against the enemy." The photograph was taken at the Canadian War Museum, Ottawa, Canada

Photoflash photograph from Pilot M. A. Mawhinney's 431 B Flight Lancaster taken at 18:34:1, two minutes before we dropped our bombs on Friday, December 15, 1944. There is lots of smoke and the target indicators can be seen in the upper right corner of the photograph. The photograph is from the Bob Middleton Collection.

304

At Croft we were living in extremely basic Nissen huts. It is amazing that after a few weeks I became accustomed to my surroundings and the place felt like home. The Nissen huts that we were living in did not have insulation on the walls or the ceiling. The only heat was from a 10 inch diameter coal burning stove. To get more heat from the stove we removed the fire bricks from the stove and filled it with more coal. We went through 3 stoves while I was there as they would eventually collapse from the heat. In the winter of 1944 and 1945 the outside temperatures did dip below freezing at night. When we woke up on winter mornings, we could see our breath as the stove would have gone out during the night. We would find frost on our blankets from our breath.

A photograph of the inside of our Commissioned Officers Quarters Nissen hut. We are huddled around the tiny stove. That is the chimney stack going through the ceiling. That is Art standing beside the stove pipe. Our hut was the same as the non-commissioned Officers huts. The photograph is from the Bob Middleton Collection.

Operation number 23 in Lancaster KB-803 designated as N-NAN on Sunday, December 17, 1944 was a 6 hour and 30 minute round trip to Duisburg, Germany at dawn. When we took off from Croft there was the illumination of a sliver of a moon. We were number 10 in order of 17 431 Squadron Lancaster crews taking part in this early morning operation. I was up at 23:00 for the midnight briefing. We were up at 02:52 and reached the target at 06:32. Over the target area we were at 18,000 feet flying at an IAS of 175 mph in the daylight. The visibility was poor with dense 10/10ths clouds. There was moderate to heavy flak. We identified and bombed using Wanganui sky markers and GEE. No results could be seen but there was a solid red glow under the clouds. We dropped one 4,000 pound cookie, and fourteen 500 pound No. 14 SBC incendiary clusters. Our squadron was usually at the end of raids and we usually carried cookies and incendiaries.

Photograph of the outboard port Merlin engine in Lancaster KB-726 at the Canadian Warplane Heritage Museum at Hamilton, Ontario. In this picture you can see all the hoses, pipes and wiring that can be damaged by enemy action or simply fail. The white bottle on the right is part of the Graviner engine fire extinguishing system. Photograph was taken by Dan Middleton.

At the end of the raids by the end of 1944 and in 1945 the German defenses were weaker as the fighters were running out of fuel and heading back to their base. Parts of the flak batteries would have been put out of commission by the end of each raid. If you had to bail out near the end of the raid it was very dangerous as the folks you just bombed wanted to kill you. A good rule was to avoid parachuting into an area you had just bombed.

As we crossed the English Channel that morning while returning on Monday, December 18, 1945 Art called Don to tell him that the port outer engine appeared to be in trouble. The oil pressure was falling, and Art could see a mist of oil trailing the engine. Don asked how serious it was. Art told Don to feather the propeller and shut off the engine.

Don asked me to quickly figure out where the nearest aerodrome was that we could set NAN down. I quickly worked out that the RAF aerodrome at West Raynham was the closest place. Don called up the control tower at West Raynham on the R/T for permission to land. Permission was granted and we landed at West Raynham at 09:21. The rest of the 431 squadron returned safely to Croft and some alternate aerodromes. This RAF aerodrome was home of two de Havilland Mosquito squadrons, numbers 141 and 239. By the time we parked N-NAN in the dispersal area we were in time for lunch. I went into the Officers' mess and discovered they had white tablecloths on the tables, and we sat down and we were served by the WAAFs. The lunch was very good, much better than the mutton that was served at Croft. Way better than the food at the USAAF aerodrome. They were serving freshly sliced roast beef. We had always heard that the food at the RAF aerodromes was not very good. That was some sort of false rumor that someone in the RCAF command must have fabricated so we would not feel so bad about RCAF food. After we had lunch Art went to work with some of the West Raynham ground crew to come up with a temporary patch for the broken pipe on the oil cooler radiator. A piece of rubber hose and some clamps did the trick to get us safely back to Croft.

This was the first time I had actually been able to go, and see, and touch, a de Havilland Mosquito. The aircraft was very impressive with the very smooth skin and tapered lines with no rivets. It was such a beautiful aircraft. I was amazed at how tremendous this aircraft was being made only of balsa wood and plywood. So much different than the wooden Avro Anson trainers we trained in. The Mosquito Mk. VIII was the fastest propeller aircraft in the war with a top speed of 436 miles per hour and a cruise speed of 295 miles per hour. The Mosquito B. Mk. XVI bomber version was unarmed and regularly dropped 4,000 pound cookies on Berlin in nuisance raids. The Mk. XVI Mosquito bomber had two 1,710 horsepower Merlin engines with 2 stage superchargers that enabled the Mosquito to fly at 37,000 feet at over 300 miles per hour while carrying a cookie. The Mosquito bomber had no armament as there was really no enemy aircraft that could intercept it. It flew way too high and fast for any German flak or searchlights. The Mk. XVI Mosquito bomber made our Lancaster Mk. X bomber cruising at 160 miles per hour seem so slow. The Mosquito was not as fast as the Messerschmitt Me 262 jet powered fighter with its top speed of 540 miles per hour, but the Mosquito pilots said that the Mosquito was more maneuverable than the Me 262.

The de Havilland Mosquito was an aircraft that was almost never built. The Mosquito was built out of wood as there was a restriction on aluminum for building aircraft and especially some new unproven aircraft. The idea that a bomber could fly so fast and so high that it did not need defensive armament sounded ridiculous to many people and in particular to Lord Beaverbrook, Minister of Aircraft Production. Finally, the Mosquito project found a supporter in Air Marshal Sir Wilfrid Freeman, Air Member for Research and Development. When Geoffrey de Havilland re-submitted the unarmed bomber for reconsideration on September 6, 1939, three days after the outbreak of the Second Word War, Freeman took up the cause and won approval for the construction of the prototype despite the high priority given to existing types of bombers. The many versions of the Mosquito aircraft went on to become marvelous fighters, bombers and recognizance aircraft. The Mosquitos that were on the West Raynham aerodrome squadrons were night fighters and intruders of the Mk. VII type.

At 19:00 on Monday, December 18, 1945 we left West Raynham and flew back 145 miles to Croft on a one hour flight.

Photograph of a de Havilland Mosquito Fighter at the Canadian Warplane Heritage Museum on Father's Day, June 15, 2014. Photographed by Dan Middleton.

Photograph of Don our Skipper posing with our favorite Lancaster, N-NAN. The photograph is from the Bob Middleton Collection.

Ray as a Commissioned Officer, our Batman, and I in late December of 1944. We are standing in front of an air raid shelter. Sometime in November of 1944 after the professional picture had been taken of the crew at Darlington Ray became a Commissioned Officer. The photograph is from the Bob Middleton Collection.

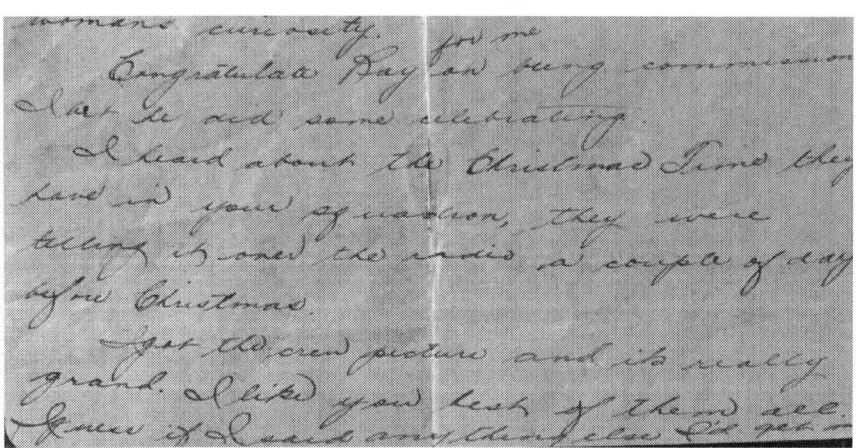

A letter that Pat wrote to me after receiving the formal picture of the crew in one letter and hearing about Ray becoming a Commissioned Officer in another letter. Photograph from the Bob Middleton Collection.

As good luck would have it after the Duisburg operation our crew was now on a 10 day leave just before Christmas 1944 and we would not have to return to battle in the skies until the New Year of 1945. What an awesome Christmas present. The package of Christmas presents had arrived from Mom and Dad. The best part of the package was the carton containing 1,000 cigarettes in packages of 20 from the Orange Lodge. One of the benefits of having that Grand Orange Lodge Travelling Certificate was the cartons of cigarettes I received 4 times while I was in England. I gave away many packages of cigarettes as I could not smoke them all by myself. I was a popular guy when a new case of cigarettes arrived. In England at that time, you bought loose cigarettes from a tobacconist and then you put them in your metal cigarette case.

Jack Cornock asked me what I was doing for our leave. I told him I was probably going to go to London and hang around there. Jack told me he had been invited to visit at his cousin's place near Carlisle a few miles from the west coast of northern England. This is a cousin whom Jack had never met. Jack's cousin owned the Tarn End House Hotel and summer resort that was 10 miles east of Carlisle two miles south of the village of Brampton. The hotel was about 30 miles farther north than Croft and 60 miles to the west. The train trip from the Eryholme station took about two hours to get to the train station at Carlisle. Jack's cousin picked us up from the train station and we drove about ten miles to the hotel.

The place was huge and absolutely beautiful with high ceilings large windows and massive fireplaces located in a beautiful rolling English countryside. The main building overlooks a small kettle lake named Talkin Tarn. Being that this was the off season and there were no guests in the hotel Jack, and I had our pick of any room we desired. Gosh, a room all to myself and it even had a sink with running water too. Sure beat the pants off the Nissen hut at Croft. The place was still quite busy with all of his cousins, friends and relatives staying there for the Christmas holiday. It was a great ongoing party with plenty of beer and alcohol for a few days. Besides the resort and hotel Jack's cousin also owned a small sheep farm that also had a few pigs. The farm had a hand cranked contraption that sliced up turnips and carrots to feed the sheep and the pigs that Jack and I were operating to help out.

311

The Tarn End House Hotel as it appeared in the 1990s. The hotel was purchased by the Hogarth family in 2018 and they are currently restoring the hotel to its original beauty. The photograph is courtesy of the Hogarth Family.

One night Jack's cousin asked me if I wanted to take this great huge Clydesdale draft horse back to the farmer that owns it. They had borrowed it to pull wagons around the property. I asked, "Well where is the farm and how do I get there?" He said, "Oh, the horse knows." So, he helped me up on the horse and told the horse "Home." So away I went down a lane and then along a road. The whole time on the road the huge hooves of the horse going clonk, clonk, clonk. Eventually the horse and I turned into a driveway to a farm and the farmer came out and greeted me. The farmer asked me who I was. I told him I was a friend of a fellow who is the cousin of the fellow that owns the Tarn End Hotel up the road. He said "Oh great let me help you down from the horse. Thank you for bringing him back." Goodness, that horse was about eight feet high, and I needed some help. We chatted for a bit while the farmer drove me back to the hotel.

While we were there, we ate great. I suppose I ate some sheep that was prepared more tastefully than the cooks at Croft did and lots of pork that was a delicacy at the time. The pigs on the farm were not actually legal to have for personal eating. Even if you raised your own meat you were supposed to be restricted to the same ration limits as the people that had to buy food. Well, we ate great. The ration coupons that we were given when we left Croft, we gave to Jack's cousin to help him out with other food he had to buy.

To help out around the place during the day we went up the hill to the farm to cut and split wood and harvest turnips and carrots. We did odd jobs around the place. Jack's cousin did not charge us anything for the accommodations and all we could eat and drink. A couple of times we took Jack's cousins and some friends to the pub just 2 miles up the road in Brampton, England. Brampton is shown on the map on page 102.

On Christmas Day we were all making quite merry and Barb one of the cousin's sisters asked me to do the polka with her. She said it was really easy and she would show me. I told her that I really did not know what to do but with some deliberation and the assistance of the three beers I said, "Sure." As it turned out I did the polka well. The polka that we were dancing was the same one the guests were doing at Mr. Fezziwig's Christmas party in the Charles Dickens *Christmas Carol* movie starring Alistair Sim.

Sometime after Christmas and before New Year's we made our way back by train to Croft. In the midst of that war, and all the operations over Germany completed, and the operations yet to do, that was a Christmas to remember forever. Thanks Jack. Before Jack and I returned we knew we still had eight to ten operations to complete before we would be screened for non-combat Instructor duties. In December 1944 we did not know how much longer the war would last or when we could go back home.

Chapter 33

HAPPY NEW YEAR 1945

On the morning of Tuesday, January 2, 1945 we walked into the briefing room and when the curtain was pulled back from the map the red line went all the way to Nuremberg, Germany. There were many groans and my stomach started to churn more than normal. That was a long 9 hour trip. This trip would be a real test of my abilities as a navigator with the 8 turning points for me to navigate with precision a long way from home.

The last time that Bomber Command visited Nuremberg, Germany was on the night of March 29 and 30 in 1944. About 800 aircraft went to Nuremberg that night and 95 aircraft and crews did not return to England. That night the sky was clear. There was a crescent moon and they had turning points but with long straight legs. They had to take a more direct route to maximize the bomb load and conserve fuel. Our aircraft were constantly harassed by Luftwaffe fighters to and from Nuremberg. At that time, our fighter escorts did not have the range to protect the bomber gaggle that far from England. Due to head winds much of the force was still over France on the return leg when the sun was coming up. Many more aircraft were write-offs after landing besides those that had Failed to Return. That was the worst night for Bomber Command of World War II. The attack was scattered and not very effective. We did not know about this early disaster as it was never really acknowledged by Bomber Command. 431 Squadron did not participate in that operation and the majority of those crews at Croft at the end of March 1944 had finished their tours by January 1945, so there were no crews on the base that would have remembered the disaster. I did not know about the Nuremberg disaster until reading about it many years later.

Looking at our trips to Nuremberg and Munich, on page 230 you can see those were direct routes as well. It was later in the war and we had fighter coverage all the way to the targets. Our fighter escorts flew high overhead, and we did not see them.

Nuremberg is in Bavaria in the southern part of Germany and was also known as Nürnberg. Nuremberg is the English way of saying Nürnberg. In the 1930s Nürnberg became the centre of the Nazi party. It was also the city that hosted the Nuremberg Trials.

Operation number 24 in Lancaster KB-827 designated as M-MOTHER on Tuesday, January 2, 1945 was a 9 hour and 19 minute, 1,540 mile round trip to bomb the armament plants at Nuremberg, Germany at night. The moon was almost full. There were only 49 RCAF bombers out of the total of 521 bombers in this operation. We were number 8 in order of 16 431 Squadron Lancaster crews taking part in this operation. The Navigator briefing was at 11:00 and the main briefing was at 12:00. We were up at 14:54 and reached the target at 19:41. Over the target area we were at 16,000 feet flying at an IAS of 160 mph. There was heavy flak that night. We were chased by some predictive flak that night and Don changed course and banked to port or starboard to escape from it. This was a long, hazardous trip. The weather was clear, and Ray identified the target by red and green TIs. He bombed on the centre of the smoke and fires as per direction from the Master Bomber. A large area was covered by fires and explosions. It was a very good attack. There were 15 very large well grouped hits with red and orange explosions. We dropped one 4,000 pound cookie, and fourteen Mk. 14 500 pound SBC incendiary clusters.

This bombing of Nuremberg caused the greatest damages to the city of all the bombing that occurred there during WWII. In total on the raid were 514 Lancasters and 7 Mosquito Pathfinders. In all 1,825 tons of high explosives and 479 tons of incendiaries were dropped by all the Squadrons involved. There was complete destruction of the Nuremberg old town with permanent damages to historic buildings and structures.

Before we could land at Croft, we had to do the 40 mile long Great

Circuit at 1,500 feet around Middleton St. George and Croft. The tower controller said, "Big Tree to Fly Swat Mother Great Circuit at 1,500." A delay landing was just what we did not want after all those flying hours. While flying over Middleton St. George we saw Lancaster KB-700 the Ruhr Express burning on the ground. The Ruhr Express had a hydraulic failure, and the flaps could not be operated which caused it to hit fast and hard while landing. It was only brought to a stop about 50 feet past the end of the runway. The pilot needed to move the aircraft off the runway as soon as possible in case of other aircraft overshooting the runway. While turning off the runway the outer starboard propeller hit a trench digging machine that a civilian worker had carelessly left at the end of the runway. The collision ruptured a fuel tank and within seconds the Ruhr Express was ablaze. The crew managed to get out safely. The Ruhr Express after 49 operations was a total loss, however. It was such a shame as the Ruhr Express, the first Canadian built Lancaster was to be flown back to Canada after operation 50 to be used in Victory War Bond drives back in Canada. All our aircraft returned safely to Croft and we finally landed at 00:04.

We could not keep any of our logs or charts that came out of the aircraft after any of our trips. We had to hand these in during our debriefing. I only have the condensed record in my own logbook of all our trips. I have always been rather miffed that we could not have our charts and records back. As it turns out it seems that I was also a sneaky navigator. At Christmas 2019 when my son, Dan brought my souvenirs out of my RCAF trunk we found my actual navigation chart for the trip to Nuremberg. The chart was folded over 8 times so it would have fit nicely into my pocket for none to see. On my navigator chart I spelled the target Nürnberg.

FTR On January 6, 1945 the Lancaster KB-821 SE-P flown by Pilot Officer Bernard Adilman and crew failed to return while on an operation to Hannau, Germany. All the members of the crew perished. All the crew members were on trip 6 of their second tour. They had been on 41 operations altogether. Three crew members are buried at Durnbach War Cemetery in Germany and the other four are commemorated at the Runnymede Memorial at Surrey, UK.

My RCAF trunk that I brought home with me. I purchased it in March 1944. It held all my belongings for the duration of my time in the UK. I was surprised everything is still in the trunk as Davey and Danny used to play with everything in the trunk when they were young children.

This is me standing at the back of our Nissen hut with my bicycle. This is the bicycle that was stolen. Notice that I was standing in snow. From the Bob Middleton Collection.

My navigation chart for our January 2, 1945 trip to Nuremberg, Germany. From the Bob Middleton Collection.

Operation number 25 in Lancaster KB-803 designated as N-NAN on Sunday, January 7, 1945 was an 8 hour and 50 minute, 1,650 mile round trip to Munich, Germany at night under the illumination of a half moon. The route we took on this operation is shown on page 230. We were number 5 in order of 9 431 Squadron Lancaster crews taking part in this operation. The Navigator briefing was at 14:00 and the main briefing was at 15:00. We were up at 18:20 and reached the target at 22:32.

On the way to Munich, we passed by the north face of the 9,000 foot high Silvretta Alps while flying over Lake Constance, Switzerland. Flying at about 7,000 feet we were seeking protection by the mountains from the probing German radar. We were a few thousand feet above the tree line and the half moon was lighting up the mountains and the evergreens growing on the face. A half-moon like that was not good for flying at night as we could be seen quite easily. Our aircraft made a marvelous silhouette against the moonlit sky. It was an absolutely beautiful surreal Currier and Ives picture postcard type of scene. I wondered what we were doing up here with all this natural beauty and we had thousands of pounds of bombs and incendiaries in the bomb bay that we were going to drop on Munich in less than one hour. It just seemed cruel and unreal. But this was total war and we had to win or become slaves to the Nazi regime.

When we reached the target area at 22:32 we were at 18,500 feet flying at an IAS of 160 mph. We were bombing the marshalling yards and factories. The visibility was poor with 10/10ths cloud with their tops at 10,000 feet. Ray identified red sky markers with green stars and bombed blind using my H2S directions. There was a great glow under the clouds, but the results were impossible to assess.

We all had a very close call that night. We had been flying in a straight course for 5 or 6 minutes after Ray had dropped the bombs and the photo flash had gone off and we should have turned around for home. The conversation went like this. Don said, "Bob shouldn't we have started the turns for our return trip?" I told Don rather rudely "I'll bloody well let you know when it is time to start the turns." There were always three 60 degree turns to start the return trip. It sounded like something was wrong with me. Don told Ray, "Go and find out what is wrong with Bob. He does not sound right." Ray actually knew what to look for as his oxygen hose had become disconnected on a previous operation one night when he could not get an astro fix for me. Ray found that my oxygen hose bayonet connector had become disconnected. The connector may have been caught on a parachute snap just after I had gone up front to look out through the canopy to see the target. I was experiencing the same effect as when I did not wear the oxygen mask in the decompression chamber in Belleville. I did not remember anything before Ray reconnected my oxygen. Like being intoxicated I was off in my own little world and I did not appreciate Don disturbing me. It was so fortunate that I had experienced the lack of oxygen two years ago in the decompression chamber in Belleville. I was not freaked out and I was able to do my job in a short amount of time. By the time I had recovered enough to give directions to Don we had gone about 30 miles past Munich. After that recovery I said to Don "See that bright star over there. That is Jupiter. Fly towards Jupiter until I get an astro fix." That would have us flying west towards home. After I had recovered a little bit more I went and took that astro fix. I gave Don a course to fly and 15 minutes later Don asked, "What is that town to the south of us?" I told Don "I think it is the town of Ulm." The rest of the crew giggled a bit because I was not quite sure where we were yet. I was still somewhat fuzzy from the lack of oxygen. Quite amazing the fellows all were joking in a situation that may have seen us shot down. But, what else could you do? Panic would not help. A little while later after passing Ulm Don said, "I see two search lights over there and I'm going to fly between them." "Sounds like a good idea Don." As we flew between the searchlights all hell broke loose. Suddenly there was flak exploding all around us.

We were probably the only aircraft in the sky as we were off course, separated from the gaggle and late. Easy pickings for the radar controlled flak guns. Jack the tail gunner asked Ralph the mid-upper gunner "What are you firing at? I don't see anything." Ralph told Jack, "I'm not firing. That smell is the cordite in the flak. That is flak exploding all around us my friend." Jack was shouting out that the flak was so thick they could taxi across it. I do not think flak had ever come that close to us at any time up until that night. We had never smelled cordite in the aircraft before and I had never seen flak so thick before. I do not remember the ride through the flak as being rough. When we returned, we found 3 one inch diameter holes in the side of the fuselage just behind the wing. We could smell the flak because it had gone through the thin aluminum skin and was smoldering inside the aircraft. The flak and the searchlights served as a good landmark. We were flying over Stuttgart, the city that had a searchlight gap over the city. Searchlights were on both sides of the town, but no searchlights were in the centre of town. Only in September 2020 did I learn that Stuttgart had several huge flak towers in the city with eight massive 128 mm flak guns that hurled huge 5 inch diameter 57 pound explosive projectiles into the sky. Each flak gun could fire at 20 rounds per minute. I think this is what was referred to as heavy flak at our briefings. We kept going and the flak and searchlights soon disappeared behind us. After flying through Hell over Stuttgart that night and getting through we considered ourselves extremely lucky. It was a very good attack on Munich. We dropped one 4,000 pound cookie, and fourteen 500 pound SBC incendiary clusters for a total of 11,000 pounds of bombs.

All our aircraft returned safely but were all diverted to RAF Winthorpe due to lousy winter weather at Croft in the north of England. Everything near Croft and Middleton St. George was fog and snow bound. Most of the squadron landed at RAF Winthorpe which is in Nottinghamshire 120 miles south of Croft. We landed at Winthorpe at 03:10. Currently the Newark Air Museum is at RAF Winthorpe.

RAF Winthorpe was a permanent Heavy Conversion Unit (HCU) No. 1661 that was flying old Sterling 4 engine heavy bombers built by Short Aircraft. The food at the aerodrome was marvelous. We had roast beef that was sliced in front of us and 4 different styles of potatoes plus all the fixings. We had desserts galore. There was a buffet that was set out the same as you would find on a cruise ship. The tables had white tablecloths. The Officers' mess was in a building that had a huge fireplace with a long hearth that extended into the room. We had that fireplace loaded with wood and we had a huge fire that was even out on that long hearth. It was such a warm pleasant place after freezing at cold and damp Croft in our non-insulated corrugated steel Nissen huts. During the 1944/45 winter at Croft the only time we were really ever warm was when we were up flying. The cabin heat in both the Halifax and the Lancaster was great. During the month of January 1945 there were a few big snowstorms, and the temperature was mighty cold below freezing. This was the worst winter in years. At Croft that winter for a few days most of the plumbing froze and there were only three toilets working. We were at Winthorpe for three days and we did not have to do a thing except relax. We were surprised the Commander of the school did not have us up doing any flying or doing some types of chores. We burnt all of their wood, ate all their food, and drank all their beer while there. They must have been glad to see the uncivilized horde of Colonials leave the place. Maybe we were treated so well since many of the crews diverted there had well over 20 combat operations. In our experiences we discovered that the Americans had the worst food. The RAF by far had the very best food and the best Officers' mess. The food at our Croft Officers' mess was somewhere in the middle.

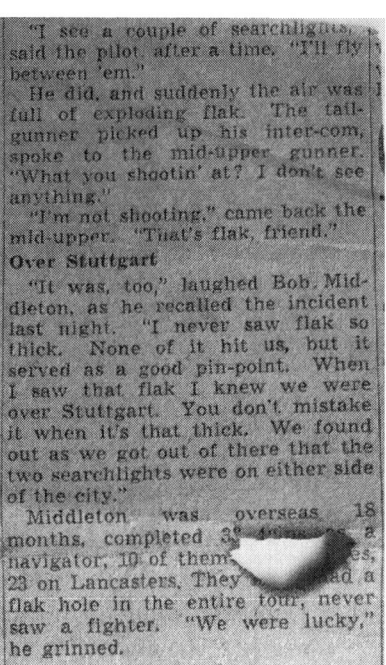

"I see a couple of searchlights," said the pilot, after a time, "I'll fly between 'em."

He did, and suddenly the air was full of exploding flak. The tail-gunner picked up his inter-com, spoke to the mid-upper gunner. "What you shootin' at? I don't see anything."

"I'm not shooting," came back the mid-upper. "That's flak, friend."

Over Stuttgart

"It was, too," laughed Bob Middleton, as he recalled the incident last night. "I never saw flak so thick. None of it hit us, but it served as a good pin-point. When I saw that flak I knew we were over Stuttgart. You don't mistake it when it's that thick. We found out as we got out of there that the two searchlights were on either side of the city."

Middleton was overseas 18 months, completed ?? ??????, a navigator, 10 of them ??????, 23 on Lancasters. They ?????? a flak hole in the entire tour, never saw a fighter. "We were lucky," he grinned.

Part of a newspaper clipping about our Munich return trip adventure from the April 27, 1945 edition of The Globe and Mail. I have always said, "We were Lucky." This photograph is what a 140 foot tall flak tower with eight 128 mm flak guns in Vienna looked like. The flak tower in Stuttgart would have looked like this one in Vienna. Notice the size of the vehicles and the nearby buildings. My actual newspaper clipping is courtesy of The Globe and Mail Inc.

323

On Friday, January 12, 1945 we finally returned back to Croft after staying at Winthorpe for those 4 marvelous days. The 95 mile flight from Winthorpe to Croft was only 45 minutes. During the war there was no communications about the whereabouts of the aircraft and crews after an operation. Everything was top-secret and the wireless or phone was not used to convey this type of information. When we returned to Croft the crew and I found that all our bicycles were gone. We were away from Croft for so long folks figured we had the chop and our bicycles were free for the taking. I lost my 3-speed bicycle I bought for £3 when I was at Honeybourne OTU. I never got it back. A few days after we returned, I went to Darlington to buy a replacement bicycle. No one back at Croft had heard anything about us before we showed up.

431 Squadron Lancaster KB-806, Pilot Officer J. R. Lightbown and crew on January 12, 1945 after their return to Croft from the same Sunday, January 7, 1945 Munich operation that my crew was on. This was the end of their tour after 32 operations. Notice all of the snow on the ground. This was also the last trip for Lancaster KB-806 named SE-X as it crashed with all the crew killed only two days later on Sunday, January 14, 1945 on the way to Merseburg, Germany. Was it the skill of the crew, luck of the aircraft or luck of the crew or was survival just random chance? This photograph is courtesy of the Lightbown family.

A few times in January we were sent out to shovel snow off the dispersal areas. We only had coal shovels, so I suspect this was more of a make work project.

FTR   On January 14, 1945 the Lancaster KB-806, SE-X of Pilot Officer M. A. MacLeod and crew failed to return after colliding with a Luftwaffe Bf 109 fighter while on a night operation to Merseburg Germany. All the crew members perished. They were buried in the Berlin 1939-1945 War Cemetery, Germany.

431 Wing Commander, Eric Mitchell's tour was finished on January 10, 1945 and Ralph Davenport became the 431 Wing Commander on January 14, 1945.

Operation number 26 in Lancaster KB-803 designated as N-NAN on Wednesday, January 17, 1945 was an 8 hour and 45 minute round trip to bomb the synthetic oil factory at Zeitz, Germany at night under the illumination of a quarter moon. The factory was about 26 miles south-east of Merseburg in the centre of a dirty brown coal mining district. We were number 7 in order of 13 431 Squadron Lancaster crews taking part in this operation. On this trip we had Pilot Officer J. A. Keates flying with us as a second pilot. The Navigator briefing was at 12:00 noon and the main briefing was at 14:00. We were up at 17:21 and sometime before we reached the target, I had just turned out my light and pulled back my curtains and went forward to stand behind Art and J. A. Keates. Suddenly out of nowhere a Focke-Wulf Fw 190 day fighter flew across our path. The Fw 190 was only about 30 feet in front of us and he must have been very surprised as well as he was banking the aircraft so sharply that his wings were almost vertical. We knew it was a day fighter because it was so close to us we could see in the light of the quarter moon the blue paint on the underside of the wings. That was too close for comfort. The two aircraft missed having a mid-air collision in the dark by less than one second. Tonight, a Luftwaffe pilot and an entire Lancaster crew were Lucky. We never saw that Fw 190 again that night. He probably had to land to change his underwear. Ray always recalled this as being "an especially frightening moment."

We reached the target at 22:20. Over the target area we were at 18,000 feet flying at an IAS of 160 mph. The visibility was clear with a slight ground haze. We identified red and green TIs to the west of the target. There was strong fighter activity and many searchlights near Frankfurt. There was a great deal of barrage flak early on but by the time we got there the flak had diminished. While we were nearing the target the Master Bomb Aimer advised us to bomb the red target indicators and not the green target indicators. We bombed on the red TIs. Only about a minute later we heard from the Master Bomb Aimer in a very calm British business like voice, "Oh. Number two can you take over? We are going down." The Master Bomb Aimer and crew were from an RAF squadron and we did not hear anything more about them. Another bomber and crew that failed to return that night.

The bombs were very well placed. Orange explosions were seen in a small area with 5 to 8 columns of black oily smoke coming from large fires. It was a good effort. The river, the railway lines, and the town of Zeitz could easily be seen from the glow of the fires. The fires could be seen for 55 miles on the return trip by Jack our rear gunner. We dropped one 4,000 pound cookie, ten 500 pound Medium Capacity bombs with 0.025 second time delay fuses and four 250 pound bombs. Most of the synthetic oil factory was destroyed. Before we arrived there that night it had been pounded by B-17s and B-24 bombers of the USAAF in the daylight. Six weeks after this raid there was no indication that any repairs had been attempted at the facility. That synthetic oil factory was so badly damaged that it was out of commission for the rest of the war. The factory employed 5,000 workers and had an output of 300,000 tons of oil. That operation would be responsible for reducing the available fuel supplies for Luftwaffe fighters. With less available fuel fewer Luftwaffe fighters would be coming up and shooting us down.

When we returned to Croft at 02:07 in the early morning of Thursday, January 18, 1945 I saw that a flight of American Army Air Force four engine B-24 Liberator bombers had landed at our aerodrome. I got up early in the morning to go out and take a look at the B-24 Liberator bombers before they left Croft. I had never seen an actual B-24 before except for pictures in magazines or in newsreels. While I was looking over a B-24 some of the American fellows from a crew came out to show me around their B-24 Liberator. They told me that they had bombed Zeitz in the daylight before we were there. I told them that we had visited Zeitz that night in the dark and that the fires they had started were still burning and could be seen from quite some distance. They asked me how on earth we could possibly find the target and bomb it in the dark. They did not think it was possible. I told them that each of our aircraft has its own Navigator and it is the Navigator's job to get his own aircraft to the target and back to home in the dark by dead reckoning. We fly at night or in the daylight not in formation but in a gaggle and we do not follow each other. They were in absolute disbelief we could fly and bomb at night and we did not need to follow a Master Navigator. I told them our Mk. XIV bombsight worked in the dark and we did not have to fly perfectly straight and level. The famous American Norden bombsight could not work in the dark and the bomber had to fly absolutely straight and level for a longer time under the control of the bomb aimer. They proudly showed me their bomb bay that held nine 500 pound bombs. That totals only 4,500 pounds per trip. I was not very impressed. I told them to come over and look at our 33 foot long bomb bay that carried 12,000 pounds of bombs as a standard load all the way to anywhere in Germany. I told them we usually carried one 4,000 pound cookie and an assortment of other the bombs and incendiaries.

The B-24 Liberator named Diamond Lil from the Commemorative Air Force Collection in Mesa, Arizona, USA visiting the Canadian Warplane Heritage Museum on June 15, 2014. Photographed by Dan Middleton.

I also told them that a Lancaster bomber with the bomb bay doors removed could carry one 22,000 pound grand slam or earthquake bomb used for penetrating submarine pens or tunnels. These American fellows who had never seen the Lancaster bomb bay before were totally impressed. One Lancaster bomber and the crew of 7 carried the same bomb load as two B-24 Liberators and 22 crew members. To me and others in Bomber Command it seemed like such a waste of bombers and crews. We had a little song about the huge amount of defensive armament and ammo and the tiny bomb load on the USAAF bombers.

There were 18,482 Consolidated Aircraft Company B-24 Liberators built from 1940 to 1945. Of this number 4,600 were manufactured by the Ford Motor Company. The B-24 Liberator holds the record as the most produced multi-engine heavy bomber in American military history. The B-24 Liberator with a crew of 11 men could generally carry about 4,000 pounds of bombs to Germany. There are currently thirteen complete B-24 Liberator bombers in existence at various museums. The B-24 was powered by four Pratt & Whitney R-1830 twin wasp 14-cylinder air cooled radial engines that produced 1,200 horsepower each.

Our crew went on a seven day leave for London on Saturday, January 20, 1945. We hung around London and went to the picture shows and spent time drinking at the many pubs. We all thoroughly enjoyed ourselves. While in London on this leave we stayed at the Savoy Hotel which was a regular commercial hotel that offered good rates for members of the armed forces. The train rides were always courtesy of the RCAF. There were still air raids sirens going off due to the German V-2 ballistic missiles that were still crashing to the earth and destroying parts of London. The V-2 missiles did not stop landing in London until the end of March 1945.

While we were on leave away from the aerodrome on Friday, January 26, 1945 the pilot known as Crash was flying our favorite N-NAN Lancaster and practicing with 3 engines not running and feathered. He had only the outer starboard engine running. He was not able to un-feather the propellers and start any of the engines. With only the starboard outer engine with a generator running and the air temperature being close to freezing the batteries were not powerful enough to operate the electric feathering oil pump in the engine oil sump to un-feather the propellers and turn over the engines. With only the starboard outer engine running the aircraft is difficult to manage and would be losing 50 feet per minute with no load on board. The dead inner engines have the hydraulic pumps that operate the landing gear, flaps and the rear turret. The flaps and the undercarriage could not be lowered as there was no inboard engine powered hydraulics.

My friend, Dan Monahan from the London, Ontario Navigation School was taking a ride in the rear turret that day when everything went sideways. When we were on training operations or in the return leg of a combat operation and we were over the English Channel or England we would take rides in the gunner's positions. The view from the gunner's turrets in the daylight was marvelous and it was fun pretending firing the guns. And after all we were just 21 years old. Dan was trapped in the rear gunner's turret without the hydraulics working. You do not want to be in the rear turret when a bomber crash lands. Sometimes there are miracles, and the turret is thrown clear from the crashing aircraft and the rear gunner ends up seriously crumpled but alive. I am sure that is the exception and not the rule. Being thrown safe is the exception like the story of Andrew Mynarski and Pat Brophy.

Dan had been having a great old time playing and having fun rotating the rear turret but, when the engines were shut down, he had the turret turned at about 45 degrees from the guns pointing straight back. If you remember the picture on page 143 of the rear gunner sitting in the fully rotated turret of the Wellington bomber, you can see the opening that you used to enter and exit the rear turret. With the turret turned halfway to 45 degrees you cannot bail out or get back into the rear of the aircraft. If the rear Air Gunner had to get out and there was no hydraulics the gunner had to rotate a tiny hand crank many turns. The rear turret has this big ring gear and at the end of the crank is a tiny pinion gear that meshes with it. As Dan was not a rear gunner and had no formal training about the rear turret, he had no idea where that tiny hand crank was located. Dan frantically called the rear gunner and asked where the hell the hand crank was located. The rear gunner quickly explained to Dan that the crank was down low on his right hand side and explained to him how to use the crank.

At this point the aircraft was getting closer to the ground with only that one engine running and since the hydraulics were not working the aircraft did not have the flaps down. Without the flaps in the down position the Lancaster no longer floats at low speed but falls fast. Dan was in a bit of a panic. Once Dan found the crank, he started to turn it in the wrong direction at first. Dan quickly turned the crank the other direction and once the opening in the turret was lined up with the rear opening of the aircraft Dan scrambled out of the turret and got into a crash position. There were no seats with seat belts in the aircraft, so the crash position involved sitting on the floor with your back to a bulkhead while facing backwards and hanging on. Only the pilot had a fixed seat with a harness. The Navigator only had a bench with a hinge that allowed the bench to fold up out of the way against the side of the fuselage. Lancaster N-NAN crash landed with wheels up 10 miles south of Croft in a field near the Village of Yafforth. Yafforth is shown on the map on page 102. Luckily, no one in the aircraft was injured. And yes, this was the same Crash that broke the back of a Halifax in October of 1944. However, our favorite Lancaster N-NAN was a write-off. Later after my return to Canada I drew the sketch of our poor broken N-NAN.

My 1945 sketch of our wrecked N-NAN Lancaster lying in a field near Yafforth in Yorkshire.

After Crash returned two days later from his last operation, number 31 on January 28, 1945 he and his crew were all screened and sent back home to Canada. Crash and crew were fortunate as the point system was still being used and after 31 operations, they had the required 120 points and were finished their tour.

Don told me when Crash was back in Canada with the RCAF he feathered an engine of a Ventura Bomber and crash landed in New York State. I heard about this crash landing from Don while he was still flying for six months after the war ended.

A Ventura bomber. From my aircraft recognition scrapbook.

Sunday, January 28, 1945 the Wing Commander had Pilot Officer C. E. Heaven, a Wireless Operator and I pick up one of our Lancaster bombers, KB-811 designated as T-TARE that had been repaired after diverting to the emergency aerodrome at Carnaby, England.

The Pilot Officer G. H. Glabelt and crew of Lancaster KB-811 T-TARE were unlucky on their trip to Zeitz, Germany on January 16, 1945. The inner starboard engine had been hit by flak and had to be shut down and the propeller feathered. They were lucky however as the Lancaster and the crew all came back safely to Carnaby, England on 3 engines without any more incidents. We had been on that same operation to Zeitz, Germany.

331

We spent 9 hours getting to Carnaby while wearing our battle dress, Mae West, carrying all our gear and parachutes. We must have looked a sorry sight to the civilians. We took the train from the Eryholme station to Leeds, changed to the train going to the Scarborough train station and then we took the bus to Carnaby. The route we took on this train and bus trip is shown on page 102. We left Croft in the morning and arrived at RAF Carnaby in the dark at 21:00. We had to stay overnight and leave in the morning. The food and the accommodations at Carnaby were good.

When I got up in the morning the sight at RAF Carnaby was incredible. There were hundreds of broken aircraft of all sorts in the fields everywhere. Some would be repaired but most of them would be used for parts and eventually melted down for aluminum for new aircraft or for pots and pans. There was heavy equipment everywhere used to move the broken aircraft. These were the aircraft that we would never see landing at Croft.

Carnaby was one of three emergency landing airfields located on the east coast of England just a few miles inland. There was Woodbridge in Suffolk, Carnaby in Yorkshire and Manston on the southeast coast in Kent. These airfields were where a pilot or another crew member would land an aircraft that had medical emergencies or suspected damage to hydraulics, undercarriage, tires, dead engines and or low on fuel. Landing at a regular aerodrome could cause great damage to the runway. Bomber Command also did not want crews at a regular aerodrome to see these aircraft crash land or return in these poor conditions. It is horribly bad for the morale of the other crews to see aircraft crashing at your aerodrome or dead airmen being removed from horribly damaged aircraft. At all three bases the southernmost east-west runway was very large. The south emergency runways were 9,000 feet long with 1,500 feet of unobstructed grass at both ends. The runways were 750 feet wide. If the landing gear of the aircraft was useless the pilot would land his aircraft on the grass at either end. The landing on the grass was softer and there would be fewer sparks generated that could set off the fuel supply or any bombs left on board.

The distance from RAF Carnaby back to Croft was only 60 miles but as ops were on, we had to do the Great Circuit at 1,500 feet until all of the aircraft had departed. There was a longer delay caused by a departing Lancaster that was stooging down the runway zigzagging from side to side across the runway. The pilot eventually taxied it onto the grass. Afterwards it was discovered the ground crew had managed to reverse the port and starboard brake controls. When the pilot pressed the port pedal to turn to port the aircraft turned starboard and when the pilot pressed the starboard pedal to turn to starboard the aircraft turned to port. This is very a confusing situation for a pilot. Imagine your confusion if your car turned to the left when you turned the steering wheel to the right and turned to the right when you turned the steering wheel to the left. We were up for 90 minutes in the daylight for that short 60-mile trip.

Ray is standing in a dispersal area beside a Lancaster tail fin. He is wearing a pair of boots with the tear away leggings. Photograph from the Bob Middleton Collection.

Chapter 34

FEBRUARY 1945 AND ONLY A FEW TO GO

Operation number 27 in Lancaster KB-808 designated as U-UNCLE on Thursday, February 1, 1945 was an 8 hour round trip to bomb the marshalling yards at Ludwigshafen, Germany at night with a bit more illumination than from a three quarters moon. We were number 9 in order of 11 431 Squadron Lancaster crews taking part in this operation. We all went to the mess at 11:15. The Navigator briefing was at 12:00 and the main briefing was at 14:00. We were up at 15:32 and reached the target at 19:24. Over the target area we were at 16,500 feet flying at an IAS of 155 mph. The visibility was 6/10ths cloud with tops at 5,000 feet. We identified green TIs and red flares with green stars. We bombed the centre of the fires and saw bursts in the centre of town. One large orange and then white explosion at 19:33 was seen about ten miles to port lasting 30 seconds. The glow from the fires under the clouds could be seen for 50 miles on our return trip. The route that was chosen was good. We could see the dummy fires that had been lit by the German ground forces in empty fields. The dummy fires were an attempt to get us to drop our bombs on their fake target indicators. Tonight, it did not work. We dropped one 4,000 pound cookie, eight 500 pound No. 14 SBC clusters and six AN/M14 thermite SBC incendiary clusters fused at 4 seconds. We all returned safely to Croft and we were back down at 23:30.

Operation number 28 in Lancaster KB-741 the Chop Kite currently re-designated as C-CHARLIE, on Saturday, February 2, 1945 was a 7 hour round trip to bomb the marshalling yards and German troop concentrations at Wiesbaden, Germany at night under the illumination of a three quarters moon. Lancaster, KB-741 had originally been designated as Y-YOKE. KB-741 was re-designated as C-CHARLIE because all of the Y-YOKE aircraft were considered bad luck by the crews and Bomber Command must have thought that we would not know that KB-741 C-CHARLIE was really KB-741 Y-YOKE. We knew it was still bad luck as the 431 and 434 Squadron Y-YOKE aircraft eventually Failed To Return. We were number 12 in order of 13 431 Squadron Lancaster crews taking part in this operation. The Navigator briefing was at 13:30 and the main briefing was at 14:30. We were up at 20:31 and shortly after we were up the supercharger on the outer starboard engine packed it in. Don shut down the supercharger and we continued on as it still ran but with less power at high altitude. Near the beginning of our tour everyone in the crew had agreed that if we lost an engine after takeoff, we would continue to the target on three engines. Before we passed the coast of England Ralph our Mid-Upper Gunner said, "Bob something is smoking above your desk." That was my H2S radar. The image on the screen on the H2S just became an out of focus line. I turned off the H2S. The GEE box packed it in a short while later when all that showed on the screen was a big green blob, so I shut that off as well. We reached the target at 23:37. Over the target area we were at 19,000 feet flying at an IAS of 155 mph. The target was the marshalling yards and German troop concentrations. The weather and the visibility were poor with 10/10ths layered cloud with tops at 19,000 feet. There was moderate flak. We had serious problems with icing that Don somehow eventually solved. We identified and bombed the target by using the glow of the fires under the clouds as the mechanical computer of the Mk. XIV bombsight packed it in and was of no use. There was a bright glow under the clouds with many small explosions. There was one very large explosion at 23:45. Cloud and high winds did not allow for an accurate assessment of the results. Just before we were landing Don had problems with getting the flaps to go down completely. We felt lucky to return back to base this night in the "Chop Kite" with all the equipment failures we suffered on this trip. On the return trip we could see the glow of the fires for 25 miles. We dropped one 4,000 pound cookie, 1,350 4 pound incendiaries and 150 4 pound type X incendiaries for a total load of 10,000 pounds. At 01:25 we jettisoned about 700 pounds of the incendiaries from 10,000 feet.

Once we landed Jack was stuck in the tail turret and he was going to chop himself out with the axe. We convinced him to hang on while we got the turret swung round for him. All of our aircraft returned safely to Croft and we were back down at 03:27. Group Captain Bob Turnbull, the Station Commanding Officer was present at our debriefing when Don said he would refuse to fly in C-CHARLIE again if it was assigned to our crew. I nearly fell out of my chair when Don said that to him. The Group Captain was visibly miffed by Don's comment but, he got away without being reprimanded. With 28 operations completed we were quite a senior crew now and that must have counted for something. No trip to the Glass House at Sheffield for Don this time. KB-741 C-CHARLIE was fixed up and was sent up again with other crews. We never flew in KB-741 C-CHARLIE again.

This is a photograph that was taken of Lancaster KB-741 Y-YOKE sometime after it arrived at Croft on October 18, 1944. I believe Ray took the picture as we considered any bomber designated Y-YOKE to be a doomed bad luck "Chop Kite." This is the Lancaster photograph that is shown on the book cover. The photograph is from the Bob Middleton Collection.

FTR   Pilot Douglas A. Magrath and crew flying in KB-741 C-CHARLIE on February 15, 1945 Failed to Return from Chemnitz,

Germany. Pilot Douglas A. Magrath and crew are buried at the Berlin 1939-1945 War Cemetery, Germany.

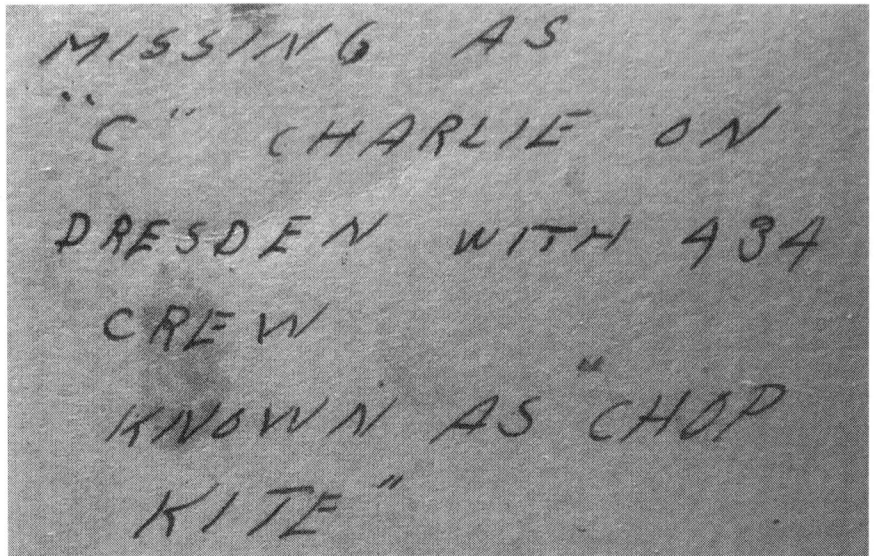

I wrote this note on the back of that previous Y-YOKE photograph when KB-741 that had been re-designated C-CHARLIE did not come back from Chemnitz on the night of February 15, 1945. This was only 13 days after we had flown in KB-741 C-CHARLIE and Don said we would refuse to fly in it again. The aircraft was on loan to 434 Bluenose Squadron when it Failed to Return. In error, I wrote Dresden instead of Chemnitz as these two operations overlapped on February 15. The Dresden operation took place from February 13 to February 15, 1945 while we were on leave. I was very disappointed not to go to Dresden as it was such a huge success and it would have been such a good test of my navigation skills.

Operation number 29 in Lancaster KB-808 designated as U-UNCLE on Sunday, February 4, 1945 was a 6 hour and 30 minute round trip to the marshalling yards at Bonn, Germany at night under the illumination of a half moon. We were number 10 in order of 13 431 Squadron Lancaster crews taking part in this operation. This was a Canadian only operation involving 200 RCAF aircraft. The Navigator briefing was at 12:30 and the main briefing was at 13:30. We were up at 17:39 and reached the target at 20:52. Over the target area we were at 18,500 feet flying at an IAS of 160 mph. The visibility was 10/10ths cloud with tops at 8,000 feet. We identified and bombed the target by GEE and the glow of the fires. It appeared to be a fairly good concentration and we could see a good glow from the fires. The route was good, and the tactics were good but the Pathfinder Force was late and it was only a fair scattered attack. The glow under the clouds from the fires could be seen for 80 miles when leaving the target area. We dropped one 4,000 pound cookie, thirteen 600 pound SBC X-type incendiary clusters for a total load of 11,800 pounds. We all returned safely to Croft and we were back down at 00:12.

We were going on another operation with all our gear on the ground in front of us. Ray took this photograph. The photograph is from the Bob Middleton Collection.

I managed to catch a cold just before our operation to Goch, Germany. The weather was so cold and rotten way up in the north of England in February of 1945. Our miserable Nissen hut only had that tiny coal stove for heat. It is a wonder we were not sicker. I did not go to see the Medical Officer about my cold and congestion as I remembered when the Medical Officer prevented Ralph from going with us to Soest on December 5, 1944. I did not want to miss the operation and I did not want my fellow crewmates to have to fly with a possibly less experienced navigator. By this point we all had 29 operations of experience. Any substitute navigator would have less experience than me. If something horrible happened to our crew while I was not with them, I do not know how I would have felt. By 29 operations together we were definitely a Band of Brothers.

Operation number 30 in Lancaster KB-811 designated as T-TARE on Wednesday, February 7, 1945 was a 7 hour round trip to Goch, Germany at night under the light of a quarter moon. This was the same repaired Lancaster that Pilot Officer C. E. Heaven, a Wireless Operator and I had picked up from RAF Carnaby on January 28, 1945. Goch is on the Netherlands-Germany border and the British army wanted to break out into the Netherlands. We were bombing German troop concentrations for an Army cooperative target. The operation was called at noon for a night takeoff. We were number 11 in order of 12 431 Squadron Lancaster crews taking part in this operation. The Navigator briefing was at 13:30 and the main briefing was at 14:30. We were up at 19:20 and reached the target at 22:20. Over the target area we were at 12,000 feet flying at an IAS of 160 mph. The visibility was poor with 9/10ths cloud. There was slight flak but there was strong German fighter activity. We identified the green and red TIs and bombed on the red TIs. The Master Bomber called the TIs too late, and he said to abandon the operation a few minutes after we dropped our bombs. The attack was considered to be fair. When we left the target, it was just a huge glow with smoke rising to 4,000 feet. Seven of 431 Squadrons' aircraft aborted after word from the Master Bomber.

As we dropped down in altitude on the way back my ears began to bother me due to the congestion from my cold. I asked Don to descend much slower than he had been descending and he did. As we dropped down to 1,500 feet my ears were in such agonizing pain it felt like someone was putting hot pokers in my ears. In the April 1942 Issue of *Air Trails* magazine an article on high altitude flying states "Any slight cold or sinus congestion will bring on the tortures of the damned when the time comes to descend." I was fortunate as we had only gone up to

12,000 feet that night. My ears hurt for many days afterwards but, I did not go see the Medical Officer.

We dropped one 4,000 pound cookie, ten 500 pound MC bombs with 0.025 seconds time delay and six 250 pound GP bombs with tail fuses. We all returned safely to Croft and we were back down at 01:13.

On Thursday, February 8, 1945 Ray and I went off to London on a ten day leave for drinking, entertainment and relaxation. It was so marvelous that every 6 week all the Bomber Command crews had a 10 day break from flying in combat. This gave us a much-needed rest from the stress of the operations. We left from the train station at Eryholme. The Eryholme train station was just a short 5 minute ride south-east of Croft.

Painting of RCAF Lancaster KB-811 T-TARE at Croft in the winter of 1945 with snow on the ground. This print is hanging in my house. By artist, Donald Kenneth Anderson, 1980. This photograph is from the Bob Middleton Collection.

Nose art on KB-811. Shes Trudy Terrific. The photograph is courtesy of the Bomber Command Museum at Nanton, Alberta.

This is a picture of my return trip ticket to London. The picture is from the Bob Middleton Collection.

Sunday, February 18, 1945 we were up at 15:30 doing Air/Sea bombing practice.

Operation number 31 in Lancaster KB-837 designated as X-X-RAY on Tuesday, February 20, 1945 was a 7 hour and 25 minute round trip to Dortmund, Germany at night under the light of a half moon. The RCAF supplied 90 aircraft of the 500 Bomber Command aircraft involved in this operation. This was the last night raid that Dortmund would experience. At the last minute during the day the target had been changed, the bomb load changed, and the petrol load changed. The discarded bombs were in piles scattered all about the dispersal area. This was a pain in the neck for everyone on the base. We had a double briefing that day and I had to prepare a second set of charts for the new target. The ground crews all had to do their work twice and then take all the unused bombs back to the bomb dump. Normally they never had to take bombs back. The armorers then had to remove all the fuses from the unused bombs. These were left all about the dispersal areas.

342

Normally we never saw the bombs lying about the dispersal area. The bombs, fuel and ammunition were generally loaded on board while we were at the briefing or resting up. No one was happy with all the extra work.

Picture of Ray posing with the five hundred bombs that had been taken off our Lancaster. The photograph is from the Bob Middleton Collection.

We were number 14 in order of 14 431 Squadron Lancaster crews taking part in this operation. Our dinner was at 16:00. The Navigator briefing was at 16:45 and the main briefing was at 17:45. We were up at 21:13 and reached the target at 01:10. Over the target area we were at 18,500 feet flying at an IAS of 155 mph. The visibility was poor with 10/10ths cloud with tops at 10,000 feet. There were numerous searchlights and many enemy fighter aircraft. Don saw many of our own aircraft shot down and fires were starting as we approached the target. We were bombing the marshalling yards and a built-up area. A bright moon above the clouds brought out the fighters. We identified the green and red TIs and bombed on the red TIs. Fires and explosions were seen over the whole target area. We dropped one 4,000 pound cookie, and ten 600 pound SBC incendiary clusters. This was a good attack, and we could see the target for 100 miles behind us on the return trip. Jack's rear turret became unserviceable during this trip. We all returned safely to Croft and we were back down at 04:36.

A day or so after we had completed 20 operations on our trip to Soest, Germany all of Bomber Command was told that now they were using a point system. Up to then a crew had to do 30 operations to complete a tour. A complete tour had now become 120 points. For any trip to Germany the crew would receive a credit of four points. For a trip anywhere else the crew received a credit of three points. After operation 20 we had 74 points towards our 120 points needed to complete our tour. The Second Dickey points of the pilot were counted in the total.

After our successful trip to Dortmund, Germany we had 118 points and 31 trips. We all got excited and said among ourselves on the way back we only had only one more trip to go. We had never counted our chicks before they had hatched before this as it was considered bad luck to do so. We stopped talking about it real quick hoping that the Big Guy up there in the heavens had not heard us. After we got out of our Lancaster and arrived at the debriefing, we discovered the points system had been scrapped and now all the bomber crews had to complete 35 operations. This is crazy. How is anyone going to survive a tour of 35 operations? By 1944 the USAAF Eighth air force crews also had to complete 30 to 35 missions to finish a tour. I guess that was our reward for counting our chicks before they had hatched.

Our next trip to Pforzheim, Germany would have been 122 points and the end of our tour but now it would only be trip 32 for the crew and 34 for Don. The tour count was actually calculated by the pilot's operations total. Don had been on two second dickeys before we flew together as a crew so thankfully the next trip after Pforzheim would be 35 trips for Don. Our last trip as a crew would be number 33 to Mainz, Germany on February 27, 1945. That was the 35 operations for Don. Thanks for doing two trips for us Don!

FTR   Lancaster KB-809 Q-QUEEN and crew number eight in the flight order flown by Pilot Officer John. W. Kopp with nine trips failed to return from the Dortmund operation February 21, 1945. John W. Kopp and the crew are buried at Reichswald Forest Cemetery, Germany.

February 22, 1945 saw us up in the air at 14:10 practicing Air/Sea bombing and we did more Fighter Affiliation.

Operation number 32 in Lancaster KB-807 designated as B-BAKER on Friday, February 23, 1945 was an 8 hour and 50 minute round trip to Pforzheim, Germany at night under the illumination of a full moon. There were 56 RCAF bomber crews taking part in this operation of 356 bombers. We were number 2 in order of 12 431 Squadron Lancaster crews taking part in this operation. We had only this operation and one more operation to go but no one spoke a word about that. The Navigator briefing was at 12:30 and the main briefing was at 13:30. We were up at 15:38 and reached the target at 20:09. Over the target area we were at 8,000 feet flying at an IAS of 165 mph. The visibility was clear with some haze. We identified the green and red TIs and bombed on the red TIs. There was only slight light flak but a strong fighter activity. Don saw many of our bombers going down leaving trails of flames and sparks. A bomber going down at night looked like a fireworks display. There were fires burning on the ground from the bombers that had been shot down that I did not see hidden away in my safe place.

We were bombing an instrument factory and the marshalling yards. The whole target area was a mass of flames with smoke up to 12,000 feet and a large explosion at 20:07. From 5,000 feet Jack could see the fires for 150 miles on the return trip from the target.

One of the most important jobs of the Flight Engineer was to keep track of how much fuel we had in the fuel tanks, the rate of consumption and which tanks the fuel was in. Art had to open and close the fuel cocks for the tanks during a trip to make certain all the engines had fuel and also keep an equal amount of fuel in the port and starboard wings to balance the aircraft. The correct aircraft balance reduced the stress for the pilot keeping the bomber trimmed level.

That night just as the wheels touched tarmac and the tail was still in the air both starboard engines sputtered and came to a stop. Somehow Art had managed to use up all the fuel in one or all the 3 starboard tanks. He had forgotten to switch between the starboard tanks or had not opened the fuel cock that equalizes the fuel between the port and starboard wing tanks. It is not possible to taxi the bomber in a straight line with engines only running on one side. In our case the bomber would have gone around in a right turning circle. We were at a stop at the side of the runway with other aircraft waiting to land. I asked Don if I should send up a red flare to warn the tower and the other bombers landing. Don told me not to and he ran up the running port engines and moved a bit closer to the edge of the runway. If I had sent off the red flare there would have been all sorts of reports to fill out and Art may have been reprimanded. Don told Art to open the balancing fuel cock to get fuel to the starboard wing and get out of the Lancaster and prime the inner starboard engine so he could start it. Art got out, climbed up on the starboard wheel and primed the inner starboard engine while Don started that engine. Once the engine was running Art climbed back in the aircraft and Don taxied back to our dispersal area on the two inboard engines. We were so very lucky that night. If those starboard engines ran out of fuel 60 seconds sooner while we were still 50 or 100 feet above the ground the Lancaster may have spun in and we all could have been killed. I do not know if Don's fantastic flying skills would have saved us that night.

Photoflash photograph of Pforzheim on February 23, 1945. © IWM Image C 5083 from the Imperial War Museum Collection.

Once we were at the debriefing there was not very much said about the error. We were just Lucky again. Except for one crew we all returned safely to Croft and we were back down at 00:25. Lancaster KB-808 U-UNCLE flown by Pilot Officer P. J. Hurley landed at the emergency RAF aerodrome at Manston due to damage by friendly incendiaries dropped on his aircraft. The crew was not injured.

That was our best attack yet out of 32 operations. Of all the Bomber Command operations this was the third in terms of loss of German life on the ground after Dresden and Hamburg. About 18,000 people were killed. In my logbook I wrote, "Best attack yet." We dropped one 4,000 pound cookie, and ten 600 hundred 4 pound SBC incendiary clusters.

INSTRUMENT CENTRE HIT

" Mass Of Flames "

These big day raids followed a heavy and concentrated attack by R.A.F. bombers on the communications and industrial centre of Pforzheim, in the Upper Rhineland between Karlsruhe and Stuttgart.

Pforzheim is an important junction on a main line leading from east to west towards the battle-front. Most of its inhabitants, engaged before the war in jewellery manufacture, both in factories and in their homes, have since the war been making precision instruments, fuses, small arms components, and similar war materials. These industries have grown in importance as the larger industrial areas have been destroyed.

The attack was the first big one to be made on Pforzheim, and crews reported that before they left the whole town was a mass of flames, with the fires completely out of control and a glow in the sky visible for 150 miles.

A clipping from an English newspaper about the Pforzheim operation. From the Bob Middleton Collection.

Throughout my story there are tragedies of aircraft exploding in the sky and crashing to the ground with total loss of life in training operations and combat operations. During the Second World War in the British Commonwealth there were about 10,000 aircrew killed in training accidents flying in aircraft from simple Tiger Moth and Fleet Finch basic trainers to all types of fighters and bombers. Of the 125,000 men in Bomber Command there were 55,573 killed on operations during the Second World War. Of the 50,000 Canadians in Bomber Command 10,250 were killed. In the US Eighth Air Force 26,000 crew members were killed in WWII. There are various old pictures of destroyed bombers in the archives. I was there and I saw the tragedies with my own eyes. I saw the flames and sparks coming from doomed aircraft and the funeral fires on the ground. At the time you simply sucked it up and in the words of the war time Prime Minister of England, Sir Winston Churchill, KBO just "Keep Buggering On."

British Prime Minister Winston Churchill, KBO outside of No. 10 Downing Street with his famous V for Victory. Lebrecht Music & Arts / Alamy Stock Photo ERH09N.

On Tuesday, October 2, 2019 the B-17G bomber owned and operated by the Collings Foundation crashed at the Bradley International Airport, Connecticut, USA killing 7 of the 13 people on board. The pictures taken at the crash site by Chris Chin are from 2019, not something that occurred in past history, 75 years and 3 generations ago. My son added these pictures as he felt it brings home to the more recent generations what we went through night and day after night and day so many years ago. The tragedy shown in these photographs took place at least 12,000 times for Bomber Command alone in combat operations. I remember vividly flying over Honeybourne OTU on the night of Saturday, July 3, 1944. I saw close up the flames of the Wellington that crashed into the bomb dump with all 7 fellows on board killed. Something went wrong while the pilot was practicing landing with an engine shut off. Such was the human cost for the liberty and freedoms that we enjoy today. With great respect to the people involved in this accident I present 3 pictures from the article taken by Chris Chin for *The Drive* newsletter. When you look at these 3 images try to imagine this happening 12,000 times and the 55,573 brave Bomber Command airmen who gave their all.

Photographs from Tuesday, October 2 and Wednesday, October 3, 2019 of the wrecked B-17G of the Collings Foundation. The photographs are courtesy of photographer Chris Chin and *The Drive* newsletter.

Sunday, February 25, 1945 found us up at 14:15 doing H2S radar practice for me and cross-country bombing practice for Ray. I loved to fly and I knew my flying days would soon be finished.

Operation number 33 in Lancaster KB-837 designated as X-X-RAY on Tuesday, February 27, 1945 was a 7 hour and 10 minute trip to Mainz, Germany in the daylight. The target for the operation was the railway and the communication centre in Mainz. We were number 17 in order of 17 431 Squadron Lancaster crews taking part in this operation. We had our meal at 06:00. The Navigator briefing was at 06:30 and the main briefing was at 07:30. We had second Pilot Officer J. W. Aldrid on board. We were up at 12:52 and reached the target at 16:30. Over the target area we were at 17,000 feet flying at an IAS of 155 mph. The visibility was poor with 10/10ths cloud with tops at 8,000 feet. We were lucky as there were no fighters about and the flak was slight. Some of the crews could see our fighter escort over the target.

We had just about arrived over the target and I was up front in my usual Nosy Navigator position when I happened to look above us and I saw another Lancaster almost directly above us with the bomb bay open with a full load of bombs. It was a really spectacular sight. Before I could snap that picture Don turned our aircraft to get out from under that bomber. I did not get the photograph, but I did live to tell how I missed that shot.

I took this picture standing behind Art on the way to Mainz. This is 10/10ths cloud flying at 17,000 feet. There were Lancasters as far as I could see. I was always happy to hear those Packard built Merlin engines running and to see all those marvelous propellers spinning. The photograph is from the Bob Middleton Collection.

The gaggle leader trailing smoke was in the wrong place way off to the port side. Don said to me. "Bob the leader is way over there to port. Should we be over there too?" I told Don. "Skip. They are too far north and to cross over there we would be crossing the paths of our other bombers." The Pathfinder Force was late and was not seen until most of the crews had already dropped their bombs. We identified the target by the green smoke puffs, and we bombed between the green smoke puffs as per instructions from the Master Bomber. It was a very scattered effort, and nothing could be observed due to the cloud cover. We dropped one 4,000 pound cookie, six 500 pound No. 14 SBC clusters and eight 500 pound M-17 SBC clusters totaling 11,000 pounds of bombs. All of our aircraft returned safely to Croft. It was the general opinion of the crews that the bombing was very scattered and not very successful. In my logbook I wrote, "Worst attack of tour." The railway yards were not hit. Most of the bombs landed 5 miles north-west of the intended target. There were 1,500 <u>tons</u> of bombs dropped and hundreds of buildings were destroyed.

This is a photograph I took over Mainz showing the first gaggle leader heading in the wrong direction a few miles to the north trailing smoke. The two alternate gaggle leaders were close by. This is what 10/10ths cloud and slight flak looked like from above the clouds. Photograph from the Bob Middleton Collection.

On our return we were number 3 in line but when Don asked for permission to land the tower controller told him to do the 40 mile long Great Circuit around Croft and Middleton St. George. We made one Great Circuit and the tower told us again. "Big Tree to Fly Swat X-RAY. Great Circuit at 1,500." After that second circuit Don got on the R/T asked what the heck was happening or something to that effect. Why are all the other crews landing while we are circling? The tower controller gave us permission to land finally. We finally landed at 20:03. When we got out of the aircraft other crews congratulated us on completing the tour. The tower controller was messing around with us because he knew it was our last operation and he wanted the other crews to be able to congratulate us on completing our tour as we got out of our aircraft. After we climbed out of a Lancaster for the last time we were all joking around and were wishing each other good luck.

Brand new Lancaster KB-837, SE-X-X-RAY. There are no operation bombs marked at the front. The photograph was taken by 431 Squadron Flight Engineer, Michael Bachinski. From the Bill Heron Collection.

When I got back that night, I was disappointed because there would be no more flying for me. Even though it was dangerous it was fun flying and after we had survived 33 Operations unscathed, we felt rather "fireproof." When you are 21 years old you are invincible and eager to take risks. Afterwards it was a relief not having my guts all tensed up in anticipation before going off on an operation. We were screened on Thursday, March 1, 1945 and would be going home. No

352

Instructor duties. No more combat operations. The end of this war was feeling awfully close so I knew I would be going home soon. I sent letters home to Pat and Mom and Dad that I had finished flying over the unfriendly skies of fortress Europe, but I did not know when I would be coming home. That would have been a huge relief for them. The rest of the crew left to return to Canada about the third week of March, but I stayed around for another three weeks. I do not know why.

Lancaster KB-807 SE-B BAKER that we took to Pforzheim, Germany on February 23, 1944. The photograph was taken by 431 Squadron Flight Engineer, Michael Bachinski. From the Bill Heron Collection.

Thursday, March 1, 1945. 13 Iroquois Squadron crews left for Manheim in the daylight at 11:15 and all aircraft returned safely.
Pilot Officer Don Rombough and all his crew were screened today, and they have been posted to the repatriation "R" Depot in Warrington. Warrington is 17 miles east of Liverpool, England, the departure points for the troop ships going to North America.

Chapter 35

33 OPERATIONS COMPLETE WAITING TO GO HOME

In the 6 months that our crew was on active operations at Croft from Friday, September 15, 1944 to Tuesday, February 27, 1945 only six aircraft and crews were lost. Fortunately, 5 members of one crew survived as POWs for the last few months of the war. One 431 Squadron Lancaster aircraft and crew perished in a training accident a few miles north of London. Out of the 33 operations our crew participated in there was only one aircraft and crew that failed to return on one of those operations. Of those 33 operations we participated in 469 aircraft went out to targets and 468 returned safely to England. An incredibly low loss rate of only 0.02%.

During the 2 months of July and August of 1944 before our crew arrived at Croft the 431 squadron had lost 16 aircraft and crews. The squadron was having a terrible time.

During the 2 months from March 1, 1945, to April 25, 1945 after our crew had finished flying the 431 Squadron lost 6 aircraft and crews.

People have asked me if our survival was because of skill or experience. You had skilled and experienced crews with over 30 operations that would fail to return. The first 5 operations for a new, inexperienced crew were generally the most risky. Many crews were lost on their first few operations. It seemed that the more operations you completed the better your chances of survival were from experience and skill you acquired but, eventually your luck could run out. I don't know if our crew of 7 lucky fellows was the lucky talisman for the entire Squadron, but I do know that surviving the tour I simply attribute to luck and when people ask me how we survived 33 operations I sometimes reply, "Can you spell LUCKY?" After each one of those 33 operations I had one real egg with bacon after the debriefing. **Luck is 33 Eggs.**

March 2, 1945.

14 431 Squadron aircraft went to Cologne for a very successful attack.

All aircraft returned safely to Croft except for SE-D that landed at RAF Woodbridge due to hydraulic issues.

March 3, 1945.

There was only training all day. Fourteen aircraft were briefed for an operation, but it was scrubbed.

March 4, 1945.

An operation was called but scrubbed just before the briefing.

March 5, 1945.

14 aircraft left for Chemnitz at 16:52. All aircraft returned safely to base. Flight Lt. Gonjec in Flight Officer Reid's crew was slightly wounded by flak.

March 7, 1945.

16 aircraft left for Desset at 16:55 and were briefed to land at Bascombe Down. All aircraft returned safely. One crew's aircraft Lancaster KB-802 SE-V piloted by John Duggan was damaged by flak and was left at Bascombe Down for repairs. The crew returned to Croft in a different aircraft.

March 9, 1945.

19 aircraft were detailed for an operation, but it was scrubbed.

March 10, 1945.

There was training all day.

March 11, 1945.

15 aircraft went to Essen in the daylight and were up at 11:50.

FTR   The Wing Commander Ralph F. Davenport and the crew of Lancaster KB-853 SE-A Failed to Return. Pilot, Ralph F. Davenport, and crew were skilled and experienced, but their luck ran out when they were hit by flak and crashed in the target area. Only 14 aircraft returned of the 15 aircraft about 18:25. 6 crew members are buried at Reichswald Forest Cemetery, Germany. 1 crew member is buried at

Venray War Cemetery, Netherlands.

I learned in August 2020 that among this crew was Rear Gunner, Hubert Bishop who had been the Mid-Under Gunner during 6 of our September 1944 operations over France. This confirmed my belief that so much of survival in the unfriendly sky with flak exploding all around you was the luck of not being in the wrong place at the wrong time. Hubert Bishop had become a Commissioned Officer by December 1944. Wing Commander Ralph Davenport had recommended him for a DFC, Distinguished Flying Cross on February 24, 1945 for, "his ability to make instant decisions in an emergency, combined with a strong sense of duty and personal courage." He received a posthumous DFC on May 10, 1945.

March 12, 1945.

15 aircraft flew to Dortmund in the daylight. Only light flak. There was 10/10ths cloud, and the results could not be seen. All aircraft returned safely.

March 13, 1945.

Operations were scrubbed.

March 14, 1945.

The Squadron raised 50 pounds towards a party for the ground crew. Section leaders were busy out collecting the money. 14 aircraft went off to Zweirbrücken, Germany. There was a little cloud and slight haze. The timing over the target was good and no opposition was encountered. All aircraft returned safely.

March 15, 1945.

15 aircraft went to Hagen at night. It was clear over the target with satisfactory results. There was only light flak but, the night fighters were out in force and our aircraft were followed from Hagen all the way back to England.

FTR   Lancaster KB-815, SE-K and crew of Pilot Officer Robert Haw Failed to Return. Robert Haw had 34 trips, 121 points and 205 hours. The crew of Lancaster KB-815 is buried at Perwijz Churchyard in Belgium.

March 18, 1945.

W. C. McKinnon from 419 Squadron arrived to assume command of the 431 Squadron due to Wing Commander R. F. Davenport's death.

March 19, 1945.

There was training all day.

March 20, 1945.

There was training all day and then a late operation was called. The crews were briefed at 23:15 and 14 aircraft were up by 01:30 on March 21. All aircraft returned safely. The aircraft KB-831 of Pilot F. G. Saunders and crew were hit by a safe 500 pound bomb just behind the outer port engine leaving a 2 foot by 3 foot hole. Through expert airmanship F. G. Saunders brought the aircraft back and landed safely at Croft.

On Saturday, March 22, 1945 14 434 Squadron aircraft and 8 431 Squadron aircraft were detailed for an operation to Hildesheim, Germany. All of the 431 Squadron aircraft had left. Later, after 7 434 Squadron aircraft had left, Lancaster KB-832 from 434 Squadron was gathering speed while in the centre of the runway and was up to 70 mph, when owing to a cross wind started to veer to port. The pilot checked the throttles on starboard slightly and as it straightened advanced the starboard throttle and then continued to the right. The port throttles were pulled right back with no change and the aircraft left the runway making a 90 degree abrupt turn to starboard. It is believed that a tire blew as it went into the mud and the landing gear collapsed. When the landing gear collapsed the propellers hit the ground and the engines stopped abruptly and a fire started between the port engines and under the port wing. The flight engineer pressed the Graviner fire extinguisher buttons, but no results were seen. As the fire spread to the bomb bay the 6,000 pounds of incendiaries began to burn along with the fuel on board.

The crew got out of the aircraft safely and ran as fast as they could run. KB-811 from 431 Squadron that was close to KB-832 was moved away from KB-832. The 434 Squadron Wing Commander had some crews start up the engines of four Lancasters which were moved farther away from the burning Lancaster. There were three Lancasters that were only thirty feet from KB-832 that were not moved as it was too dangerous for the crews. The fire crew went out to put out the fire, but they were recalled quickly. There is no way water will extinguish incendiaries. Only sand will extinguish incendiaries. Water makes the magnesium incendiaries burn hotter. Thirty-seven minutes after the fire started the 4,000 pound cookie exploded. Lancaster KB-832 vanished with total destruction. KB-811 was slightly damaged. The 3 other Lancasters that were not moved away were written-off as they were filled with so many holes from the debris of the exploding bomb, the Lancaster pieces and rocks from the bomb crater. The bomb crater was 50 feet across and 25 feet deep. A hole that deep in the ground would have contained enough soil and rocks to fill about six dump trucks. There was debris scattered everywhere on the base. It took more than a day to clean up the mess.

Photograph of a cookie exploding at Croft on Saturday, March 22, 1945. The photograph was taken by the Squadron photographer at Croft, LAC Poste from Woodstock, Ontario. Just as LAC Poste took the photograph, he was knocked flat by the blast. The photograph is courtesy of the Bomber Command Museum in Nanton, Alberta, Canada.

I was riding my bicycle at the time on the way to a depot to get a part for my bicycle when I saw three fellows lying in the ditch beside the road. The fellows yelled at me to get off my bicycle and jump in the ditch. "Don't you see that Lancaster on fire over there?" I had seen it. "That burning Lancaster has a cookie on board. Get off of your bicycle and get in the ditch with us." Before I knew it I was blown off of my bicycle by the blast and I was lying on the road. I was at least one mile from the explosion. The wind from the blast, the sound and the rising column of smoke and debris from the blast was incredible. There were pieces of Lancaster scattered all over the aerodrome and a house not very far away had the slate roof completely demolished. In the photograph the larger dark spots are believed to be Merlin engines. Later that day I picked up a piece of a gun sight that had an electric lamp that illuminated the graticule. The lamp was still good. I donated that piece to the Air Force Museum at Trenton, Ontario, Canada 20 years ago. I had never been on the receiving end of one of our cookies before. The blast from one cookie was devastating and we would drop hundreds of these 4,000-pound cookies on targets on every operation.

FTR   On Saturday, March 22, 1945 Lancaster KB-808 SE-Y-YOKE and crew piloted by Pilot Officer John P. Duggan with 32 trips, 121 points and 220 hours failed to return from Hildesheim. The aircraft was hit in the bomb bay by flak on the run to the target. The cookie and aircraft exploded instantly. This was the last Y-YOKE aircraft at Croft. Pilot Officer John P. Duggan and the crew are buried at the Hanover War Cemetery, Germany. The rest of the Squadron's aircraft returned safely.

Photograph after Lancaster KB-808 SE-YOKE exploded after being hit by flak on the trip to Hildesheim, Germany. The photograph is courtesy of Don Root, son of the Mid-Upper Gunner, Clayton Root

Photograph of the crater left by the explosion of the cookie. That is me with my bike. The two photographs of Croft show how barren and dismal Croft was while I was there. Photograph is courtesy of and copyright by David Walker, grandson of the owners of the farm beside Croft.

March 24, 1945.

10 aircraft carried out a successful raid on the benzoyl plant at Mathias Stinnes near Essen, Germany. There was no cloud cover, and the bombing was accurate. There was little or no opposition and all the aircraft returned safely.

March 25, 1945.

14 aircraft went to Hanover, Germany. Pictures showed good results. It was a well pranged target. One aircraft KB-874 was damaged by flak and returned to Manston.

March 29, 1945.

There were no operations today. Cleaning, redecorating, and painting of A and B flight officers' quarters.

March 31, 1945.

15 aircraft went off to Hamburg, Germany this morning. There was 10/10ths cloud over the target with light flak. Enemy jet fighters were seen attacking the gaggle. This operation was not a piece of cake. The crew of Pilot Heaven claimed one fighter destroyed and one damaged. The crew of T. S. Pattison claimed one fighter damaged.

FTR Lancaster KB-859, SE-UNCLE and crew piloted by P. J. Hurley Failed to Return. Pilot P. J. Hurley and crew had 21 trips and 121 hours. Pilot P. J. Hurley became a POW in Stalag Luft 1. Six crew members were killed and are buried at Becklingen War Cemetery, Germany.

April 1, 2, 1945.

High winds so there were no operations today.

April 3, 1945.

13 aircraft went to Meisburg, Germany. It was a good raid and all the aircraft returned safely.

April 6, 1945.

No operations today. Our eighth Victory Loan bond drive today. All the boys keenly were interested, and they sold $11,150 in bonds.

April 7, 1945.

13 crews were briefed on a raid, but it was scrubbed. The briefings and all the hours cramped the bond drive so only $6,800 of bonds were sold.

April 8, 1945.

14 crews went off to bomb Hamburg, Germany in the evening. Since

the briefings were late in the afternoon, we pushed the bond drive hard and sold $10,600 today. All the aircraft landed away safely and returned on April 9.

April 10, 1945.

16 aircraft and crews went off on a raid to Leipzig, Germany. It was a good prang and all our aircraft returned safely to Croft.

April 11, 1945.

No flying today due to bad weather. To date the boys have sold $40,000 worth of Victory Loan bonds. We reached our bond sales target.

Chapter 36

<u>ON MY WAY HOME</u>

I left Croft on Thursday, April 12, 1945 for the last time with some other mates from the base. I could not leave Croft without my Longines RAF Navigators watch being taken back. I tried to sneak the watch out with me but, Jack Sisman, the Navigation Officer asked me, "Bob what's that on your wrist?" He took back my watch after I sheepishly took it off my wrist and handed it to him.

Photograph of a Longines RAF Navigators watch listed on EBay. These watches currently list for $3,000 USD. The photograph is courtesy of Greg Beaumont (EBay seller ID Slake25)

I said goodbye to the staff and the ground crew who had taken such good care of us. I'll be glad to never see any mutton again as long as I live. The food at Croft was so bad I am sure the cook must have been skimming and putting extra money in his pockets. To this day I will not eat lamb in any shape or form. We were taken by lorry to the Eryholme train station. The train pulled out about 11:00 for a 6 hour ride to the Warrington repatriation depot just west of Manchester. The bunch of us were unloaded from the train about 18:00 that night and we went to the barracks for a dinner of macaroni and cheese. When you were hungry anything tasted good and at least it was not mutton.

On Friday, April 13, 1945 we hung about Manchester for the day and did some souvenir shopping. It was so strange and different. I was not on a five day leave and, in a few days, I would not be going back to the terror in the skies over Germany. I was on my way home.

April 13, 1945.

16 431 squadron crews went off to bomb Kiel, Germany. The bomb timing was bad. All our aircraft landed away. One aircraft blew a tire upon landing so two crews were diverted.

On Saturday, April 14, 1945 I left Manchester by train with a few hundred other fellows all heading home. Our destination was Liverpool, England where we would be sailing home on the American troop ship USS *Mount Vernon*. We arrived later that night and had dinner when we arrived at a canteen. I boarded the *Mount Vernon* about 22:00 that night. There were 1,000 Commissioned Officers assigned to living quarters in the hold of the ship. We all had beds of sorts. I was quick and managed to get a bed. The beds were all bunk bed style in three levels. The frames were made up of vertical pipes and horizontal pipes. There was a sheet of canvas lashed to the horizontal pipes with a thin mattress thrown on top of that. There was only 20 inches between beds three high, and you had to be very careful not to rise too fast as you may bash your head on the pipes above you that supported the mattress above you. The non-commissioned officers only had hammocks to sleep in.

April 15, 1945.

14 431 Squadron crews were back at Croft prepared for a raid but it was scrubbed just as the briefing ended. To date $49,700 worth of Victory Loan bonds have been sold.

Postcard of the *SS Washington* before it was requisitioned by the US Navy and became the USS *Mount Vernon*. Postcard is from the Dan Middleton Collection.

It was early Sunday, April 15, 1945 and I got up and was served some greasy pork for breakfast that I did not care too much for, but it was still better than the mutton at Croft. The Captain of the ship was E. P. Eldrege. The *Mount Vernon* pulled away from her berth at 07:40. Altogether on the ship were about 3,500 military passengers including 390 members of the RCAF. The *Mount Vernon* could carry 6,000 troops.

The *Mount Vernon* had previously been the luxury ocean liner named SS *Washington.* She was launched in May 1933 and served routes from New York City, USA to Plymouth, England and to Hamburg, Germany. In 1935 the SS *Washington* was advertised as the largest liner ever built in America. The *Mount Vernon* had a gross tonnage of 23,626 tons, was 667 feet long with a beam of 86 feet. The speed of the ship was twenty knots. The *Mount Vernon* was about 70 feet shorter and ten knots slower than the *Mauretania*, the ship I had come over to England on. On the deck were four 5 inch guns, four 3 inch guns and eight 0.50 caliber machine guns. The US Navy acquired the SS *Washington* for use as a troop ship on June 16, 1941. In December of 1941 the *Mount Vernon* was steaming to Cape Town, South Africa to pick up troops. While the ship was passing near Cape Horn word arrived that Japan had attacked Pearl Harbor. The United States of America immediately declared war on Japan and joined in the fight to free occupied Europe from Nazi domination. The Japanese had attacked the "Sleeping Giant" a fictional quote from the 1970 Hollywood movie *TORA, TORA, TORA*. Japanese Admiral Yamamoto reportedly wrote in his diary, "I fear all we have done is to awaken a sleeping giant and fill him with a terrible resolve." The 2001 movie, *Pearl Harbor* used the "Sleeping Giant" quote.

President Roosevelt had created the lend-lease agreements with England and the Commonwealth countries in preparation for a World War that the majority of Americans wanted nothing to do with. President Roosevelt did all he could to help his Allies around the world. It was a European war that Americans were trying to ignore until Japan dragged the USA into the now complete world conflict. Ian Dagnall computing / Alamy Stock Photo H4E0DK.

At 9:30 AM this day a memorial service was held for the late President Roosevelt who had passed away on Thursday, April 12, 1945. President Franklin Delano Roosevelt or FDR as he was also referred to had served as the President of the USA for three terms from March 4, 1933 to April 12, 1945. In retrospect it is so sad that after President Roosevelt had seen the USA through the Great Depression, WWII in Europe and the Pacific, he passed away just a few days before the demise of Adolf Hitler on Monday, April 30, 1945 and Victory in Europe on Tuesday, May 8, 1945. In just a few more days he would have seen the end of the Second World War in Europe that the Allied Forces had worked towards since the beginning.

A little bit after noon I saw that two British destroyers the HMS *Cavendish* on our port side and the HMS *Carron* on our starboard side 2,000 yards off our bow. Almost like flying in bombers, with all our turning points to confuse and trick the enemy U-boats, the troop ship did not travel in a straight direction for more than a few hours. They sailed a zigzag course. You do not steer in a straight line too long to avoid contact with German U-boats. After we had been on our way for an hour we could hear and see depth charges going off a few miles away. I can only guess someone detected U-boats in the vicinity. Once out at sea the *Mount Vernon* steamed at 23 knots directly across the Atlantic Ocean in a zigzag plan and did not go way down south like the *Mauretania* did on the trip from Halifax to Liverpool, England. The threat of attack by German U- boats must have been very low by the middle of April 1945.

April 16, 1945.
13 431 Squadron aircraft took off from Croft for a late night raid on Schwandorf, Germany. This was the first night operation in some time. All of our crews returned safely from the operation after a quiet trip. It was a long, hard grind blessed with little opposition.

April 19, 1945.
At Croft there were no operations today. A bottle of Scotch whiskey was put up as a raffle. For a $50 bond you received a raffle ticket. We sold another $1,400 in bonds so we are up to $53,450.

April 20, 1945.
This was another quiet day today at Croft. Training and one battle order was prepared but that was scrubbed.

As we turned north sailing up the American east coast the weather became very stormy and the Atlantic Ocean violent with huge crests. The ships speed had been reduced to only 15 mph. At only 667 feet long the *Mount Vernon* was long enough that it could ride over the crest of three waves. A fourth crest was too much, and the bow of the ship would fall into the trough and disappear 10 feet under the ocean and then reappear and rise up back into the air. As the bow went down into the ocean the water came up to the closed windows on the promenade deck. The bow of the ship was cordoned off as it was so dangerous. You could easily be washed over the side and disappear forever. The crew allowed us to stand at the stern of the ship. Standing at the stern of the ship was an exhilarating experience, better than any roller coaster ride at the CNE. Nowhere near as exciting and terrifying as when our pilot, Don would corkscrew our bomber to escape danger over Germany, however. The deck at the stern of the ship would go down to within about ten feet above the surface of the Atlantic Ocean and then a few moments later the stern would be 40 feet above the Atlantic Ocean. I never did see the propellers but, they must have come very close to the surface. And yes, I was standing at the stern hanging over the railing holding on for dear life. Out of the thousands of folks onboard I was the only fool standing out on the deck in that storm. There were shuffleboard courts running the length of the deck at the stern of the ship. I was having a marvelous time playing shuffleboard by myself that day. The ship was rolling quite slowly, and I was eventually able judge how hard to push the shuffles depending on whether the stern was rising or falling.

Later I was looking at the sides of the ship and watched the seams of the ship. The plates of the hull of the *Mount Vernon* were riveted together. As the ship went up and down, and the water crashed against the ship, I thought I could see the seam of the plates moving slightly. As the stern rose the water appeared to be swirling around in the seams between the plates and then got squeezed back out of the seams as the stern went back down. It was almost like the hull of the ship had gills and the ship was breathing. One thing that I realized on this trip is that I do not get seasick, and I do not get airsick. I always found this amazing, especially on the days that the Atlantic Ocean was so rough. Many poor fellows were overcome with seasickness.

April 21, 1945.
Victory Loan bond drive at Croft closed at $55,950 worth of bonds sold at 431 Squadron.

April 22, 1945.
15 431 Squadron aircraft went off for a raid on Bremen, Germany in the daylight. Due to heavy cloud over the target the crews were told not

to bomb. It was a wasted effort. All of our aircraft returned safely back at Croft.

The Consolidated PBY Catalina or Canadian Canso from the Canadian Warplane Heritage Museum collection. Photograph is courtesy of the Canadian Warplane Heritage Museum at Hamilton, Ontario.

Once the weather cleared I saw that we were constantly accompanied by PBY Catalina flying boats. One would leave and then another would appear to take over the task of overseeing our safety. The PBY Catalina was an amazing aircraft used for many tasks at sea. The PBY Catalina in some configurations had a range of 3,000 miles while cruising at 120 miles per hour. There are records of Catalina flying boats being airborne for 26 hours in operations such as search and rescue and of escorting ships like the *Mount Vernon*.

April 23, 1945.

There was training all day back at Croft. Awards were given out today. Pilot B. M. Kaplansky for expert airmanship while under fire by enemy fighters. Pilot D. E. Gomyrl was wounded in the shoulder by flak while over the target and was unable to pilot the aircraft. He gave expert directions on flying the aircraft home and then took over the landing even though one arm was useless. Pilot F. K. Saunders received a DFC for piloting his aircraft safely home with a hole in the port wing made by a bomb falling through the wing.

The Martin Mariner PBM flying boat picture is from a 1943 magazine clipping in my aircraft recognition scrapbook. From the Bob Middleton Collection.

A Martin Mariner PBM flying boat approached us from the bow and was flying alongside the *Mount Vernon* for quite some time appearing almost stationary. The ship was travelling about 23 miles per hour with the wind and the wind was blowing quite strong at about 80 miles per hour. The Mariner was probably traveling at airspeed of 100 miles per hour into the wind. The Mariner eventually passed the ship, but it took quite some time. A while later just as the Mariner had passed the stern it turned around in a shot and came back flying in the other direction and it went past us like a fighter aircraft with that 80 mph tail wind. The Martin Mariner was built as a compliment to the Consolidated built PBY Catalina. The Y in PBY stood for Consolidated and the M in PBM stood for Martin Industries. The PBM had a range of 3,000 miles.

On Monday, April 23, 1945 the Channel Pilot and tugs picked us up. At 22:52 we docked at Pier No. 6 at Newport News, Norfolk Virginia, USA. When I got off the ship, I looked back at the bow that was now sitting about 35 feet above the water. I was totally amazed that a few days earlier that bow had been going 10 feet under the water in those huge waves. I was almost home and so far from the conflict that was still going on in Europe. I was on the North American continent.

On the morning of Tuesday, April 24, 1945 I disembarked the *Mount Vernon* and said goodbye to my new shipboard friends that I never saw again. Later that morning I boarded the pool train bound for Montreal, Quebec, Canada.

April 25, 1945.

Back at Croft 15 aircraft went to bomb gun positions on the island of Wangerooge, Germany on a daylight operation. The raid had good results. Sadly, on this last 431 Squadron operation of the war, two of our aircraft both with almost new crews collided mid-air over the target area. Both of the aircraft and the crews were lost.

FTR   Lancaster KB-831 SE-E and crew piloted by Barry D. Emmet with only one operation and five flying hours. 5 crew members are remembered at the Runnymede Memorial Surrey, UK. 1 crew member is buried at the Sage War Cemetery, Germany. 1 crew member is buried at the Becklingen War Cemetery, Germany.

FTR   Lancaster KB-822 SE-W and crew piloted by Douglas G. Baker with only one operation and five flying hours. 5 crew members are remembered at the Runnymede Memorial Surrey, UK. 1 crew member is buried at the Sage War Cemetery, Germany. 1 crew member is buried at the Kviberg Cemetery, Sweden.

I arrived at the Manning Depot in Montreal on Wednesday, April 25, 1945 where I was served a dinner of macaroni and cheese. I was really back in Canada, my country. I had left a year and a half ago. I was lucky as many served over in England for two or three years and two tours. The odds of surviving a second tour are so much less than your first tour. I felt so lucky to have survived 33 operations without a scratch over enemy occupied Europe. As soon as I was in the Montreal Manning Depot, I sent a telegram to my Mom and Dad and my fiancée Pat informing them that I would be arriving at Union Station in Toronto at 5 PM the next day on Thursday, April 26, 1945. Up to this telegram I had not informed anyone at home that I had left Croft. No one knew when I was coming home or what ship I was travelling on. If this information was generally known the information ran the risk of being discovered and then having a U-boat lying in wait for us somewhere. Sinking a troop ship full of 4,000 fully trained personnel was a jackpot for the enemy. I stayed overnight at the Montreal Manning Depot.

On Thursday, April 26, 1945 I arrived home at Toronto Union Station. I do not know what I was expecting when I got off the train. I had not seen any family or my fiancée, Pat for 18 months since I left Toronto for my departure for England at Halifax on Monday, October 18, 1943. The anticipation and butterflies in my stomach were almost the same as getting in a bomber as who knows what I should expect. The train pulled into Toronto about 5:00 PM. I stepped off the train and just as my feet hit the ground of Union Station, Pat who wearing flowers in her hair and was wearing a beautiful white suit, jumped into my arms. I knew I had arrived in heaven. I had arrived back home; I had survived all the hellish terrors in the skies over occupied Europe and done my part to save the world from one evil tyrant and his thugs.

ONE FLAK HOLE was all F.O. Bill Middleton's plane suffered in a tour. Here he is home with his fiancee, Patricia McIntyre.

The newspaper picture from page four of the Friday, April 27, 1945 edition of The Toronto Daily Star. The Toronto Daily Star reporter managed to get my name incorrect, however. My brother's name is Bill.

When I got off the train photographers from The Toronto Globe and Mail and The Toronto Daily Star snapped our pictures together and the reporters took down our story. That story is on page 323.

lustry
nt
by Drew

Recreation and
t, under a sep-
lister, will be
Government, if
ultimate object
share of tourist
an ever before,
this announce-
i address to the
: (central), at
lotel. The new
rdinate and ad-
s activities re-
and tourist in-
be aided and
tion of an On-
il consisting of
various bodies
rist travel and
d.

1st and travel
rection of Tom
'remler praised
se absorbed by
Mr. Drew ap-
stance of the
in selling On-
of the United
scribed as "160
foot-loose peo-
nly the surface
try had been
d.

'preters to the
at the British
the Premier
interpreters of
sh partnership
ing up of that
the English-
re in Ontario
y of bringing
pact upon the
nation.
I to the mines,
culture, is our
ry. One of the
tribute to the
war is this;
we bring here

An unserviceable compass caused FO. Bob Middleton some flak-happy moments over Stuttgart but the young navigator came out of it "without a hole" and last night got home to Toronto. He is shown with Miss Patricia Mc-Intyre.

Unhurt in Flak Shower After Compass Fails

Loan Sale
Though St
Wash Out

If Toronto's wee
give the Eighth Vi
vassers a break soo
to be an upheaval t
the Berchtesgaden
like a Maypole da
school. At least,
some of the 700 as
terday after slosh
streets for the th
day.
But notwithstan
tance of housewive
vassers to park th
on polished hardwo
still buying fairly
drop in the total as
previous loans was
city's total for the
000, bringing the t
days up to about 3
city's $250,000,000 s
loan statisticians p
16.1 per cent of th
in 16.66 per cent
time.
Capt. Mahoney on t
They aren't vi
alarm, at all, but
since the rampage
day, the City Ha
scheduled for eve1
have been washed s
They hope today: t
noontime crowd wi
to hear Capt. J. G
landed in Normand
did "hush hush"
reaches for some
The parade which
last Saturday will
uled for this week
day there will be a
than 4,000 sea, air s
cadets.
Troops of Militar
are continuing the!
on their $1,235,00(
yesterday reached
mark when sale

The newspaper picture from page 4 of the Friday, April 27, 1945 edition of The Globe and Mail. The reporter did not get the story correct. We actually received three small holes over Stuttgart. Use of the photograph is courtesy of The Globe and Mail Inc.

On April 27, 1945 Back at Croft a daylight operation was planned but scrubbed. The Squadron had the honor of playing host to Mr. and Mrs. Vincent Massey, the Canadian High Commissioner in London. The guests appeared pleased with the appearance of our Squadron. After today there were no more operations at Croft. There was some training.

On May 10, 1945 11 431 Squadron Lancasters flew to Juvincourt, France to pick up 240 POWs and 2 RCAF crews. The POWs were brought to Westcott, UK for repatriation.

May 11, 1945 22 crews started 4 days of intensive ground school in preparation of bringing 431 Squadron Lancasters back to Canada to become part of Tiger Force for the fight in the Pacific. Between May 14 and May 31 of 1945 all the training was completed.

On May 31, 1945 20 Lancasters from 431 Squadron left from Middleton St. George and eventually landed at Moncton, New Brunswick. In total 141 RCAF Lancasters made the trip to Moncton. The Tiger Force Lancasters were to have been stationed on Okinawa Island, about 965 miles south of Tokyo. The war ended before any RCAF Lancasters left Canada.

Chapter 37

HOME IN TORONTO

It was marvelous being home in Toronto from the war over there. I did miss the excitement and the flying some days. We all had a pretty good idea that the war in Europe would be over almost any day now. It had been reported that Adolf Hitler had committed suicide on Monday, April 30, 1945. A few days later Berlin fell to the Russian Army and on Monday, May 7, 1945 Germany surrendered unconditionally at Reims, France.

On Tuesday, May 8, 1945 the Second World War in Europe officially ended. This was VE Day, Victory in Europe. Me and what looked like the rest of Toronto went over to Yonge Street to celebrate. Pat was working for the Consumers' Gas Company on Toronto Street and she could not get the day off. It was a huge party. The Toronto Daily Star did not print the newspaper that day.

431 Squadron Wing Commander W. F. McKinnon wrote in the 431 Squadron logbook on May 8, 1945, "Today is VICTORY IN EUROPE DAY. Eleven months from D-Day our armies have forced the Germans to capitulate. No. 431 R.C.A.F. Squadron the Famed Iroquois has played its part in the hammering of the fortress of Europe. While this is a day of great jubilation still one can't help remember that this victory has not been gained without loss. Since its formation on 11th November 1942, No. 431 Squadron suffered the following casualties: Total number killed: 301. Total number of POWs: 104. Total number of

aircraft lost: 75. Let us not forget these gallant airmen that made this victory possible."

During the time that Wing Commander W. F. McKinnon wrote about the 431 Squadron had flown 2,257 sorties in 168 operations.

ADDRESS REPLY TO:
THE SECRETARY,
DEPARTMENT OF NATIONAL DEFENCE FOR AIR,
OTTAWA, ONTARIO.

OUR FILE J.37180
REF. YOUR
DATED

ROYAL CANADIAN AIR FORCE

Ottawa, Ontario.

16th May, 1945.

Flying Officer R.J. Middleton,
8 Ashbridge Avenue,
Toronto, Ont.

Dear Flying Officer Middleton,

        The rapid and successful development of the Royal Canadian Air Force and its outstanding contribution towards the defeat of Germany, would not have been possible without officers like yourself who have rendered most valuable service in the Canadian war effort.

        On the occasion of your release from active service in the Royal Canadian Air Force, I wish to convey to you my sincere appreciation of your faithful service.

        Please accept my best wishes for your happiness and every success in the future.

        Yours sincerely,

(J. A. Easton)
Group Captain,
for Chief of the Air Staff.

Thank you letter from the RCAF for my service. From the Bob Middleton Collection.

When I returned home many people wanted to hear about my adventures flying in bombers over Europe. Mr. Butler the owner of a paper factory was very interested in my stories. My Aunt Lil did the washing and pressing of his drapes and linens. At Christmas he would bring us boxes of the self-adhesive strips of colored paper that we made paper chains with. He told me that I should be writing a diary of all that happened over those past two years before I forgot the stories. I never did write it down then but 75 years later we are writing it down and most of the memories are intact.

After I had been home for a couple of weeks my Dad arranged a job for me at the Post Office in the Registered Letter department. I started at the Post Office around the beginning of June. My job was to sort through registered letters and fill out registered letter tags to go with the registered letters. These were all filled out by hand. There were about 20 people in the department. I was working with some old duck that moved like molasses in January. It did not matter how fast I was because he would give me more to do. For every ten forms and slips I filled out he did three. Pat would come down to the Post Office every day and meet me and we sat on the front steps while I had my lunch. The hours were from 5:00 PM to 1:00 in the morning. Once we finished all the forms that had to be processed, we could leave early. I generally left about midnight. After all the training I had been through and all the risky flying over occupied Europe I was beside myself with boredom. Oh, I wish I was still flying. One day I asked the boss what I had to do to quit. He told me he needed one week's notice. I gave him the notice right there. In seven more days, I was finished with the Post Office. In 1945 a full-time work week was 5 and one half days. I had off half of Saturday and all day Sunday.

Ken Locke who was one of my friends from Danforth Tech told me that he was working for the Bell Telephone Company and the job was good and paid well. Ken suggested I should go apply. Ken lived two doors south of Pat's house. I applied at the Bell Telephone Company. They did not have any outside linesmen jobs available as these jobs were being held open for returning veterans. Bell had openings in the drafting department and my time at Danforth Tech and my Navigator experience provided the prerequisites so on July 3, 1945 I ended up working as a Bell Telephone Company draftsman. When I started with

Bell Telephone Company the regular starting pay was $88 per month. Because I had served in the war, I was paid $100.64. That was certainly commendable of the Bell Telephone Company for treating veterans well. The work was great and all the folks I worked with were marvelous. At lunch break I would sketch my memories of my days with the RCAF.

I turned 22 on Sunday, July 15, 1945. This same day the last blackout area in Britain in the west end of London was lifted. Most of the blackout in Britain had ended in April 1945. All the lights were back on just as Vera Lynn had promised us in her song, *When The Lights Go On Again*. The next day, July 16 the plutonium bomb, "Trinity" with a 22,000 ton explosive yield was successfully detonated in the New Mexico desert and the nuclear age had begun. The next day the news was given to President Harry S. Truman at the beginning of the Potsdam Conference. The three leaders, Winston Churchill of Britain, Harry S. Truman of the USA, and Joseph Stalin of the USSR decided how to administer Germany, what the new Europe would look like and who was going to control which countries. At the conference President Truman announced they had successfully tested an atomic bomb and were prepared to use one against a city in Japan. The Allied forces had weighed the consequences of the use of nuclear bombs or a conventional invasion by sea and the continued bombing destruction of Japan by air. It has been estimated that the combined military and civilian casualties on both sides in an invasion of Japan would have been in the millions. The hope was that one bomb dropped on one city possibly killing 70,000 people instantly would end the war without any more loss of life or any further destruction of Japan. It was feared the Japanese soldiers and citizens would have fought to the bitter end. If millions of people on both sides of the conflict had been killed in a long, protracted conventional invasion of Japan how would historians have written history if the atomic bombs were not used when available to reduce the loss of life by 2 million people?

Russia had already forced the surrender of the Japanese in China in Operation August Storm. Over 80,000 Japanese civilians and soldiers were killed. About 600,000 Japanese were taken prisoner. By August 9, 1945 Russia was ready to invade the northern islands of Japan. That would have been a horrible slaughter of the people in northern Japan.

The Japanese military invaded China in 1931 and created a puppet state. For 14 years the Japanese murdered and subjugated the Chinese people. The Russians and the Chinese would have invaded Japan and the Chinese soldiers would probably have exacted a terrible revenge on the Japanese. The northern Japanese islands would have probably remained in Russian control the same as the German controlled territories that Russia had invaded in Europe. The world may have been faced with a Communist North Japan and a Democratic Republic of South Japan. There would have been no stability in the region. On July 26, 1945 the Potsdam Declaration, was issued by the group to Japan calling for their unconditional surrender. The declaration warned of "prompt and utter destruction" if Japan failed to surrender unconditionally. The Japanese leaders refused to surrender and on August 6, 1945 the uranium bomb, "Little Boy" with an explosive yield of 15,000 <u>tons</u> was detonated over the city of Hiroshima. About 70,000 people were killed instantly and another 70,000 people died from the effects of radiation. In comparison, all the bombs and incendiaries that were dropped by 2,000 bombers on Duisburg, Germany on October 15, 1944 amounted to a yield of 6,800 <u>tons</u>.

My cousin Wilf Fry who was in the Canadian Army and stationed in Victoria, British Columbia in 1945 wrote me a letter the next day that expressed the sentiment of 2,159 weary days of war. "What do you think of this new bomb the Japs are getting thrown at them? It shouldn't last long, now." Imagine if you can what the sentiment would be if our current world war against COVID-19 does not end until 2025.

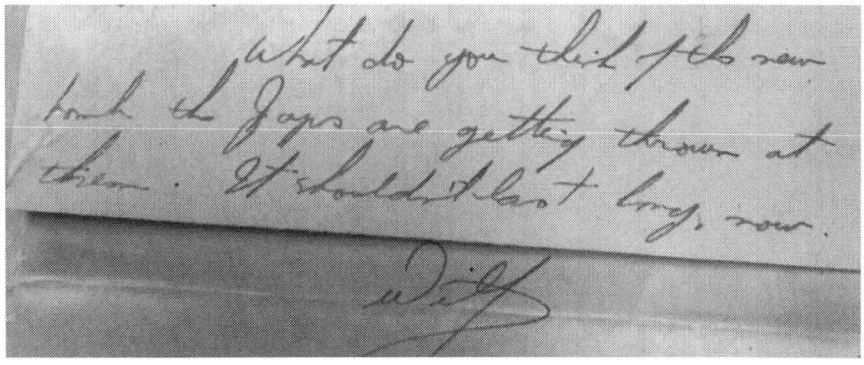

Part of the letter my Cousin Wilf Fry wrote to me on August 7, 1945. The photograph is from the Bob Middleton Collection.

There was still no acceptance of the surrender terms from the Japanese government. The Allies waited until August 9, 1945 when the plutonium bomb, "Fat Man" with an explosive yield of 21,000 <u>tons</u> was detonated over the city of Nagasaki. There were about 70,000 people killed in Nagasaki. The Japanese government agreed to an unconditional surrender on August 15, 1945. That day became known as Victory in Japan Day, VJ Day. There were huge parties in the streets of all the Allied nations that day. The VJ Day parties were the largest in the United States. This year August 15, 2020, marked the 75th anniversary of VJ Day. The surrender documents were signed by Japan on board the battleship USS *Missouri* on September 2, 1945.

I spent many hours shaping out of balsa wood the various aircraft that I had flown in England. Until the late 1940's there were no plastic model kits of the Wellington, Halifax or Lancaster. I still have these wooden models. Somehow, I had kept them away from my two sons who would have loved to see if they could fly. I shocked Dan in May 2020 when I told him I still have them. He was sure Dave and he had destroyed those models years ago.

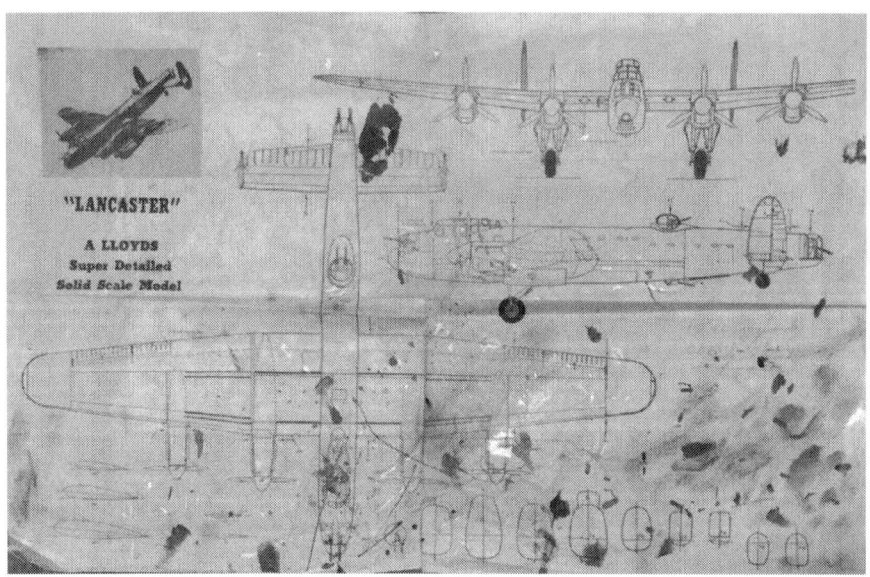

Scale model plans for the Lancaster bomber that I carved from wood. On this plan the Lancaster is shown with a lower turret. Lancaster bombers were never built with the lower turret. I used this plan to carve and shape a model of the Lancaster. I drew the H2S blister around that turret. The photograph is from the Bob Middleton Collection.

Photograph I took in 1946 of my solid balsa wood models of a Wellington, a Halifax Mk. III and a Lancaster I built while living with Mom and Dad in 1945 and 1946. The photograph is from the Bob Middleton Collection.

My bomber models photographed in 2020. The Wellington is a plastic model. The wooden Wellington fell off a shelf and I never rebuilt it. Photograph was taken by Dan Middleton.

A few months after I had been working with the telephone company, I applied for my Veterans' Land Grant loan, under the VLA (Veterans' Land Act from 1942). Back then the clerks at the Veterans' Land Administration did everything for you. You told them the information and the clerk filled in the forms. No self-serve or online nonsense back then. I told the clerk that I was being paid $100.64 per month and he wrote down $164.00 per month. Looked good to me and I left it alone. I figured it may help get me a loan when I needed it.

A few days before Christmas 1945 I proposed to Pat, and we announced our wedding day would be July 18, 1946. Ray and his wife sent us a congratulations telegram on Christmas Day 1945.

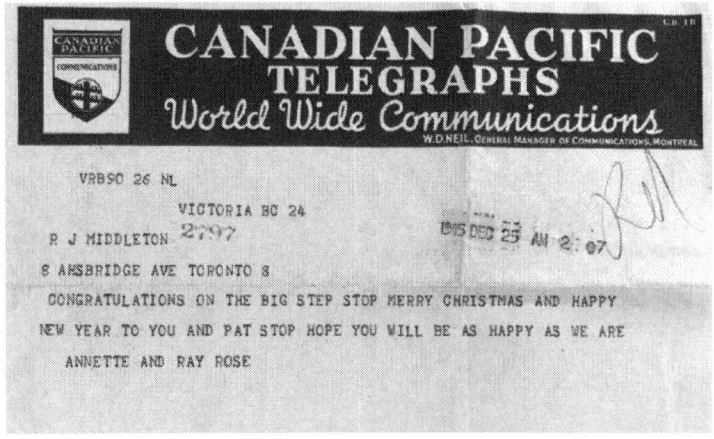

Merry Christmas, 1945 telegram from Ray and Annette Rose. The telegram is from the Bob Middleton Collection.

Pat's brother, Bill McIntyre was married to Irene Scharfe on Saturday, May 4, 1946. After 2 years in the Canadian Army Bill enlisted in the RCNVR, Royal Canadian Naval Volunteer Reserve from August 9, 1944 to November 28, 1945 and was an Electrical Artificer in the Navy. He was stationed in Ottawa when he met Irene. Irene was a clerk living in Ottawa and working on the preparation of the national census. Bill was always very secretive about his work with the Navy. On February 7, 1945 he was recommended for advancement in the naval Electrical Department for, "Special ability in the draughting-room work." After the war Bill worked in the Engineering department of Ontario Hydro for 36 years until he retired in 1981. He received the honorary title of Engineer for his work there.

Irene and Bill's wedding photograph. The photograph is courtesy of Robert McIntyre and Laurel Wheeler.

Photograph at my wedding shower thrown by the folks in the Telephone Company Drafting department. The photograph is from the Bob Middleton Collection.

Our wedding picture from a well-worn negative. Pat made her own wedding dress and I bought a new suit. Photograph from the Bob Middleton Collection.

Pat and I were married at St. Matthew's Presbyterian Church located on the south-west corner of Eastwood Road and Gainsborough Road at 3:00 in the afternoon on Thursday, July 18, 1946. Pat made her own wedding dress, and I bought a new suit. The location of the church is indicated by the ♥ on the page 30 map. In attendance were my family and friends and Pat's family and friends. The reception and dinner were at the church. Doris McKeown was Pat's Maid of Honor and my cousin Ted Fry was my Best Man.

For our honeymoon we drove off in a cab to Bonnie View Inn summer resort on Lake Kashagawigamog in the Haliburton Highlands and stayed there for two weeks. I believe the cost of that cab ride was about $30 one way. Like many fellows who had been overseas I did not have a driver's license or a car in 1946. I could fly a Tiger Moth aircraft but, I could not drive a car. In 1948 I took a driving course with School of Safe Driving at a downtown Toronto location and passed the driving test. I required a license to drive a telephone company vehicle. Our first car was a 1938 Chevrolet that I purchased for $600 in 1948. Cars were expensive as automobile factories were still ramping up to produce consumer vehicles after 6 years of producing military vehicles.

The wedding head table. Seated beside Pat is her best friend, Doris McKeown. Sitting beside Doris was one of Pat's friends at the Consumers' Gas Company. Sitting beside me is my cousin Ted Fry. Photograph from the Bob Middleton Collection.

My Dad and Mom with Pat and I. People think Dad and I look like deer in the headlights. Photograph from the Bob Middleton Collection.

Pat's Mom and Dad with Pat and I. Photograph from the Bob Middleton Collection.

Chapter 38

BUILDING OUR HOME

While working in the Bell Drafting department I met Dane Gibson, an outside Plant Engineer. Dane was also a Navigator in the RCAF who had flown in Wellington bombers in North Africa during 1942. During one operation that he was flying on, their aircraft was shot down and had to ditch in the Mediterranean Sea. They were rescued by a British patrol boat. Dane suffered a head injury in the crash and had a plate in his head. Dane who became a good friend and my next door neighbor told me one day that he was going to be building a house using the Veterans' Land Act grant. To qualify for the grant a veteran had to purchase a piece of land at least 1 acre in size. Dane had purchased a 1 acre lot from McNab Realty and managed to have it legally subdivided into two half acre lots. The property was in the middle of nowhere in Scarborough just south of Kingston Road and a mile west of Markham Road. He told me that an RCAF friend, Al Asher who was going to build a house beside him but, Al changed his mind because his wife felt it was too far from Toronto and civilization. In 1948 there was only one traffic light for the 6 miles along Danforth Avenue and Kingston Road from Main Street all the way to Markham Road. The half acre lot was $1,000. I worked out how much it would cost me to build a house and I went to the Bell Credit Union to apply for my Veterans' Land Loan in order to buy the land and materials.

The clerk at the credit union looked over all information I had given and asked me if I was still being paid $164 per month. I said, "Oh, someone must have put down an incorrect amount. I'm being paid $137 per month." I had been given quite a few raises since I had started with the Telephone Company. I was a bit worried if I made enough to qualify. She told me that was enough income to qualify for the loan. The Veterans' Land Act granted me $6,000 at 3.5 percent interest which was half of the going mortgage rate in 1948. I was allowed to use $600 of that to purchase furnishings and appliances and I only had to pay back two thirds of the $5,400. All together the house project would cost me $8,000. Pat and I had $1,450 in cash and we took a small loan from the Bell Credit Union for $347.00. I am still a member of the Bell Credit Union and in 2017 I received a glass ornament from them for being a customer for seventy years. I am the only member of the Bell Credit Union that has been a member for more than seventy years.

Before we decided to build a house, we had been looking at prebuilt houses in Scarborough. There were some very nice two story houses west of Fallingbrook Road and south of Kingston Road for $12,000. On Hague Avenue west of Warden Avenue there were some nice five room bungalows with forced air heating for $5,800. At Birchmount Road and Kingston Road there were five room bungalows for $9,000. After living in our parents' homes for so long on the tiny lots we decided it would be nice to have a large property where we could breathe.

We were building the house from a plan that Dane had seen in a home magazine. I took those and drew up the plans for both of our houses for the Scarborough Township and for the VLA. The plans were OK because they were approved. We started building our house in the middle of nowhere on Faircroft Boulevard in Scarborough in August of 1947. I surveyed the location of the house myself. It was not a kit so there was no precut material. Every piece of wood was cut with a hand saw, every hole was bored with a bit and brace drill and every nail was driven home by a hammer. I still have that hammer. The basements of both mine and Dane's houses were dug out at the same time by a bulldozer in the spring of 1947. The building inspector had told us that the hole for the basement had to be four and a half feet deep. Both of our basement foundations were dug six inches shy of the four and a half feet deep. Before we got much further, we found out the Inspector had made a mistake and the hole needed to be five and one half feet deep plus another one half foot deeper around the perimeter for the foundation wall footings. It would cost too much money to have the bulldozer come back so I dug out by hand with a shovel 18 inches of clay from the hole that was about 25 feet by 30 feet.

A photograph of what building a house will do for your physical condition. Somewhat different looking than I was in my shaving cream picture at Croft on page 281. The photograph was taken at the Windermere Lodge. Photograph from the Bob Middleton Collection.

The hole had straight sides, so I had to heave the clay out of the hole up onto the surface. I could heave a shovel full of clay from the centre of the hole up to the top. This amounted to about 42 yards of clay enough to fill three large dump trucks. That was a great deal of digging and I had great muscles to show for it. After I dug out my basement, I helped Dane dig his basement deeper.

I had a little bit of yellow sand in one corner so that made my life somewhat easier. Dane's basement hole was about half yellow sand which helped even more. The house beside Dane had a basement that was all yellow sand. It poured rain one day and at the end of the rain I had 12 inches of water in the basement hole. Dane had 6 inches of water in the basement hole and Dane's neighbor had no water in the basement hole.

You have to have blocks for the foundation of the house but, back then you had to supply the block manufacturer with the cement equal to the amount required for the blocks you ordered. It was next to impossible for the average guy to obtain cement. Through the Veterans' Land Act I was allotted a large enough quantity of cement to make the blocks and the concrete for the footings. I took the bags of cement to Argo Block on Kennedy Road north of Lawrence Avenue to have the blocks made. In 1948 that was a long way. The blocks were shipped to our property. Dad and I mixed the cement and poured the footings for the foundation walls and posts. Once the footings were set adequately my Dad laid all the blocks. The blocks were very green as they were only a few days old. Concrete takes 28 days to cure to full strength. We had to carry the blocks carefully by lifting with both hands from the base. If we picked up the block with one hand using the webs the block would break. Because the blocks were so green the mortar bonded to the blocks very well and in 2020 there are still no basement wall cracks or leaks. Not those many years previously Dad had been a hod carrier and he was quite good at laying the foundation blocks. Dad knew everything about laying bricks and block. I did the mortar mixing and the transporting of the blocks and mortar. This took us many weekends as Dad was still working in 1947. Once the foundation was laid we started to build the ground floor on top of it. It is quite an amazing feeling to be sitting in a lawn chair on the floor of your own house that you are building with your own two hands.

Pat and I started out on a three day vacation to Niagara Falls sometime in August 1948. Back then there was no QEW so the entire trip each way took about six hours along Kings Highway 2. As we were going through Etobicoke we saw a truck going the other way that was carrying a full load of bags of cement. We still did not have any cement for the basement floor. The Veterans' Land Act did not allow me that much cement and we did not know where to buy cement. We turned around and followed the truck to a house near Sunnyside. I asked him if I could by 25 bags of cement if I paid in cash and he agreed. I rented a trailer and made two trips between Sunnyside and the house. That took the rest of the day and in the end, it was too late to go to Niagara Falls.

Me standing in the snow behind our house in 1949. Photograph is from the Bob Middleton Collection.

I hired Doug Brown, the fellow who had laid the basement floor for my brother-in-law, Bill McIntyre, to do my basement floor. I rented a small cement mixer with a gasoline engine to mix the cement. One part cement, two parts sand and three parts gravel was the formula. Dad and I spent all of October 8, 1948 filling the mixer, mixing, emptying the mixer and moving the cement by wheelbarrow to the north-west basement window that we dumped the cement through. The cement I bought turned out to be quick setting and very strong. It took a great deal of muscle by Doug to level and float smooth that quick setting cement floor. Doug blessed the cement and that basement floor a few times that day. Doug gave me a handwritten 10 year warranty. I still have the warranty paper. That floor has never developed a crack to this day.

We had the foundation ready before the winter and I was building the main floor during the winter of 1947 and 1948.

Me putting some more nails in the siding at the back of the house. I put most of these boards up by myself.
Photograph from the Bob Middleton Collection.

The job in the Bell Telephone Drafting department was great. I met Reg Stark there and we are still friends after 75 years. The job was going well but we were classified as clerks the same as the female switchboard operator clerks. In 1948 the male clerk draftsmen were being paid more than the female operators so the Telephone Company gave the male clerks a raise of only $10 per month. The female clerks received a greater raise. This was no good as we were not going to see a decent raise for years until the male and female pay rate was the same. The outside linesmen were in a different classification that was making more money so Reg and I gave our notice to the Drafting department in the summer. We were transferred to the outside linesmen crews at the beginning of November 1948 and the weather was sure cold that year.

By this time, I had been building my house in Scarborough with only hand tools. My muscles and my stamina were quite high, so the outdoor manual work was no effort for me. Back in those days if you were installing just one or two poles for a phone service you dug those by hand. No auger was sent to do the job. The foreman of the crew I worked in was Slim Dunnit who was quite a likeable character. The first job I went out on with the crew was installing lines and poles for a VLA suburb north-west of Ellesmere Road and Kennedy Road in the north end of Scarborough. This was in the middle of nowhere in 1948. Slim and the guys with the truck dropped me off and told me to start digging a hole six foot deep for a pole. Doug took off with Don Shaw driving the truck and said they would be back later to help me dig and then drop in the 35 foot long pole. I am sure this was my initiation, and they were probably laughing all the way to the coffee shop. The first 36 inches of the ground I had to go through was frozen solid. All I had for tools was a round mouth long handled shovel, a narrow long handled shovel with the head set at 90 degrees for removing the dirt out of the hole and a six foot long pinch bar for chopping at the frozen dirt in the hole. After the hour I spent digging the hole I was quite warm. The crew came by about an hour after I had finished and were just amazed the hole was complete. I had muscles everywhere. We dropped the pole in and backfilled the hole. We all went off to a local restaurant for a company paid lunch. This northern part of Scarborough north of Ellesmere was considered out of our normal territory and that entitled us to a company paid lunch. Slim always tried to get us assignments outside of our area so that we could get free lunches.

I became really good at digging holes and climbing up poles with my belt and the spurs on my boots. Even though it was winter I really enjoyed the work and my co-worker's company. I stayed on the line gang for 8 months. All the time I was working on the line gang I was also building our house.

Bill, Irene, Pat and I had all been hanging around together and we became the best of friends for many years. Pat and Irene in a very short time became adopted sisters. We would visit each other every other weekend before and after we had children.

Pat and Irene considered themselves to be adopted sisters. The photograph is courtesy of Rob McIntyre and Laurel Wheeler.

After my stint on the line gang, I was sent to the Mount Pleasant Garage which is just north of Eglinton Avenue where I became an equipment installer for both residential and commercial locations. This was another very good job which I did for about 7 years. I was working at many locations and I was never bored. We were installing equipment at Frigidaire where they were manufacturing jet engine turbine blades. I still loved aircraft and really liked watching the manufacturing process for those blades.

About 1954 I was promoted to a PBX, Private Branch Exchange Installation Foreman. I was responsible for the installation of the cable and jack switchboards that are only seen in movies and museums now. This was another really great job and I went around to many companies helping them design their phone system. These PBX switchboards were still seen in many company reception areas as late as the 1980s.

A photograph of a small PBX board. The photograph was taken by Dan Middleton.

Pat and I are showing off our new shoes at Pat's parent's backyard. Behind us is Irene McIntyre. Photograph from the Bob Middleton Collection.

Bill and I worked on building each other's houses. Bill had purchased a full 1 acre lot in North York north of Sheppard Avenue just east of where Highway 404 is now. Bill and Irene's house is still standing and is currently the home of their daughter Laurel and her husband Dennis.

Chapter 39

MEMORIES OF FAMILY AND FRIENDS

Our first son Dan was born on Wednesday, November 19, 1952.

Our second son Dave was born on Saturday, January 28, 1956. A few days after Dave was born, we brought him home in a big snowstorm.

By 1956 when I was 33 years old, I had been suffering with problems with my tonsils for so long that I decided to have them out. One morning in March a week before Easter in April of 1956 I went to the Lockwood Clinic on the corner of Bloor Street and Jarvis Street by myself to have the tonsils out. The Lockwood Clinic was an old house that had been converted into the clinic. The procedure room had been the dining room of the house. The doctor and nurse sat me down in a dentist style of chair in the middle of the dining room. I had no idea of what I was in for. They started the procedure at 10:00 AM with a long needle of local anesthetic the doctor injected into the back of my throat. That hurt. Back then used needles were sterilized and then reused a few times. I was then totally frozen and could not feel a thing. I could sense things being pulled in my mouth, but it did not hurt. Yes, I was completely conscious. I can tell you why you are knocked out for this procedure. Just read on. Then the doctor took a tool with a loop of wire and placed the loop over the tonsils. That loop reduced in size and cut off each tonsil. It seemed like something out of a torture scene in a spy movie. I cannot imagine anything less sharp to cut the tonsils off than what he used. Just as I thought the doctor had finished, he said, "I missed a piece." In he went and cut that piece out. I ended up with a very sore throat. At 11:30 AM when the procedure was done, I was taken to a room with a bed and a side table. On the side table was a glass of ginger ale and a bowl of ice cream. I wanted nothing to do with any of that. As the anesthetic wore off the pain began, and I eventually fell asleep. My sleep was constantly interrupted by the bell at St. Paul's Anglican Church next door.

Pat with Davey and Danny in summer 1957. Danny is wearing the striped shirt. Photograph is from the Bob Middleton Collection.

When I woke up the next the day the ice cream was completely melted, and I was not interested in the ginger ale. After I had recovered sufficiently the clinic called a cab to take me to Pat's parents' house at 78 Ashdale Avenue. Pat's Mom was helping Pat take care of our second son Dave who was born three months earlier. When I got to their house Pat made me some eggnog as I absolutely could not eat anything. I could barely swallow. I drank the eggnog. After a couple of days, I drove us all back home to Faircroft Blvd. in Scarborough. I was not able to go to work for an entire week as I was not able to swallow solid food. I lived on eggnog. On the Tuesday after the Easter Monday holiday, I went to work. The boss looked at me and asked how I felt. I think I must have looked lousy. I told him I was OK. He told me to go home and recover. I was not back to work until another week had gone past.

After I had been a PBX Installation Foreman for 7 years, I went back to the Repair department at the Mount Pleasant Garage for a year.

From there I was sent to work for the CO, Central Office as the Equipment Foreman at many different central office exchanges. I spent a few years at Maple, Donlands, Markham, Eglinton and Ernest Avenue. I worked at Ernest Avenue before it opened and started it up and cut it over. I was the Equipment Foreman for the 490 exchange at Ernest Avenue for 5 years. When it opened the exchange acquired 6,000 phone numbers from the Hickory exchange and 6,000 phone numbers from the Baldwin exchange.

Wymbolwood Beach Lodge Resort at Tiny Beaches on the south end of Georgian Bay was a fabulous resort we started going to with Bill and Irene and their children Robbie and Laurel in 1962. This was the first of eight summer vacations our two families spent there together. That first vacation there Bill and I must have been bored and itching for something to do. We had not built a house or garage for many years. For a few days we ended up helping Art Dunsford, the owner of the lodge and his son Reese build a new garage. I think that put us in the good books with the Dunsford family for years after that. They always had room for us at the lodge.

During the summers when we were not at Wymbolwood Beach Lodge our family and Bill's family spent many Saturdays at Musselman's Beach, north of Toronto or the Heart Lake Conservation area in Brampton, west of Toronto. Bill and his son Robbie spent many hours playing catch at both of those parks. Rob is currently a coordinator of a baseball league in The Beach in Toronto.

During the late 1960s and early 1970s we travelled many times to the east coast of Canada. For the summer of 1967 we travelled out to Cape Breton with Irene and Bill and their kids. We stayed with Irene's cousin at his house on the ocean. We visited PEI, Nova Scotia, and Cape Breton. I drove the Cabot Trail in one day. In 1969 we ventured all the way to PEI in our 1967 Buick Skylark pulling a tent trailer. It rained most of the time on this trip once we were east of Quebec. All I could say for the rain was that it kept those tiny trailer tires cool. On one trip to the east coast in 1972 we rented a tent trailer and Dan's girlfriend Debbie Troop came with us to Nova Scotia.

Our son, Dan married Debbie Troop on May 12, 1973. Our son, Dave married Dianne Charles on May 21, 1981.

After working at Bell Canada (Bell Telephone Company), for 39 years I retired on my 60th birthday in 1983. I was paid out as if I were still working until I was 65. It was an offer no one should refuse.

We went out to visit Dave and Dianne many times after they moved out to Alberta. We took many trips out west to visit them. We travelled out there by every way possible. We travelled there by car, train, airplane and one time just to experience it, by Gray Coach bus. On that bus trip we took many books with us.

On our 1984 trip out west we went to Johnston Canyon in Banff, Alberta. The photograph was taken by Dave Middleton.

Pat continued to work at her job as a secretary to Dr. Arthur Axelrad at the University of Toronto until she retired in 1987 at age 62. I had lots of time to peruse my hobbies while I was waiting for Pat to retire. For those 4 years I became the person who prepared dinner for us so that dinner was ready for Pat when she came home.

Pat and I started square dancing in the 1980s with Bill and Irene. We would go out dancing once or twice a week and also went to special square-dancing events outside of Toronto. We continued until about 2010 when the square dance callers were retiring. Eventually the places offering weekly square dancing were too far away.

Pat and I at a square dance conference in Calgary, Alberta in 1986. Dave and Dianne were living in Parkland, a subdivision in Calgary. Photograph was taken by Dave Middleton.

For almost 20 years I was involved with a volunteer group of men who serviced and maintained mechanical braille typewriters for the Canadian Institute for the Blind until those mechanical machines were partially replaced by electronic technologies.

Photograph taken of me, Bill Bauld and Jim Endicott, repairing braille machines by Toronto Star reporter, Ken Faught. The photograph was in the October 1, 1999 edition of The Toronto Star. Getty image 1231913774.

The Canadian built Mark X Lancaster FM-213 at the Canadian Warplane Heritage Museum in Hamilton went through an eleven year restoration from 1977 to when it first flew again on September 24, 1988. It was given the designation VR-A in recognition of Mid-Upper Gunner, Pilot Officer Andrew Mynarski for his act of heroism on June 13, 1944 that earned him a posthumous Victoria Cross. Pat and I were there for that first flight since it was retired in 1963 and placed on a pylon in Goderich, Ontario. We had been to the museum many times over those years of restoration of FM-213 to see the progress. If Hamilton had not been so far away from Scarborough, I would have been a volunteer in the restoration group.

Pat and I went to 5 air crew reunions over the years. The first reunion Pat and I attended was in Winnipeg, Manitoba in 1988. This was a huge event and there were at least 6,000 aircrew and their guests registered. This was a very special occasion because 2 of my crew members and their wives attended. In attendance was our Pilot Don Rombough and his wife Kay from Gananoque, Ontario and Bomb Aimer Ray Rose and his wife Annette from Victoria, British Columbia. It was a great reunion, and we attended all the events and parades. This was the only reunion with any members of our crew.

In 1992 Pat and I attended the 6th Commonwealth Wartime Aircrew Reunion in Winnipeg, Manitoba. I had a great time talking to all the "Old Airmen." This was the last reunion we attended outside of Ontario.

At a reunion at the Toronto Royal York Hotel, September 2nd to 6th, 1999, I purchased a VHS tape of the Halifax Recovery Project.

For my 80th birthday in 2003 Dave and Dan bought me a flight in the Mynarski Lancaster VR-A at the Canadian Warplane Heritage Museum in Hamilton.

Halifax NA337 was ditched in Lake Mjøsa, Norway in 1945. It was recovered from 750 feet of water and brought to Trenton, Ontario in 1995. Between 1995 and 2009 Pat and I regularly visited the restoration work of the Halifax NA-337 at the National Air Force Museum of Canada in Trenton, Ontario. I wish I lived closer to Trenton as I would have enjoyed being a volunteer working on the Halifax restoration. The Halifax NA-337 dedication ceremony we attended was on November 5, 2005.

Pat and I celebrated a combination of our 67th wedding anniversary and my 90th birthday on July 27, 2013. The photograph was taken by Dan Middleton.

Photograph of Pat and I at the wedding of granddaughter Christine and John on August 17, 2013. The photograph was taken by Dan Middleton.

Ray Rose, our 24 year old Bomb Aimer returned home to Victoria, British Columbia where he worked in the jewelry store and eventually took over from his father and ran the store until he retired in 1986. Pat and I visited with Ray and Annette a few times at their home in Victoria, British Columbia over the years. Ray passed away in the spring of 2015 at the age of 95.

When Don Rombough our Pilot returned, he worked at and eventually owned the family motel in Gananoque, Ontario.

Jack Cornock our Rear Gunner joined Air Canada in Toronto, Ontario and worked there in administrative positions until he retired. Jack retired to the town of White Rock, British Columbia. Pat and I visited him in British Columbia once.

Ralph Hamel our Mid-Upper Gunner went back home to Saskatchewan and his wheat farm after his tour.

Ken Smith our Wireless Operator returned home, and we heard that he had moved to Hawaii and no one really heard anything about him.

He never sent letters to any of us or replied to letters from me. I think he did not want to remember anything about our service with the RCAF.

Art Morency our Flight Engineer sat or stood beside the Pilot and saw everything that he saw. Don spoke with Art a few times on the phone over the years after the war. After the war, the rest of us never heard from Art. For many men, flying in bombers in unfriendly skies was a terrifying experience that they tried to forget as soon as possible.

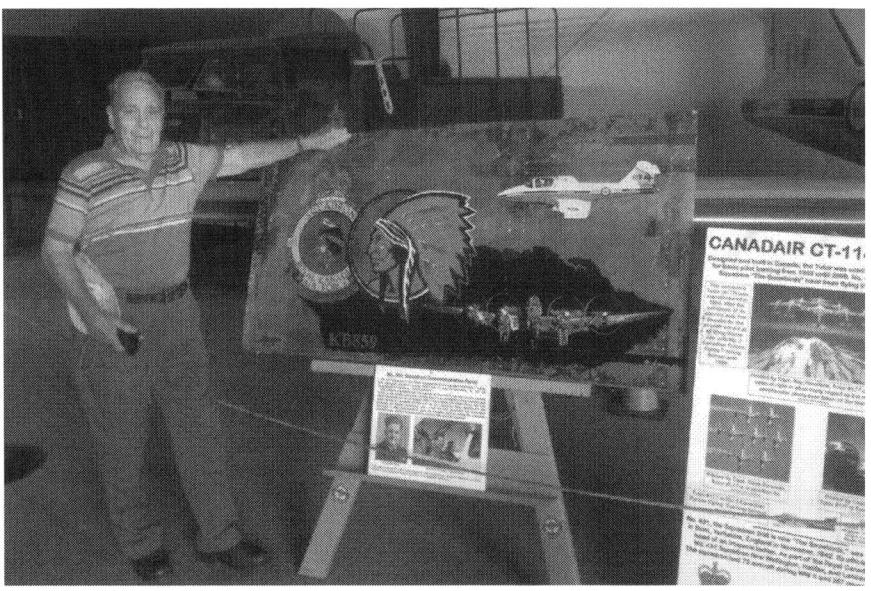

Me at the Bomber Command Museum in Nanton, Alberta on Sunday, August 18, 2013. This day was Pat's 88th birthday. The painting is of the Snowbirds and 431 Iroquois Squadron. In 1978 the Canadian Snowbirds aerobatic team was assigned the 431 Iroquois Squadron designation. The photograph was taken by Dan Middleton.

In the last few months of WWII Bomber Command, Sir Arthur Harris and Prime Minister Winston Churchill received a great deal of negative publicity over the bombing of Germany cities. The German propaganda machine made sure that the civilians of Britain and North America received horrible pictures of dead people and greatly inflated the numbers of the dead in bombed out German cities. Just after the end of WWII the British Commonwealth Army and Navy surviving members received medals in recognition of their effort in the war. The bad press that Bomber Command received delayed the creation of the Bomber Command bar until 2013. Sixty-eight years after WWII ended the British and Canadian governments finally awarded the few remaining members of Bomber Command a Bomber Command bar. The negative sentiment against those men who risked their lives in the hostile skies over occupied Europe ran so deep that it took that long to recognize our contribution to end that war. Any Bomber Command veteran who wanted the bar had to fill out a form and mail it into Veterans Affairs. I was in the very first group to receive the Bomber Command bar.

My bar was presented to me August 26, 2013 by the Minister of Veterans Affairs, Julian Fantino at the Canadian Forces College in Toronto, Ontario. Ray, like many Bomber Command veterans received their bar through Canada Post with no ceremony. Ray was disappointed to say the least with the lack of a ceremony.

I received my Bomber Command bar on August 26, 2013. The photograph was taken by Pat Middleton.

The Bomber Command Bar. Photograph taken by Dan Middleton.

My beloved Pat passed away a few days after Christmas in 2013. That was the Christmas of the terrible ice storm in the GTA and 8 days of blacked out electricity in our part of Toronto. We had been married for 67 wonderful years.

For the 2014 Remembrance Day events at the Canadian Warplane Heritage Museum in Hamilton an organization assembled together 12 former Lancaster aircrew members. Seven of us each representing a position in the Lancaster sat down and pretended to go through a briefing for a wartime operation for CHCH TV. The event attracted television news crews from CHCH TV, CTV TV and CBC TV. I was interviewed by all three networks and appeared on all three that night.

My interview by CHCH TV journalist Pamela Vanmeer. Photograph taken by Dan Middleton.

Lancaster crew members gathered at the Canadian Warplane Heritage Museum on November 11, 2014. I am in the back row on the far left. Photograph taken by Dan Middleton.

Wednesday November 11, 2015 Dan and I were at the Canadian Warplane Heritage Museum. After the Remembrance Day Ceremony Tina Travale, the woman in the picture on my right came up and gave me a big hug and thanked me for my service in Bomber Command. Carla Dicesare her sister is on my left. During the 1940s Tina 4 and Carla 2 were children living in Nazi occupied Amsterdam, Netherlands. During this time regular Bomber Command night operations flew over the Netherlands on their way to and from Nazi targets for many years. These operations involved four engine Halifax bombers with 14-cylinder Bristol Hercules engines and four engine Halifax and Lancaster bombers with 12-cylinder Rolls-Royce Merlin engines. The sound from each of these aircraft is unique. Tina never saw the bombers as these flew at night with no lights. There would be hundreds of aircraft in each operation. The sound overhead from these aircraft would last for quite a while. Tina's parents told her that the men in those aircraft would rescue them from the terror and horror of the Nazi occupation. The crews that operated those aircraft did rescue them. Tina currently lives near the Hamilton airport. Living near an airport you hear aircraft of all kinds. In September 1988, the restored Canadian built AVRO Lancaster dedicated to Andrew Mynarski flew for the first time since the 1950s. 32 years ago VR-A, the Mynarski Lancaster flew over Tina's head. Tina told me that she immediately wept tears of joy and thankfulness upon hearing the sound of the four Merlin engines she had not heard for 44 years. She recognized immediately the sound overhead of her unseen childhood heroes.

Photograph taken of Tina, me and Carla at the Canadian Warplane Heritage Museum after the 2015 Remembrance Day Ceremony. Photograph taken by Dan Middleton.

Photograph of Carla 2 and Tina 4 taken in Amsterdam during 1943. Photograph is courtesy of Carla Dicesare and Tina Travale.

There is an airpark on Skylark Drive in Guelph, Ontario that is the home to the Tiger Boys Club that restores and flies vintage Tiger Moth and Fleet Finch trainers. Every year for 10 years I had gone there with Pat, my son, my grandson and and his family to watch and also fly in those vintage Tiger Moth and Fleet Finch aircraft at the airpark. Each year on the third full weekend in September the Tiger Boys have an open house where they offer 30 minute rides in a Tiger Moth or a Fleet

Finch for $100. We did not fly in 2019 due to rotten weather. The event was cancelled in Sepember 2020 due to COVID-19.

With my son, grandson, granddaughter-in-law, and great-grandkids in 2017. The photograph is from the Bob Middleton Collection.

Flying with great-grand kids Kate and Andrew in 2018. Photograph taken by Dan Middleton.

It is such an indescribable thrill to fly with my great-grandchildren in the Thurston Jackeroo modified four seater version of the Tiger Moth trainer that I learned to fly in 1942. Who would have thought I would be flying in a Tiger Moth with my great-grandchilren 76 years later in 2018. The Thurston Jackeroo Tiger Moth that flies with the Tiger Boys in Guelph, Ontario is the only airworthy example of the aircraft in the world. The Jackeroo Tiger Moth at Guelph also has the distinction of being used in France before the evacuation at Dunkirk in May and June, 1940.

Victoria Day 2018 found Dave, Dan and I riding in the Lancaster VR-A at the Canadian Warplane Heritage Museum in Hamilton. Dave treated us for the ride. It was an amazing 90 minute trip we will all remember forever. When I was flying in Lancasters in 1944 and 1945 I had never dreamed that I would be flying in a Lancaster 73 years later with my sons.

My son Dan had brought along a sound pressure meter to measure how loud the engines were on the Lancaster. The engine noise I was subjected to for hours gets the credit for much of my hearing loss. When all four engines were running while we were sitting on the ground the sound level was 110 decibels under the mid-upper turret. This is the sound level of a healthy automobile horn at 3 feet. Once we were in the air cruising at 2,000 feet standing beside the pilot the sound level was 122 decibels. A jet aircraft 200 feet away at takeoff is 118 decibels. When we were flying operations at 15,000 feet and had a full load of bombs and fuel onboard it must have been even louder.

The weather that morning was beautiful and sunny with just a bit of haze. The usual trip is over Niagara Falls and then over Toronto. It was Victoria Day and we were not allowed to fly over Toronto. Instead, we flew over Niagara Falls and then out over Lake Erie and the area along the north shore of Lake Erie. I stood in the mid-upper turret for quite some time watching the scenery going by. My son Dan tells me that after we got out of the Lancaster I remarked. "It sure was nice not having people shooting at us."

Me riding in the mid-upper turret of the Canadian Warplane Heritage Museum Mynarski Lancaster VR-A on May 21, 2018. Photograph from the Bob Middleton Collection.

Our Canadian Warplane Heritage Museum Lancaster crew on May 21, 2018. From left to right: Crewman Dave Finnamore, Dan Middleton, Dave Middleton, Copilot Bill Craig, Bob Middleton, Pilot Leon Evans, Flight Engineer Craig Brookhouse and fellow passenger Mark Whiteman. The photograph was taken by Dianne Middleton.

I met with Dan, my grandchildren and great-grandchildren on August 13, 2019 at the National Air Force Museum in Trenton, Ontario for lunch and a tour of the museum. Before we met the grandchildren and great- grandchildren the Museum Director, Kevin Windsor asked if I would like to speak to a group of Air Cadets that were meeting at the museum. I spent about 20 minutes speaking with a very eager group of young people.

I spent half an hour inside the Halifax bomber sitting at the Navigator's bench with my grandson, Chris speaking with him and the Museum Director, Kevin Windsor. There are probably not many RCAF Bomber Command WWII veteran RCAF Navigators left that get to do that. There is the photograph of that event on page 200. My granddaughters Julie and Lisa also spent 30 minutes touring inside the Halifax with Kevin Windsor.

Photograph of Halifax NA-337 with my son Dan, my grandchildren and my great-grandchildren taken in August 2019. Left to right back row: Lisa, Julie, Dan, Bob, Andrew, Chris, Kate and, Colin. Left to right front group: Aiden, Zara, Lili and Joy. The photograph was taken by the Museum Public Relations photographer, Theo Czerny-Holownia and is courtesy of the National Air Force Museum of Canada in Trenton, Ontario.

My son Dave and his family with me on August 20, 2019 at the Bomber Command Museum in Nanton, Alberta. Left to right: Dianne, Dave, Leigh, Bob, Christine, Poppy, John and Holly. The photograph was taken by a Bomber Command Museum volunteer.

In November 2019 my son, Dave was home for a visit. Dave, Dan and I had the wonderful opportunity to go together to the Remembrance Day Ceremony at the Canadian Warplane Heritage Museum. It had snowed the night before and we almost did not go. The Lancaster and Mitchell did not fly overhead that day as the weather was poor and there were icing conditions. The men and aircraft are too valuable to lose. Many times, at Croft during the winter we would not takeoff under those same conditions. Operations would be scrubbed. These aircraft do not have deicing equipment. We all spoke with many people there. I was interviewed by CHCH television reporter, Kelly Botelho and I appeared on the CHCH television news that night. We left the Museum about 2:00 PM. I think we were the last people to leave. Even with the rotten weather that day there were about 3,500 people in attendance. On the way home we stopped for a great lunch at Breezy Corners family restaurant on Highway 6 about 10 miles north of Hamilton.

Photograph of Dan, Dave and I at the 2019 Remembrance Day Ceremony at the Canadian Warplane Heritage Museum in Hamilton, Ontario. There was a big snowstorm that day and the VR-A Lancaster did not fly over at 11:00 that day. It is too dangerous for the Lancaster to fly in those conditions.

Chapter 40

<u>2020</u>

2020 has been quite a year so far. In early March 2020 Amy Spowart, the President and CEO of the National Aviation Hall of Fame had invited me to attend and speak at the Gala Event at the Arsenal of Democracy in Washington, D.C. on May 8, 2020. I was going to be riding in the Canadian Warplane Heritage Museum Lancaster VR-A over Washington, D.C. on May 7, 2020, the airshow practice day. The Arsenal of Democracy Airshow was going to be amazing with 100 WWII vintage military aircraft flying. This did not happen as COVID-19 is currently visiting the world.

We are waiting for this dreaded COVID-19 virus to pass over us and we are waiting for an effective vaccine. I appeared in a 60 second clip on a CBC National News Pandemic Diaries series with three other WWII veterans on Thursday, April 29. We veterans commented about how similar our feelings of this pandemic are to the early days of WWII when the Allies were taking a shellacking. A good quote from Jeanne Tweten, a 98 year old RAF aircraftwoman was, "Keep calm and carry on."

This is the first time in at least 25 years that my family and I have not attended the Father's Day event at the Canadian Warplane Heritage Museum that was closed due to COVID-19. I am Membership Chairman of our local Aircrew Association and the Treasurer of our local Bell Pioneers Club. I do a great deal of work on the computer maintaining the records for the clubs.

Dan and I socially isolating at my house on the 75th Anniversary of VE Day, May 8, 2020.

My current house that Pat and I built in Scarborough in 1947 and 1948. The photograph was taken by Dan Middleton.

This keeps me very busy and occupied. I belong to a computer club and we spend an hour on Saturdays on Zoom meetings. My half acre lot keeps me very busy spring, summer and fall. My son Dan and I meet for a socially distanced lunch in the backyard once a week.

This summer was incredibly long and hot. The lawn was so dry and my vegetable garden suffered with a lack of water. I told Dan that this was what the summer of 1952 was like a few months before he was born.

My 97th birthday was on Wednesday, July 15, 2020. My son Dan and I went for diner at a socially distanced patio at the Stone Cottage Inn on Kingston Road near Scarborough Golf Club Road. Dan arranged a birthday party for me at the Quarry Restaurant in Scarborough on July 18, 2020. This date would have been our 74th wedding anniversary.

Photograph of Dan and I at the Stone Cottage Inn on July 15, 2020 for my 97th birthday. The photograph was taken by our server.

My brother's wife Marie's 90th birthday was on July 13th and we had a double birthday party with a cupcake birthday cake. To keep socially distanced and stay in our own "bubbles" we were sitting at three tables separated by 6 feet. At one table was my brother, Bill, his wife Marie, their daughter Patti. At the second table was my grandson Chris, his wife Amanda and their two children Kate and Colin. My nephew Rob McIntyre was seated at the end of their table. It was great to see all those folks after so many months in isolation from them.

A few days after my birthday I received an email message from the Snowbirds, "On behalf of all Snowbird team members, we wish Mr. Middleton a very happy 97th birthday." Dan had informed the Snowbirds Chief Warrant Officer, Bruce Byers that it was the 97th birthday of a WWII era 431 Squadron "Warrior of the Air."

Photograph of my 97th birthday party at the Quarry Restaurant on July 18, 2020. At one table was my brother, Bill, his wife Marie and their daughter Patti. At the second table was my grandson Chris, his wife Amanda and their two children Kate and Colin. My nephew Rob McIntyre was seated at the end of their table.

On the CBC special I appeared on in April there was also Pilot, Reg Harrison who had served with 431 Squadron the same time I was at Croft. I do not remember him as he had been away for 15 weeks recovering from burns sustained from an explosion during a landing at Croft on March 15, 1944. Reg and our crew flew on the operations of November 27 and 30, 1944. Reg was screened after his 19th operation on November 30. Reg and crew were lucky to survive another crash landing. After 3 crash landings and one bailout the CO feared his luck would soon run out. Dan had noticed that Reg Harrison had received a plaque in 2018 as an honorary member of the Canadian Forces Snowbirds Team. I did not know it but a few weeks later Dan began enquiring if I could become an honorary Snowbird as well. This was about the same time that the Snowbirds Team had a terrible accident in Kamloops, British Columbia a few moments after takeoff when the engine failed due to a bird strike. Sadly, Captain Jennifer Casey, the Squadron's Public Relations Officer died in the accident.

Monday, August 10th this year I received a very special VE Day coin from the RCAF for Veterans of WWII. Photograph was taken by Dan Middleton.

Early in September Dan suggested that we should visit the Canadian Warplane Heritage Museum on Sunday September 27, 2020 for a late Father's Day visit since the museum was closed during the Father's Day weekend due to the COVID-19 lockdown. Chris my grandson and his family would meet us there for the visit. Little did I know this was a ruse to get me there for a presentation of an honorary Snowbirds member plaque. I fell for it completely.

We were sitting down having lunch with museum volunteer, John Desramaux when my grandson Chris and family showed up. A little while later a friend of Dan's from the 431 Facebook group Steve York and his wife showed up. Dan introduced us saying he had invited Steve to meet me since we would be at the museum. A few other people showed up from the 431 Facebook group. A bit later Ron Passmore his wife and another member of the Danforth Tech Society showed up. Dan said he had invited them to meet me as well because they had assisted Dan with photographs and documents from Danforth Tech. I was having a marvelous time answering questions and telling stories of those times in the RCAF, while at a "social distance", to the group of people I was surrounded by. A short while later author and historian, Ted Barris showed up. He is a good friend of mine. I did the technical proofreading of his 2018 *Dam Busters* book. I figured he was there working on sales or working on a new book. I was becoming a little suspicious of why all these people were at the museum.

While I was speaking with all my new friends Dan asked me if I wanted to go look at the Lancaster. I told him, "I have seen the Lancaster before. I have flown in it." I was enjoying speaking with people. Dan convinced me to go to the other side of the museum with him to go see the Lancaster. When we got there, I saw Ted Barris standing behind a podium and an easel beside him had a collage of my old photographs. I sat down; Ted introduced me and related to the audience a short version of my biography. I was taken by complete surprise. When Ted finished, he introduced Dan who presented me with the Snowbirds Honorary plaque and a framed print of a Snowbird formation signed by the current members of the team. That story can be found at: tedbarris.com/2020/09/30/luck-is-33-eggs.

After Dan brought out the Snowbirds cap and put it on my head I asked, "When do I get a ride." I am now an Honorary Snowbird. I understand that I am one of three 431 Squadron honorary members. Many photographs were taken, and I spent another hour speaking with the people that had come to honor me for my RCAF service in helping to keep the wolves from the door so many years ago.

My Honorary Snowbird plaque I received Sunday, September 27, 2020. The photographs were taken by Dan Middleton.

Family picture after the presentation of my Honorary Snowbird plaque. I was allowed to have my mask off for the photograph. From left to right is Steve, Amanda's stepfather, Sue, Amanda's mom, great-granddaughter Kate, granddaughter-in-law Amanda, great-grandson Colin, great-grandson Andrew, great-granddaughter Joy, grandson Chris, Me, Ted Barris and my son Dan. There are four generations of the Middleton family in this photograph. The photograph is courtesy of Ted Barris.

I hope you have enjoyed this story of my life. I wish everyone health and happiness in the future and let's beat the pants off COVID-19!

Lest we forget

EPILOGUE

A mere week after I was inducted into the Honorary 431 Snowbirds Society my son, Dan was contacted by Andrew Spearin, the Director of Sharp End Studio in Hamilton, Ontario. Andrew wanted to get my contact information from Dan and speak with me. He had seen Dan's post on the RCAF 6th Bomber Command Facebook group. Andrew Spearin and his creative team in partnership with the Canadian Warplane Heritage Museum in Hamilton, Ontario are creating a virtual reality video game encompassing all the steps through the BCATP, British Commonwealth Air Training Plan, training in the UK and ultimately flying actual combat operations in Bomber Command.

The video game is titled *Valiant Effort* and takes a civilian after he joined the RCAF starting as a LAC, Leading Aircraftman, ITS, Initial Training School and then through all the trades. Once the player has graduated from his trade they will join up as a crew at OTU, Operational Training Unit, change to 4 engine bombers at HCU, Heavy Conversion Unit and finally RCAF 419, Moose Squadron. The player must earn graduation from each level before advancing to the next level just as the RCAF airmen had to.

Andrew Spearin called me about a week later and we spoke for an hour about my experiences and about his project. He invited me to go a flight in Lancaster VR-A with his camera crew. I told him I was not really comfortable climbing up the ladder and into the belly of the Lancaster. Andrew contacted Dan and asked him if he could twist my arm somewhat. My son contacted Emily Millar and Laura Hassard-Moran at the Canadian Warplane Heritage Museum and asked them if they could arrange to have a mechanics platform and stairs set up beside the Lancaster to make it easier for me to climb in. Lancaster Pilot, Leon Evans contacted Dan on October 23 that they would have the steps in place for me. Dan called me and told me that everything was set up for me with the set of stairs. Dan used his persuasive powers and the next day I called Dan back and said, "Sure, I'll go. Do they still have the seat for me?" Dan told me they were holding it for me. I told Dan, "It sure would be fabulous if you could fly with me too. I'll feel a bit guilty leaving you down there on the ground." A few hours later Andrew contacted Dan and told him there was another seat available for him. Dan called me the next day and told me he was going too. This was going to be marvelous. Dan told Andrew that I was "over the moon." The flight was arranged for Wednesday, November 4 at 11 AM. Dan would pick me up in Scarborough and then take me back home later in the day. I usually drive myself to Dan's house in Brampton and then he drives to and from the museum and I drive home from his house. Dan figured it was going to be a huge day and I would probably be exhausted.

This is my current virtual video game image to be used in the game *Valiant Effort*.

We arrived at the Canadian Warplane Heritage Museum for our 10 AM pre-flight briefing. Dan and I met Andrew Spearin, the camera crew and other members of Sharp End Studio. We chatted with the Lancaster crew for a while and then met up with some of Dan's Facebook friends and Dan's high school friend Dan Garry. Dan had told them about our trip.

My grandson Chris and his two boys Colin and Andrew showed up a short while after the briefing. The flight was delayed a few hours, so we all sat down for lunch in the hanger. We watched the museum crew move the Dakota out of the hanger.

After lunch I was interviewed by CBC TV journalist Trevor Dunn. Ted Barris had contacted the CBC and suggested that an interview with Andrew Spearin about the *Valiant Effort* game and me would be a great Remembrance Day week spot. I spoke with Trevor for about 40 minutes. While I was speaking there was a crowd of people gathered around listening to my stories. Off camera Trevor and I talked some more.

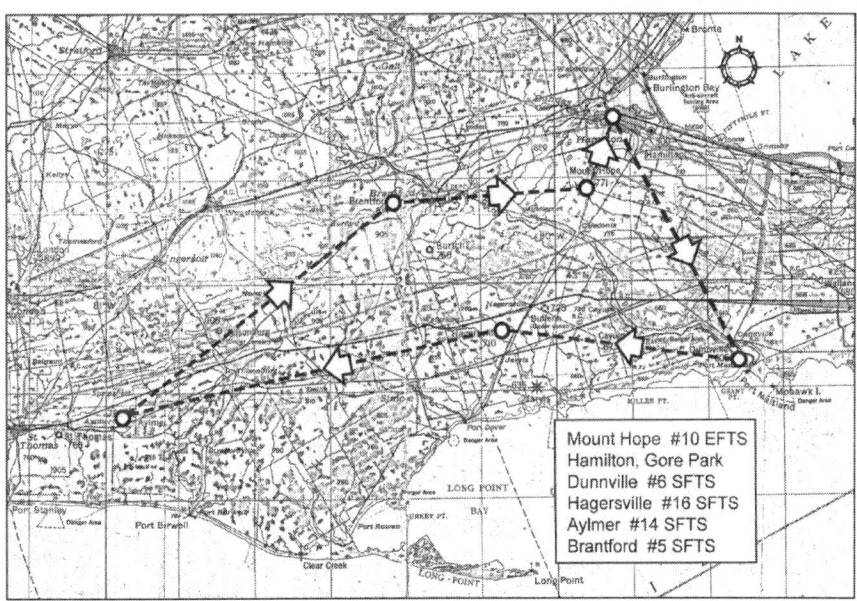

Mount Hope #10 EFTS
Hamilton, Gore Park
Dunnville #6 SFTS
Hagersville #16 SFTS
Aylmer #14 SFTS
Brantford #5 SFTS

The route of the Wednesday, November 4, 2020 flight in Lancaster VR-A. This was map scanned from my 1942 London AOS map.

Once all of the Sharp End Studio's cameras and sound gear was installed in VR-A and it was ready to go we received word that we were ready to fly. We all climbed onboard VR-A about 1:30 PM. The set of stairs they had set up at the side of the aircraft was great. The ladder is too challenging when your knees have been around 97 years.

The number four, starboard outer engine was started first and then the rest of the engines. The Merlin engines were making their noisy music. Just a few minutes after we sat down, we were airborne at 1:35 PM. This was my second flight in Lancaster VR-A in $2^{1/2}$ years.

I was so pleased that I made it up the steps and was inside VR-A once again for another adventure. That is the CBC TV News camera on the left. Photograph by Dan Middleton.

Our flight plan took us north to Hamilton then south-east to Dunville home of No. 6 SFTS. From there we flew west and passed over Hagersville No. 16 SFTS and then on to Alymer No. 14 SFTS. From there we headed north-east to Brantford No. 5 SFTS and then back to

Mount Hope. During our 45 minute, 138 mile long route we were flying at an altitude of 2,000 feet at 207 mph. The sky was clear, and the weather was fairly warm. Owing to the warm temperature the ride was a bit bumpy and I stayed in my seat most of the time. The view through the little windows between the horizontal stringers of the fuselage was great.

After we returned to the museum, we had our group picture taken and then stayed at the museum speaking with many people. My grandson, Chris, great grandsons, Andrew, and Colin climbed in and looked around inside. Dan's friend Dan Garry and his friend had a ride in the Lancaster as the tug pushed it into the hanger.

After we left the museum Dan, Chris, Andrew, Colin, and I went to dinner at East Side Mario's in Hamilton. In Hamilton there was still indoor dining available. Dan drove me home to my house in Scarborough and dropped me off at 7:00 PM. I was pleasantly tired, and I settled into my favorite chair. About 2 hours later I woke up and went upstairs to bed. What a great day I had.

Our Canadian Warplane Heritage Museum Lancaster crew on November 4, 2020. From left to right: Sound Engineer Mark McNeilly, Flight Engineer Randy Straughan, Copilot Leon Evans, Pilot Bill Craig, Dan Middleton, Bob Middleton and Andrew Spearin. The photograph was taken by Chris Middleton.

A few days later Ron McKeen, the Evening Producer for the CBC Metro Morning talk show on FM radio called me. He asked if I would do a phone interview on the Monday, November 9, 2020 show with host, Ismaila Alfa at 7:40 in the morning. I said sure. Ron gave me some coaching and a sample of the questions that Ismaila may ask. The interview went well. I hope I got across the message of how much so many people gave so that we can enjoy the lives we have today.

 **CF Snowbirds** @CFSnowbirds · 35m   ···
Bob Middleton was a navigator with No. 431 (Bomber) Squadron during World War Two - he flew 33 missions over Europe on Lancasters and Halifaxes. This year, at age 97, he was named an Honorary Snowbird. Thank you for your service 🙏 #RemembranceDay 🌷 #cfsnowbirds

Royal Canadian Air Force and 2 others

The Snowbirds Facebook post recognizing my service in the RCAF during WWII. The post was supplied by Lt. Becky Major, CF Snowbirds Public Affairs Officer.

The same day the CBC TV News spot that Trevor Dunn produced from the interview at the Canadian Warplane Heritage Museum on November 4, 2020, aired at 6:55 PM on the CBC Toronto News. Trevor Dunn asked me what I thought of on Remembrance Day. I told him, "My thoughts are the same as everyone else. I think of those that were in the fight and those that did not return." Dan has shared the clip of the show with many friends and all of them are very impressed and have thanked me for my service with the RCAF during WWII.

Lt. Becky Major, the Canadian Forces Snowbirds Team Public Affairs Officer posted a genuinely nice post about me and my Bomber Command service on Facebook, Twitter and Instagram on Tuesday, November 10, 2020, at 1:00 PM. By 11:00 AM, Wednesday I had 3,000 likes, 306 shares and 144 comments. Not bad for a 97 year old guy. There are so many people out there that appreciate the sacrifices of our armed forces.

It is now Remembrance Day 2020. We are not gathering today, but we are celebrating virtually, with family, watching the television and listening to the radio. It is a time to be thankful for the outcome of the Second World War. I will remember my crewmates and all the other men and women who were there and those who gave up their lives for our freedoms. We need to pass on our stories while we are still here to tell them. We need to educate our countrymen of what was done by the generations before them before the stories are forgotten. If it was not for the commitment of the scientists and inventors, people in the army, the navy and the air force, and the leadership of all, it may have been a vastly different world. Let us not take for granted what we have and what was fought for. For me it has also been luck, the Luck of 33 Eggs.

Post Script

Thursday, April 29, 2021, the book, "LUCK IS 33 EGGS" was published by Amazon KDP.

Robert Middleton on Thursday, May 6, 2021, when he held his finished book in his hands for the first time. We called it, "Happy Book Day."

Robert signing his book at the National Air Force Museum at Trenton, Ontario a few days after his 98th birthday. Left to right. Joan Rombough and Bev Miller (Rombough) nieces of Pilot Don Rombough. Lucy Knorr (Hamel) and Wade Knorr. Daughter and grandson of Mid-Upper Gunner Ralph Hamel.

The last outing with the family of Robert's grandson and his son Dan to the Annual Tiger Boys open house at the Guelph Airpark on Sunday, September 19, 2021.

Sadly, on Wednesday, October 13, 2021, at age 98 Robert Middleton, "broke the surly bonds of earth," to navigate among the stars in heaven that he had trusted many years ago. Godspeed Robert and thank you.

WWII RAF and RCAF Phonetic Alphabet Aircraft Names

A   APPLE
B   BAKER
C   CHARLIE
D   DOG
E   EASY
F   FRED
G   GEORGE
H   HOW
I   INK
J   JIG
K   KING
L   LONDON
M   MOTHER
N   NAN
O   OBOE
P   PETER
Q   QUEEN
R   ROGER
S   SUGAR
T   TARE
U   UNCLE
V   VICTOR
W   WILLIAM
X   XRAY
Y   YOKE
Z   ZEBRA

The RAF and the RCAF used a different phonetic alphabet than the Joint Army/Navy radiotelephony alphabet used by the USAAF in WWII.

Glossary

A&AEE	Aeroplane and Armament Experimental Establishment
AOS	Air Observer School
AWOL	Absent Without Official Leave
BCATP	British Commonwealth Air Training Plan
BCIS	Bomber Command Instructors School
BST	British Savings Time
CNE	Canadian National Exhibition
CFJIC	Canadian Forces Joint Imagery Centre
Cookie	High Capacity blast bomb
CW	Continuous Wave
CWHM	Canadian Warplane Heritage Museum
DFC	Distinguished Flying Cross
DRO	Daily Routine Orders
EA	Electrical Artificer. Competent Naval electrical technician
EFTS	Elementary Flying Training School
FIDO	Fog Investigation and Dispersal Operation
FTR	Failed to Return
GMT	Greenwich Mean Time
GP bombs	General Purpose bombs
HC bombs	High Capacity bombs
HCU	Heavy Conversion Unit
HMS	His Majesty's Ship or Her Majesty's Ship
IAS	Indicated Air Speed
IFF	Identification Friend Foe
ILS	Instrument Landing System
ITS	Initial Training School
LAC	Leading Aircraftsman
LD fuses	Long delay fuses

MC bombs	Medium Capacity bombs
NAAFI	Navy, Army, Air Force Institutes
NCO	Non-Commissioned Officer
OGU	OGU was an experimental landing system
OTU	Operational Training Unit
PFF	Pathfinder Force
POW	Prisoner of War
R/T	Radio Telephone
RAE	Royal Aircraft Establishment
RCAC	Royal Canadian Armored Corps
RCAF	Royal Canadian Air Force
RCNVR	Royal Canadian Naval Volunteer Reserve
RMS	Royal Mail Ship
SAP bombs	Semi-Armor Piercing bombs
SBA	Standard Beam Approach
SBC	Small Bomb Containers
SFTS	Service Flying Training School
SOC	Struck Off Charge, the military was officially finished with the airframe
SS	Single Screw Steamship or Steam-powered Ship
TI	Target Indicator
Trolley ACC	Trolley Accumulator
USAAF	United States Army Air Force
USN	United States Navy
USS	United States Ship
UTC	Coordinated Universal Time
VLA	Veterans Land Grant Act

BIBLIOGRAPHY AND SOURCES

The major source of information concerning the memoirs of Robert J. Middleton comes from his own historical accounts and personal knowledge of events as they occurred, as a primary source. Photographs, letters, personal documents, family background information and his flying logbook all come from Robert J. Middleton's own stories and personal collection of artifacts and memorabilia. Details of other sources can be found in the acknowledgements.

Below is a biographical list of all the publications that have helped with putting this book together. The publication dates are from the editions that were consulted. These many not be from the first year of publication.

Bardua, Heinz *STUTTGART IM LUFTKIEG* (Klett-Cotta, 1985)

Bishop, Chris *LUFTWAFFE SQUADRONS 1939-45 THE ESSENTIAL AIRCRAFT IDENTIFICATION GUIDE* (Amber Books, 2012)

Botting, Douglas and the editors of Time-Life Books *THE GIANT AIRSHIPS* (Time-Life Books, 1980)

Bowman, Martin W. *LANCASTER REAPING THE WHIRLWIND* (The History Press, 2016)

Bowman, Martin W. *LEGACY OF THE LANCASTERS* (Pen & Sword Aviation, 2013)

Bowman, Martin W. *The Wellington Bomber Story* (The History Press, 2011)

Bowyer, Chaz *Supermarine Spitfire* (Chartwell Books Inc., 1980)

Bowyer, Michael J. F. *AIRCRAFT FOR THE MANYA DETAILED SURVEY OF THE RAF'S AIRCRAFT IN JUNE 1944* (Patrick Stephens Ltd., 1995)

Buchan, A. F., Borthwick, R., Wadden, William R. *AVIATION MATHEMATICS* (Houghton Mifflin Company, 1942)

Burns, Michael *SPITFIRE! SPITFIRE!* (Blandford Press Ltd., 1986)

Campbell, James *The Bombing of Nuremberg The gripping recreation of the most disastrous Allied night raid of World War II* (Doubleday & Company, Inc., 1974)

Cole, J. A. *Lord Haw-Haw The Full Story of William Joyce* (Faber and Faber Limited, 1987)

Cotter, Jarrod and Blackah, Paul *AVRO LANCASTER 1941 onwards (all marks) Owners' Workshop Manual* (Haynes Publishing, 2010)

Dungan, T. D. *V-2 A Combat History of the First Ballistic Missile* (Westholme Publishing LLC, 2005)

Dunmore, Spencer and Carter, William *REAP THE WHIRLWIND THE UNTOLD STORY OF 6 GROUP, CANADA'S BOMBER FORCE OF WORLD WAR II* (McClelland & Stewart Inc., 1992)

Eckhertz, Holger *D DAY Through German Eyes* (DTZ History Publications, 2015)

Ethell, Jeffrey L. *KOMET The Messerschmitt 163* (Ian Allan Ltd., 1978)

Falconer, Jonathan *HANDLEY PAGE HALIFAX 1939 onwards (all marks) Owners' workshop manual* (Haynes Publishing Group, 2016)

Falconer, Jonathan *RAF BOMBER COMMAND 1939 to 1945 Operations Manual* (Haynes Publishing, 2018)

Feesey, Donald W. *THE FLY BY NIGHTS RAF BOMBER COMMAND SORTIES 1944-45* (Pen & Sword Aviation, 2007)

Ford, J. Brian *German Secret Weapons blueprint for Mars* (Pan/Ballantine, 1972)

Frankland, Noble *bomber offensive the devastation of Europe* (Ballantine Books Inc., 1970)

Gibson, Guy VC, DSO, DFC *Enemy Coast Ahead-Uncensored The Real Guy Gibson* (Crécy Publishing Ltd., 2005)

Grant, William Newby *P-51 MUSTANG* (Bison Books, 1988)

Grehan, John and Mace, Martin *Bomber Harris Sir Arthur Harris' dispatch on war operations 1942-1945* (Pen & Sword Aviation, 2014)

Hastings, Max *BOMBER COMMAND CHURCHILL'S EPIC CAMPAIGN THE INSIDE STORY OF THE RAF'S VALIANT ATTEMPT TO END THE WAR* (Touchstone, 1979)

Hewer, Howard *IN FOR A PENNY IN FOR A POUND THE ADVENTURES AND MISADVENTURES OF A WIRELESS OPERATOR IN BOMBER COMMAND* (Stoddart Publishing Co. Ltd, 2000)

Jackson, Robert *Bomber! Famous Bomber Missions of World War II* (St. Martin's Press, Inc., 1980)

Johnson, 'Johnny' George *THE LAST BRITISH DAMBUSTER One man's extraordinary life and the raid that changed history* (Ebury Press, 2014)

Johnson, G. O. Air Marshal C.B., M.C. *THE R.C.A.F. OVERSEAS THE SIXTH YEAR* (Oxford University Press, 1949)

Lomas, Harry *ONE WING HIGH Halifax Bomber-the Navigators' Story* (Airlife Publishing Ltd., 1995)

Murray, Iain Dr. *DAM BUSTERS Owners' Workshop Manual 1943 onwards (all marks and models)* (Haynes Publishing, 2013)

Murray, Iain Dr. *VICKERS WELLINGTON Owners' Workshop Manual 1936 to 1953 (all marks and models)* (Haynes Publishing, 2012)

Page, Ron and Cumming, William *FLEET THE FLYING YEARS* (The Boston Mills Press, 1990)

Periscope Film LLC. *V-1 ORIGINAL WWII GERMAN MANUALS FOR THE V-1 "BUZZ BOMB"* (Periscope Film LLC.)

Peden, Murray *A THOUSAND SHALL FALL* (Canada's Wings Inc., 1982)

Price, Alfred *THE LUFTWAFFE 1933-1945 Volume III* (Arms and Armor Press, 1982)

Robson, Martin Dr. *THE LANCASTER BOMBER POCKET MANUAL 1941-1945 Air Ministry* (Conway, an imprint of Anova Books Ltd., 2012)

Rolfe, Mel *FLYING INTO HELL The Bomber Command Offensive Recorded by the Crews Themselves* (Grub Street, 2004)

Sweetman, Bill and Watanabe, Rikyu *Mosquito* (Janes's Publishing Company Limited, 1981)

Sweetman, John *THE DAMBUSTERS RAID* (Motorbooks International, 1990)

Taylor, Frederick *COVENTRY THURSDAY, 14 NOVEMBER 1940* (Bloomsbury Paperbacks, 2015)

Taylor, Frederick *DRESDEN TUESDAY, FEBRUARY 13, 1945* (HarperCollins Publishers, 2004)

Taylor, W. R. and Moyes, Philip J. R. *Pictorial History of the RAF Volume Two 1939-1945* (Ian Allan Ltd., 1980)

Unknown *Concentration Camp Horrors* (Radiola, 1978)

Ward, Chris *6 GROUP BOMBER COMMAND AN OPERATIONAL RECORD* (Pen & Sword Aviation, 2019)

Westermann, Edward B. *flak GERMAN ANTI-AIRCRAFT DEFENCES, 1914-1945* (University Press of Kansas, 2001)

Wicks, Ben *NO TIME TO WAVE GOODBYE* (Stoddart Publishing C. Limited, 1988)